T0320892

Human Development in an
Unequal World

Human Development in an Unequal World

K. Seeta Prabhu
Sandhya S. Iyer

OXFORD
UNIVERSITY PRESS

Oxford University Press is a department of the University of Oxford.
It furthers the University's objective of excellence in research, scholarship,
and education by publishing worldwide. Oxford is a registered trademark of
Oxford University Press in the UK and in certain other countries.

Published in India by
Oxford University Press
2/11 Ground Floor, Ansari Road, Daryaganj, New Delhi 110 002, India

© Oxford University Press 2019

The moral rights of the authors have been asserted.

First Edition published in 2019

ISBN-13 (print edition): 978-0-19-949024-0
ISBN-10 (print edition): 0-19-949024-4

ISBN-13 (eBook): 978-0-19-909566-7
ISBN-10 (eBook): 0-19-909566-3

Typeset Bembo Std 10.5/13
by Tranistics Data Technologies, New Delhi 110 044
Printed in India by Gopsons Papers Ltd., Noida 201 301

Dedicated with gratitude to
The Universal Force that guided and made all things happen
&
Parents and K.R. Prabhu—husband, guide, philosopher, and friend
for encouragement and support

—K. Seeta Prabhu

Mom and Dad for their Blessings, and to the 'Three' pillars in my life
for their encouragement and support

—Sandhya S. Iyer

Contents

Boxes, Figures, and Tables

FIGURES

Abbreviations

AIDS	Acquired Immune Deficiency Syndrome
ALP	Accelerated Learning Program
AP	Andhra Pradesh
ASDS	Kenyan Agricultural Sector Development Strategy
ASER	Annual Status of Educational Report
BNA	Basic Needs Approach
BRAC	Bangladesh Rural Advancement Committee
BRT	Bus Rapid Transit
CAREC	Regional Environment Centre for Central Asia
CCT	Conditional Cash Transfer
CEDAW	Convention on the Elimination of Discrimination against Women
COP	Conference of Parties
COP21	Conference of Parties, Paris 2015
CPM	Capability Poverty Measure
CPR	Common Property Resource
CRISE	Centre for Research on Inequality, Human Security and Ethnicity
CSG	Child Support Grant
CSW	Commission on Status of Women
CUP	Cambridge University Press
CV	Coefficient of Variation
DAC	Development Assistance Committee
DDS	Deccan Development Society
DEDAW	Declaration on the Elimination of Discrimination against Women

DSD	Department of Social Development
DSDW	Department of Social Welfare and Development
E5	Emerging 5
ECOSOC	Economic and Social Council
EEC	European Economic Community
EG	Economic Growth
EHDI	Extended Human Development Index
EKC	Environmental Kuznets Curve
EOLSS	Encyclopaedia of Life Support Systems
ESCAP	Economic and Social Commission for Asia and the Pacific
ESDP	Education Sector Development Program
ESRC	Economic and Social Research Council
EU	European Union
EURODAD	European Network on Debt and Development
FLFP	Female Labour Force Participation
FPO	Farmers Producers Organization
G20	Group of Twenty
G7	Group of Seven
G77	Group of Seventy-Seven
GAD	Gender and Development
GDI	Gender Development Index
GDP	Gross Domestic Product
GEI	Gender Equity Index
GEM	Gender Empowerment Measure
GGEI	Global Green Economy Index
GGI	Gender Gap Index
GHG	Greenhouse Gases
GHI	Global Hunger Index
GID	Gender Index of Development
GII	Gender Inequality Index
GNH	Gross National Happiness
GNI	Gross National Income
GNP	Gross National Product
HCR	Head Count Ratio
HD	Human Development
HDCA	Human Development and Capabilities Association
HDI	Human Development Index

HDPI	Human Development Poverty and Inequality
HDR	Human Development Report
HI	Horizontal Inequality
HIC	High-Income Country
HIV	Human Immunodeficiency Virus
HMIS	Health Management Information System
HPI	Human Poverty Index
HRD	Human Resource Development
ICSU	International Council for Science
ICT	Information, Communication and Technology
ICUN	International Union of Conservation of Nature and Natural Resources
IDIP	Index of Development of Intellectual Potential
IDRC	International Development Research Centre
IEAG	Independent Expert Advisory Group for Data Revolution on Sustainable Development
IGES	Institute for Global Environmental Strategy
IHDI	Inequality Adjusted Human Development Index
IHDS	Indian Human Development Survey
ILO	International Labour Organization
IMF	International Monetary Fund
INR	Indian Rupees
ITO	International Trade Organization
IUCN	International Union for Conservation of Nature
KEK	Kosovo Energy Corporation
LIC	Low-Income Country
LLI	Level of Living Measurement
LMIC	Low- and Middle-Income Country
MDG	Millennium Development Goal
MECOVI	*Programa para el Mejoramiento de las Encuestas de Hogares y la Medicion de Condiciones de Vida* (Regional Programme for Improvement of the Surveys and Measurement of the Living Conditions in Latin America and the Caribbean.)
MEW	Measure of Economic Well-Being
MGNREGA	Mahatma Gandhi National Rural Employment Guarantee Act

MIC	Middle-Income Country
MPI	Multidimensional Poverty Index
MPLA	Muslim Personal Law Application Act
NAM	Non-Aligned Movement
NCAER	National Council of Applied Economic Research
NEP	New Economic Policy
NGO	Non-Governmental Organization
NIEO	New International Economic Order
NSRT	North South Round Table
NSS	National Sample Survey
NWFPs	Non-Wood Forest Products
O8	Other 8
OBOR	One Belt One Road
ODA	Overseas Development Assistance
OECD	Organization for Economic Cooperation and Development
OPEC	Organization of the Petroleum Exporting Countries
OPHI	Oxford Poverty and Human Development Measure
ORS	Oral Rehydration Solution
PCI	Per Capita Income
PES	Payment for Ecosystem Services
PFA	Platform for Action
PISA	Performance for International Student Assessment
PPP	Purchasing Power Parity
PQLI	Physical Quantity of Life
SAL	Structural Adjustment Loan
SAP	Structural Adjustment Programmes
SASSA	South African Social Security Agency
SDGI	Sustainable Development Goals Index
SDG	Sustainable Development Goal
SDI	Social Development Index
SDSN	Sustainable Development Solutions Network
SE	Social Exclusion
SGRs	Strategic Grain Reserves
SHGs	Self-Help Groups
SIGI	Social Institutions and Gender Index
SPM	Standard Particulate Matter

TFR	Total Fertility Rate
TISS	Tata Institute of Social Sciences
TWSP	Training for Work Scholarship Programme
UBI	Universal Basic Income
UN	United Nations
UNAIDS	United Nations Programme on HIV and AIDS
UNCED	United Nations Conference on Environment and Development
UNCTAD	United Nations Conference on Trade and Development
UNDESA	United Nations Department of Economic and Social Affairs
UNDP	United Nations Development Program
UNEP	United Nations Environment Program
UNESCO	United Nations Educational, Scientific and Cultural Organization
UNFCC	United Nations Framework Convention on Climate Change
UNICEF	United Nations International Children's Emergency Fund
UNRISD	United Nations Research Institute for Social Development
UNU–EHS	United Nations University Institute for Environment and Human Security
UNU–WIDER	United Nations University World Institute for Development Economics Research
USAID	United States Agency for International Development
USD	United States Dollar
VI	Vertical Inequality
WAD	Women and Development
WCED	World Commission on Environment and Development
WeD	Well-Being in Developing Countries
WHO	World Health Organization
WID	Women in Development
WWID	World Wealth and Income Database

WIDER	World Institute for Development Economics Research
WRC	Women's Rights and Citizenship
WSSD	World Summit on Sustainable Development
WTO	World Trade Organization

Preface

The values of freedom and justice are central to human flourishing and well-being. These values have been focal points of debates for several centuries. Arguments in favour of human flourishing are pertinent as societies in contemporary times are getting increasingly fragmented into multiple identities and social categories. The 'Unequal World' represents the conjunction of human unfreedoms due to deprivations and inequalities in multiple realms. Experiments of the MDGs, and currently the SDGs, reflect the complexities in human progress, wherein the frameworks have renewed the focus on people, even as the processes that drive the outcomes continue to be hinged on the past. The twenty-first century development trajectory presents numerous challenges in terms of rising inequality within nations, heightened vulnerability and concerns about sustainability.

The human development concept owes its formal debut to the intellectual contribution and sagacity of thinking of Mahbub ul Haq and Amartya Sen, who together laid its foundations. The term 'human development' gained currency after the publication of the first Human Development Report (HDR) by the United Nations Development Programme in 1990. While advocacy on the human development approach that is rooted in equity and justice has been hugely successful and the concept firmly established in the development lexicon, it has not been able to transform the ethos of *doing development* significantly. Ritual obeisance to the concept and using the Human Development Index as a summary measure to indicate human progress has relegated the more transformative potential of the paradigm to the sidelines. Consequently, *development as usual* seems to be the predominant mode, and the more valued dimensions of well-being and flourishing seen as esoteric preoccupations rather than real world concerns. Meanwhile, empirical assessment has acquired an enhanced acceptance and several new human-centred indices have been computed and debated, even as the theory that underpins this assessment is still evolving.

It is in such a setting that this book seeks to bring back people-centred development paradigms to the forefront, and help refocus development on the centrality of peoples' choices and freedoms. This volume is anchored in the human development paradigm and examines a range of issues that reflect the dimensions of an unequal world. Set within the broader framework that includes processes, institutions and actors, it explores both analytical and empirical realms.

Human Development in an Unequal World is the fulfilment of a promise that we made to ourselves while teaching and interacting with students over the past two decades. During the course of our deep engagement as researchers, teachers, and practitioners with the concept and its applications, we faced moments of exhilaration and exasperation. On the one hand, the concept struck a chord in our hearts as it seemed to diagnose and pinpoint accurately the maladies of the current development trajectory. On the other hand, it was frustrating to watch the indifferent attitude of mainstream theorists and their dismissive attitude towards what they felt was merely a *do good-er* preoccupation.

The engagement with the world of practice was both from the outside as consultants and from within the system since one of us worked in the United Nations system. The deep interaction with various governments, in an attempt to change the way development was delivered to people, brought us face-to-face with the anachronistic, top-down, paternalistic, target- and beneficiary-oriented development approach. In the few instances where the paradigm was accepted, it was done narrowly, following the Human Development Index and its thrust on education, health, and per capita income. The ambitious attempt to introduce human development curriculum at the university level got off to an enthusiastic start but floundered thereafter from lack of ready-to-use resources and trained teachers.

Against this backdrop, our principal aim has been to provide an integrated exposition of the human development and capabilities approach. The chapters negotiate various facets of the human development approach, including its conceptual arsenal, methodological tools, as well as the applications. The book is written by two economists who have worked largely in the discipline of development studies, and hence, reflects this orientation.

There has been considerable literature expounding the human development approach that has been supported both by the UNDP and the HDCA. Hence, our attention is directed towards a more informed reader who is familiar with the subject but is yet to comprehend its many dimensions. Our attempt is to bring within the reach of students in developing countries the more advanced concepts and approaches to enable a more meaningful engagement with the paradigm. At the same time, being acutely aware of the need to ensure that the fundamental premises and concepts in the nature of prior readings are understood, we have included in the annexures a succinct summary of the main ideas. Policy implications and important contemporary issues have been highlighted to facilitate the readers to connect concepts with practice.

The book evolved over a span of few years, and during this period, the global policy environment has become extremely dynamic. The arrival of the Sustainable Development Goals agenda has led to a quest to identify and explore interconnections, terminologies, and tools. We have recognized these changes and tried to incorporate most, if not all, of these developments within the realm of the conceptual framework within which they are situated. We emphasize the need for a paradigmatic shift in the way development is interpreted and driven. Placing peoples' lives in people's hands is an imperative that can no longer be ignored.

A book of this nature would not have been possible except for the support and encouragement we received in ample measure from numerous institutions, peers, students, and practitioners across various disciplines. Special mention must be made of the intellectual environment at the Tata Institute of Social Sciences (TISS), where much of the manuscript was written and finalized. The lively academic debates and discussions and the multidisciplinary ethos of the Institute provided an opportunity to imbibe the rich perspectives emerging from sociology, philosophy, ethics, and related disciplines. We thank the former director of Tata Institute of Social Sciences, Professor S. Parasuraman, for the encouragement and for providing intellectual space by way of Tata Chair professorship to Seeta Prabhu. The Institute's research grant provided us the wherewithal to engage crucial research assistance that helped us to wade through this vast exercise.

We benefited greatly from the numerous opportunities presented to us over an extended period during the preparation of the manuscript to discuss various parts of the book with eminent scholars. To mention a few: Seeta Prabhu received a fellowship at the Institute of Advanced Study, Shimla; delivered lectures at the South Asian University, New Delhi, the Institute of Human Settlements, Bengaluru, and the University of Mysore. Internationally, Expert Group Meeting Measuring Human Development in Asia and the Pacific: Present and Future, Lao PDR; lectures at University of Mongolia, Ulan Bator, University of Afghanistan, Kabul; and training sessions on human development to UN and non-UN officials at New York, Bangkok, Jakarta, and Aceh helped us in obtaining insights into country-specific experiences and issues. Presentations across various conferences and seminars, including Think Tank 20 meetings and processes in Germany, India, and (currently) Argentina and Bangladesh helped us to shape critical perspectives about contemporary challenges of globalization and development in the Global South. We were also aided by interactions with scholars and researchers from the Institute for Development Studies, Sussex, UK; German Development Institute-DIE, Bonn; Shanghai Institute for International Studies, China; Human Sciences Research Council, South Africa; African Research Universities Alliance, Ghana; Research and Information System for Developing Countries, New Delhi; Observer Research Foundation, Mumbai; and Gateway House, Mumbai. The process of learning and relearning human development dynamics in an ever-changing world has been by far the most fascinating process for us.

Our gratitude to two anonymous referees of the manuscript whose insightful comments helped us identify contemporary challenges of human development, both in terms of conceptualization and evaluation. We are grateful to various fellow academicians who took time off their busy schedules to give substantive comments on earlier drafts of chapters. Individual chapter reviews by Aromar Revi, A.K. Shiva Kumar, Alakh Sharma, Anuradha Rajivan, M.H. Suryanarayana, R. Sudarshan, Sanjay Reddy, Sunil Nandaraj, Sukhadev Thorat, T. Palanivel, Vibhuti Patel, Mrutuyanjaya Sahu, and Meenakshi Kathel enabled us to strengthen the chapters considerably. While we have incorporated their important suggestions to the extent possible, we take full responsibility for the gaps that still remain.

The draft benefited a great deal from the excellent research assistance received from Toral Gala, whose commitment to the subject and attention to detail lightened our burden on several fronts. The support provided by young researchers Ananya Chakraborty, Paramjeet Chawla, and Pareen Sachadeva was invaluable as we raced towards meeting publishing deadlines.

Last but not least, the completion of this ambitious endeavour would not have been possible without consistent support of our families. We are grateful for their encouragement and for also for cheerfully bearing with the *externalities* that our exacting work schedules imposed on them.

We expect the volume to be of interest to both academicians as well as practitioners engaging with development studies and alternative development paradigms. The chapters are designed to provide a critical perspective and should be of particular interest to research scholars in universities. We do hope that this modest contribution to the literature will spur further research and applications in the years to come and contribute to the more widespread teaching of the subject in universities and institutions of higher learning.

K. Seeta Prabhu
Sandhya S. Iyer
October 2018

1 Introduction

1.1 PLACING PEOPLE AT THE CENTRE OF DEVELOPMENT

Development has remained an intriguing phenomenon. The unequal world we experience today is a curious amalgam of the opposing forces of globalization and people-centric development exerting their sway over development processes and policies worldwide. The enhanced opportunities for human freedom and emerging newer perspectives of development, where people are active participants, coexist with growing protectionist tendencies that could restrict and stifle freedoms and achievements made thus far. The unequal world is not only a reflection of uneven distribution of material resources, but also of inequalities in opportunities in terms of access to entitlements and those emerging from gender, class, caste, ethnicity and race, in turn translating into unequal human development outcomes.

The phenomenal economic growth experienced by countries over the last half a century has been unprecedented in human history. The shedding of the erstwhile legacy of colonialization also led to a shift, whereby both developed and developing countries contributed to the determination of the global agenda, albeit at differing rates. While the rapid economic progress of the developing countries had its positive impact in raising average growth rates that the world has experienced, the backlog of unresolved challenges in these countries, largely related to the distribution of the gains of economic growth, has affected the sustainability of global outcomes. It is ironic that despite its stupendous success on several fronts, the development mosaic of the twenty-first century is overcast with the challenges of multidimensional poverty, inequality, climate change and uncertainties with respect to economic progress.

At this juncture, it is worthwhile to recall the alarm raised by Dudley Seers[1] back in 1969, where he pointed to the need to clarify the 'true meaning' of development: should it aim to enhance rates of economic growth or to tackle poverty? Is development enabling job creation or creating joblessness? What has been happening to inequality? The questions that Seers raised had to do with the nature of development that countries experienced in the post–World War II period and highlighted the circumstances that spurred the quest for a more people-centred paradigm.

The 1970s witnessed numerous political struggles for freedom across the world. The shedding of the shackles of colonialism led to large-scale adoption of the democratic system of government: at least thirty countries in Europe, Asia, and Latin America transitioned to the democratic form.[2] This phenomenon virtually doubled the number of countries that adhered to democratic governance structures, even though there were wide differences in the type and extent of democracy actually practiced. The fall of the Berlin Wall in 1989 and the disintegration of the Soviet Union into fifteen separate countries in 1991 symbolized the struggles and the eventual triumph of the human spirit against all odds.

Further, on the economic front, even as the forces of globalization gathered strength during the 1970s and 1980s and spurred economic growth, it deepened a sense of disquiet about the prevailing development paradigm. The quadrupling of oil prices in 1973 by the Organization of the Petroleum Exporting Countries (OPEC) and a further increase in 1979 triggered a huge debt crisis[3] in the 1980s. Increasing and unsustainable debt service obligations led several developing countries into a debt trap, compelling them to resort to financial support from the International Monetary Fund (IMF) and the World Bank through stabilization and structural adjustment packages.[4] The impact of these packages on countries was quite devastating, particularly for developing countries in sub-Saharan Africa, which already had high levels of poverty and inequality. Negative growth rates experienced by these countries resulted in deterioration in living conditions of the poor in the absence of adequate safeguards to protect the vulnerable sections. Fiscal stringency led to cuts in real per capita expenditure on social sectors, particularly on education and health in sub-Saharan Africa and Latin America. Its impact on social attainments was reflected in the decline in school enrolment rates, rise in drop-out rates, and increase in the extent of under-nutrition.[5]

Although social sector policies were designed to be a part of the 'adjustment package', in reality the focus was more on trade policies, public finance, public enterprises, and the agriculture sector. Evidence from 1980 to 1993 indicated that less than 1 per cent of the 3,040 conditionalities imposed by the IMF and World Bank were related to social sectors, while most of the provisions were add-ons and were trivial in magnitude to make any real difference to the situation on the ground.[6]

These circumstances deepened the determination of scholars and development practitioners to shift the axis of assessment of development away per capita income towards a more holistic concept of people's well-being that included both material and non-material outcomes. It was with this motive that Mahbub ul Haq[7] questioned the growth strategies adopted by developing countries that seemed to disproportionately benefit the rich. He positioned poverty as a moral issue and argued in favour of a more direct attack on it to reduce deprivation. Amartya Sen,[8] in his Tanner lectures, questioned the very domain in which equality is sought to be achieved. He pointed out that it was necessary to move beyond utility, which represented only the mental reaction of individuals, to the more meaningful realm of basic capabilities.

Numerous discussions were held at a global level, including at the North South Round Tables (NSRTs) organized under the aegis of the International Society for Development (ISD) on the dimensions of development that are truly valuable. These bipartisan dialogues on the issues faced by both developed and developing countries provided a unique platform for the birth in 1990 of the human development approach[9] that placed people at the centre of development. It was through these NSRTs that the idea of a human-centred development paradigm found its natural expression and a recommendation for preparing annual reports on the numerous discussions was made.[10] While it was not the only experiment that provided an alternative framework to counter the growth-led approach of the past, human development has certainly gained greater legitimacy as a developmental alternative in theoretical and empirical terms, and in terms of guiding policy dialogue.

Over the past quarter century of its people-centric existence, guided by the core philosophy of well-being, freedom, and human flourishing, the human development paradigm has enabled substantive deliberations on a range of issues such as liberty, participation, conflict, and social cohesion. Thus, the debates on development today no longer hinge solely on raising the levels of per capita income, but have moved towards measuring the quality of the development process as a whole. The tireless efforts of scholars and institutions globally have resulted in this mammoth transformation.

The theoretical importance of the human development paradigm arises from the fact that it brought back into the understanding of development a value-based concept that focused on the Aristotelian notion of human flourishing that at once transcended the narrow interpretation dominated by economic growth. Being embedded in the processes of equity, productivity, empowerment, and sustainability, the new paradigm provided an analytical framework that was holistic, integrated and relevant to the contemporary development landscape. Further, it identified self-respect, dignity, choice, and freedoms as crucial elements, and thus imbued the much-needed human element into development that had been increasingly assuming the nature of a mechanistic, technical exercise. Capabilities and entitlements, the core constituents of the human development approach, brought freedoms, choices, endowments, and conversion factors to the forefront of analysis and provided a stark counterfoil to the prevailing paternalistic and welfare-oriented approach to development. This more integrated analytical framework also shifted the perception from instrumental notions of development to the intrinsic value of development and what it means for people. By rebutting the premise of the utilitarian paradigm, which staunchly held that actions of individuals are rooted in self-interest, the human development approach provided a value-based alternative embedded in equity and justice.[11]

The Human Development Index[12] (HDI), the aggregate measure that was introduced along with the human development concept in 1990 as an alternative measure of development, captured people's imagination. Even though it might not have succeeded in unseating Gross Domestic Product (GDP) per capita as a measure, it managed to drive home the point that measuring human progress goes beyond income, and must include other dimensions that matter to humans. Despite being trapped by its own success, with human development being most often equated with HDI, the human development concept is nonetheless here to stay. The annual publication of the Human Development Reports (HDRs), which introduced innovations in measures of development, capturing dimensions of inequality in indices relating to human development and gender, has been a historic contribution to development literature. The debate has also been successful in reshaping the notion of poverty from a unidimensional income perspective to one that is multidimensional.

Before we proceed with our discussion of various perspectives on human development, we will explain some of its key elements as a prelude to what follows in other chapters. Section 1.2 discusses how the human development approach is centred on choices and freedoms. Section 1.3 presents the prominent approaches and pathways that preceded the human development approach, while Section 1.4 highlights the backlogs of the twentieth century. The last section presents the rationale and chapter scheme of the book.

1.2 CHOICES AND FREEDOMS

The human development approach emerged from the overwhelming ambition of scholars and practitioners to place *equity and justice* as integral components of the development paradigm. It is not as though concerns towards equity and justice did not exist in the philosophy of the dominant development paradigms. Such concerns held centre stage in the utilitarian philosophy of Jeremy Bentham, in the libertarian approach propagated by Robert Nozick, and in the notion of justice articulated by John Rawls. However, the notion of justice as conceived by these frameworks was rather limited and coloured by subjective biases of various kinds. While the utilitarian paradigm emphasized material well-being to the extent of exclusion of non-material components, Nozick's and Rawls's emphasis was on liberties and freedoms to the extent of exclusion of material well-being.[13]

A few crucial questions to ask while assessing development paradigms are as follows: why do people matter? What is the role of the individual in the larger collective? Can the individual 'self' achieve the 'good' for all? Can the pathway of the 'self' pose a constraint to the possibilities of 'selfless' behaviour? What are the roles of cohesion, compassion and solidarity in fostering development?

Central to these norms of justice are the philosophical contributions of Aristotle and Immanuel Kant. While Aristotle's arguments were rooted in metaphysics, understood broadly as 'the search for what there is and what things in general are', for Kant the moral law that 'exercises on the human heart by way of reason alone' was important. Both Aristotle and Kant were concerned with the 'self' and the 'real' foundations of human flourishing, which hinged more on the achievement of non-material progress rather than on material outcomes. They argued that societies are driven by individuals and each individual determines his/her notion of well-being on the basis of certain decisions. Only 'good' decisions would yield fair outcomes.

The notion of the 'self' emphasized by Aristotle and Kant was very distinct from the notion of the 'individual' that occupied centre stage in the utilitarian, Rawlsian and libertarian schools of thought. Utilitarians equated an individual's utility with his/her own pleasure, with the assumption that the individual will act in the general interest of society. Rawls extends this to interpersonal comparisons of relative advantage in terms of a *difference principle* across social primary goods comprising 'rights, liberties and opportunities, income and wealth and the social bases of social respect'.[14] Libertarians like Nozick[15] see no role for the state to help individuals who were unluckily born with few resources, hence poor, weak, and sick. They argue that it is for individuals in society to decide whether to help such people by giving their own resources as a gift. Any redistribution that might occur as a result would only be due to voluntary decisions of individuals to transfer some of their assets in pursuit of some moral values. The 'self-seeking' individual in the utilitarian and libertarian systems exercises individual choice and the distribution of benefits occurs from the individual decision. However, it is uncertain whether such a self-centric framework results in fairness in welfare distribution.

Sen, while rejecting both the utilitarian position and the Rawlsian construct of social primary goods, argues that what is important to value is not goods but *what goods do to people*. He clarifies that the well-being of individuals lies not only in what they achieve for themselves, that is, 'well-being achievement', but also in what they are *free to achieve*.[16] Thus, what is required in a metric of well-being is neither primary goods nor utility, but something that is distinct from them. He calls this 'capability', the freedom to achieve a range of 'functionings'.[17] It is this philosophy that influenced the shaping of the human development concept and its definition in 1990 as 'the process of enlarging the range of people's choices'.

The distinctive feature of the Aristotelian ethic is that it values only 'good' outcomes for human flourishing. Aristotle explains that individual choices are reflections of the socio-cultural milieu of the society and that such actions, which are in accordance with societal arrangements and valuations, enhance social welfare. The rest are considered 'bad' values and morals.[18]

Thus, Sen's question, 'Equality for What?', draws our attention to the fact that inequalities in a society need to be understood from the standpoint of how individual freedom is an outcome of both individual choice as well as societal norms. The utilitarian interpretation is simplistic in that social justice is achieved when total utility is maximized through *equal treatment of everybody's interests*. This sum-ranking procedure assumes that society is rightly ordered and that there are institutions that enable people's achievement of the greatest satisfaction.

Therefore, in comparing the human development approach with other approaches, we see several points of contention. In the Rawlsian framework, poverty and inequalities enter indirectly through their influence on choices, freedom, and fairness of opportunities. For the libertarians, the presence of a formal institutional framework is a crucial platform for voice and empowerment, although, in societies that are inherently unequal, such presence may not ensure equal access of legislative and judicial mechanisms to all. These advantages fall short of capturing the presence of multiple forms of poverty and inequalities that create inherent disparities in freedoms of access, process, and opportunity in society. The Aristotelian and Kantian perspectives re-centre the human being to the larger metaphysical notions of equality, justice and freedom that get embedded in the notion of the *good*. Thus, the human development approach rekindles the idea of human well-being as encompassing expansion of freedoms resulting in human flourishing in all its dimensions.

1.3 PATHWAYS FROM THE PAST

Prior to the emergence of the human development approach, several influential approaches such as Human Resource Development (HRD), the basic needs and human rights attempted to bring a people-centric focus into the development paradigm. Subsequently, the human security approach also gained some importance. We highlight the main features of these approaches in what follows.[19]

Human Resource Development

The HRD approach revolves around the concept of human capital, which owes its existence to the analytical work of Theodore Schultz, Gary Becker, and Jacob Mincer during the 1960s. The human capital concept pointed out for the first time that just as investment in physical capital yields returns over a period of time, individuals also contribute to production through their embodied education, skills and on the job training.[20] It is therefore logical that such investments made by individuals be considered human capital. This approach was in sharp contrast to the then prevailing view of treating education and health as consumption goods.

The HRD approach values human beings for their contributions in promoting and sustaining the growth of the economy. Its malleability to theorization, estimation, and forecasting led to its ready acceptance by policymakers, who were able to integrate the notion of human capital into productivity models, which was otherwise classified generically as 'labour' in the classical growth models. This approach became hugely influential also because it enabled computation of private and social rates of return to investments in education and health, which in turn enabled policy decisions to be based on such estimates.

However, over the years, this very advantage became a constraint, as the viewpoint of perceiving education and health purely as enhancing the productive capability of individuals led to a neglect of the intrinsic value of knowledge and health for their own sake. The restrictive view of education in particular, linking it largely to enhancing efficiency in the production of commodities or services at the cost of ignoring its role in augmenting information, knowledge, communication, and the ability to express opinions in the society as a whole, was a serious drawback.[21]

Moreover, the use of cost-benefit analysis itself was flawed. It required a rigid separation between economic and non-economic aspects in estimating rates of returns that did not have logical underpinnings.[22] The approach also ignores how the structure of human capital formation affects the social relations of production and the evolution of class relations—factors that have a profound impact on the process of accumulation of human capital.[23]

Blaug criticized the human capital theory on its own logic. According to him, the human capital theory is a sterling example of the use of 'methodological individualism', which professes that all social phenomena are to be traced back to their foundations in individual behaviour.[24] This is a contentious claim, as most analysts believe that individual behaviour is shaped by social, cultural, and environmental factors. Social phenomena cannot be reduced to individual responses alone, since the whole is different from the sum of its individual constituents.

The human capital notion provided a boost since the Great Depression of the 1930s to the policy initiatives of the then industrialized countries, as they could justify the intensive use of humans as labourers and workers to enhance productivity and efficiency. However, the developing countries faced serious challenges in adopting this approach as they were in the initial stages of industrialization and their efforts stymied by having to simultaneously raise the standard of living, educate people, tackle poverty, mortality and morbidity issues, with very limited resources.

Basic Needs

Gradually, by the 1970s, there was a shift away from the individualistic-human capital framework to a people-centric welfare approach characterized by the basic needs approach. Emerging out of the work of the International Labour Organisation (ILO) World Programme in the 1970s, the basic needs approach was articulated powerfully by the team led by Paul Streeten.[25] Streeten argued that unlike the income and employment approach propagated by the HRD framework, the basic needs approach focuses on mobilizing *particular* resources for *particular* groups.[26] Its critical contribution consisted in moving beyond the income component as a measure of poverty and emphasizing the importance of physical services and commodities such as health, sanitation and hygiene, nutrition, education, shelter, and other prerequisites in order to enhance the productivity of the poor. Haq describes the basic needs approach as the 'conceptual forerunner of human development'.[27] Basic needs encompass both material and non-material needs. However, there is no universally accepted definition of basic needs nor of what developmental effort is required to meet basic needs.

Generally speaking, *basic needs* reflect a set of priorities set by individuals or societies for action, and are eminently linked with outcomes of development that focus on the poor and the destitute. The approach required a restructuring of the production processes with the aim to enhance income earning opportunities and ensure adequate supply of basic goods and services to the poorest in the society.[28] High priority is given to components of current consumption by the poor in the short run, with the assumption that it would reduce the current deficit and also stimulate growth in subsequent periods.

Adoption of the basic needs approach provides a country or region with the opportunity to define a standard of living that is considered the minimum acceptable level, which can then be used to identify group or groups of people falling below the minimum. However, the orientation is driven largely by the progress of this target group and/or indicators of the minimum. This also leads to oversimplification of the process of tackling and/or eliminating poverty. Poverty eradication is often constrained by social segregation and structural and institutional rigidities that are prevalent in a society[29] but not given due attention during the endeavours to ensure basic needs. The approach also strengthens the paternalistic orientation of the state, and the choices and voices of people are not given due attention.

Human Rights

Protecting human dignity and promoting the right to life came to the forefront during the processes that led to the independence of countries in the developing world, encompassing partition of countries and formation of nation-states. These processes, along with the compulsions arising out of incessant wars and conflicts associated with the Cold War era and the rise of the Non-Alignment Movement, enhanced the role of the state in committing itself to protection of human dignity and promoting the right to life. While the United Nations' (UN) Universal Declaration of 1948 set the tone for national governments to take responsibility in ensuring basic human rights to citizens, its scope was largely confined to legal provisions pertaining to civic and political rights. Subsequent movements, including those by the non-governmental organizations, led to redefining the scope and content of human rights beyond the political realm to encompass social and economic rights.

The economic upheavals of 1970s and 1980s due to Structural Adjustment Programmes (SAP) re-emphasized the responsibility of the duty bearers, namely, the national governments, towards the claim holders, namely, the citizens. This is reflected in the adoption of Right to Education (1960), Right to Health (1978) and Right to Work (1948), all of which were discussed and were included in various UN declarations. With the declaration of the Right to Development[30] in the 1986 UN General Assembly, the pressure on national governments for the provision of social and economic rights gathered momentum.

The fundamental features of human rights include universality and inalienability, indivisibility, and interdependence and interrelatedness.[31] While human rights often trigger legislation, it is not their constitutive characteristic. Implementation of human rights is not confined to the legally recognized rights, and the protection of human rights or political and moral entitlements need not take coercive means or punitive legislations. Rights can be secured through other means and processes—'communication, advocacy, exposure and informed public discussion'.[32] Sen underlines that if entitlements are rights of the people, then they have a mutual relationship with duties. That is, it is a duty that these rights are protected even though it may often be difficult to identify who the duty bearer is. In the case of human rights, where there is no single duty holder and hence they cannot be enforced by the courts, other democratic means such as action by the legislature, media, and civic protests may be required for them to be asserted.

Human rights include economic and social freedoms that are significant and socially influential, yet often unrealized due to institutional weaknesses. For example, the right to health is often not realized in many developing countries due to the lacunae in the institutional framework that is responsible for its implementation. These lacunae, however, should not prevent its being recognized as a human right. Human rights play an instrumental role in reinforcing public accountability as they provide 'countervailing power' to people which enables them to 'voice' their demands.

The bridge between state-led development and market expansion on the one hand, and growing land alienation, deepening inequalities, and growing capitalistic exploitation on the other, led to movements by civil society to ensure human rights. By the 1990s, the human rights discourse expanded its frontiers to evolve into a rights-based approach that empowered the people facing challenges of government failures and market-led alienation.

Human Security

With the growing process of militarization of countries globally and the increased threat across boundaries, the human security approach gained prominence. Classical international relations theories treated security as being mainly concerned with peace-keeping, refugee crisis, and humanitarian aid. The emergence of the concept of human security shifted the focus from the narrow realm of territorial security to a broader concept of people's security.[33] Human security is anchored in freedoms, and connects different types of freedoms—freedom from want, freedom from fear, and freedom to act on one's own behalf. As per The Commission on Human Security, its role is 'to protect the vital core of all human lives in ways that enhance human freedoms and human fulfilment'.[34]

Gasper[35] considers human security as a combination of human development, basic human needs, and human rights. Alkire views human security as 'a minimal or basic or fundamental set of functions related to survival, livelihood and dignity'.[36] In other words, human security is concerned with the rudimentary thresholds of a subset of human capabilities that people consider important to be protected even in troubled times. For example, if being well-nourished is one of the human capabilities, ensuring minimum requisite amount of food security to people for their survival and further expansion of other capabilities becomes an area of interest under human security.

There are four basic features of the human security concept as articulated by Amartya Sen. First, unlike the conventional approach where the focus is on territories, Sen's focus is on people and their security. Following from this, the second feature is that the security of persons is viewed within an overall context of living. Third, the thrust is on basic principles including life, death, and dignity of persons. Lastly, the approach takes into consideration the stability or instability of the fulfilment of basic priorities of living. Thus, this concept looks at threats to the fulfilment of basic priorities in the lives of ordinary persons.

The broader connotation of human security serves as a bridge between the human development and peace themes, though the merger has not been smooth. Both concepts are concerned with basic capabilities, but the difference is that while the former focuses on the changes in the levels of human development, the latter is concerned with conditions that influence those levels and the stability of the attainments per se.

1.4 BACKLOGS OF THE TWENTIETH CENTURY

Many countries have witnessed unprecedented growth over the past five decades. Trends indicate that world population increased by twenty-three-fold and world GDP by 300-fold during the last millennium, resulting in an increase in world per capita income by about fourteen-fold. The growth achieved by some countries during the past twenty-five years has been remarkable, as fifteen countries, comprising over a fourth of the world's GDP and half the world's population, have grown at a fast rate.[37] There has also been improvement in human development indicators with the index improving by 41 per cent globally between 1970 and 2011. More hearteningly, the low HDI countries improved their HDI value by 61 per cent.[38]

This high level of growth has, however, come at the great cost of rising inequality of income and massive environmental degradation. Milinovic[39] estimated that between 1988 and 2008, the real income of the top 1 per cent globally increased by over 60 per cent whereas the bottom 5 per cent registered stagnancy in their real income. The financial and economic crisis of 2008 further affected the already deteriorating situation. Subsidies on items such as food and fuel were slashed in over 100 countries despite rising food prices. Further, wage bills have either been cut or capped in ninety-eight countries and rationalization of social safety nets are on the agenda of eighty countries, at a time when there should actually be increased protection to shield the poor from adverse circumstances. Labour flexibilization reforms are ongoing in thirty countries, eroding workers' rights. Rising inequality of incomes and increasing vulnerability of the poor due to recurring economic crises and resource depletion caused by environmental degradation has also aggravated social unrest. ILO[40] confirms that out of seventy-one economies for which data were available, the risk of social unrest increased in forty-six economies between 2011 and 2012.

The rapid growth of the world economy, involving intensive use of resources, has also led to catastrophic impacts on the natural ecosystem. Climate change is no longer a distant possibility but a lived reality as is evident from rising global temperatures, which were, on average, 0.75 degrees Celsius higher in the 2010s than at the beginning of twentieth century. It is estimated that the atmospheric temperature could rise by as much as 2–5 degrees Celsius or even higher if the current level of emissions is sustained, leading to devastating impacts on the earth. Human activities are estimated to have already surpassed three out of ten environmental thresholds or planetary boundaries,[41] namely, climate change,[42] rate of biodiversity loss,[43] and nitrogen cycle.[44] Some of the already visible impacts are food and water scarcity, rising sea levels, extinction of biodiversity, and extreme weather conditions including storm, forest fires, drought, flooding, heat waves, and other irreversible changes in the ecosystem.[45]

The world is truly at the crossroads, and sustainability in its myriad dimensions including economic, social, and political realms is on top of the agenda of researchers and thought leaders. The advent of the Sustainable Development Goals (SDGs), with a much more comprehensive and integrated agenda than the preceding Millennium Development Goals (MDGs), reflects the priority given to more holistic global development. It is in this context that the human development paradigm assumes renewed importance.

1.5 RATIONALE OF THE BOOK AND CHAPTER SCHEME

The persistence of the challenges of inequality, climate change, and unsustainable growth renders it not only imperative, but also an opportune time, to reorient the prevailing development perspective with the guiding philosophy of human development so as to enable a more systematic linkage to be forged between economic growth, capability enhancement, choices, and well-being. While over the past quarter century of its existence, the human development paradigm evolved both conceptually as well as methodologically, its use has not been as widespread as was originally envisaged, as scholars and institutions have largely focused on individual dimensions of the approach. Though this use led to a deeper understanding of these constituents of freedoms, the lack of an integrated approach limited the prospects of a more forceful perspective of human development to emerge as a possible alternative paradigm.

This book is an attempt to fill this gap, as it seeks to provide an integrated understanding of the theoretical evolution of the discipline of human development and its core applications thus far. The volume provides a lucid exposition of the key dimensions of the capability and human development approach, and presents the main debates and discussions in a convenient and ready-to-understand format without diluting their richness. Numerous examples, drawn from development experience across several developing countries, demonstrate the application of the human development approach in practice, thereby demystifying it. The book presents perspectives on both the conceptual evolution and as well as empirical dimensions of the human development approach over the past three decades and is a modest contribution towards furthering its enhanced understanding. The book is intended to aid an objective assessment and comprehension of the human development approach among research scholars, academics and development practitioners, all of whom can influence and foster human flourishing in its multiple dimensions.

Chapter 2 explains in detail the notions of *functionings and capabilities*. It discusses the multilayered phenomena of capabilities in the form of as threshold, internal, external, and complex capabilities. It explains how they provide valuable understanding about the conversion factors that are involved in the translation of resources to capabilities and capabilities into functionings. It critically evaluates the capabilities approach and emphasizes the importance of the role of endowments and entitlements as factors influencing human well-being. The chapter also elaborates the role of *entitlements and endowments* in contributing to human flourishing and well-being. The unique feature of the chapter is the presentation of an integrated analytical framework that traces the pathways to human development through equity, sustainability, empowerment, and productivity processes. In addition, the chapter discusses HDI and the challenges relating to its computation.

Chapter 3 reflects on the meta-questions of human flourishing, well-being, and justice, and critically examines ideas of choices, well-being, and freedom from a human development standpoint. Freedom is the pivot around which human development revolves, where freedoms are of two kinds—personal freedom and process freedom—each with different public policy implications. The chapter discusses both process and opportunity freedoms and distinguishes them from other conventional notions of freedom. It also deals with the process of choice and the act of choice at the individual level and its relationship with human flourishing. Further, the role of agency is highlighted, where both individual as well as collective agency is important to bring about change in society.

Chapter 4 discusses the methodological issues pertaining to human development analysis. It critically reflects on the role of GDP as a measure of human progress, and points to the shift in the discourse from unidimensional to multidimensional measures. In the light of significant efforts towards deriving alternative measures of well-being that include multiple dimensions, the issues relating to composite indices, such as indicator selection, weightage given, and the combination of numerous dimensions in one index, are examined. A key perspective highlighted in the chapter is the challenge posed by *missing and empty indicators*, as well as missing and unreliable data. While cautioning researchers on these issues, the chapter points towards the need for better data reporting. Additionally, it argues in favour of extending the human development approach to the process of data generation using participatory methods, particularly at a time when the SDG mandate extends over 230 indicators, many of which are also necessary for monitoring at the local level.

Unravelling the linkages between economic growth and human development has assumed urgency in the current era where development processes no longer follow historical patterns. Chapter 5 juxtaposes the relationship between them in the light of the globalization process and the varying outcomes of human development across countries. The analysis of linkages between GDP and HDI over the past three decades across countries shows that the process is extremely dynamic in nature and that human development outcomes do not follow a defined trajectory. This is particularly evident in the analysis of backlogs in human progress, where we find the dominance of joblessness, impoverishment, displacement, and migration. The chapter concludes that economic growth and human development cannot be viewed as disconnected processes as they influence each other in multiple ways.

Chapter 6 critically examines the role of social sector policies in enhancing human freedoms against the backdrop of the globalization process and the SDGs that are anchored in the human development ethos. We argue that the agenda of human development policymaking is to identify and promote *public goods* that enhance basic capabilities and, thereby, human well-being. Drawing from the empirical experience of countries, four stylized facts that contribute to the effectiveness of social sector policies are presented. The stylized facts emphasize the role of initial conditions, redistributive measures, and synergies of integrated policies. Select innovative measures across countries that address human development challenges are discussed with a view to identifying unique policy initiatives. The chapter highlights the need to distinguish between the pathways of policymaking that enhance comprehensive outcomes and those that lead only to culmination outcomes.

Chapter 7 argues that the analysis of poverty and inequality cannot be conducted in independent silos as they have numerous interconnections. The human development approach requires the adoption of a multidimensional lens to poverty and inequality, as deprivations go beyond income dimension and encompass non-income aspects such as basic capabilities. The chapter further elaborates that poverty emanates from socio-cultural differentiations and the resultant horizontal and vertical inequalities could cause capability losses. Policies to address such inequalities would need to pay heed to the differing initial conditions and recognize ethnicity, class, women's agency, and spatial concerns.

Chapter 8 presents an intersectional analysis of women's human development outcomes through the lens of gender and social relations on one hand, and the nature of public policies implemented on the other. Against the backdrop of women's movements, the central preoccupation of the chapter is to explain women's marginalization process, wherein critical gaps in the formation of basic capabilities across men and women in the society are identified. Differences in human development outcomes not only stem from differences in access and opportunity freedoms, but also exist on account of differences in endowments and entitlements. Thus, the real concerns about women's human development achievements are regarding capability deprivation and inequalities in access to labour markets, access to social opportunities, political participation, and access to social protection. It is argued that purely entitlement transfers through state policy will not be able to resolve the issue. The numerous efforts to assess human development outcomes of both women and men in terms of quantitative and qualitative dimensions have been able to capture only some part of this multilayered phenomenon. Despite refinements over the years, the multidimensional measures of Gender Development Index, Gender Empowerment Measure, and Gender Inequality Index presented by the United Nations Development Programme (UNDP) continue to capture only a small portion of the gamut of gender-based outcomes in society.

Chapter 9 explains the importance of broadening the purview of sustainability to include environmental, economic, and social dimensions. The rationale for this more comprehensive view lies in the fact that people face multiple vulnerabilities due to disaster-related risks, macro-economic shocks, political turmoil, and ever-expanding social inequalities. Therefore, this chapter argues for the need to anchor all actions in the pathway of strong sustainability as sustaining ecosystems and their services, and maintains that ensuring environmental rights for present and future generations is important from the point of view of ensuring intergenerational equity. This can be achieved by adopting an *institutionally integrated view* of a freedom-centred approach that strengthens the foundations of sustainable human development through promotion of basic capabilities, collective freedoms, and social cohesion.

Discussing human development issues at the national level without being mindful of the global architecture that can enable or hinder the same would be an exercise in futility. In recognition of this, Chapter 10 reflects on the broader engagement of global policymaking in influencing pathways to human progress. Widespread globalization and *crony* capitalism have undermined the *agency* of countries in shaping national policies. At the developmental level, this trend has been countered through global dialogues across countries that have sought to secure global public goods through MDGs and SDGs. For instance, at the political level, the rise of an international forum of governments and banks (G-20) demonstrates the resolve to provide an alternate platform for dialogue on contentious issues. The chapter puts forth the argument that the *unequal world* today is gearing towards fostering notions of equity and justice, which are key to the human development paradigm. The rejuvenation of the global architecture is imperative as the onslaught of economic crisis, environmental fragility, and worsening of social inequities is cutting across economies in both the developed as well as the developing world. In such a milieu, it may be worthwhile to revive the dialogue process beyond the SDG mandate, to encompass economic and political issues *a la* the North-South Roundtables platform of yore.

NOTES AND REFERENCES

1. Pointing to the false identification of development with only economic growth that was measured singularly in terms of national income, Seers argued that this narrow interpretation was convenient as it facilitated analysts to avoid confronting the real problems of development. The fundamental questions that Seers raised had to do with the very meaning of the term 'development'. For further details, see Seers, D. 1969. 'The Meaning of Development'. IDS, Communication Series No. 44, University of Sussex, p. 5.

2. The third wave of democracy was preceded by the first and second waves of democracy, but each of them was also followed by a reversal wave. For details, see Huntington, S.P. 1993. *The Third Wave: Democratization in the Late Twentieth Century* (Vol. 4). Norman: University of Oklahoma Press.

3. For example, the debt burden of countries in sub-Saharan Africa was estimated to have doubled between 1980s and 1990s.

4. Both sets of policies were based on a common logic steeped in the neo-classical paradigm with its naïve belief in the functioning of the markets to

ensure allocative efficiency and in the belief that individual pursuit of self-interest maximizes social welfare. Since state intervention in the economic sphere is believed to be the root of all evil, the dominant recommendation of the two institutions was to roll back the involvement of the State to let markets function freely.

5. There was a decline in social spending per head of 26 per cent in sub-Saharan Africa and 18 per cent in Latin America between 1980–5 (Stewart, F. 1991. 'The Many Faces of Adjustment'. *World Development* 19 [12]: 1847–64). In Tanzania, gross enrolment ratio fell from 92.8 to 72.2 per cent between 1980–5 (Kakwani, N., Makonnen, E., and Van Der Gagg, J. 1990. 'Structural Adjustment and Living Conditions in Developing Countries', Working Paper PRE #467, Welfare and Human Resources Department, World Bank, Washington, DC). In a ten-country analysis, Cornia observed that during the stabilization period nutritional status declined or remained constant in all the countries except South Korea (Cornia, G.A. 1987. 'Economic Decline and Human Welfare in the First Half of the 1980s', in *Adjustment with a Human Face: Protecting the Vulnerable and Promoting Growth* [Vol. 1], ed. G.A. Cornia, R. Jolly, and F. Stewart, pp. 11–47. Oxford: Clarendon Press).

6. Alexander, N.C. 2001. 'Paying for Education: How the World Bank and the International Monetary Fund Influence Education in Developing Countries'. *Peabody Journal of Education*, 76 (3/4): 285–338.

7. Haq, M. ul. 1976. *The Poverty Curtain: Choices for the Third World*. New Delhi: Oxford University Press.

8. Sen, A. 1980. 'Equality of What?', in *Tanner Lectures on Human Values* (Vol. 1), ed. S. McMurrin, pp. 195–220, Cambridge: Cambridge University Press.

9. We use the terms human development approach and human development paradigm interchangeably. The human development discourse has evolved its own distinct concept, theory, and methodology to warrant being termed a paradigm. It has also provided a unique approach towards shaping policy advocacy.

10. This idea was later taken up by UNDP in the form of annual HDRs and Mahbub ul Haq was invited to lead a team at the UNDP and prepare the first HDR, which was published in 1990. The contribution of the NSRTs to the evolution of the human development approach is discussed in Annexure D.

11. Sen contends that in their attempt to establish what is just or establish a set of just principles that are essential to design just institutions governing society, these traditional political philosophies disclose little as to how to identify and reduce injustice. For further details, see Sen, A. 2009. *The Idea of Justice*. London: Penguin.

12. The HDI is a summary measure of three dimensions—income, knowledge, and long and healthy life.

13. These paradigms are discussed in greater detail in Annexure A.

14. Rawls, J. 1999. *A Theory of Justice*. Cambridge, MA: Harvard University Press, p. 54.

15. Nozick, *The Meaning of Development*.

16. Sen, A. 1993. 'Capability and Well-Being', in *The Quality of Life*, ed. M. Nussbaum and A. Sen. New York: Clarendon Press, p. 453.

17. Functionings are understood as the 'valuable beings and doing' of people. These foundational notions are discussed in detail in Chapter 2 of this volume.

18. For more, see Crisp, R. and Sounders T.J. 1999. 'Aristotle: Ethics and Politics', in *From Aristotle to Augustine: Routledge History of Philosophy* (Vol. 2), ed. D. Furley, pp. 109–46. London; New York: Routledge.

19. More details about the four approaches in comparison with the human development approach are given in Annexure B.

20. Human capital was defined as 'stock of skills and productive knowledge embedded in people'. See Rosen, S. 1989. 'Human Capital', in *The New Palgrave Dictionary of Economics* (Vol. 2), ed. J. Eatwell, M. Milgate, and P. Newman, pp. 681–90. London: Macmillan Press, p. 682.

21. The human capital theory has been criticized for its overwhelming emphasis on the benefits of education in the labour market. Machlup, in an analysis of screening mechanism, showed that for the assessment and selection process while hiring people, especially at entry levels conducted by firms, educational qualifications of applicants serve as signals of desirable qualities that an employer is looking for. For more, see Machlup, F. 1984. *Volume III: The Economics of Information and Human Capital*, as a part of Knowledge: Its Creation, Distribution and Economic Significance. Princeton: Princeton University Press; Tan, E. 2014. 'Human Capital Theory: A Holistic Criticism'. *Review of Education Research* 84 (3): 411–45.

22. A minimum level of education influences several non-economic dimensions such as a person's own consciousness, inter-personal behaviour and the like, which are valuable. Moreover, education also leads to non-tangible benefits such as enhanced self-respect and dignity, the value of which to the individual may be difficult to measure. None of these aspects are taken into account while computing rates of returns to investment in education.

23. For details, see Bowles, S. and Gintis, H. 1975. 'The Problem with Human Capital Theory: A Marxist Critique'. *American Economic Review* 65 (2): 74–82.

24. For details, see Blaug, M. 1976. 'The Empirical Status of Human Capital Theory: A Slightly Jaundiced Survey'. *Journal of Economic Literature* 14 (3): 827–55.

25. Streeten, P., Burki, S.J., Haq, U., Hicks, N., and Stewart, F. 1981. *First Things First: Meeting Basic Human Needs in the Developing Countries*. New York: Oxford University Press.

26. Streeten, Paul. 1979. 'Basic Needs: Premises and Promises'. *Journal of Policy Making* (1): 136–46.

27. Haq, M. ul. 1995. *Reflections on Human Development*. Oxford: Oxford University Press, p. vii.

28. For details, see ODI. 1978. 'Basic Needs', Briefing Paper No. 5, Overseas Development Institute, London.

29. For details, see Ghai, D. 1978. 'Basic Needs and its Critics'. *IDS Bulletin* 9 (4): 16–18.

30. UN General Assembly. 1986. 'Declaration on the Right to Development'. A/RES/41/128. Accessible at http://www.un.org/documents/ga/res/41/a41r128.htm.

31. For details, see UN General Assembly. 1948. 'Universal Declaration of Human Rights'. 217(III). Paris. Accessible at http://www.un.org/en/universal-declaration-human-rights/.

32. Sen, A. 2004. 'Elements of a Theory of Human Rights'. *Philosophy and Public Affairs* 32 (4): 315–56, p. 345.

33. The concept of human security came into prominence after it was proposed by the UNDP in the 1994 HDR; although the concept was defined earlier in the Beveridge Commission Report as 'freedom from want and freedom from fear'. See Beveridge, W.H.B. 1942. *Social Insurance and Allied Services*. London: Her Majesty's Stationery Office; UNDP. 1994. *Human Development Report 1994: Human Security*. New York: Oxford University Press.

34. Commission on Human Security. 2003. *Human Security Now*. New York: United Nations Publications, p. 4.

35. Gasper argues that like the human development approach, human security also focuses on reasoned freedoms; like the basic human needs discourse, it emphasises prioritization; and like the human rights' discourse it is unwilling to sacrifice anyone. For details, see Gasper, D. 2005. 'Securing Humanity: Situating "Human Security" as Concept and Discourse'. *Journal of Human Development* 6 (2): 221–45.

36. Alkire, S. 2003. 'A Conceptual Framework for Human Security', Working Paper, Centre for Research on Inequality, Human Security and Ethnicity, p. 24.

37. Commission on Growth and Development. 2008. *The Growth Report: Strategies for Sustained Growth and Inclusive Development*. Washington, DC: The International Bank for Reconstruction and Development; The World Bank. Accessible at http://documents.worldbank.org/curated/en/120981468138262912/pdf/449860PUB0Box3101OFFICIAL0USE0ONLY1.pdf; 14 September 2018.

38. UNDP. 2011. *Sustainability and Equity: A Better Future for All*. New York: Palgrave.

39. Milanovic, B. 2013. 'Global Income Inequality in Numbers: In History and Now'. *Global Policy* 4 (2): 198–208.

40. ILO. 2013. *World of Work Report 2013: Repairing the Economic and Social Fabric*. International Institute for Labour Studies, Geneva: ILO.

41. As proposed by Rockström, J., Steffen, W., Noone, K., Persson, Å., Chapin III, F.S., Lambin, E., Lenton, T.M., Scheffer, M., Folke, C., Schellnhuber, H., Nykvist, B., De Wit, C.A., Hughes, T., van der Leeuw, S., Rodhe, H., Sörlin, S., Snyder, P.K., Costanza, R., Svedin, U., Falkenmark, M., Karlberg, L., Corell, R.W., Fabry, V.J., Hansen, J., Walker, B., Liverman, D., Richardson, K., Crutzen, P., and Foley, J. 2009. 'Planetary Boundaries: Exploring the Safe Operating Space for Humanity'. *Ecology and Society* 14 (2): 32.

42. Climate change as measured by atmosphere carbon dioxide concentration (parts per million by volume) and change in radiative forcing (watt per metre square) was proposed at 350 and 1, respectively. As against this, the measured levels of the indicators in 2009 were at 387 and 1.5, respectively.

43. The proposed boundary for the rate of biodiversity loss as measured by extinction rate (number of species per million per year) is ten and the current status is higher than 100.

44. The amount of N2 removed from the atmosphere for human use (millions of tonnes per year) is proposed to be thirty-five but the current status is 121 today.

45. Stern, N. 2007. *The Economics of Climate Change: The Stern Review.* Cambridge: Cambridge University Press.

2 The Concept

Since its formal debut in 1990, the human development paradigm has progressed steadily in successive years to capture popular imagination as an alternative development paradigm. Its nuanced dialect, explicit recognition of diversity of human beings, and innovative methodologies not only provided a platform for critical reflection but also rekindled interest in the core values of development. The human development paradigm gained increased acceptability across the world and secured for itself a seat at the high table of global development discourse. Defined initially as 'the process of enlarging the range of people's choices',[1] it ushered in an ethical, value-based concept of development and restored the illustrious tradition of Aristotle for whom 'wealth is evidently not the good we are seeking, for it is merely useful and for the sake of something else',[2] and Kant, who reiterated that one should 'so act as to treat humanity, whether in thine own person or on that of any other, in every case as an end withal, never for as a means only'.[3] Aristotle's focus on the *human-ness* of human beings formed the basis for integrating moral values into the human development approach. The importance given to *choices* draws from Aristotle's view that the ability to choose a *way of life* in accordance with what a person considers to be *good* is the essence of being human.[4] Human beings choose acts on the basis of the extent to which they contribute to '*eudaimonia*'[5] or 'living in a way that is well-favoured by God',[6] more commonly interpreted as happiness or flourishing. Aristotle combines the emphasis on rational choice with its being in consonance with moral virtue.

Sen's critical perspective on interpersonal comparisons in welfare economics of reaching *impossibilities in distribution* re-ignited the possibilities of attaining social welfare by broadening in general the informational base that includes ownership of primary goods and resources, and in particular differences in converting them into capability to live well. Influenced by the Kantian notion of public reasoning, Sen discussed the possibilities of enhancing social welfare by bridging the reasoning and enabling comparisons of the information base.[7]

The basic choices specified in the definition of human development were to lead a long and healthy life, to be knowledgeable, to enjoy a decent standard of living, and to be able to enjoy substantive freedoms including political freedom, guaranteed human rights, and self-respect. The decade of the 1990s saw significant clarification about the contours of the approach in terms of core components (entitlements, functionings/capabilities), processes (equity, productivity, sustainability, and empowerment), and ethical dimensions (freedoms, opportunities, and agency). The definition of human development has been deepened and broadened in successive HDRs,[8] even as its basic thrust on choices, freedoms and opportunities continues. In the twentieth anniversary edition of the HDR, UNDP provided a broadened definition of human development, which states: 'Human development is the expansion of people's freedoms to live long, healthy and creative lives; to advance other goals they have reason to value; and to engage actively in shaping development equitably and sustainably on a shared planet. People are both the beneficiaries and drivers of human development, as individuals and in groups'.[9] Further, the 2016 HDR states that 'human development is about enlarging freedoms so that all human beings can pursue choices that they value'.[10] Moreover, there is an explicit recognition that the trajectory of human development encompasses multiple pathways. For example, the development experience of the early industrialized countries in Europe demonstrates how the spin offs from enhanced economic growth can be utilized to invest in human resources whereas the experience of East Asian economies illustrates how early massive public investment in education and expansion of health care could lead to accelerating growth rates and achieving greater opulence within a relatively short time span.

The transition of the human development paradigm from being a philosophy to providing guiding principles for policy and setting the institutional agenda has been interconnected and impressive, although, in some cases, the transition has been rather disjointed. More importantly, its formal expression in the writings of Haq[11] and Sen reversed the way in which the means and ends of development were perceived. This meant that the tradition started during the post–World War II period, of according precedence to GDP per capita as the principal end worth pursuing and people acting as a means to achieve it, was reversed. The human development paradigm positioned development of the people as the end while economic growth was considered as an important means to achieve this end.

In 1990, UNDP initiated the preparation of annual HDRs that succeeded in putting forth *two* ideas: (*a*) that development needs to be assessed not in terms of GDP per capita alone, but in terms of people; and (*b*) that the expansion of the range of people's choices is at the crux of the development project.[12]

The human development paradigm's evolution owes much to the efforts of Haq and Sen. Haq engaged with the formulation of the people-centric approach as a planner in Pakistan and within the UN system. He also played a crucial role in the NSRTs on development in the 1970s.[13]

This chapter reflects critically on the conceptual and methodological advancement of the human development paradigm: it raises questions related to what, why, and how. Section 2.1 introduces concepts of functionings and capabilities that have become central to the human development approach. This is followed by two sections (2.2 and 2.3) that discuss various forms of capabilities and the transitions and challenges posed by conversion factors. Section 2.4 discusses the importance of the inclusion of entitlements and endowments in human development analysis. Section 2.5 discusses the importance of the HDI in translating concepts into measures. The intersections of entitlements, capabilities, and processes of human development are presented in Section 2.6, and Section 2.7 discusses the shaping of the human development paradigm with the help of multidimensional indicators such as the HDI. The last section presents the emerging challenges in enlarging people's choices.

2.1 ABOUT FUNCTIONINGS AND CAPABILITIES

The human development approach evolved systematically to encompass a range of dimensions of development. Its refined expression of the individual's *notion of good*, societal norms of human flourishing, and intersectionality of rules, norms, structures, and practices is significant as it provides an advanced theoretical framework for human progress.[14] The earliest effort to deepen the perspective on social welfare was contained in Sen's conceptualization of capabilities as the ability to convert primary goods and resources to substantive freedoms that people have. Functionings, defined as 'the various things a person may value doing or being'[15] are a result of deliberate choice. An activity is considered worth doing for its own sake as happiness resides in the performance of one's function.

The connotational complexity is that functionings comprise not just what human beings *do* but is also what human beings *are*—what their state is—which is also an object of assessment. This is in keeping with the core aspect of human development that people are valuable in themselves—they are not just a *means* but also the *ends* for whom development takes place.[16]

The notion of *beings* is not esoteric. It can be easily understood with everyday examples such as being healthy and nourished, being safe, being educated, being employed, and so on. Similarly, *doings* are not merely those that enable one to earn an income but include simple everyday activities such as being able to visit loved ones, travelling, caring for a child, voting in an election, taking part in a debate, and so on, or more complex doings such as achieving self-respect, being socially integrated, and so on.

A question that immediately arises is whether functionings consist of what are universally considered to be morally *good* beings and doings or if it is possible for beings and doings generally considered undesirable or morally *bad* to also be included. In other words, is there a moral reasoning to be attached to *beings* and *doings*? Can universal *bads* like taking drugs or killing a person be treated as functionings? As functionings are 'beings and doings that people value or have reason to value',[17] several universal *bads* such as committing violence, taking drugs, and so on can be assumed as not being valuable or as actions that people will not have reason to value. This does not rule out however, that theoretically there exists a possibility that these could be considered valuable by an individual or a group of individuals in society.

Another tricky issue relates to income as a functioning. While income is considered an essential constituent of functionings, it is considered useful only up to a certain point. This limitation challenges the unfettered weight given to income for expansion of individual choices in mainstream development discourse. On this, Sen asserts, 'individual claims are to be assessed not by the resources or primary goods the persons respectively hold, but by the freedoms they actually enjoy to choose between different ways of living that they can have reason to value'.[18] Thereby, Sen extends the notion of *ends* within the human development approach to one that enhances actual freedoms to pursue things that an individual values. He further states that it is 'adequate to concentrate on the means to freedom, rather than on the extent of freedom that a person actually has'.[19] As different individuals have differing levels of resources and primary goods, the conversion of these available means could lead to achievement of varying levels of freedoms—the ends.[20] The case of Devi, discussed in Box 2.1, illustrates this succinctly.

The focus of evaluation in the human development paradigm is not merely on *commodities*, but on what individuals do with them. For example, the object of assessment is not consumption of food per se, but rather what the food does to the person. Hence, being nourished is a functioning while consumption of food is not. Moreover, if resources are different from functionings, resource requirements would vary depending on the community in which one lives. In the conventional utilitarian approach, the assessment ends at the stage of distribution of goods and services, whereas the functionings viewpoint considers what these goods and services *do to people* as their object of assessment.[21]

The list of valuable functionings is long and open-ended, lending itself to a variety of interpretations. Included in its gamut are the 'utilitarian value of "being happy"', the liberal value of "acting freely" and "being able to choose", and the Rawlsian value of "having self-respect," alongside more concrete functionings such as being in good health and being adequately fed.[22] This leads to a concept of well-being that is 'broad and partly opaque'.[23] Functionings are most commonly used for evaluation of states of *goodness*, the prime example being the HDI, which ranks countries according to attainments on knowledge, health, and income fronts.

BOX 2.1   Functionings of Child Labour in India

Devi, aged ten, youngest in the family that works in the match industry of Sivakasi, uses her forefinger to fold small pieces of wood into a box. Relentlessly, she spreads the paste on a piece of paper, wraps the box, and throws it into the pile. Both her parents and her three older brothers work as agricultural labourers.

Sivakasi, a small township in Tamil Nadu, a state in Southern India is a much-publicized centre of child labour. Several industries thrive there: match, fireworks, and printing industries. Most children belong to villages within a range of about 20 miles. These children are transported by bus 3–4 hours on average one-way for a 12-hour workday for in conditions that include the use of chemicals and inflammable material. Each matchbox is made manually. Younger children (between four and ten years) earn between 7 and 10 Indian rupees (INR) a day, while older children earn about INR 10–15 a day.

The situation in Sivakasi attracted public attention in 1976 when a bus capsized and many children were fatally injured. None of the children had ever been to school. During the series of deliberations in the Parliament, the elected member from Sivakasi argued that 'child labour is an economic problem and should be tackled accordingly without causing hardship to the families of child labourers and also without upsetting the industries which have created employment'.

The above evidence indicates a lack in two crucial functionings: adequate income and knowledge. Children like Devi live in several developing countries; they face multiple challenges in supplementing household income and facing contingencies. Failure in one of the functionings would cause rigidities in securing the other. The frontier of expanding literacy as a functioning played a crucial role in Sri Lanka and South Korea, where governments directly provided elementary education for all. In India, however, primary education was not compulsory until 2005 and thus the possibility of ameliorating poverty through education has yet to gain momentum. Realities of Sivakasi reverberate in other sites of bonded labour, casual labour, and illegal migrant labour across the world even today.

Source: Weiner, M. 1991. *The Child and the State in India*. New Delhi: Oxford University Press.

The importance of strengthening functionings that are crucial for human life has been highlighted by the SDGs. In Table 2.1 we present facts and figures for select goals that point to globally widespread deprivations in functionings despite the rapid economic progress achieved since the post–World War II period. It is a matter of consternation to note that as of 2014, over 800 million people across the world were struggling to fulfil basic human needs, pointing to the urgent need to shift policy focus towards these important dimensions of human life.

The formation of functionings is a complex process as realizing a functioning is dependent on the real opportunities available to achieve them. This brings in the notion of capabilities, a key concept within the human development paradigm. Capability is a person's real freedom or opportunity to achieve functionings. Stated differently, capability is 'substantive freedoms he or she enjoys to lead the kind of life he or she has reason to value'.[24] Thus, while travelling is a functioning, the real opportunity to travel is the corresponding capability. The distinction between functionings and capabilities is one of between the realized and the effectively possible. In other words, the difference is between achievements on one hand, and freedoms or valuable opportunities from which one can choose on the other.

Capability is defined in the functioning space and represents alternative functioning combinations from which a person can choose one combination. Capability is often considered to be similar to a budget set and represents the set of real opportunities that are available to an individual. However, it is not a mere summation of functionings. The presence of opportunity freedom to utilize functionings into meaningful outcomes for, say, a better standard of living is crucial.

It is important to note that the terms capability and capabilities are used interchangeably in the literature though the connotation of these two terms is slightly different. A significant expansion of the capabilities approach can be attributed to scholarly explanations by Sen and Martha Nussbaum. Section 2.2 discusses Nussbaum's perspective at length. Capability is a term used by Sen to refer to the opportunity to choose a *set of functionings* that is valuable and that people have 'reason to value'.[25] Once functionings are viewed as a set, there is scope to include interrelated functionings in the same set. For example, the functioning of being healthy is interrelated with the functioning of

TABLE 2.1 Identification of Functionings in the SDGs

Goal	Fact	Functionings Backlog
No poverty	836 million people still struggle for the most basic human needs	Deprivation in basic entitlements
	One in five persons in developing regions lives on less than USD 1.25 per day	Deficiency in provision of social protection
No hunger	One in every four persons still goes hungry in Africa, and 66 million primary school-age children across the developing world attend classes hungry	Calorific deficiency
	As of 2014, 795 million people are estimated to be chronically undernourished, and over 90 million children under the age of five are dangerously underweight	Nutritional deprivation
Good health and well-being	Poor nutrition causes nearly half (45 per cent) of deaths in children under five—3.1 million children each year	Child mortality
	Each year, more than six million children die before their fifth birthday	
	Maternal mortality ratio in developing regions is 14 times higher than in developed regions	Lack of access to maternal health
	Since 2000, global mortality rates due to malaria and tuberculosis have fallen by 58 per cent and 41 per cent, respectively	Poor access to health care
Quality education	57 million children remain out of school	Low access to education resulting in education deprivation
	103 million youth worldwide lack basic literacy skills; more than 60 per cent of these are women	Low mean and expected of schooling

(continued)

TABLE 2.1 (*Continued*)

Goal	Fact	Functionings Backlog
Gender equality	Girls face barriers to enter schools	Low gender parity in education
	Women employed as unpaid workers in most sectors; low labour force participation rate outside in non-agricultural sectors	Low women's participation in labour markets
Clean water and sanitation	663 million people are still without improved drinking water	Lack of access to safe drinking water
	1.8 billion people globally use a source of drinking water that is fecally contaminated	Health and water deprivation
	2.4 billion people lack access to basic sanitation services such as toilets or latrines	Lack of access to sanitation facilities
	Nearly 1,000 children die each day due to preventable water and sanitation–related diarrhoeal diseases	Lack of access to safe drinking water
	Floods and other water-related disasters account for 70 per cent of all deaths related to natural disasters	Environmental vulnerability
Affordable and clean energy	3 billion people rely on wood, coal, charcoal, or animal waste for cooking and heating	Lack of access to safe fuel
Decent work and economic growth	Global unemployment increased from 170 million in 2007 to nearly 202 million in 2012	Lack of income opportunities
	Nearly 2.2 billion people live below the US poverty line of USD 2	High job vulnerabilities
	470 million jobs are needed globally for new entrants to the labour market between 2016 and 2030	Growing pressures of youth unemployment

Source: Formulated by authors from http://www.undp.org/content/undp/en/home/sustainable–development-goals.html; 8 February 2018.

having safe drinking water and proper sanitation. Different functionings that are valuable for enhancing the capability of a child include aspects such as being nourished, being educated, being able to learn, and live in an enabling environment at home and society. Sen reiterated the need for a relatively small number of centrally important capabilities such as education, health, nutrition, civil, and political liberties, human dignity, and so on. However, he desisted from providing a capability list as it is not in keeping with the pluralistic and democratic nature of the capability approach.[26]

The perceptions regarding what constitutes basic capabilities could vary widely across communities and countries. An interesting example given by Trani, Bakshi, and Rolland,[27] using Sen's conceptualisation of capabilities, brought to the fore the fact that bodily integrity, access to shelter, health, education, and wealth would be considered basic capabilities in most contexts. Yet, in the case of Afghanistan, they found that people accorded much higher weights to aspects such as love, care, and community participation. Despite being deprived of some basic capabilities, respondents in their survey found positive perception of well-being if they conformed to their social roles and are supported by their families.

2.2 FORMS OF CAPABILITIES

Over the past two decades, there has been significant exploration of the concept of capabilities, involving its components and characteristics. Originally conceived as a *set of functionings*, capabilities have now been examined in a more dynamic fashion including several layers and processes.

Nussbaum suggested a list of essential capabilities known as *central human capabilities*, which focus on what it means to live a life with *human dignity*. She argues that an individual must attain a certain *threshold level in the enlisted ten capabilities* to enable him/her to 'live in a truly human way'.[28–29] Nussbaum's list[30] provides normative content to the capability approach and ensures wide applicability by including cross culturally specified capabilities. Her list includes life; bodily health; bodily integrity; senses, imagination, and thought; emotions; practical reason; affiliation; other species; and play and control over one's environment. We argue that this should be viewed as *threshold capabilities* as these also represent the set of functionings that protect the individual from deprivation, discrimination, vulnerabilities, and unfreedoms and are foundations that would enable individuals to expand human freedoms.

Figure 2.1 provides an understanding about the multilayered capabilities concept. Basic capabilities[31] are elementary innate powers that every individual possesses and are essential for the expansion of other more advanced capabilities. Sen considers them to be a person's ability to do certain basic things. There is no rigidity in this classification. It essentially deals with the notion of how individuals seek to expand their choices through two forms of capabilities: internal capabilities and external capabilities.

Internal capabilities are matured, developed conditions of the individual that enable the person to exercise the required functions. Sometimes, internal capabilities develop only as the body grows, with time and supportive environment: for instance, a person's ability to exercise political choice or a child's ability to play and learn a language. However, this notion is a little problematic as speech, love, gratitude, and so on, are largely actions of individuals, and in order to consider them as capabilities, we may have to examine the opportunity freedoms available to the new born child. The notion of internal capabilities largely locates the notion of functionings without considering oppor-

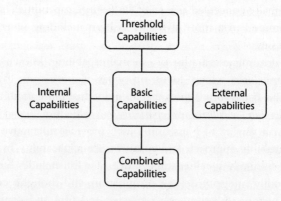

FIGURE 2.1   Conceptual Representation of Central Capabilities
Source: Formulated by authors.

tunity freedom. Though there is a certain acceptance of the notion of internal capabilities, it is yet to be fully explored critically.

External capabilities are driven through processes where internal capabilities of individuals interact with the external context. Foster and Handy,[32] while providing a list of external capabilities, state that external capabilities are those that enhance capabilities of an individual due to his/her access to another person's capabilities or due to 'direct human relationships'. For example, a nutritionist, apart from providing professional advice and care to his/her patients, also takes care of the health needs of her family, friends and colleagues by providing useful tips regarding healthy living. Thus, it is the external capabilities of his/her family, friends and acquaintances that are enhanced because of certain capabilities possessed by her.

Basu and Foster[33] also highlight the significance of external capabilities by illustrating three cases: first, that of a low-skill job that requires reading and writing skills; second, that of agricultural extension workers who disseminate information on effective agricultural techniques to be used through brochures; and third, that of a medical facility in a nearby village whose staff distributes pamphlets on preventing diseases and infection and various services that the facility offers. They remark that though all the three cases are intrinsically linked to literacy, unlike case one that required the person herself to be literate, cases two and three are instances of external capabilities since they rely on the access of a literate person who can and is willing to provide the required literacy services.

Combined capabilities may then be defined as internal capabilities combined with external conditions that are necessary for the exercise of human functions. For instance, in a non-democratic set-up, the citizens of the nation may possess the internal capability to exercise freedom of speech and expression but not the combined capability required for the same.

This hierarchical evolution provides an analytical lens whereby formation of functionings occurs through a range of processes that are within the control of the individual and are also influenced by the milieu in which he/she is present.

One of the key challenges in the use of the term capability is that it is commonly used by people to indicate skills or capacity. For example, in common parlance one could say that A is capable of playing football whereas B is not. However, this is not the sense in which the term is used in the capability approach. Gasper[34] points to three different connotations of the term:

1. P capability, indicating inborn potential which relates to innate abilities
2. S capability, indicating acquired skills and abilities
3. O capability, which is opportunity capability

Sen's usage relates to O capability while Nussbaum's usage includes elements of P and S capability as well.[35] Sen's analogy of functionings as being akin to a budget set and a person with pocket full of coins being able to buy many different combinations of things indicates that a person has the possibility of choosing many different life paths from given functionings. Thus, capability is composed of two equally important parts, namely, functionings and opportunity freedom.[36]

The choice of functionings to form the capability set is indeed an *individual* choice. However, individual choice is influenced by social arrangements.[37] Though at the individual level the decisions on what is considered valuable are taken by the individual concerned, collectively arriving at *valuable beings and doings* is an entirely different process. Societal preferences on which functionings set is valuable is an issue that can be resolved only through public reasoning.[38] Sen is optimistic that a consensus can be arrived at through informational broadening. He also acknowledges that the process of societal consensus requires not only acting on the basis of given individual preferences, but also entails being sensitive to the fact that such preferences and norms develop through public discussion and interactions that facilitate the emergence of shared values and commitments.[39] Further, social arrangements do not need a complete social ordering of all possibilities. A workable solution could be arrived at on the basis of partial orderings, wherein there is contingent acceptance of particular provisions, though social unanimity may remain elusive. A striking example of such consensus was the ratification of the MDGs by a large number of member countries of the UN in 2000 followed by a similar consensus on the SDGs more recently in 2015.

Apart from capabilities at the individual level, collective capability is also an important component that merits attention. Collective capability is acquired by people in the process of pursuing lives that they value. Collective capabilities are not a sum of individual capabilities but are 'new capabilities that the individual alone would neither have nor be able to achieve if he or she did not join a collective'.[40] Collective capabilities influence individual choice by affecting the individual's perception of the *good* and determining his or her ability to achieve these functionings. For example, in developing countries, Farmers Producers Organisations (FPOs) are an institution that enhances the collective capabilities of small and marginal farmers. The FPOs mobilize small and marginal producers of agricultural commodities to form alliances, which enable them to collectively build their capacity and leverage marketing and production strength. These FPOs enable the farmers to enhance collective capabilities such as their ability to undertake investment, access information and technical assistance, and use of appropriate inputs. They also improve the risk-bearing capacity of farmers and enhance their income earning potential.

2.3 CONVERSION FACTORS: TRANSITIONS AND CHALLENGES

The manner and extent to which any resource benefits an individual depends on how it meets divergent human needs, the opportunities available to individuals, and how social arrangements facilitate or hinder their access to such opportunities. The capability approach pays particular attention to the diversity across individuals, both in their own choices as well as in their personal, social and environmental factors, which influence the extent to which resources can be converted into functionings and capabilities.

Human diversity is recognized in two ways: first, by recognizing plurality of functionings and capabilities as the evaluative space; and second, through an explicit focus on personal and socio-environmental conversion factors of commodities into functionings. To illustrate, food is a resource that enables a person to be well nourished, a capability. As Sen[41] pointed out, the transition process from obtaining the food to converting it into nutrition depends on the person's metabolic rate, which varies depending on body size, age, sex, activity levels, and so on, all of which are *personal factors*. In addition, *social factors*, such as religious beliefs that determine norms in regard to the amount and kinds of food that a person can consume, can also influence functionings. For example, vegetarians do not consume meat and eggs, vegans do not consume dairy products in addition to meat as it is against their beliefs; this, in turn, could influence people's nutritional levels. *Environmental factors* such as lack of safe sanitation and drinking water can also lead to parasitic diseases that inhibit the absorption of nutrients by the body. It is evident that overall, the social and institutional context affects conversion factors and the capability set directly.[42]

The conversion of resources into functionings can be distinguished at two levels: (*a*) from resources to capability; and (*b*) from capability to functionings (see Figure 2.2). Thus, the conversion from resources to functionings is through capability. Personal, social, and environmental factors play a key role in this conversion, particularly in the first level (from resources to capability), whereas agency emerges at the forefront at the second level. Here, agency[43] is 'constructively valuable'[44] in the achievement of being well educated, healthy, well nourished. The constructive value of the agency lies in the agent's selection, weighing and trading of capabilities.

Chiapperò-Martinetti and Salardi[45] operationalize conversion factors into a 'functioning production function', measuring conversion of resources (inputs) to achieved functionings (outputs) associated with being healthy, being educated, and living in a safe and healthy environment. However, functionings are not only determined by resources used

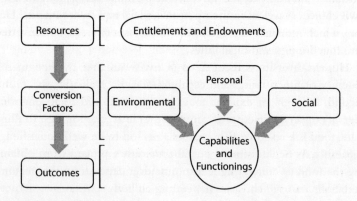

FIGURE 2.2 Conversion Factors
Source: Formulated by authors.

but also by technology under process. Conversion factors—personal, social, and environmental—act as constraints and determine the conversion rate. They use micro sample survey data on both qualitative and quantitative variables generated by the Italian Central Statistical Office for the purpose. In a similar study, Binder and Broekel[46] measure conversion efficiency in the UK and indicate that the same amount of resource like food can result in differing levels of nutrition for individuals, depending on the strength of conversion factors.

The issue of evaluation of a capability set faces huge informational challenges. Since the capability set is defined in the space of functionings, one way to judge the capability set would be from the point of view of functionings.

Sen[47] identifies three different ways in which this can be done:

1. Using the entire set of options open to the person, involving weighing the options available in some way.
2. Selecting only the option that is actually *chosen* by the person, amounting to looking at only the 'focal point of the set'.
3. Focusing on *maximally valued option* from the capability set.

The use of either option 2 or 3 is termed to be 'elementary evaluation' as the full range of options available is not explored for the assessment.

Exercising the first option would be informationally demanding as it would require gathering information on interpersonal variations to understand how capability actually translates into functionings. This means that one has to contend with a host of conversion factors that operate at the individual or household level. It is also difficult to understand what the individual capability set might be, as this would require an analyst to reckon with not only the capability set under consideration but all the alternative sets that are available and considered before a choice is made. Such an evaluation may not be possible if the elements in the capability set are not fully ordered, since future rankings may be unknown. Even if future tastes are known partially, it will lead only to a partial ordering of the elements. Moreover, the core of the argument of the capability approach is that considering what is actually chosen is unsatisfactory, true assessment should be of the full range of possibilities that are available.[48]

Fuzzy set theory has been often applied to capabilities, as it can theoretically consider the plurality of functionings and the plurality of alternative possibilities in the capability set from which an individual chooses a set.[49] However, even this effort falls short of the requirement, as most applications have only examined achieved functionings and not how they relate to capability sets. If the key to evaluation of capability is to attach importance to the freedom to have alternatives rather than just the chosen combination, then the informational challenges are indeed huge and cannot be overlooked.

Alternatives 2 and 3 avoid the informational challenge by focusing only on either achieved functionings or on the maximally regarded option. The reduced informational requirements in both cases render it operationally simpler to manage. However, such an evaluation can only qualify to be an *elementary evaluation* as compared to a full evaluation, since it fails to take into account the entire range of options available to a person from which a set is chosen. When the value attached to the maximally regarded option is taken to represent the entire capability set, the evaluation resembles the conventional uni-focal approach.

A question that naturally arises, then, is how the capability approach is different from the conventional approach that considers only achievements (or functionings) and not *possibilities* or *opportunities* that existed? Sen answers this question by pointing to the conceptual difference that exists between the two approaches. In the conventional utilitarian approach, the focus is on the functioning combination that the person actually has, whereas in the elementary evaluation using the capability approach, the focus is on the chosen functionings. The availability of various options enters the evaluation, even though the assessment is based on the alternative that the person actually chose (option 2), or on the 'most choosable functioning combination that the person had the opportunity to choose'[50] (option 3). To illustrate, if one wants to evaluate the health status of an individual, according to alternative 1, one will have to list all the elements that determine the health status and the weights associated to each of these elements, such as genetic make-up, age, income status, list of communicable and non-communicable diseases that one is exposed to, level of hygiene and sanitation in the environment where he/ she lives, his/her health history, list of social factors that affect health habits and usage of health care services, accessibility and availability of health care services, and so on, where the list can be infinite or indefinite. Thus, choosing one particular element from the capability set becomes difficult. When resorting to alternatives 2 and 3, life expectancy is used universally to represent the health status of a person. This is because it is widely accepted as a representative of the whole set or a chosen option that is a *focal point of the set* and also the most valued option in the capability set.

2.4 SOME EMERGING CONCERNS

The capability approach made a significant contribution to the development of an alternative lens by evaluating developmental outcomes, and is now firmly established in the lexicon of development theory and practice. Drawing from Aristotle's notion of *eudomonic* well-being that goes beyond the narrow and hedonic utilitarian calculus, it highlights the virtues that define humanity.[51] The major contribution of this approach has been a focus on human beings as ends in themselves, highlighting their *beings and doings* and focusing on the human potential and its conversion into actual outcomes. It provides space for a Kantian conception of moral freedom which contrasts starkly with the view that reduces human beings to merely 'strict maximizers of a narrowly defined self-interest'.[52] In the process, the approach carves out an entirely different pathway of normative assessment, bringing into question the assumptions used by conventional economics, particularly that of similarity of preferences across individuals and their responses to given situations.

The distinguishing feature of the approach is its cross-cultural nature that is achieved by defining functionings in a very generic manner, thereby making it applicable across different settings. At the same time, the approach recognizes that individuals may accord different weights to functionings. The weights depend on what people value and have *reason to value*, which is an acceptance of the plurality of ways of living. Importantly, it explicitly factors in the differential rates of conversion of capabilities into functionings depending on personal, social and environmental conversion factors that individuals face, and thus acknowledging situations where *equality of resources could translate into multiple and diverse outcomes*.

Although at once intriguing and complex, the capability approach has made a substantive contribution to both development thinking and development practice. Nonetheless, many concerns remain in the articulation of key concepts as well as in assessing them, some of which are addressed in what follows. The issues raised are only indicative and not exhaustive of the rich literature on the subject.

First, assume that a person may value fasting in contrast to starvation, which is forced fasting. Though there may be a *reason to value* such a functioning, the choice of fasting occurs when individuals' basic capabilities enable them to make informed choices, whereas in the case of starvation, individuals are constrained in their basic functionings to achieve basic capabilities of nutrition. Thus, even as the capability approach rests on the pivot of functionings that people value and have 'reason to value', it places choices and presence of public reasoning central to human freedom and collective well-being.[53] Here, we need to be cautious as though public reasoning could broaden the perspectives of those who participate, societal judgements about what constitutes a *good life* could lead to restrictions on individual liberty. Even as this fear is well founded, since capabilities encompass a range of resources, processes and opportunities that overlap, individual preferences and liberty are protected.

Second, another issue is the capability approach's exclusive focus on individual capability and the complete neglect of collective capability. Ibrahim defines collective capability as capabilities that are 'newly generated functioning bundles a person obtains by virtue of his/her engagement in a collectivity that help her/him achieve the life he/she has reason to value'.[54] Stewart[55] points out that the preoccupation with the individual has meant that the capability approach neglects social institutions and competencies. But the approach adopts ethical individualism and not methodological or ontological individualism,[56] while also recognizing the social moorings of individual choices. The process of expansion of capabilities occurs through agency, freedom, and empowerment.

Third, in the process of seeking equality and human freedom, the capability approach fails to recognize the importance of solidarity. Several societies in modern times are individualistic; the capability approach too, in its liberal individualist orientation, prioritizes 'individual liberty, not social: the freedom to choose, not to belong'.[57] Another related aspect is that Sen's concept of functionings is not well defined and could refer to 'ability to perceive opportunities, ability to formulate choices, ability to make choices, and ability to act'.[58] A similar problem is experienced with the concept of well-being. This approach limits the understanding of differences in the degrees and types of *happiness* or the distinction between the terms *happiness* and *pleasure*.[59] That said, capabilities and functionings are part of a continuum that facilitate alternate interpretation. Thus, their contribution to overall human freedom and well-being cannot be considered in isolation.

Fourth, the capability approach focuses on 'what goods do to people'. This brings together two aspects; a person's ability to do certain things, and the state produced by the goods in the person.[60] Cohen argues that the former can be treated as a capability, and the latter one represents what he calls 'midfare'.[61] Sen agrees with Cohen in so far as the distinction is concerned but asserts that he is mistaken in interpretation. We, too, agree with this perspective, as capability is the process towards enlarging human freedom, and doings and beings are critical for their own sake. The distinction between functionings and capability is an essential part of the capability approach.

Fifth, assessing the state of well-being using the capability approach is problematic, since most often one must rely on what Sen calls 'elementary evaluation', which essentially means that the best value in the capability set is assigned to the set as a whole.[62] The problem with such an evaluation is that the elements of the set may not be fully ordered. Even if the assessment is made using partial orderings of functioning vectors on well-being, to be cast in the spirit of the capability approach it would be necessary to consider not only what has been achieved but what *could be achieved*. It needs to borne in mind that human well-being is a dynamic process ingrained in the socio-economic and cultural milieu, and there could be individual level variations in achieved functionings.

Sixth, the open-ended and undefined theorization is a boon and a bane. Even though a range of freedoms can be captured in the capability approach, yet, several commentators[63–64] have critiqued the non-availability of a list, reasoning that any evaluative study developed on the capability approach will require selection of a list of capabilities to be analysed.[65] However, there is also a strand of thought arguing that ethical theorists are not obligated to provide a list of capabilities or decide on behalf of people what should be evaluated, since this would be against democratic principles. A list must necessarily emerge through social discussion and public reasoning, since any close-ended list will not encompass the diverse human dimensions and various social and institutional dimensions that people value and have *reason to value*. The issue is still being actively debated and defies a solution as the proponents and opponents are equivocal in their respective viewpoints.

Lastly, albeit theoretically, the capability approach has been expansive in nature, non-availability of corresponding and reliable data sets in the existing international and national data systems, continues to be a challenge.[66] However, the popularity of the capability approach being used in several research studies highlights efforts to transcend some of the shortfalls highlighted above.[67] This points to the potential that remains underexplored.

2.5 ENDOWMENTS AND ENTITLEMENTS

We will now discuss other important concepts that guide the expansion of human freedom and flourishing: entitlements and endowments. The entitlement approach acquired importance in the context of Sen's analysis of famines (the Indian province of Bengal in 1943, Bangladesh in 1974, Ethiopia in 1974), where he pointed out that the occurrence of famines was less due to shortages of food and more due to the failure of the poor to secure their entitlements. The term 'entitlement' is used to denote 'the set of alternative commodity bundles that a person can command in a society using the totality of rights and opportunities that he or she faces'.[68] The term is used more in the sense of what the law guarantees and supports, and does not have a moral connotation of what *a person is normally entitled to*. According to Gasper,[69] entitlement 'is an extension of the concept of purchasing power to cover acquisition potential as a whole'.

What, then, are the entitlements of people in a society? How do these entitlements get realized? Figure 2.3 provides a framework for understanding entitlements and endowments.

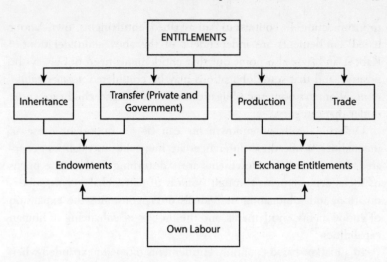

FIGURE 2.3   Entitlements and Endowments
Source: Formulated by authors.

Endowments refer to a person's set of resources including their own labour power. Dworkin[70] identifies two categories of endowments: natural and social. Natural endowments include a person's physical and mental health and ability, general fitness and capacities, and wealth, fixed, and financial assets. It also includes labour power, which is his or her innate capacity to produce goods or services that others will pay to have. In addition to the natural endowments mentioned earlier, social endowments that include the social structures and processes that affect a person's ability to 'generate impersonal resources and realize their ambitions' may also be important.[71] A person's religion, gender, race, historical experience, and background are all elements of social endowments. In fact, these are the very factors that could cause and perpetuate inequalities in society.

Watts[72] points out that empowerment is a prerequisite to securing entitlements. Often a woman's entitlement depends on the extent and nature of her negotiation within a household. Kabeer and Aziz[73] point to transfers within the family that depend on (*a*) a woman's independence, (*b*) the extent to which she neglects her own well-being for the rest of the household, (*c*) the culturally relative perception of what a contribution is, and (*d*) the extent to which women are subject to intimidation. In contrast to 'kin ascribed' entitlements, 'own-labour based' entitlements are independent of the above considerations.[74] Kabeer and Aziz also point out that entitlements need not always be positive, and that some obligations may be considered *negative entitlements*. Women's domestic obligations of cooking and child care come under that category.

Differing levels of endowments can be an important cause of inequalities. While these differences are inevitable, inequalities generated through social endowments are a disturbing feature. The praxis of social arrangements through systems of patriarchal norms, subordination, and subjugating individuals often constrains the expansion of endowments, entitlements, and the process of enhancing of human capabilities.[75]

In a market-based economy, entitlements often are expanded when an individual acquires alternative capabilities by exchanging one's own bundle. This is what Sen calls *exchange entitlements*. Exchange entitlements are more feasible to acquire in a market-based economy as compared to a socialist economy, where private ownership of assets is either restricted or not prevalent. However, socialist economies may have higher levels of social security provisioning, which would enhance the entitlements of all citizens. Sen includes social security[76] and net taxation[77] in the definition of entitlements.

An exchange entitlement is defined as 'the set of alternative bundles of commodities that he can acquire in exchange for what he owns'.[78] Sen identifies four types of processes that impact entitlements in a market economy. Trade-based entitlements comprise entitlements that are obtained through trading what one owns, including one's own labour power. Production-based entitlements are entitlements that one gets by arranging production through the use of one's own or hired resources. Own labour entitlements include the entitlements that accrue from the use of one's own labour power including those entitlements that are acquired through trade and production. Finally, inheritance and transfer entitlements refer to the entitlement to own what is given by another person who owns the asset or resource.

The total entitlements that a person secures, thus, depend on endowments and those acquired through exchange. This represents the set of alternative possibilities that confront a person or a household. *Exchange entitlement mapping* or *E mapping* reflects the rules, conditions, and

BOX 2.2 Homelessness and Entitlements

Access to housing enables a person to expand one's capabilities. It provides shelter where an individual can rest, store his or her belongings, and maintain clean and sanitary conditions. It also serves as a reference point—a place where one can engage in different activities and facilitate social and political participation. Therefore, it enables the achievement of various potential functionings and states of well-being that make a house a home. As a commodity, housing enables interaction between what the commodity contributes to the user and what the user contributes.

However, obstructions such as extremely low endowments, absence of entitlements due to lack of explicit welfare orientation by the state or lack of social systems could lead to absence of right to land and right to articulate one's need. In addition, low purchasing power, low accessibility and availability, and lack of opportunities and freedoms to exercise functionings, which contribute to states of well-being, can lead to homelessness. Homelessness is a condition that occurs due to four categories or reasons: rooflessness, houselessness, insecure housing, and inadequate housing. In the context of Nussbaum's list of capabilities, homelessness refers to deprivation of bodily health, bodily integrity and control over one's environment.

In Delhi, India, a homelessness survey was conducted in 2010 by the Government of Delhi with the objective to address the needs of the homeless population and restore their rights. The study had a sample size of nearly 55,000 and analysed the distribution of homeless people across the state, their origin, caste, period of homelessness, age and gender distribution, occupation, ancestral work, access to basic amenities, sleeping spaces, sex ratio, literacy levels, causes of homelessness, and problems faced by homeless people. Its major observations are: (a) the majority of the homeless are men and young adults (over 85 per cent); (b) the majority of homeless people are working and are productive citizens of the city (nearly 69 per cent); (c) the motivation to migrate is a result of the poor state of the rural economy; (d) most of the homeless people sleep on pavements and at workplaces, cook their own food, and rely on water from unsafe sources; (e) a large number of the homeless are children (over 20 per cent); (f) the ratio of homeless girls falls sharply as they enter puberty and adulthood; and (g) harassment from the police is a major problem homeless face besides the other difficulties.

Source: Evangelista, G.F. 2010. 'Poverty, Homelessness and Freedom: An Approach from the Capabilities Theory'. *European Journal of Homelessness* 4: 189–202; Government of Delhi. 2010. *Homeless Survey 2010*. New Delhi: Project Management Unit; GNCTD–UNDP Project; Administrative Reforms Department.

processes that affect how entitlements are derived from one's endowment. In explaining the phenomenon of starvation due to famines, Sen[79] contends that factors determining exchange entitlements of an individual would include not only surplus production of food grains, but also distribution and availability of the produce equitably to all in society. The presence of diverse processes in each of the categories influences exchange entitlements both through volume of food supply and via the population distribution or demography in society.

The type of endowments and entitlements depend both on state action and the mode of production in the operation in the economy. Box 2.2 provides an example in the context of homelessness to explain the role of the state in the form of affirmative policies to tackle entitlement failures in society. In a series of primary surveys on the public distribution system in India, Drèze and Khera[80] have highlighted the fact that the implementation of Right to Food Act 2013 has converted the legal entitlement of existing food security programmes of the Government of India, empowered local population to demand effective implementation of schemes, and contributed to human agency. The claim to entitlements is not limited to only material well-being but is also reflected in the transformation to nonmaterial welfare.

The capability sets that Sen alludes to in his writings, as well as the list of capabilities that Nussbaum provides, include many entitlements that are emphasized by the human rights movement. In fact, entitlements or capabilities cover both the first generation of human rights such as political and civil rights and second-generation rights encompassing economic and social rights. Nussbaum[81] equates human rights to her notion of combined capabilities, because they require an interaction of internal with external capabilities in order to exercise a particular functioning. Take the example of Alia, who has completed her primary education with good grades. However, she is unable to pursue secondary education because of the absence of separate toilets for girls and boys in schools. Thus, her capability to pursue higher education is curtailed due to the absence of enabling external conditions. Similarly, even though the government promotes and disseminates information regarding family planning, uneducated people may not be able to gather this information and benefit from it.

2.6 PROCESSES AND INTERCONNECTIONS

The synthesis of the human development and capabilities approach through the prisms of capabilities and entitlements has revolutionized the development arena. Today, the language of capabilities has emerged as a prominent alternative as it lends precision and supplementation to the language of rights. Political participation, right to free exercise of religion, right to free speech, and so on are best secured when the relevant capabilities to function are present in people. The capability approach has enabled a better understanding of inequalities through its focus on *beings and doings* of people. Importantly, it can highlight inequalities that women suffer inside families, particularly inequality in access to resources and opportunities, educational deprivations, failure of household work to be recognized as *work*, and insults to bodily integrity. Another advantage of the capability approach over the language of rights is that it is not linked sharply to any particular cultural or historical tradition—a shortcoming that the language of rights suffers from as it is often associated with the European Enlightenment, even though its component ideas have deep roots in many traditions.

Capabilities and entitlements together determine human development outcomes. The processes of strengthening them can be driven by enhancing equity, productivity, sustainability, and empowerment, which represent the means to a plurality of ends. Denuelin and Shahani[82] classify these processes as pillars of human development. The notion of pillars was introduced in Haq's *Reflections on Human Development*.[83] We prefer to call them *processes*, as the larger meta-question of human development is that of human flourishing, human freedom, and human well-being, of which the ethical fulcrum is that of freedoms, opportunities, and agency.

The human development framework emerging from the range of processes and interconnections is presented in Figure 2.4 as a four-quadrant system. The framework identifies four distinct and highly interrelated paths to human development. As is evident, these paths represent the four processes of human development:

1. Equity-led path to human development.
2. Productivity-led path to human development.

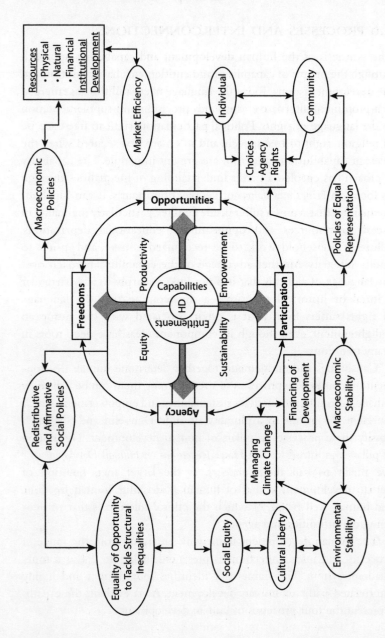

FIGURE 2.4 Analytical Framework
Source: Formulated by authors.

3. Empowerment-led path to human development.
4. Sustainability-led path to human development.

We argue that the identification of specific pathways of development through any of the processes requires a mix of primary institutions and actors. This framework brings together the pillars/processes of human development along with the main actors involved in actualizing the human development outcomes. While human development could be triggered through any of the processes, outcomes can be accomplished only when the other paths of human development are also involved in the later stages. The interplay of the processes with institutional actors provides an interesting perspective in operationalizing human development: Quadrant I on equity deals with the role of public action; Quadrant II on sustainability concerns itself with the role of the individual/community with physical and human ecology at various levels; Quadrant III deals with simultaneous interplay of human agency and market; and Quadrant IV shows how processes are a reflection of the role of government policies in driving effective development of markets.

A failure to understand the interconnectedness of these processes could lead to a gradual erosion in the depth and vigour of human development progress leading to a vicious trap, which could result in lopsided economic growth or lopsided human development outcomes.[84] Economic growth and human development linkages often seek to explain the process of expansion of human choices but have provided limited theoretical explanations about their interconnections. The emergence of a vicious trap, resulting in either lopsided economic growth or lopsided human development outcomes, can be traced to the weak interconnectedness among the processes of development.[85]

Why Does Equity Matter?

Equity is a comprehensive aspect encompassing equality of opportunity in multiple dimensions such as economic, social, cultural, and political. The notion of justice and equity in the human development approach is interpreted within the realm of capabilities.[86] It captures differences in opportunity freedoms and thereby recognizes heterogeneities among individuals. It encompasses both inter- and intra-generational dimensions. Equity is sought to be achieved in the realm of access to opportunities rather than in functionings that constitute end results.

While seemingly simple in its articulation, the principle of equity has powerful ramifications that necessitate a restructuring of the prevailing economic and power relations. Where initial conditions in terms of asset and wealth distribution are unequal, pursuing equity in capabilities could involve taking politically sensitive measures comprising redistribution of productive assets such as land, income and credit and other measures that could improve capabilities and entitlements.

The human development approach reorients the debate of equity from a solely individual-driven process to include actions initiated by the state. Affirmative public action takes centre stage wherein there is a role for both the state and peoples' participation. The concept of equity also implies that the rights of women, minorities, and other traditionally excluded groups are taken into account. Many of these measures were implemented in the East Asian countries and we discuss one such example in Malaysia in Box 2.3. The Malaysian experience shows that affirmative state polices in education simultaneously enable the reduction of economic and social inequalities.

The realization of this process calls for a unique state–society relationship. It is assumed that on one hand, enhanced capabilities and entitlements will be achieved through the state-led implementation of redistributive and affirmative social policies, as on the other hand social transformations at the individual and household level overcome inter- and intra-generational inequalities.

Role of Productivity in Bridging Opportunities

The process of enhancing human freedom for achieving higher growth rate and sustainable development outcomes 'requires investment in people and an enabling macroeconomic environment for them to achieve their maximum potential'.[87] For operationalizing the efficiency principle, it is necessary to demonstrate that the chosen initiative is indeed the one that offers the best results in expanding choices and enabling optimum use of opportunities by people. As

BOX 2.3   Affirmative Action in Malaysia

In the 1960s, Malaysia was beset with wide ethnic inequalities between the Bumiputera, or *son of the soil*, comprised of the Malays on one hand, and the minority population comprised of the Chinese and Indians on the other. The historical domination of the minorities in higher-skilled and income occupations in the urban areas was in sharp contrast to the Bumiputera, who were employed mainly in agricultural activities and lower-skilled jobs. In 1957–8, the mean income of the Malays was less than the half of that of the Chinese.

The Government of Malaysia, through a series of affirmative actions in the New Economic Policy (NEP) in 1971, introduced quotas for Bumiputeras in public universities along with special scholarships for overseas study. It also established new schools and universities for the Bumiputeras. Special quotas were introduced to enhance employment opportunities in the government sector, alongside schemes to promote small and medium sized enterprises.

As a result, between 1970 and 2000, the enrolment percentage of Malay students in tertiary institutions doubled, registrations of Bumiputera professionals increased from 5 to 37 per cent, and employment in professional, technical, and related work increased by 8.7 per cent for the Bumiputera as against 5.4 per cent for Chinese professionals. The NEP also contributed significantly to poverty reduction by almost 41 per cent from 49.3 per cent in 1970 to 7.5 per cent in 1999.

Examples of similar affirmative action in other countries include employment and education quotas for the scheduled castes (SCs) and scheduled tribes (STs) in India, and the Employment Equity Act in South Africa.

Source: Cheong, K.C., Nagraj, S., and Lee, K.L. 2009. 'Counting Ethnicity: The National Economic Policy and Social Integration'. *Journal of Economic Studies* 46 (1): 33–52.

stated earlier, income as a functioning represents a means that could lead to achievement of varying levels of freedoms—the ends. The linkages with access to livelihoods and quality jobs in this regard cannot be ignored. Structurally and institutionally, highly iniquitous labour markets could derail opportunities for investments in people. Thus, macroeconomic policies that are narrowly defined to enhance growth rates of only physical and financial capital may enhance human capital of a select few, but could lead to exclusion of the population at large.

The human freedom approach to the process of enhancing productivity places importance on conditions of work, dignity, and much neglected aspects of accounting for individual values. Thus, productivity involves monetary as well as non-monetary rewards to the use of one's time. Since income is only a means of human flourishing, monetary rewards are not the sole parameter on which productivity can be assessed.

It is necessary that there exists a supportive environment for people to attain their full potential. The structure of the economy and the extent to which the benefits of development are reaped by the poorer sections also have a bearing on the relationship between productivity enhancement and human development. For example, in Indonesia between the 1970s and 1980s, productivity enhancement of the agricultural sector stemming from structural reforms such as land consolidation, investment in rural infrastructure, and subsidies to key agricultural inputs such as fertilizers, resulted in a rice boom. The rising incomes led to sharp reduction in poverty and malnutrition,[88] highlighting how paying attention to the neglected areas through appropriate investments can lead to productivity enhancements, which in turn contribute to positive human development outcomes. The Nepal HDR 2014 examines the relationship between levels of human development and productivity in nine regions. The empirical analysis across seventy-five districts of Nepal indicates a positive relationship between productivity levels and HDI values, and a negative correlation between labour productivity and poverty. The Report also highlights that structural change and economic transformation are closely associated with productivity enhancement in major sectors.[89]

Human capabilities expand the frontiers of individuals, in turn enhancing their exchange entitlement. This, as stated earlier, reorients the role of markets, which would otherwise distinguish individuals on narrowly determined human capital parameters.

In this era of dynamic transformation of economies, the role of the governments and markets needs rethinking.[90] The larger assumption here is that state-led microeconomic policies enhance basic capabilities and implementation of appropriate macroeconomics policies would mediate market-led institutions. Nayyar[91] raised concerns about placing overwhelming importance on markets in contributing to development. According to him, the momentum of globalization has reduced autonomy of nation-states in matters of economic policies and excluded people without income or sufficient assets, and capabilities. Productivity in an era of economic fragility would be contingent on effective implementation of policies.

The linkages can be explained in the following manner: productivity contributes to economic growth through improvements in market efficiencies. Markets are treated as being indispensable in the larger development process but are driven by larger macroeconomic policies designed by the government. While some analysts[92] view the governments and markets as substitutes, Streeten[93] argues that government should incorporate markets as powerful instruments of planning.

In an evaluation of growth effects of human development among Indian states, it was found that though the high rate of economic growth helped enhance per capita income, literacy rates and health seeking behaviour, there were limits to the ability of growth and market-led mechanisms to reduce income poverty, education dropout rates, and infant mortality rates.[94] This evidence reiterates the importance of the role of affirmative and redistributive policies along with economic growth in securing human development outcomes.

Empowerment and People's Participation

Empowerment—the freedom to shape and exercise choices that affect people's lives—is a foundational feature of human development that distinctively sets it apart from other approaches to development. It refers to 'people's active legitimized engagement in the policies and practices that influence their lives'.[95] Empowerment is about processes that lead people to perceive themselves as entitled to make life choices, whether they are at the level of policymaking, implementation, or management. It implies that people need to be involved at every stage, not merely as beneficiaries but as active participants who are able to pursue and realize goals that they value and have reason to value.[96]

Participation can be fostered both at the individual as well as community levels, wherein individuals and groups develop capacities to undertake action based upon individual or collective rights. Empowerment often requires a transformation of power relations in all spheres of life. This strikes at the roots of existing unequal power structures and thereby supports longer term processes of development.[97]

Empowerment can be more than an instrumental concept. Taken together with equity and productivity, this path contributes to transformative development whereby the process of development not only provides material benefits to people, but also enriches and transforms them into active agents in development. The example of Grameen Bank in Bangladesh illustrates this clearly (see Box 2.4). Over the years the Bank has secured livelihoods of the poor and ensured participation of women in decision making processes, both at the individual and societal levels.

In a democratic nation, citizens have the entitlement of right to speech and expression, and right to information. Collective action

---

BOX 2.4　　Empowering Women: The Case of Grameen Bank

The Grameen Bank, or the rural bank, established in 1983 in Bangladesh, provides a powerful example of empowerment of women through microcredit for small scale self-employment generating activities. Women accounted for 96 per cent of the total members of the Bank and owned 97 per cent of the Bank's shares, whose total collective savings accounted to USD 1.2 billion in 2012. The easy provision of credit and increased savings empowered several disadvantaged women and female-headed households. By actively participating in leadership roles at Grameen Bank, these women are increasingly being involved in decision-making within the household and the community. Further, it has also contributed to social empowerment. The Bank has listed *sixteen decisions* that the person who avails loans from the bank will follow, including commitment to improving education, nutrition, sanitation, and housing status of the family. This has further strengthened women's position and agency to achieve social development goals.

Source: Economic and Social Commission for Asia and the Pacific (ESCAP). 2013. *Empowering Women Economically: Illustrative Case Studies*. Bangkok: United Nations.

and people's participation provide a voice to the masses in the larger process of economic growth. Drèze and Sen[98] emphasize the presence of liberal spaces and people's action in advancing human development outcomes. According to them, society is both a beneficiary and benefactor of the choices regarding development. The presence of passive communities would result in ineffective formulation and implementation of development policies. Platteau[99] lays equal importance on the role of non-formal institutions such as interpersonal relations, cultural practices, and societal structures in securing against risks and vulnerabilities on one hand, and ensuring social security for households on the other. Thus, it becomes crucial to understand the nature and extent of entitlements and capabilities achieved by the communities in securing themselves from vulnerability. Social cohesion across strata provides a powerful mechanism of peoples' voices and action.

Democratic processes provide voice to the excluded and marginalized sections of the population. As Drèze and Sen[100] point out, it is essential to distinguish between government and state, though the terms are often used interchangeably. As a concept, the state includes not only the government but also the legislature that formulates rules, the political systems that oversee democratic processes, the role played by opposition parties, and basic political rights upheld by the judiciary. Further, '[a] democratic state makes it that much harder for the ruling government to be unresponsive to the needs and values of the population at large'.[101] Mukherjee[102] reiterates that the presence of affirmative policies of reservation in the political processes has provided an enabling condition for vulnerable social groups in India, both in local planning and in asserting ownership of forest resources.

Thus, human agency—the ability to pursue goals that one values and has reason to value—entails human motivation that goes beyond self-interest. The ability to decide and act on the basis of what a person values, or has reason to value, even if the action is not to personal advantage is an important aspect of human behaviour. It could extend to paying attention to the *conditions* and *consequences* of choice that determine what is possible for people to imagine or do[103] and to creating conditions wherein agency and choice are possible without fear of retribution.[104]

Sustaining Outcomes

Sustainability is a term that is understood largely as pertaining to the environment. Its definition is deeply influenced by the 1987 UN Report of the World Commission on Environment and Development (WCED) entitled *Our Common Future*, popularly known after its chairperson as the Brundtland Commission Report.[105] This Commission defined sustainability as 'development that meets the needs of the present without compromising the ability future generations to meet their own needs'. This is very different from the understanding of sustainability professed by the ecological school as maintenance of ecosystem resilience', where the focus is on the 'bounce back' capacity of the ecosystem to respond and recover after a disturbance.[106]

The human development approach goes beyond these realms and understands sustainability in terms of capabilities and freedoms. It defines sustainable human development as 'the expansion of the substantive freedoms of people today while making reasonable efforts to avoid seriously compromising those of future generations'.[107] This is similar to the definition given by Sen where sustainability is defined as 'the preservation, and when possible expansion, of the substantive freedoms and capabilities of people today "without compromising the capability of future generations" to have similar—or more—freedom'.[108] Sustainability, as per this approach, includes many more dimensions apart from environmental sustainability, such as economic, social, and cultural sustainability. Financial sustainability refers to the way in which development is financed, and emphasizes that development should not lead countries into debt traps. Social sustainability points to the way in which social groups and other institutions are involved in ensuring participation and involvement and avoiding disruptive elements. Cultural liberty and respect for diversity are other important values that can contribute to socially sustainable development.

Equity is inextricably linked with sustainability. While equity is largely viewed as intra-generational, sustainability refers to inter-generational equity, implying that equity and sustainability are two sides of the same coin. Examples of successful development initiatives—such as those in Niger (details in Box 2.5), where equity and sustainability

BOX 2.5   Regenerating Natural Resources for Sustainable Development

Niger faces development challenges on multiple fronts, mainly on account of its massive desert-like topography further aggravated by the pressure on the existing, scarce natural resources owing to more than 3 per cent annual rate of growth in population. The resultant deforestation and overgrazing further exacerbate desertification and soil erosion, leading to food insecurity.

In 1983, an integrated development programme involving farmer managed natural regeneration, now known as 'Sowing Seeds of Change in Sahel', was introduced in Maradi, one of Niger's poorest and densely populated areas. This programme managed natural regeneration through adoption of traditional knowledge and skills, but took particular care of tree characteristics and community needs. The programme successfully reforested 5 million hectares (about 4 per cent of the country's land), benefiting both from growing forests and from their density. The programme improved cereal yields, food security, animal productivity, biodiversity, income generation by selling firewood and timber, and improved livelihood of about 2.5 million people. The example highlights the importance of local community agency and participation for solving local problems and reducing poverty.

Source: UNDP. 2012. *Case Studies of Sustainable Development in Practice: Triple Wins for Sustainable Development*. New York: UNDP.

went hand in hand in natural resource regeneration—demonstrate that these two processes are not necessarily opposed to each other.

The sustainability path to human development focuses on improving individual and collective freedoms and agency of society through a thrust on social equity, cultural liberty, and environmental and macroeconomic stability. Such a path enables the integration of participation and agency, and helps in expanding human freedoms and aggregating opportunities across generations.

The four processes of human development, namely equity, productivity, empowerment, and sustainability, are intrinsically interlinked and need to be pursued together. Ensuing text provides detailed discussion about this. Success in any one principle will depend on its ability to take cognizance of the others as well. For example, unless education opportunities are widely spread and people in all sections of the society are able to take advantage of secondary education, economic growth itself may not be sustained.

2.7 SHAPING OF HDI

In 1990, the concept of human development was ushered along with its principal measure, the HDI. Drawing heavily on capabilities approach, the HDI can also be seen as the translation of the concept of basic capabilities into a quantitative measure of progress. The chief architects of the HDI, Haq and Sen, began their discussion on alternatives to GDP per capita in early 1980s, and by 1990, they could develop the HDI as a rival to the GDP per capita measure. Their effort was to provide a simple measure that was not as 'vulgar'[109] as GDP per capita, and yet has the ability to focus on something more meaningful, like human life. Box 2.6 presents the rationale for the birth of the HDI.

As we stated earlier, this was not the first experiment at integrating economic and non-economic measures in a composite index, yet it became a watershed for transforming the methodologies used for such assessment and served as a practical platform to integrate various tools simultaneously. As compared to other efforts to incorporate non-economic dimensions in alternate measures, a simpler methodology advanced by Haq and Sen was more effective in integrating both dimensions effectively.

The HDI comprises *three* main components: knowledge, long and healthy life, and standard of living. The standard of living, or the income dimension, was included because it denotes command over resources needed for a decent living, and serves as a proxy for all other dimensions that were not included. HDI mainly represents functionings across three dimensions to evaluate states of *goodness*, and ranks countries according to attainments on income, education and health criteria.

Life expectancy was used as a proxy for long and healthy life, and reflected a common belief that a long life was valuable in itself, and that adequate nutrition and good health were contributory factors.

Knowledge as a component included literacy and good quality education necessary for learning and knowledge building, as well as for productive life in a modern society. Income was included to measure command over resources. Data scarcity on many of the vari-

BOX 2.6   Haq and Sen's Rationale for the Birth of HDI

Acutely aware of the need for a measure to challenge the supremacy of GDP per capita as a marker of progress, Haq and Sen led the effort to create a new composite index that, while including GDP per capita, went beyond it and reflected people's achieved well-being.

There are six major concerns that governed the search for a new measure to represent human development levels of nations. First and foremost, it was necessary that the HDI captured the choices of people, since human development is defined as enlarging the range of people's choices. While several choices could be included, the effort was to measure a few key choices apart from income to be combined into a composite index. Stemming from this concern was the second consideration of keeping the index simple and easy to compute so as to facilitate its widespread use. Hence, it was decided to keep the dimensions limited to the most basic of choices. Third, the preference was to use a composite index rather than numerous individual indices. Technical issues related to aggregation of multiple indicators were resolved through scaling, and equal weights were assigned to the dimensions to reflect that they were all equally important, clearly signalling that there is no substitutability among the dimensions. As the variables chosen for constructing the indices are estimated using different units of measure, they are normalized prior to constructing a composite measure. Fourth, a clear decision was made to include both economic and social choices within the same index to indicate the synergy between social and economic progress. Fifth, the coverage and methodology of HDI was to be kept flexible to enable it to be refined it once it was out in the public domain. This would enable a response to possible critiques as well as to take into account better data sets that might become available in the future. Finally, though it was evident that the data required for the computation of HDI were not available across all countries and often the data were unreliable or dated, a bold decision was taken to proceed with the ranking of countries and use the rankings to pressurize the governments to improve their data systems.

Source: Haq, M. Ul. 1995. *Reflections on Human Development*. Oxford: Oxford University Press.

ables such as access to land, credit, and other resources led per capita income to be used as a proxy, since data on the indicator were readily available and computed across nations regularly. The lack of comparability of per capita estimates across countries posed a tricky issue. This was resolved by adjusting the estimates for purchasing power parity that reflects the ability of currencies to purchase commodities in an economy. In order to factor in the diminishing returns that accrue by transferring income at higher level to human capabilities, the logarithm of real Gross National Product (GNP) per capita was used as an income indicator.

The indicators of the education dimension have been revised in 1991 and 1994. In 1990, the education index comprised only adult literacy rate. It was revised in 1991 to add mean years of schooling. In 1994, mean years of schooling was replaced by average gross enrolment ratio for primary, secondary, and tertiary education.

The three dimensions were combined into a composite index by giving equal weights, sending out an unambiguous message that all the three dimensions were equally important in promoting human development, and none of them could be used as a substitute for another. Goal posts were set for each indicator, which reflected *natural zeros* and the *aspirational goals* from which component indicators were standardized. A country's achievement was set in accordance with this norm, and the resultant HDI score reflected the country's achievement relative to the outcomes attained by other countries or in the same country relative to other indicators. The values of the composite index ranged between 0 and 1, indicating the extent to which there is complete absence of functionings achievements and the highest possible that can be attained.

The dimension index was calculated as follows:

$$\text{Dimension index} = \frac{\text{actual value} - \text{minimum value}}{\text{maximum value} - \text{minimum value}} \quad (2.1)$$

The dimension index was applied to each indicator. The education index comprises two indicators—mean years of schooling and expected years of schooling. Thus, the education dimension would have *two*-dimension indices. Equation 2.1 is first applied to each of the two indicators, and then the arithmetic mean of the two resulting indices is taken. Each dimension index reflects a proxy for capabilities. Anand and Sen[110] argued that while the income dimension in HDI is equally crucial, there are limits to the extent to which income could contribute to the enhancement of capabilities. Each subsequent dollar in income would have a smaller effect on expanding capabilities. The logarithm of income is strictly concave, and the average of the logarithms of incomes tends to increase as the given total income is more equally distributed.

Once the dimension indices are estimated, the aggregate HDI is computed as a geometric mean[111] of the three dimensions: standard of living, education, and health, with all the three dimensions being given equal weights. Haq[112] justifies the use of equal weights that 'all these choices were very important and that there was no apriori rationale for giving a higher weight to one choice than to another'.

$$HDI = (I_{health} \cdot I_{education} \cdot I_{income})^{1/3} \qquad (2.2)$$

The HDR statistical tables provide data on essential indicators of human development, namely population trends, health and educational attainments, national income and composition of resources, work and employment, health security, status of fundamental human rights treaties, international integration, perceptions of well-being, and the like. It also provides a dashboard of indicators on gender gap and economic, environmental and social sustainability.

Although the HDI was introduced in a hesitant and tentative manner, it surprised its own founding father with its widespread acceptability, which is attributed to its policy relevance. Overall, the HDI has served a useful purpose in holding up a mirror to national governments, whose performance as to whether they succeeded in combining economic progress with social development can now be assessed. The seriousness with which national governments consider their HDI rankings is evident from the severe contestations to the ranks put out annually. It has also led to measures within individual countries that focus specifically on the dimensions on which HDI indicates as lacking. With the increasing use of disaggregated HDRs across geographical regions and social groups, HDI has emerged as an important tool to highlight differential achievements and identify lagging regions as well as groups with respect to key social indicators. Despite its shortcomings, HDI transformed the development discourse and succeeded in dethroning GDP as the sole indicator of human progress. Countrywide assessments by national and international agencies now routinely refer to HDI along with GDP per capita in assessing the socio-economic progress of the nation. Its popularity and large-scale use in policy analysis has vindicated Haq's strong faith in the simplistic measure that included both economic and social dimensions as an alternative to per capita income.

Several critics argue that HDI is a limited measure and does not mirror the range of choices that people have, and that it provides a narrow and truncated picture of human development.[113] Some experts contest the dimensions neglected in the HDI, particularly political freedom and environment. The HDI is silent on the distributional concerns in the areas of gender, income, region, ethnicity, and occupation.[114] The enthusiasm to expand the purview of HDI has often made it unrecognizable, so much so that it has distanced itself from the original purpose of highlighting key dimensions that matter for human progress.

Srinivasan[115] points to the fact that, since the indicators relating to literacy and life expectancy have natural limits, the index largely tends to capture the performance of the developing countries. The countries with higher initial levels of attainment have very little scope for further improvements. Since the HDI is designed to measure change in attainments levels, it results in capturing the performance of developing countries to a greater extent and that of the developed countries.

The presence of a positive correlation between per capita income with other dimensions of the HDI is a serious constraint that was raised by several scholars.[116] Since income influences education and health attainments, they argue that there is little to be gained in including additional indicators. Despite these concerns, the human development index has stood the test of time and fulfilled the original purpose for which it was devised. While it has not been successful in unseating GDP per capita as a measure, it has acquired an importance that is hard to deny, as all assessments of well-being invariably refer to the HDI as one of the important barometers of development.

★★★

Being human-centric in nature, the human development approach includes both capabilities and entitlement processes that shape freedoms, choices, and well-being. The formation of basic functionings and capabilities occurs through a range of processes that lead to plurality of outcomes, which also enhance choices. Being influenced by numerous social science disciplines, its theoretical framework has transcended rigid disciplinary boundaries. Blazing a new trail, the human development approach does not hesitate to suggest that value judgements would be required on an ongoing basis for its operationalization. Similarly, on account of its ethical moorings, the approach has immense implications for understanding equity and justice. The human development paradigm places people at the centre of development and reorients the notion of empowerment and peoples' participation as intrinsic values. The human development approach is often criticized for leaning towards liberal philosophy and for placing overwhelming importance on individual choice, which may or may not contribute to overall well-being.

Nonetheless, it needs to be recognized that the approach is still in its evolutionary phase, with scholars continuously exploring its many dimensions and enriching it in the process. Its dynamic nature has unintended consequences as it is often criticized simultaneously on the grounds of being too narrow as well as being, too broad, and still incomplete, reflecting, in a sense, both the expectations from the approach as well as its current state of development.

Further, some analysts consider the approach to be too esoteric, while others have successfully applied it to developmental projects on the ground.[117] Some of the impending constraints seem to be raised partially due to the complexities in conceptualization and measurement. Yet, the uniqueness of the human development approach and its ability to explain human choices and behaviour succinctly even as it recognizes heterogeneities at the community level have helped shape a narrative distinct from a predominantly utilitarian approach.

Drawing from the above discussion, it emerges that the human development approach has built the notion of *people-centric* development well beyond its predecessors such as human resource development, the basic needs approach, the human rights and human security approaches. The human development approach encompasses capabilities, entitlements, freedom, and sustainability, each of which is valued intrinsically. At its most fundamental point, it considers individual freedom to be at the core of well-being rather than merely contributing to individual aggregation. Moreover, the role of the state is not within the narrow construct of welfare state, but one that has substantive responsibility in building capabilities, implementing redistributive polices, enhancing the potential of markets, and protecting the environment for the future. The thrust on public action uniquely links state action with the individuals and communities as equals in the development process.

NOTES AND REFERENCES

1.   UNDP. 1990. *Human Development Report 1990: Concept and Measurement of Human Development.* New York: Oxford University Press, p. 5.

2.   Aristotle. [1980] 2009. *The Nicomachean Ethics,* trans. D. Ross (Revised Edition). Oxford: Oxford University Press, p. 7.

3.   Kant, I. [1873] 2008. 'Chapter 2', in *Fundamental Principles of the Metaphysics of Morals,* trans. T.K. Abbott. New York: Cosimo Classics.

4.   For an elaborate discussion on the notion of *choice,* see Chapter 3 of this volume.

5.   Where *eu* in Greek means well and *daimonia* means divinity or spirit.

6.   Chung, P.S. 2012. *The Hermeneutical Self and an Ethical Difference: Inter-Civilizational Engagement.* Cambridge: James Clarke and Co, p. 77.

7.   Sen, A. 1999. 'The Possibility of Social Choice'. *American Economic Review* 89 (3): 349–78.

8.   For more details on the definition of human development across various HDRs, see Alkire, S. 2010. 'Human Development: Definitions, Critiques and Related Concepts', Human Development Research Paper, 2010/01, UNDP, New York.

9.   UNDP. 2010. *Human Development Report 2010: The Real Wealth of Nations: Pathways to Human Development.* New York: UNDP, p. 22.

10.   UNDP. 2016. *Human Development Report 2016: Human Development for Everyone.* New York: UNDP, p. 1.

11.   Haq, M. Ul. 1972. 'Let Us Stand Economic Theory on Its Head: Joining the GNP Rat Race Won't Wipe Out Poverty'. *Insight.*

12.   A detailed discussion on the role of global institutions in furthering the human development paradigm is presented in Annexure D.

13.   See Annexure D for more on NSRTs.

14.   The immediate question arising from the definition is: who decides what is valuable? It is the individual who decides on the value of any being or doing and hence his or her valuation is what is taken into account. Questions such as what is considered valuable collectively and how one arrives at collective choice from individual choices will be dealt with later in this chapter.

15.   Sen, A. 1999. *Development as Freedom.* New York: Oxford University Press, p. 15.

16.   For a detailed discussion about differences in means and ends notions, see Annexure C.

17. Alkire, S. 2008. 'The Capability Approach to the Quality of Life', Working Paper prepared for the working group Quality of Life, Commission on the Measurement of Economic Performance and Social Progress, Paris, p. 5.

18. Sen, A. 1990. 'Justice: Means versus Freedoms'. *Philosophy versus Public Affairs* 19 (2): 111–21, p. 114.

19. Sen, 'Justice: Means versus Freedoms', p. 115.

20. Discussion on conversion factors is presented in detail in Section 2.3.

21. Sen elaborated rather differently. He argued that relative poverty occurs due to differences in the weights attached to different functionings, valuable though they may all be. For more, see Sen, A. 1993. 'Capability and Well-Being', in *The Quality of Life*, ed. M. Nussbaum and A. Sen, pp. 30–53. Oxford: Clarendon Press, p. 31.

22. Sugden, R. 1993. 'Welfare, Resources, and Capabilities: A Review of Inequality Re-examined by Amartya Sen'. *Journal of Economic Literature* 31 (4): 1947–62.

23. Sen, A. 1992. *Inequality Reexamined*. Oxford: Oxford University Press, p. 48.

24. Sen, *Development as Freedom*, p. 87.

25. Sen, *Inequality Reexamined*, p. 81.

26. Sen, A. 2005. 'Capabilities, List, and Public Reason: Continuing the Reason', in *Amartya Sen's Work and Ideas: A Gender Perspective*, ed. Bina Agarwal, Jane Humphries, and Ingrid Robyens, pp. 335–9. London; New York: Routledge.

27. Trani, J.F., Bakhshi, P., and Rolland, C. 2011. 'Capabilities, Perception of Well-Being and Development Effort: Some Evidence from Afghanistan'. *Oxford Development Studies* 39 (4): 403–26.

28. Nussbaum, M. 2000. *Women and Human Development: The Capabilities Approach*. Cambridge: Cambridge University Press, p. 74.

29. It is interesting to note that even such a staunch supporter of the market paradigm as Adam Smith placed importance on human dignity and the ability to 'appear in *publik* without shame'. For further details, see Smith, A. [1776] 1976. 'Chapter 2, Book V', in *An Inquiry into the Nature and Causes of the Wealth of Nations* (Vol. II), ed. R.H. Campbell and A.S. Skinner. Oxford: Claredon Press.

30. See Nussbaum, M.C. 2011. *Creating Capabilities*. Cambridge, MA: Harvard University Press.

31. The term *basic capabilities* was used for the first time by Sen as 'a person being able to do certain basic things' (Sen, A. 1980. 'Equality of What?', in *Tanner Lectures on Human Values* [Vol. 1], ed. S. McMurrin, pp. 195–220. Cambridge: Cambridge University Press, p. 218). Further, Sen uses the term basic capabilities to refer to certain threshold level of capability—'the ability to

satisfy certain elementary and crucially important functionings up to certain level' (Sen, *Inequality Reexamined*, p. 45).

32.   Foster, J. and Handy, C. 2008. 'External Capabilities', OPHI Working Paper Series no. 08, Oxford Poverty & Human Development Initiative (OPHI), Oxford.

33.   Basu, K. and Foster, J.E. 1998. 'On Measuring Literacy'. *Economic Journal*, 108 (451): 1733–49.

34.   Gasper, D. 1997. 'Sen's Capability Approach and Nussbaum's Capabilities Ethic'. *Journal of International Development* 9 (2): 281–302.

35.   To illustrate from the Nussbaum's list of central human capabilities, *practical reason* and *senses, imagination, and thought* are associated with S capability, and *play* and *emotion* are associated with P capability. See Nussbaum, *Women and Human Development*, pp. 78–80.

36.   The concept of opportunity freedom has been addressed in Chapter 3 of this volume.

37.   As per Nussbaum, social arrangements also complement individual capabilities. For more, see Nussbaum, *Women and Human Development*.

38.   For more, see Qizilbash, M. 2011. 'Sugden's Critique of the Capability Approach'. *Utilitas* 23 (1): 25–51; Sugden, R. 2006. 'What We Desire, What We Have Reason to Desire, Whatever We Might Desire: Mill and Sen on the Value of Opportunity'. *Utilitas* 18 (1): 33–51.

39.   Sen, *Development as Freedom*.

40.   Ibrahim, S. 2006. 'From Individual to Collective Capabilities: The Capability Approach as a Conceptual Framework for Self Help'. *Journal of Human Development* 7 (3): 397–416, p. 404.

41.   Sen, *Inequality Reexamined*.

42.   Robeyns, I. 2005. 'The Capability Approach: A Theoretical Survey'. *Journal of Human Development* 6 (1): 93–117.

43.   The notion of agency is discussed in subsequent sections and at length in Chapter 3 of this volume.

44.   Crocker and Robeyns comment that Sen's usage of the constructive value could encompass both intrinsic and instrumental value of agency. Crocker, D. and Robeyns, I. 2009. 'Capability and Agency', in *Amartya Sen*, ed. M. Christopher, pp. 60–90. Cambridge: Cambridge University Press.

45.   Chiapperò-Martinetti, E. and Salardi, P. 2008. 'Well-Being, Process and Conversion Factors: An Estimation', HDCP-IRC Working Paper Series 3/2008, Human Development, Capability and Poverty International Research Centre.

46.   Binder, M., and Broekel, T. 2008. 'Conversion Efficiency as a Complementing Measure of Welfare in Capability Space', MPRA Paper 7583, University Library of Munich, Germany.

47. Sen, A. 1987. *Commodities and Capabilities*. Oxford: Elsevier Science Publishers.

48. A variety of methods have been suggested on how this may be done. See, for example, the literature on the application of fuzzy set theory to capabilities initiated by Chiapperò-Martinetti, E. 1994. 'A New Approach to Evaluation of Well-Being and Poverty by Fuzzy Set Theory'. *Giornale degli Economisti e Annali di Economia* 7 (9): 367–88.

49. See also Foster, J. 2010. 'Notes on Effective Freedom', OPHI Working Paper No. 34, OPHI, Oxford: University of Oxford; Herrero, C. 1996. 'Capabilities and Utilities'. *Review of Economic Design* 2 (1): 69–88; Pattanaik, P. and Yongsheng, X. 1990. 'On Ranking Opportunity Sets in Terms of Freedom of Choice'. *Recherches Économiques de Louvain* 56 (3–4): 383–90.

50. Sen, A. 1994. 'Well-Being, Capability and Public Policy'. *Giornale-degli-Economistie-Annali-di-Economia* 53 (7–9): 333–47, p. 334.

51. Dean, H. 2009. 'Critiquing Capabilities: The Distractions of a Beguiling Concept'. *Critical Social Policy* 29 (2): 261–78, p. 264.

52. Crocker, D.A. 2008. *Ethics of Global Development: Agency, Capability and Deliberative Democracy*. Cambridge: Cambridge University Press, p. 152.

53. See Sugden, 'What We Desire, What We Have Reason to Desire, Whatever We Might Desire'; Qizilbash, 'Sugden's Critique of the Capability Approach'.

54. Ibrahim, 'From Individual to Collective Capabilities', p. 398.

55. Stewart, F. 2005. 'Groups and Capabilities'. *Journal of Human Development* 6 (2): 185–204.

56. According to Robeyns, ethical individualism refers to 'who or what should count in our evaluative exercises and decisions ... and only, individuals are the units of moral concern' (Stewart 2005, p. 107). However, the distinction between methodological and ontological individualism is fuzzy. Ontological individualism is stated as 'only individuals and their properties exist, and that all social entities and properties can be defined by reducing them to individuals and their properties' (Stewart 2005, p. 108) and methodological individualism presumes 'everything can be explained by reference to individuals and their properties only' (Stewart 2005, pp. 107–8).

57. Dean, 'Critiquing Capabilities', p. 297.

58. Gasper, D. 2002. 'Is Sen's Capability Approach an Adequate Basis for Considering Human Development?'. *Review of Political Economy* 14 (4): 435–61, 456.

59. See Giri, A.K. 2000. 'Rethinking Human Well Being: A Dialogue with Amartya Sen'. *Journal of International Development* 12 (7): 1003–18.

60. Cohen, G.A. 1993. 'Equality of What? On Welfare, Goods and Capabilities', in *The Quality of Life*, ed. M. Nussbaum and A. Sen, pp. 9–29. Oxford: Clarendon Press.

61. Cohen, 'Equality of What?', p. 18.

62. Sen provides a way out by suggesting that the very act of *choosing* be incorporated in the functioning vector. Once this is done, elementary evaluation may be used for all assessments, according to Sen (*Commodities and Capabilities*, p. 44). However, Gasper ('Sen's Capability Approach and Nussbaum's Capabilities Ethic') cautions that if one were to rely on elementary evaluation and use only a distinguished element or only one option for assessment, the capability approach would resemble the conventional approach of having only a unidimensional focus.

63. Sen recognizes that the capability approach does have certain limitations in empirical analysis as 'the extensive coverage of freedoms is sometimes seen as a problem in getting an "operational" approach to development that is freedom-centred' (*Development as Freedom*, p. 24). The capability approach is seen to be seriously handicapped by the lack of a widely agreed list of basic capabilities. Amartya Sen is averse to specifying a capability set as, according to him, any list of valuable functionings will go against the freedoms of the individuals.

64. For instance, Nussbaum, M. 1988. 'Nature, Functioning and Capability: Aristotle on Political Distribution'. *Oxford Studies in Ancient Philosophy* 1: 145–84; Roemer, J. 1996. *Theories of Distributive Justice*. Cambridge: Harvard University Press; Sugden, 'Welfare, Resources, and Capabilities'.

65. Comim states that the operationalization of the capability approach is constrained by its counterfactual nature. He argues that if capabilities are potential sets of *beings and doings* and not achieved states, and even if capability is high for an individual, he or she may choose not to actualize it and may prefer to have other forms of freedom. In such cases, the information basis may not permit capture of counterfactual situations. For more details, see Comim, F. 2001. 'Operationalizing Sen's Capability Approach'. Paper presented at Justice and Poverty: Examining Sen's Capability, The Von Hügel Institute, St. Edmund's College, University of Cambridge, Cambridge.

66. Discussion on data challenges is available in Chapter 4 of this volume.

67. For specific applications of the Capability Approach, refer to Alkire, *Human Development*, p. 35.

68. Sen, A. 1984. *Resources, Values and Development*. Oxford: Oxford University Press, p. 497.

69. Gasper, D. 1993. 'Entitlements Analysis: Relating Concepts and Contexts'. *Development and Change* 24 (4): 679–718, p. 683.

70. Dworkin, R. 2002. *Sovereign Virtue: The Theory and Practice of Equality*. Cambridge, MA: Harvard University Press.

71. Pierik, R. and Robeyns, I. 2007. 'Resources versus Capabilities: Social Endowments in Egalitarian Theory'. *Political Studies* 55 (1): 133–52, p. 145.

72. Watts, M. 1991. 'Entitlements or Empowerment? Famine and Starvation in Africa'. *Review of African Political Economy* 51: 9–26.

73. Kabeer, N. and Aziz, R. 1990. *Gender Divisions in Food Production and Food Entitlements: Case Studies from South Asia and West Africa.* Teaching text for UNFPA Programme in Population and Development. The Hague: Institute of Social Studies, p. 42.

74. Kabeer, Naila. 1994. *Reversed Realities: Gender Hierarchies in Development Thought.* London, New York: Verso.

75. For more on this, see Adams, A.M., Cekan, J., and Sauerborn, R. 1998. 'Towards a Conceptual Framework of Household Coping: Reflections from Rural West Africa'. *Africa* 68 (2): 263–83; Fraser, N. 2014. *Justice Interruptus: Critical Reflections on the 'Postsocialist' Condition.* New York, London: Routledge; Kabeer, N. 1999. 'Resources, Agency, Achievements: Reflections on the Measurement of Women's Empowerment'. *Development and Change* 30 (3): 435–64; Molyneux, M. 2002. 'Gender and the Silences of Social Capital: Lessons from Latin America'. *Development and Change* 33 (2): 167–88.

76. Sen, A. 1981. *Poverty and Famines: An Essay on Entitlement and Deprivation.* Oxford: Oxford University Press, p. 6.

77. Sen, *Resources, Values and Development*, pp. 454–5.

78. Sen, *Poverty and Famines*, p. 3.

79. Sen, *Development as Freedom*.

80. Drèze, J. and Khera, R. 2017. 'Recent Social Security Initiatives in India'. *World Development* 98 (C): 555–72.

81. Nussbaum, M. 1997. 'Capabilities and Human Rights'. *Fordham Law Review* 66: 273–300.

82. Deneulin, S. and Shahani, L. 2009. *An Introduction to the Human Development and Capability Approach.* London: Earthscan.

83. Haq, M. Ul. 1995. *Reflections on Human Development.* Oxford: Oxford University Press.

84. Ranis, G. and Stewart, F. 2005. 'Dynamic Linkages between Economic Growth and Human Development', DESA Working Paper No. 8, Department of Economic and Social Affairs (DESA), United Nations, New York.

85. See Chapter 5 of this volume for detailed analysis.

86. For a comparative understanding of the distinctions in the notion of equity and justice, see Annexure A.

87. Haq, *Reflections on Human Development*.

88. Thorbecke, E. 1991. 'Adjustment, Growth and Income Distribution in Indonesia'. *World Development* 19 (11): 1595–614.

89. Government of Nepal. 2014. *Nepal Human Development Report: Beyond Geography—Unlocking Human Potential.* Kathmandu: UNDP.

90. For details see Pierre, J., ed. 2000. *Debating Governance: Authority, Steering and Democracy.* Oxford: Oxford University Press.

91. Nayyar, D. 2002, 'Towards Global Governance', in *Governing Globalisation: Issues and Institutions*, ed. D. Nayyar, pp. 3–18. Oxford: Oxford University Press.

92.   See for example, Krueger, A.O. 1990. 'Government Failures in Development'. *Journal of Economic Perspectives* 4 (3): 9–23.

93.   Streeten, P. 1984. 'Dichotomies of Development', in *Pioneers of Development*, ed. G.M. Meier and D. Seers, pp. 337–61. Washington, DC: Oxford University Press.

94.   Iyer, S.S. 2010. 'Public Intervention, Institutions and Human Development in India: Theory and Evidence', in *Democracy, Development and Decentralisation in India: Continuing Debates*, ed. S. Corbridge and C. Sengupta. New Delhi: Routledge.

95.   Maggis, K. and Shinn, C. 2008. 'Emergent Principles of Social Sustainability', in *Understanding the Social Dimension of Sustainability*, ed. J. Dillard, V. Dujon, and M. King, pp. 15–44, New York: Routledge, p. 23.

96.   See Alkire, *The Capability Approach to the Quality of Life*; Dean, 'Critiquing Capabilities'; Gasper, 'Entitlements Analysis'; Robeyns, I. 2000. 'An Unworkable Idea or a Promising Alternative? Sen's Capability Approach Re-Examined'. Discussion Paper 00.30, Centre for Economic Studies, University of Leuven, Belgium; Robeyns, 'The Capability Approach'.

97.   Participation is critical for human development. However, since human development is also concerned with individual fulfilment, and active participation enables people to realize their full potential and thereby make their best contribution to society, it can be an end in itself. For institutional perspective on participation, see UNDP. 1993. *Human Development Report 1993: People's Participation*. New York: Oxford University Press.

98.   Drèze, J. and Sen, A.K. 2002. *India: Development and Participation*. Delhi: Oxford University Press.

99.   Platteau, J.P. 1991. 'Traditional Systems of Social Security and Hunger Insurance: Past Achievements and Modern Challenges', in *Social Security in Developing Countries*, ed. E. Ahmad, J. Drèze, J. Hills, and A. Sen, pp. 112–70. Oxford: Clarendon Press.

100.   Drèze and Sen, *India*.

101.   Drèze and Sen, *India*, p. 45.

102.   Mukherjee, N. 2002. 'Measuring Social Capital: Forest Protection Committees in West Bengal'. *Economic and Political Weekly* 37 (29): 2994–7.

103.   See Kabeer, 'Resources, Agency, Achievements'.

104.   Further, see Petit, J. 2012. 'Empowerment and Participation: Bridging the Gap between Understanding and Practice'. UNDESA Expert Group Meeting on Promoting People's Empowerment in Achieving Poverty Eradication, Social Integration and Productive and Decent Work for All, United Nations Headquarters, New York, 10–12 September.

105.   WCED. 1987. *Our Common Future (Brundtland Report)*. United Nations World Commission on Environment and Development. Oxford: Oxford University Press.

106. Harris, J.M. 2003. 'Sustainability and Sustainable Development'. *International Society for Ecological Economics* 1 (1): 5.

107. UNDP. 2011. *Sustainability and Equity: A Better Future for All.* New York: Palgrave.

108. Sen, A. 2009. *The Idea of Justice.* London: Penguin, pp. 251–2.

109. See for more details Sen, A. 2010. 'Introduction by Amartya Sen', in *Human Development Report 2010: The Real Wealth of Nations: Pathways to Human Development*, by UNDP. Oxford: Oxford University Press.

110. Anand, S. and Sen, A. 2000. 'The Income Component of the Human Development Index'. *Journal of Human Development* 1 (1): 83–106.

111. In the original methodology used in 1990, the arithmetic mean was used for aggregation across the three dimensions. It was changed to the geometric mean subsequently.

112. Haq, *Reflections on Human Development*, p. 48.

113. For instance, see Lind, N.C. 1992. 'Some Thoughts on the Human Development Index'. *Social Indicators Research* 27 (1): 89–101; Sagar, A. and Nijam, A.1998. 'The Human Development Index: A Critical Review'. *Ecological Economics* 25 (3): 249–64.; Srinivasan, T.N. 1994. 'Human Development: A New Paradigm or Reinvention of the Wheel?'. *The American Economic Review* 84 (2): 238–43.

114. For details, see Akder, P., and Halis, A. 1994. 'A Means to Closing Gaps: Disaggregated Human Development Index', Human Development Report Office Occasional Paper 18, UNDP, New York; Hicks, D.A. 1997. 'The Inequality-Adjusted Human Development Index: A Constructive Proposal'. *World Development* 25(8): 1283–98.; Kelley, A.C. 1991. 'The Human Development Index: "Handle with Care"'. *Population and Development Review* 17(2): 315–24; Trabold-Nübler, H. 1991. 'The Human Development Index—A New Development Indicator?'. *Intereconomics* 26 (5): 36–43.

115. Srinivasan, 'Human Development'.

116. For example, Ivanova, I., Arcelus, F.J., and Srinivasan, G. 1994. 'Information Validity and Axiomatic Characteristics of the Human Development Index', Working Paper 94–010, University of New Brunswick, New Brunswick; McGillivray, M. 1991. 'The Human Development Index: Yet Another Redundant Composite Development Indicator?'. *World Development* 19 (10): 1461–68; McGillivray, M. and White, H. 1993. 'Measuring Development? The UNDP's Human Development Index'. *Journal of International Development* 5 (2): 183–92.

117. For instance, see Alkire, S. 2002. *Valuing Freedoms: Sen's Capability Approach and Poverty Reduction.* Oxford: Oxford University Press; Comim, F., Qizilbash, M., and Alkire, S., eds. 2008. *The Capability Approach: Concepts, Measures and Applications.* Cambridge: Cambridge University Press.

3   Human Flourishing and Well-Being

Human evolution has been strengthened by the confluence of ideologies, identities, and cultures. Although human history is often viewed in terms of *the West and the rest*, it is the contextualization and cross-learning across experiences that are crucial for human freedom. Humans are born free, and freedom is an inbuilt drive to survive, propagate, socialize, and preserve their families and communities. Past global experience has witnessed fascinating challenges in terms of negotiation of values, ethics, and choices relating to freedom.

The abolition of slavery was one such experience. The first step was taken in 1926, when the League of Nations defined the singular threat to freedom in the form of slavery as 'the status or condition of a person over whom any or all of the powers attached to the right of ownership are exercised'.[1] Ironically, even though slavery has been abolished globally and human societies have achieved tremendous progress over the years, discrimination in various forms continues to remain the core challenge to human freedom.

Liberal thinkers of the Enlightenment period like John Locke, Jean-Jacques Rousseau, and Immanuel Kant argued that though human beings are born free, the influences of the social milieu mediate the very nature of freedom through the process of civilization, resulting in what they called subservient freedoms. These subservient freedoms are often conditional on the nature of the prevalent social contract. The thinkers believed that freedoms are best achieved in a civilized society rather than in a 'chaotic', 'uncivilized' one.[2] Yet, utilitarians argued that mere expansion of material well-being and the ability to choose commodities would reflect the presence of freedom as material well-being increases individual freedom. The progression to welfare is through the spread of utilities based on a sum ranking of individual utilities.

If humans are *free* at birth, constraining them merely to material choices is certainly narrow. Sen points that '[s]ubstantive freedoms direct attention to the ends that make development important'.[3] The notion of human flourishing and explanation of metaphysical outcomes of material and non-material well-being have been pertinent to human history. Human freedom and choices are the pivot around which the human development approach revolves. Viewed as the possession of capability to achieve valuable human functionings, freedoms refer to actual opportunities people have, given their personal and social circumstances, as well as the processes that allow for such choice and action to be undertaken.

The literature on freedom, choices, and well-being abounds in both epistemological and ontological realms. The challenge is that all the three outcomes—choices, well-being, and freedom— are intrinsically important for human flourishing and have been common elements across various philosophical approaches. The capability approach repositions these crucial elements within the meta-narrative as contributing to human flourishing via the values of ethics and justice that it provides. Being sensitive to heterogeneity and relying on a broader informational base, the capability approach draws attention away from income towards capabilities. The need to debate and reorient the thesis on human freedoms is particularly important at this juncture because contemporary forms of capitalism or neoliberalism have integrated economies but disintegrated societies, and thereby, enhanced vulnerabilities, precariousness, and discrimination.

Against this background, this chapter raises the question of why freedoms are valuable. The question is traced through a series of theoretical notions and frameworks of freedoms, choices, agency, and well-being. Section 3.1 analyses why understanding and cherishing the constituents of freedom matter. Section 3.2 discusses the value of well-being; Section 3.3 builds on that discussion and raises a critical question on choice—why does choice matter? Section 3.4 addresses the nature of agency and democracy. The last section highlights the challenges of sustaining human freedoms.

3.1 CONSTITUENTS OF FREEDOM

Expansion of freedom is both a *primary end* and the *principal means* of development. For example, freedom of speech is intrinsically important to an individual and a constitutive part of development. When such freedom is lacking, people experience a sense of deprivation even though they may enjoy relatively high levels of material prosperity.

For example, the sudden emergence of the massive political demonstration, led by Beijing students in June 1989 at Tiananmen Square on the occasion of Hu Yaobang's death, challenged the centre's control over the pace of reform, as well as the party's control of political articulation. Hu Yaobang was a liberal reformer, who had been unseated for his struggle towards political and economic reform. The public memorial service commemorating the death of Hu Yaobang provided the platform for civil society struggles to showcase resistance to political hegemony, loosening of political power and access to public spaces.[4] The use of force by the government, which led to the death of a large number of demonstrators, was widely seen as curbing the freedoms of people. In such scenarios, people are likely to feel stifled due to lack of basic freedoms, even if the country makes rapid economic progress.

Freedoms, too, are valuable for instrumental reasons as they enable people to enhance their capability set. Sen identifies five categories of instrumental freedoms: political freedoms, economic facilities, social opportunities, transparency guarantees, and protective security. Interactions of various types of freedom improve capability set and human well-being. For example, the right to information enables a person to demand accountability from public service providers, in turn improving the efficiency of delivery of public services, such as elementary education and primary health care, which promote better human development outcomes. Freedom comprises actual opportunities people have, given their personal and social circumstances, as well as the processes that allow freedom of action and decision. Opportunity freedom relates to 'real opportunities we have of achieving things that we can and do value'.[5] Process freedom is defined as the 'process of autonomous choice—having the levers in one's own hands'.[6] Personal process freedom is recognized as agency.

The opportunity and process aspects of freedom, while being distinct, are not entirely disjointed. For example, lack of freedoms, or *unfreedoms*, such as the inability to escape premature mortality (or prevent morbidity) and involuntary starvation, could be attributed to the absence of elementary opportunities. Unfreedom could also be caused by unjust processes of marginalization and exclusion, which in turn, limit people's opportunities.

The capability approach emphasizes opportunity freedom while recognizing that process freedom is important for exercising opportunities. Strictly speaking, process freedom is outside the ambit of the capability approach and is part of the larger construct of development as freedom. We may recall that capability in Sen's articulation is interpreted primarily in terms of opportunity—O freedoms in Gasper's classification, rather than P and S freedoms. It is then only natural to focus on opportunity freedom. Sen clearly states that

> Although the idea of capability has considerable merit in the assessment of the opportunity aspect of freedom, it cannot possibly deal adequately with the process aspect of freedom, since capabilities are characteristics of individual advantages and they fall short of telling us enough about the fairness or equity of the processes involved, or about the freedom of citizens to invoke and utilise procedures that are equitable.[7]

However, innate potential and skills play a crucial role in determining a person's agency, which in turn influences processes. In Nussbaum's interpretation, they are an integral part of capabilities. If one were to go by her broader interpretation, then process freedoms indirectly enter the capability approach.

The distinction between opportunity freedom and process freedom has very critical implications for public policy. If governments were to focus only on enhancing opportunity freedoms, that narrow focus could lead to the attainment of *culmination outcomes*—only final outcomes without taking any note of the process of getting there. This is in contrast to achieving *comprehensive outcomes*, or taking note of the processes through which the culmination outcomes come about.[8] Thus, culmination outcomes are concerned only with the outcomes and not the process of reaching those outcomes, whereas comprehensive outcomes are those that pay attention to both the outcomes and the processes that enable the attainment of specified outcomes (see Box 3.1 for details).

BOX 3.1　Comparing Comprehensive and Culmination Outcomes

The fertility reduction in China and the Indian state of Kerala illustrates the difference between the two types of outcomes. Both regions have had remarkable success in reducing the Total Fertility Rate (TFR) from over 5 per cent in 1960s to less than replacement level (1.5) in the 1990s. The routes taken by the two countries to achieve this outcome were, however, completely different. Kerala's sharp reduction in fertility rate since 1961 till present times has been an outcome of sustained efforts of state-led policies that promoted schooling and education in general and women's capabilities and empowerment in particular. China also achieved remarkable reduction in the fertility rate from 5.2 in 1971 to below replacement level TFR in 2001. However, this decline was achieved by imposing in 1979 the *one-child policy* as the official family planning policy. The policy imposed fines on income on the family having more than one child (barring a list of exceptions). This imposition by the government on an important aspect of freedom of individuals did achieve the required reduction in fertility rate within a short period of time, but curbed individual freedom on reproductive decisions. Kerala, on the other hand, had a long history of according importance to female education, which in turn led to a decline in fertility rate as a result of voluntary decisions of families. The outcomes that China achieved in fertility reduction can be called *culmination outcomes*, whereas Kerala's fertility reduction, which paid attention to processes leading to fertility reduction, led to *comprehensive outcomes*. Predictably, comprehensive outcomes turn out to be more sustainable than culmination outcomes.

Source: George, M.V. 2010. 'The Fertility Decline in India's Kerala State: A Unique Example of Below Replacement Fertility in a High Fertility Country'. *Canadian Studies in Population* 37 (3–4): 563–600.

3.2 UNDERSTANDING THE VALUE OF WELL-BEING

At the outset, it is necessary to distinguish the notion of *well-being* from that of being *well off*. While well-being is a subjectivist view in terms of a mental state, and is related to something internal that a person achieves, being *well off* is related to opulence and denotes command over things that are external to a person's being. Sen defined human well-being as 'a person's ability to do valuable acts or reach valuable states of being'.[9] It has been a subject of abiding interest for everyone who is interested in development as well-being seems to reside at the very core of human concerns. While the concept seems intuitively clear, it is in its application that we are confronted with numerous variations and interpretations. In this section, we will focus only on the relationship between capability and well-being rather than delve into the vast literature on well-being.

Well-being has *two* variants—subjective well-being and objective well-being. Subjective well-being is a person's aggregate perception of 'feelings of happiness, satisfaction or fulfilment', while objective well-being is 'achievement/functionings in non-feeling dimensions that are valued as reflectively important, e.g. physical and mental health, longevity, security'.[10] In a study in the city of Kolkata in India, Biswas-Diener and Diener[11] attempted to understand the subjective well-being of people residing in slums. Their research underlines the observation that though the slum dwellers were deprived of some of the basic capabilities, they still measured high on subjective well-being associated with the satisfaction derived from various life domains. This subjective well-being arose from the satisfaction gained from social relationships and the importance the subjects of the study associated with this dimension.

There is no conclusive positioning of the subjective–objective derivatives as yet. The expansive literature certainly enables us to understand the differences between the hedonic and eudemonic approaches. While the former focuses on happiness and defines well-being in terms of pleasure attainment and pain avoidance, the latter emphasizes meaning and self-realization and defines well-being in terms of the degree to which a person is fully functioning. The orientation of the capability approach, through process and opportunity freedoms, is to engage with the subjective and objective notions of well-being.

There is some uneasiness among capability theorists in regard to subjective well-being as it is unable to recognize *adaptive preferences*— an inability that could lead to erroneous conclusions while judging the states of being of individuals. Adaptive preferences refer to the phenomenon where, for example, individuals faced with persistent deprivation adapt their preferences in consonance with their circumstances. This can vitiate the assessment of their true state of well-being. For example, a woman in a male-dominated social setting might perceive that her freedoms are satisfactory even though she has limited mobility and is compelled to move around only in family circles and not step out of those invisible boundaries. If asked about her subjective well-being, she might perceive her well-being levels to be high despite being deprived of basic freedoms as she has adapted to her situation. Under such circumstances, the assessment of well-being using subjective measures could be seriously flawed.

In keeping with its focus on freedoms, the capability approach distinguishes between two distinct aspects of well-being and agency. For Sen, the 'primary feature of well-being is seen in terms of how a person can "function", taking that term in a very broad sense'.[12] The approach draws a distinction between well-being achievement and well-being freedom, and between agency achievement and agency freedom.

Well-being freedom is defined as 'one's freedom to achieve those things that are constitutive of one's well-being'.[13] It implies that the person has the *freedom to do* things, but also the *freedom not to do*. The often-cited example of two persons, one fasting and the other starving, provides a clear illustration relevant to this discussion. The actual well-being achieved by the fasting and the starving person is identical, but there is a crucial difference in their freedoms being exercised. The fasting person remains hungry out of choice—he or she has chosen not to eat—whereas the second person starves out of compulsion. This difference, Sen claims, is crucial to the understanding of well-being. Freedom is not viewed as being merely instrumental but as a constitutive part of a person's well-being.

3.3 CHOICE: WHY DOES IT MATTER?

Understanding choices is important since choices and decisions reflect the intersection of individuals within the social milieu, where the role of customary practices impacts an individual's transition from functionings to capabilities. Individuals live in societies, and social conformity determines the formation of freedom. As individuals seek to expand their individual freedom, it contributes to collective freedom and collective choices. In an Aristotelian society, individuals seek the *good* and move away from *bad* choices. Human flourishing expands through positive choices. The human development approach draws on this thought, and defines the role of human agency as the ability of the individual to contribute to collective freedom. Agency, liberal freedoms, and democracy are, therefore, useful mechanisms of society that lead to human progress. The presence of a judicious mix of opportunities and institutions is crucial in this regard.

The human development paradigm has reoriented the importance of strengthening people's choices in development through its core processes of equity, productivity, sustainability, and empowerment. Why are choices so ingrained in the human development and capability approach? Who decides what is valuable? What are its constituents that delineate it from the utilitarian approach to *choice*? Haq considers choice as being infinite and one that can change over time. He argues, 'People often value achievements that do not show up at all, or not immediately, in income or growth figures: greater access to knowledge, better nutrition and health services, more secure livelihoods, security against crime and physical violence, satisfying leisure hours, political and cultural freedoms and a sense of participation in community activities'.[14] Thus, the process of enlarging people's choices entails creation of an enabling environment for people to enjoy long, healthy, and creative lives.

The linkages between choice and capabilities can best be understood in relation to the notion of human freedom. According to Sen, well-being can be defined as the freedom of choice to achieve the things in life that one has reason to value most for his or her personal life. 'Freedom of choice' can be viewed as the opportunity that all individuals should have to achieve the functionings *they have reason to value*.[15] The choices people make during their life depend on their capabilities, which impact their well-being outcomes. It is the individual who decides the value of any *being* or *doing*, and hence it is his or her valuation that is taken into account. But this process of choice is not individualistic; rather, it is connected to the socio-cultural and economic practices. Each individual is *bound* by them; they can either be enabling or constraining in nature. These constraints on choices, whether on income or non-income aspects, hold people back from their preferred choice. Therefore, questions that assume importance include: what is considered valuable collectively? How does one arrive at a collective choice from individual choices? How does the capability approach to choices enable individuals to enhance well-being and freedom, both at the individual and societal levels?

If capabilities and functionings are treated as determining well-being and freedom, then the focus on selection of dimensions should also be guided by the notion of *reason to value.* How does one determine the dimensions of capabilities? For example, how does one make a choice between immunization against communicable diseases and medical treatment to ensure a healthy life? While the former is promotional and has positive externalities, the latter is preventive in nature. Both options contribute to expansion of human capabilities, but the processes are different to prevent suffering from communicable diseases like malaria and to secure a healthy lifestyle that encompasses promotional dimensions of mental and physical well-being to achieve overall health outcomes. In this regard, evaluation of capabilities would have to be more nuanced to identify these distinctions. Thus, estimation of choice becomes complex as by its very nature, it also would have to capture the presence of individual constraints and processes. Thus, estimation of choice becomes complex since, by its very nature, it also would have to capture the presence of individual constraints. Sen,[16] therefore, argues that as the calculations of the capability set are being based on observed achieved functionings, they need to be interpreted with caution.

It is equally interesting to observe that both individual and collective choices tend to influence and reinforce each other. For example, the choice to send a girl child to school defines the levels of capabilities of the girl, as well as the capabilities achieved by of the head of the household; his/her ability to transform gender relations in the household is driven by the choices made by social institutions. At the macro level, the choice to provide political freedom and liberal spaces is as crucial as making a choice between investing in military expenditure and public goods, as is everything else within the realm of human development. Broadly speaking, the objective of development is the expansion of individual capabilities or freedoms. These can be defined as functionings (*doings* and *beings*). The focus is on functionings rather than abilities as the purpose is to evaluate progress.[17] Capabilities are the real freedoms people have or the opportunities and choices available to them.

Osmani[18] emphasizes that individuals make choices on the basis of the ordering of their preferences among the capabilities. Instead of weighing preferences narrowly on the sole basis of the person's self-interest (as in the mainstream utilitarian approach), choices within the capability approach reflect values that a person holds as well as those that are shared with others in society. An individual does not form values in a vacuum—he or she does so only through interactions with the rest of society. A study by Deneulin and McGregor[19] shows that individual choices are driven by social construction of meaning. Therefore, the choices hitherto viewed as individual choices are often guided by social and cultural norms. The evidence of Muslim weaver communities in Bangladesh presents an interesting relationship between choices and capabilities. It was found that societal views affect, and are even in conflict with, individuals' self-evaluation. While weavers took pride in their work as it requires considerable skill and dedication, the caste system extended low social status to this community. Thus, even individuals may make their choice of freedom, their functionings vector is socially embedded.

There are *two* facets related to the notion of choice: *the act of choice* and *the process of choice.*[20] Narrowly defined, the act of choice can be viewed as commodity vectors held, as presented in the utilitarian approach. The broader view of act of choice, proposed by the capability approach, interprets the functionings–preference relationship on the basis of identity of the chooser, the capability menu of selection, linkage between choice–making decision of the individual within the constraints of social norms. Here, the outcomes of the choice can vary and reflect the problems of economic, political, and social behaviour of the individual and the society as well.[21] Second, the process of choice of capabilities could be based on a range of conflicting considerations. While, in case of the utilitarian approach, goods with the highest marginal utility tend to be selected, such is not the case with respect to the process of capability selection. For example, a girl may drop out of education not because she has made a choice to discontinue, but because there may be no girls' toilets in the school. Thus, explaining girls' education capabilities necessitates a thorough reflection of their educational achievements as well as the institutional and structural provisioning of other services that enhance overall capabilities. It is therefore, argued that the process of choice is not merely reflected in achieved functionings but also in the set of feasible functionings (referred to as the person's capability) that needs to be part of the overall evaluative framework.

Additionally, it is important to note that the role of choice in contributing to human freedom includes individual as well as collective responsibility. Sensitivity to self-imposed constraints and socio-cultural, political, and behavioural norms is equally important.[22] The solidarity and obligation to others in the society would take the form of self-imposed choice constraints. Thus, collective sensitivity of the society, markets, and state-led policies could enable the implementation of suitable industrial policies, wherein adoption of renewable energy sources could guarantee safe and clean air for all, both for the present and the future generations. This self-imposed choice constraint could have a bearing on what Sen calls maximizing an individual's functionings.

Emerging as equally pertinent in this larger understanding of capabilities is the close influence of individual choice behaviour and collective choices. Unlike the utilitarian approach, choice in the capabilities expansion visualizes a certain form of interconnectedness between being individualistic and having a collective orientation. Not all visions of well-being and strategies people may wish to adopt will necessarily be compatible with one another.

3.4 AGENCY AND PARTICIPATION

Agency is a powerful concept, introduced by Sen as a core pillar of the capability approach. The term agency is used initially to denote human motivation going beyond self-interest and refers to the ability of deciding and acting on the basis of what a person values or has reason to value even if the action is not to one's personal advantage. Agency achievement refers to the person's success in the pursuit of the totality of his or her considered goals and objectives.[23] As Kabeer comments, 'Agency is about more than observable action; it also encompasses the meaning, motivation and purpose which individuals bring to their activity, their sense of agency, or "the power within"'.[24] Alkire characterizes agency as 'effective power as well as direct control'.[25]

In its generic connotation, a person's agency is enhanced not only through one's actions, but also when something he or she values occurs, even if the person had nothing to do with the occurrence but would have chosen it if there had been an opportunity and the means to contribute to it.[26] For example, we may abhor corruption and want to be part of an anti-corruption movement that is active in the country, but are unable to participate in it due to either logistical or other reasons. However, if the country's parliament passes an anti-corruption law or appoints an ombudsman to monitor corruption in response to the movement, our agency is enhanced despite us not being part of the movement. This is in keeping with Sen's belief that 'a person's ability to achieve various valuable functionings may be greatly enhanced by public action and policy'.[27]

It is important to recognize that the concept of agency, by acknowledging that people may pursue goals that may not be goaded only by self-interest alone, alters with one stroke the longstanding image propagated by the dominant conventional paradigm of a self-centred human being pursuing maximization of utility as an ultimate goal. What emerges instead in the capability approach is a more humane picture of an *ethical individual* that decides and acts on the basis of values he or she has reason to value or those that are in line with his or her conception of the *good*.

Also, this concept of agency dispels the need of a paternalistic state that is doling out assistance to passive recipients and of 'paternalistic benevolence of social reformers'.[28] Sen proposes a more participatory version of agency, in which an individual himself/herself brings 'things about by his/her own efforts or plays an "active part" in some collective action which may be termed as instrumental agency'.[29]

This version of agency brings to the fore the idea that rather than being passive recipients of development assistance, individuals and groups should be active participants in bringing about change. Both realized agency and instrumental agency contribute to 'agency achievement',[30] which refers to the person's success in the pursuit of the totality of his or her considered goals and objectives.

Interpreted from the viewpoint of freedom, *agency freedom* refers to 'one's freedom to bring about achievements one values and which one attempts to produce'.[31] It relates to what the person is free to do and achieve in the pursuit of whatever goals or values he or she regards as important. A person's agency aspect is to be understood in the context of his or her aims, objectives, allegiances, obligations, and in a broad sense, a person's conception of the good. Individual agency is 'inescapably qualified and constrained by the social, political, and economic opportunities available to us'.[32] Box 3.2 illustrates this with an example of Bangladeshi women.

Well-being and agency are two interlinked but distinct concepts, although their conceptual boundaries are fuzzy. Sen states that well-being and agency 'cannot but be different at a foundational level, since the role of a person as an "agent" is fundamentally distinct from (though not independent of) the role of the same person as a "patient"'.[33] Emphasis on enhancing the agency of an individual implies that his or her position, relationship, actions, and commitments have greater weight in the society than before. Additionally, well-being freedom concentrates on a particular objective, and can be assessed more easily than agency freedom, which is broader and not linked to anything in

---

BOX 3.2   Well-Being Freedom and Agency Freedom

Well-being freedom and agency freedom can be mutually reinforcing, where exercise of agency freedom can lead to the exercise of well-being freedom. For example, self-help groups (SHGs) are a means of empowering the poor by providing them with skills and enabling women to engage in productive work that leads to enhancement of their standard of living. By associating with a SHG, the poor folk exercise their agency freedom and act to promote individual and community goals. This exercise of agency freedom leads to promotion of well-being freedom since it provides the means for improving their standard of living. In turn, this also leads to the promotion of both well-being and agency achievement. However, it is not necessary that agency freedom and well-being freedom move in the same direction. It is possible to conceive of situations where an enhancement in agency freedom may be detrimental to both well-being achievement and well-being freedom. The life of Nelson Mandela, the noted South African leader, provides an example of how the exercise of agency freedom led to a decline in his well-being achievement as he was imprisoned and freedom of movement was restricted. His well-being freedom was also affected as his ability to choose the elements of the capability set that constitute his well-being was restricted.

Source: Ibrahim, S. 2006: 'From Individual to Collective Capabilities: The Capability Approach as a Conceptual Framework for Self Help'. *Journal of Human Development* 7 (3): 397–416.

particular.[34] Moreover, well-being and agency have dissimilar roles in moral accounting. The aspect of well-being is important in judging a person's advantage, whereas the agency aspect is important in assessing what a person can do in line with his or her conception of the good. In agency freedom, the person is seen as a doer and a judge. In well-being freedom, the person is seen as a beneficiary whose interests and advantages need to be considered.

Notwithstanding the above statements, individual agency is a powerful means of transforming society itself. Spectacular examples of individual agency leading to social transformation are legendary. For example, through the exercise of his agency, Nelson Mandela challenged the colonial rulers in South Africa on apartheid, and succeeded in changing the prevailing social arrangements to ensure equality and dignity of human beings. Abraham Lincoln's efforts to free the American society of the system of slavery, Mahatma Gandhi's struggle for India's independence against the British, and Aung San Suu Kyi's non-violent struggle to establish democratic rules and values in the Republic Union of Myanmar are striking examples of individual agency being able to question, and subsequently change, social and political arrangements in their respective countries. Several other instances of questioning social values and using their individual agency to bring about transformation abound at local levels in countries around the world. While local initiatives may lack the grandeur and scale of the examples we have cited above, they are nonetheless important in demonstrating the power of individual agency.

Agency can be practised by a group of individuals with individual agency acting as a gateway in promoting collective agency. Collective agency influences results that might not have been possible by an individual agent: through collective action, several individual agents can together bring about a more substantial positive change not only in the lives of the respective agent, but also in the community or society at large.[35] This involves exercise of human freedoms by a group of individuals in order to pursue goals of a group or a collective that go beyond individual well-being concerns. Collective agency is both instrumentally and intrinsically valuable.[36] Instrumentally, it promotes participation in local decision-making, creating a sense of self-esteem, and greater access to economic opportunities and resource sharing. Intrinsically, it influences the values and beliefs of the individual, as values are a product of the social context circumscribing an individual and not uniquely a product of his or her preferences. Moreover, both collective agency and individual agency reinforce each other, since individual agency widens the probability of collective action, while collective agency promotes the act of individual agency. Collective agency is thus an important medium for the poor through which they can pressurize a change in political and social structures by challenging unequal power relations.

Collective agency shapes collective achievements. For example, in the Menia region in Upper Egypt, extensive expansion of the quarry sector led to a significant increase in the number of quarry workers.[37] These workers, in general, were young graduates, unemployed people, farmers, and even children. Due to abject poverty and unemployment, they were compelled to work in unsafe and unhealthy environments. Absence of legal rights or social insurance that would compensate them in case of work-related accidents was an issue. In order to improve work conditions and demand accountability from the government through social insurance, the workers collected signatures from more than 550 members from their work community in order to pressurize the local administration. This action also attracted attention from the media, public officers, and the national trade union of miners and quarry workers in Cairo, which helped them voice their demands for better services. This act of collective agency of the quarry workers enabled them to enhance their choices and capabilities. The government announced universal health and social insurance for all quarry workers, which otherwise would not have been possible through individual agency. By acting collectively, individuals were not only able to exercise agency freedom but also improve their agency achievement.

★★★

Moral equality of each individual, irrespective of differences in caste, creed, and gender, is at the core of both the liberal and capability approaches. Both streams believe that human beings must be treated with dignity and respect. In addition to this core belief, the liberals interpret freedoms as *non-interference* both from the state and fellow citizens, whereas the capability approach interprets freedom in more positive terms as *possession of capability* to achieve valuable human functionings. Non-interference alone may not enable a person to live a life of freedom. For example, a person who is poor, uneducated, and unemployed might encounter no interference from the state and fellow citizens, but his or her well-being is seriously undermined as he or she lacks the required capacities and opportunities to live a life of freedom. This individual may in fact welcome state interference in the form of support towards fulfilling the basic needs of food, shelter, and clothing. Societies can be deemed to treat their members unequally not only when they interfere or restrict, but also when they permit people to live in poverty and suffer capability deprivation.[38] This would, of course, mean that the state or government would need to intervene, though largely for redistributive purposes. Such intervention is deemed to be acceptable by the capability theorists as long as it does not impinge unduly on an individual's freedoms and choice.

The capability approach's view of freedoms also distinguishes itself from the utilitarian notion of *market freedoms*. The contemporary form of utilitarianism, neoliberalism, interprets freedoms by ensuring property rights and non-interference by the state, which are in turn seen as resulting in market efficiency. The influence of this viewpoint is reflected in the widespread adoption of national and global policies to remove trade barriers, and support privatization and liberalization. The resultant shrinking space for social welfare policies does not receive much attention. It is ironical that the very process of *promoting* freedoms has resulted in increasing wealth and income gaps, and the denial of the right of the poor to live a life of dignity, free from acute deprivations.

As compared to this narrow and instrumental view of freedom, the capability approach promotes positive freedoms that are intrinsically valuable. It recognizes that capabilities make a direct contribution to the choices of individuals and extend the opportunities available to them, resulting in their *effective freedom*. Freedom is important both intrinsically and for instrumental purposes. It encompasses both process and opportunity freedoms.

The notion of well-being that emerges from the capability approach has raised a set of concerns about the nature of its conceptualization. The emphasis on capabilities could be a constraint, as it tends to prioritize individual liberty over social compassion and social solidarity. The thrust tends to be towards enhancing freedom to choose rather than on the need to belong.[39] The assumption that the individual would be free from the power relations within which his or her identity and life chances are shaped is an oversimplification of the process of civilization and flourishing. Although the approach is sensitive to social heterogeneity of capabilities, the consideration that social arrangements and social relations can continue to manifest and contribute to structural inequality is strangely ignored.

Another point of discussion is the distinction between well-being freedom and agency freedom. A broad definition of well-being freedom would include agency. But the very fact that such a distinction is made seems to indicate that it does not. The need to devise the notion of agency freedom arises because it is required to complete the requirements of the capability approach. Moreover, to add to the confusion, the concept of agency freedom is also not fully specified. The conceptual fuzziness is evident in the way in which well-being freedom is outlined. For an individual, it includes the option of *to do* or *not to do*, which is in the realm of agency. Agency freedom can be considered to be broad if it considers freedom to pursue goals and allegiances not connected to one's personal life.

Excessive categorization of agency freedom and choices seems to obscure the process of understanding pathways to human freedom. Given this obscurity in the distinctions between the two concepts, Nussbaum does not consider the distinction useful, and attributes it to the 'vestiges of utilitarianism inside Sen's non-utilitarian project'.[40] The central thrust of the capability approach is to provide moral and ethical foundations of human freedom that are driven by the inter-relationships between well-being freedom and agency freedom. The contestation between the two continues to be blurred, and requires further deliberation.

NOTES AND REFERENCES

1. See League of Nations. 1926. 'Article 1', in *Slavery Convention, Geneva, September 25th 1926*. Geneva: League of Nations.
2. Sen, A. 2009. *The Idea of Justice*. London: Penguin.
3. Sen, A. 1999. *Development as Freedom*. New York: Oxford University Press, p. 3.
4. For more information, see C. Lagerkvist, J. 2014. 'The Legacy of the 1989 Beijing Massacre: Establishing Neo-Authoritarian Rule, Silencing

Civil Society'. *International Journal of China Studies* 5 (2): 349–69; Tsou, Tang. 'The Tiananmen Tragedy: The State–Society Relationship, Choices, and Mechanisms in Historical Perspective', in *Contemporary Chinese Politics in Historical Perspective*, ed. Brantly Womack, pp. 265–95. Cambridge; New York; Port Chester; Melbourne; Sydney: Cambridge University Press.

5.　Sen, A. 1993. 'Markets and Freedoms: Achievements and Limitations of the Market Mechanism in Promoting Individual Freedoms'. *Oxford Economic Papers* 45 (4): 519–41, 522.

6.　Sen, 'Markets and Freedoms', p. 522.

7.　Sen, A. 2004. 'Elements of a Theory of Human Rights'. *Philosophy and Public Affairs* 32 (4): 315–56, p. 336.

8.　Sen explains that 'there is a distinction between "culmination outcomes" (that is, only final outcomes without taking any note of the process of getting there, including the exercise of freedom) and "comprehensive outcomes" (taking note of the processes through which the culmination outcomes come about)'. See Sen, *Development as Freedom*, p. 27.

9.　Sen, A. 1993. 'Capability and Well-Being', in *The Quality of Life*, ed. M. Nussbaum and A. Sen, pp. 30–53. Oxford: Clarendon Press, p. 30.

10.　Gasper, D. 2006. 'What Is the Capability Approach: Its Core, Rationale, Partners and Dangers', Working Paper No. 428, Institute of Social Studies, The Hague p. 4.

11.　Biswas-Diener, R. and Diener, E. 2001. 'Making the Best of a Bad Situation: Satisfaction in the Slums of Calcutta'. *Social Indicators Research* 55 (3): 329–52.

12.　Sen, A. 1985. 'Well-Being, Agency and Freedom: The Dewey Lectures 1984'. *The Journal of Philosophy* 82 (4): 169–221, 197.

13.　Sen, A. 1992. *Inequality Reexamined*. Oxford: Oxford University Press, p. 57.

14.　Haq, M. Ul. 1995. *Reflections on Human Development*. New York: Oxford University Press, p. 14.

15.　For more, see Alkire, S. 2007. 'Choosing Dimensions: The Capability Approach and Multidimensional Poverty', in　*The Many Dimensions of Poverty*, ed. J. Sibler, pp. 89–119. New York: Palgrave Macmillan; Muffels, R.J., Tsakloglou, P., and Mayes, D.G., eds. 2002. *Social Exclusion in European Welfare States*. Cheltenham: Edward Elgar Publishing; Nussbaum, M. 1997. 'Capabilities and Human Rights'. *Fordham Law Review* 66: 273–300; Sen, A. 1983. 'Poor, Relatively Speaking'. *Oxford Economic Papers* 35 (2): 153–169; Sen, *Development as Freedom*; Sen, 'Elements of a Theory of Human Rights'.

16.　Sen, A. 1989. 'Development as Capability Expansion'. *Journal of Development Planning* 19: 41–58.

17.　For more on this, see Stewart, F. 2013. Capabilities and Human Development: Beyond the Individual—The Critical Role of Social

Institutions and Social Competencies, Occasional Paper 2013/03, United Nations Development Programme, New York. Accessible at http://hdr.undp. org/sites/default/files/hdro_1303_stewart.pdf; 10 January 2018.

18.   Osmani, S.R. 2016. 'The Capability Approach and Human Development: Some Reflections'. *UNDP Human Development Report Think Piece*. Accessible at http://hdr.undp.org/sites/default/files/osmani_template.pdf; 15 October 2017.

19.   Deneulin, S. and McGregor, J.A. 2010. 'The Capability Approach and the Politics of a Social Conception of Well-Being'. *European Journal of Social Theory* 13 (4): 501–19.

20.   Osmani provides a detailed discussion the question of 'why choice?' (Osmani, 'The Capability Approach and Human Development').

21.   Sen's 'Maximization Act of Choice' has both individual and collective representations. Unlike the utilitarian approach, where consumer choices determine consumer welfare, choices in the capability approach can either be by the individual or by someone else who chooses it for him or her. For more, see Sen, A. 1997. 'Maximization and the Act of Choice'. *Econometrica: Journal of the Econometric Society* 65 (4): 745–79.

22.   Basu and López-Calva call these basic functionings and supervenient functionings; Sen had earlier called them refined and unrefined functionings. Refer to Basu, K. and López-Calva, L.F. 2011. 'Functionings and Capabilities', in *Handbook of Social Choice and Welfare,* ed. K. Arrow, A. Sen, and K. Suzumura, pp. 153–87. Amsterdam: Elsevier; Sen, 'Capability and Well-Being'.

23.   Sen, *Inequality Reexamined*, p. 56.

24.   Kabeer, N. 1999. 'Resources, Agency, Achievements: Reflections on the Measurement of Women's Empowerment'. *Development and Change* 30 (3): 435–64, p. 438.

25.   Alkire, S. 2008. 'Concepts and Measures of Agency', OPHI Working Paper 9, University of Oxford, Oxford, p. 6.

26.   As Crocker comments, 'My agency freedom is enhanced, not only when I actually do something, but when something I value occurs even when I had nothing to do with its occurrence but would have chosen it had I *had* the chance and the means'. See Crocker, D.A. 2008. *Ethics of Global Development: Agency, Capability and Deliberative Democracy.* Cambridge: Cambridge University Press, p. 153.

27.   Sen, 'Capability and Well-Being', p. 44.

28.   Crocker and Robeyns use 'realised agency' to distinguish it from a more instrumental version of agency that Sen seems to have relied upon in his writings. They suggest a more convenient classification that arranges the different notions of agency discussed above in three groups of (*a*) agency of others, (*b*) indirect agency, and (*c*) direct agency. See Crocker, D. and Robeyns,

I. 2009. 'Capability and Agency', in *Amartya Sen*, ed. M. Christopher, pp. 60–90. Cambridge: Cambridge University Press; Sen, *Inequality Reexamined*.

29. Sen, *Inequality Reexamined*, pp. 57–8.

30. Sen, *Inequality Reexamined*, p. 56.

31. Sen, *Inequality Reexamined*, p. 57.

32. Crocker, *Ethics of Global Development*, p. 151.

33. Sen, *Development as Freedom*, p. 190.

34. 'Whereas well-being freedom is freedom to achieve something in particular, viz., well-being, the idea of agency freedom is more general, since it is not tied to any one type of aim.' (Sen, 'Well-Being, Agency and Freedom', p. 203.)

35. Ibrahim, S. 2014. 'Women's Fight against FGM in Upper Egypt', in *The Capability Approach: From Theory to Practice*, ed. S. Ibrahim and M. Tiwari, pp. 52–72. Basingstoke: Palgrave Macmillan.

36. Ibrahim, S. 2006. 'From Individual to Collective Capabilities: The Capability Approach as a Conceptual Framework for Self Help'. *Journal of Human Development* 7 (3): 397–416.

37. Ibrahim, S. 2010. 'When the State is Absent, Can the Poor Step In? Accessing Basic Services through Collective Agency'. Mimeo. Paper presented at the 7th Annual Conference of the HDCA, Amman, Jordan, 21–3 September.

38. Alexander, J.M. 2004. 'Capabilities, Human Rights and Moral Pluralism'. *The International Journal of Human Rights* 8 (4): 451–69.

39. Dean, H. 2009. 'Critiquing Capabilities: The Distractions of a Beguiling Concept'. *Critical Social Policy* 29 (2): 261–78, p. 267.

40. Nussbaum's own conception of freedom is more political in nature and capabilities are valued as freedoms to pursue a partial political conception of well-being. For more, see Nussbaum, M.C. 2011. *Creating Capabilities*. Cambridge, MA: Harvard University Press, p. 200.

4   Measuring Human Progress

Measurement strongly affects the actions of policymakers, as 'what we measure, affects what we do'.[1] Measurement of human progress gathered momentum ever since the publication of global HDRs commenced in 1990, and led to several countries preparing their own national and sub-national HDRs.[2] The HDRs were, by design, meant to be tools for policy action. Indeed, the HDRs have actively highlighted several important issues concerning people and articulated their perceptions and priorities, and have been effectively used for shaping development policies.

With the advent of the MDGs in 2000, periodic reporting requirements mandated that MDG Reports be prepared by national governments. The latest addition to the global reporting, albeit voluntarily by national governments, has been the SDG agenda with a wider range of goals and indicators. The steadily expanding range of dimensions and the innovations introduced in terms of indices and indicators in various reports at the national and global levels have led to huge demands being made on data systems. There is much more effort now than ever before to report on an expanded *range of people's choices* leading to unprecedented efforts in compiling data as several hitherto unmeasured dimensions, largely qualitative in nature, are sought to be brought within the fold of quantification.

Historically, progress was sought to be measured largely in the economic dimension by the per capita GDP measure. With the setting up in the 1940s of the Bretton Woods institutions, namely, the IMF and the World Bank, GDP per capita emerged as a natural choice to monitor economic progress and assess the extent of financial assistance to be provided to developing countries. Further, the ascendency of economics as a discipline also intensified the search for more precise tools and measures, a need that the GDP per capita indicator fulfilled. Further, the conceptual framework of the neoclassical approach also found an ideal match in the GDP per capita measure. It is interesting to note that the neoclassical approach's focus on satisfaction of material needs and its penchant to gloss over the differences in physical characteristics and valuation mechanisms of individuals resonated well with the per capita GDP indicator's thrust on measurable material dimensions to the neglect of non-material dimensions.

It is intriguing how GDP and GDP per capita, which originated essentially as measures of economic activity, came to be increasingly used as measures of well-being. This happened despite the cautionary note by Simon Kuznets,[3] the chief architect of the US national accounting system, in his recommendations to the US Congress in 1934. He warned the Congress that the GDP was not to be used as a measure of well-being as it excluded from its computation a number of services, such as those of women and other members of family, relief and charity, services of owned durable goods, and so on. In his view, GDP was meant to be a precise and *specialized instrument*, which aimed to measure only the market value of goods and services produced in the formal sector or of those produced by paid labour.

Over time, the importance and influence of this indicator increased, resulting in its application to numerous uses for which it was never originally designed. This prompted Stiglitz to comment that 'GDP is not wrong as such but is wrongly used', and challenged the growing 'GDP fetishism' in formulating public policy.[4]

Notwithstanding the rising popularity of GDP per capita, numerous dissenting views questioned its use as an overall indicator of progress.[5] Haq was one of its foremost critics, and pointed out that GDP as a measure is truncated, since it records only economic activity as reflected in market transactions, thereby ignoring other types of natural and social capital.[6] Moreover, GDP is not designed to account for inequalities and when used to measure changes over time, it related measures fail to capture changes in the structure of both prices and quantities that it values. More alarmingly, GDP as a measure does not have any ethical grounding as several activities and commodities that are decidedly bad for 'society as a whole' get imputed in its expenditures.[7]

Although several efforts were made to capture the non-GDP measures of progress, the HDI emerged as a frontrunner and dramatically transformed the narrative of multidimensional measures. Although it is criticized as being conceptually weak and empirically unsound—and Sen did admit so—Haq dismissed the criticism, explaining that '[w]e need a measure ... of the same level of vulgarity as the GNP [Gross National Product]—just one number—but a measure that is not as blind to social aspects of human lives as the GNP is'.[8] Despite its shortcomings, the HDI has transformed the development discourse and has succeeded in dethroning the GDP as the sole indicator of human progress. Its popularity and large-scale use in policy analysis have vindicated Haq's strong faith in the simplistic measure that included both economic and social dimensions as an alternative to per capita income.

The emergence of human development indices has led to a resurgence of debate on issues pertaining to indices, measures, and dimensions that go beyond traditional GDP per capita. At another level, HDRs have also triggered enormous interest in measuring dimensions hitherto uncaptured in statistics. This is reflected in innovative measures presented in various HDRs and research papers. Another valuable contribution of these reports is in terms of presenting data on a large number of indicators that together provide important insights into the quality of life and well-being of people across the globe.

Since the early 1990s, there has been an exponential growth in the experiments relating to multidimensional measures, mostly based on the HDI methodology. This has been a welcome change from the unidimensional narrative accounting for simplistic relationships between variables. Today, there is an increased acceptance of the intersectionality of dimensions and processes of human well-being, and a willingness to devise indices to capture it. Laudable as these efforts are, they do not advance the practice of assessing development as they seldom step beyond the safe confines of the HDI methodology, which even Haq and Sen acknowledged as being *crude*.

This chapter presents the core elements of the debate relating to human development data and indicators. The subject specific chapters to follow contain the methodology relating to poverty and gender related indices such as Human Poverty Index (HPI),

Multidimensional Poverty Index (MPI), Gender Development Index (GDI), Gender Empowerment Measure (GEM), and the Gender Inequality Index (GII) that have been presented in global HDRs. Our thrust in this chapter is to engage with the broader issues and challenges relating to indicators, approaches, and institutional mechanisms for reporting data on human development. The discussion is set against the background of the SDGs for contemporary relevance. In this context, the questions related to quality of indices generated, rationale of research design, and the very methods through which data are generated and compiled continue to be issues that require greater deliberation and analysis. The cause is not furthered by the continued inadequacy and inability to overhaul data systems to meet the demands of the twenty-first century. This chapter focuses on these issues, which we believe require urgent attention, and are essential for building robust data systems that reflect the core elements of the human development paradigm.

Section 4.1 discusses the genesis of the measures of human well-being and the numerous experiments that have taken place in recent times. Section 4.2 raises the concern about missing and empty indicators. Section 4.3 discusses issues about improving quality of data systems. Section 4.4 presents the human development approach to data generation; the last section highlights the crucial issues emerging from attempts to measure human development.

4.1 MEASURES OF HUMAN WELL-BEING

The limitations of the GDP-related measures have spurred efforts to propose modifications in the way in which the GDP indicator is computed and used. A common modification proposed by several researchers was to take note of the environment and sustainability dimension in national systems of accounts.[9] For example, Nordhaus and Tobin's Measure of Economic Well-Being (MEW)[10] included valuation of leisure and services from consumer durables, and rated health and education expenditure as investments rather than as consumption. Further, it deducted from the GNP estimate the share of certain universal *bads* such as defence expenditure, pollution, congestion, and crime, so that GNP as a measure can truly represent material and non-material well-being. In a similar attempt, Ahluwalia and Chenery[11] attempted to overcome the insensitivity of GDP growth rate towards rising income inequalities by proposing two alternatives: (*a*) by attaching equal weights to each decile of income; and (*b*) by attaching poverty weight—that is, according higher weight to the income growth of the bottom 40 per cent. This measure rectified the GDP for differences and changes in income distribution. However, the inherent limitations in the coverage and processes that need to be adopted, along with limitations of data availability, acted as constraints to their wide acceptance and application.

The more recent Stiglitz–Sen–Fitoussi Commission,[12] adopting a forward-looking approach, recommended five ways in which deficiencies of the GDP in national accounting could be addressed. These include emphasizing indicators other than GDP, improving empirical measurement of activities such as provision of education and health services, according importance to the household perspective, adding information about the distribution of income, consumption, and wealth to data on average levels of these dimensions, and widening the scope of what is being measured, particularly that of economic activities that take place outside markets. These recommendations are yet to be implemented on a wide scale exposing the GDP-related measures to numerous deficiencies.

Moving away from measures that used GDP per capita as an indicator, early efforts at measuring social dimensions of development can be traced back to 1954 when the UN set up a committee of experts on International Definition and Measurement of Level of Living. An interim guide to governments and research organizations superseded it in 1961, and suggested a list of indicators on levels of living that were internationally comparable.[13] Subsequently, several measures of human progress were proposed between 1970 and 1990. These measures can be grouped into two categories: first, those that devised composite measures comprising of both income-related as well as social dimensions; and second, those that completely eliminated the use of GDP per capita and related income measures in the composite index.

The Level of Living Index (LLI), measured across twenty countries in 1966 by United Nations Research Institute for Social Development (UNRISD), is an example of the first category of measures. The index comprised three categories of needs: physical needs measuring health, nutrition, and shelter; cultural needs measuring education, security, and leisure; and higher needs measuring *income above a threshold*.[14] The HDI included the standard of living component along with longevity and knowledge,[15] and is an important example of an index that was designed to capture the socio-economic progress of nations. It spelt out the basic capabilities that an individual must have in order to participate in and contribute to society. Few could challenge the importance of these universal basic capabilities that every person requires to lead a worthwhile life. More recently, in 2011, the OECD initiated a research programme under its Better Life Initiative, and has been computing an index of human well-being comprising indicators from three domains: material conditions, quality of life, and sustainability, each of which in turn comprises several dimensions.[16]

A prominent example of the second category of measures which were computed without using income as a dimension is the Physical Quality of Life Index (PQLI) proposed by Morris.[17] This index assessed the ability of a country to meet the basic needs of its people. PQLI was a composite index of three indicators across 120 countries: life expectancy at age one, infant mortality rate, and literacy rate. Some of the other measures that succeeded in attracting international attention include the Socioeconomic Development Index (SDI) by UNRISD in 1970, the General Index of Development (GID) in 1972 by McGranahan et al., and the Human Suffering Index in 1987 by Camp and Speidel.[18] In a review of over twenty such indices, McGillivray and Noorbakhsh[19] argued that these indices often comprised select components of well-being along with an array of indicators to capture them. Nonetheless, most efforts often failed to substantively justify the choice of indicators with sound conceptual reasoning.

Another important attempt to extend the arena of assessment was a bid to measure political freedoms. Dasgupta[20] computed a political and civil rights index to capture the extent to which people were able to express their opinions openly without fear of reprisals. He found that barring a few exceptions, most notably Botswana, Columbia, Gambia, India, and Sri Lanka, where these rights were respected, on an average, the results were dismal. He observed that there was nothing commendable in the state of affairs in a large number of the countries sampled, and the extremely poor countries seemed simply unable to afford the luxury of political and civil rights. In a similar vein, the HDR 1992 computed a Political Freedom Index encompassing five dimensions: personal security, rule of law, freedom of expression, political participation, and equality of opportunity. The index compared the relationship between political and civil freedom with the HDI scores of countries, and found a direct relationship between them. Medium and low HDI countries failed to ensure even fundamental political freedoms such as ensuring the rule of law and equality of opportunities.[21] Subsequent annual reports however discontinued its computation due to political sensitivities.

The ongoing concern with the environment has spurred efforts to measure its dimensions. The UNEP launched the Green Economy Initiative, and as a part of the initiative, in collaboration with thirty-five partner organizations, it proposed the Global Green Economy Index (GGEI) in 2010. As many as thirty-two indicators were included in the index within its four main dimensions of leadership and climate change, efficiency sectors, markets and investment, and the environment and natural capital. The top performers in the GGEI 2016 included the Nordic countries (Sweden, Norway, and Denmark), Brazil, Costa Rica, and Zambia. The report states that 'many countries—some being among the fastest growing economies in the world—remain "stuck" in dirty, unsustainable economic models. Despite their leadership at the recent Conference of Parties (COP21) in Paris, both China and the United States continue to rank poorly on the GGEI, even though they both realize better perception results as targets for green investment and innovation'.[22–23]

The HDRs have spurred a plethora of innovations in the measurement of newer dimensions. Evidently, the enthusiasm to capture numerous perspectives on development led to a variety of formulations that include happiness-adjusted income to environmentally-adjusted income, from child development to Information, Communication and Technology (ICT) development. We will not undertake a review of this large array of measures, as it is beyond the scope of this chapter. Excellent reviews of such indices are readily available for readers interested in the subject. Yang[24] has prepared an inventory of 101 composite measures of human well-being and progress put forward since the first HDI, covering a broad range of concepts and construction methodologies. Similarly, a review of gender-related indicators[25] and of composite indices of human development by Gaye and Jha,[26] and a more recent update by Lengfelder and Cazabat[27] are useful for readers interested in pursuing this aspect of measurement. Among these innovations, the Happiness Index of Bhutan has captured people's imagination and spurred similar efforts at the global level. Box 4.1 presents some details on this index.

BOX 4.1 World Happiness Index

Gross National Happiness (GNH) has been a guiding philosophy of the Government of Bhutan for several decades. The Bhutanese GNH Reports have been published since 2010. The concept of GNH comprises nine domains of human well-being: (*a*) psychological well-being; (*b*) health; (*c*) education; (*d*) time use; (*e*) cultural diversity and resilience; (*f*) good governance; (*g*) community vitality; (*h*) ecological diversity and resilience; and (*i*) living standards. In practice, the GNH Index identifies achievement in 66 per cent or six of the nine domains as comprising 'happiness'.

Following the example of Bhutan's valuing happiness as a 'fundamental human goal', the UN General Assembly passed the resolution 'Happiness: Towards a Holistic Approach to Development' in 2011. Following the UN high-level meeting on happiness and well-being, the first World Happiness Report was issued in April 2012, revealing international comparisons of quality of life. Several developments have contributed to the acceptance of happiness as a measure of social progress as well as a goal of public policy. These include OECD's acceptance of people's subjective well-being as a central agenda.

The six key variables used to explain happiness differences among countries and through time are income, healthy life expectancy, having someone to count on in times of trouble, generosity, freedom, and trust, with the latter measured by the absence of corruption in business and government. As per the 2017 World Happiness Report, while Norway tops the global happiness rankings, China, the USA, and Bhutan are found to be less happy than before. Further, although income differences matter in poorer countries, differences in mental and physical health, work life, and personal relationships explain major variance in happiness within countries.

Source: Centre for Bhutan Studies and GNH Research. 2016. *A Compass Towards a Just and Harmonious Society: 2015 GNH Survey Report*. Thimpu: Languiphkha; Helliwell, J., Layard, R., and Sachs, J. 2017. *World Happiness Report 2017*. New York: SDSN; OECD. 2013. *OECD Guidelines on Measuring Subjective Well-Being*. Paris: OECD Publishing; UN General Assembly. 2011. *Happiness: Towards a Holistic Approach to Development*. A/RES/65/309. Accessible at http://repository.un.org/bitstream/handle/11176/291712/A_RES_65_309-EN.pdf?sequence=3&isAllowed=y; 17 January 2018

The latest index to make its appearance on the global platform is the SDG index,[28] computed in 2016 by the Sustainable Development Solutions Network (SDSN) and Bertelsmann Stiftung, comprising seventy-seven indicators. This was followed by SDG Index in 2017 with an expanded range of eighty-three global indicators. The questions raised about the relevance and meaning of an index with numerous indicators of varying hues and measurement methods has led analysts to lean increasingly towards a 'dashboard' of multidimensional indicators that eschews aggregation and is gaining popularity as multiple dimensions are sought to been assessed simultaneously. The SDG dashboards presented by SDSN and Bertelsmann Stiftung have been quite popular.

On the positive side, many of the indices have been excellent advocacy tools and have strengthened the debate on neglected human dimensions in the development process. It was perhaps no coincidence that there was a significant rise in the number of UN-sponsored world conferences addressing various social issues starting from the World Summit for Children in 1990, and followed by conferences on sustainable development in 1992, human rights in 1993, population in 1994, social development and women in 1995, among others. These conferences were able to mobilize public opinion across countries in favour of addressing important dimensions of human well-being. The HDRs together with the indices provided both analytical vigour and a tool for advocacy at these UN gatherings.[29] The indices and the HDRs have also contributed to policy initiatives.

On the negative side, however, the ever-increasing dimensions and number of indicators in such composite indices raise doubts about what the index actually represents. Very often the theoretical model underlying the index is fuzzy, the inter-relationships between indicators are not scrutinized adequately, and the weighting system used is unclear. Another shortcoming is the lack of a critical lens while combining stock and flow variables. Even the HDI has fallen prey to this phenomenon. For example, in the HDI, stock variables such as adult literacy and life expectancy are combined with flow variables such as income per capita and gross enrolment ratios.[30] Moreover, several indices ignore the lagged effects of some variables on others. For example, government expenditure on education in the past few years would bear fruit after a lag to reflect in enhanced literacy rates or enhanced average number of years of schooling. Indices that are computed seldom consider such refinements, and are engaged largely in correlating current levels of indicators with each other to draw inferences.

4.2 MISSING AND EMPTY INDICATORS

The importance of accurate measurement using indicators that are important from the point of people's lives can hardly be overemphasized. They are critical in terms of policy initiatives of the government, as wrong indicators (or wrongly measured indicators) can lead to wrong policy conclusions and play havoc with the lives of millions of people.[31]

The proliferation of innovations in measuring human development and its related measures has led to a huge demand for various types of data, not all of which are readily available with statistical systems. The widening range of indicators and indices point to the increasing expectations and demands from global, regional, and national statistical systems, which need to undertake special efforts to generate, compile, and report such data. The challenge is often compounded by the fact that the relevant statistical systems are seldom consulted before framing indicators and indices; demands are made post facto on the system to provide data on newer dimensions. With the growing use of data, not only by the policymakers but also by the media, civil society, academia, international agencies, and donors, the statistical systems are burdened with demands for data on an ever-increasing range of issues. However, these demands are being made at a juncture when institutions and governments around the world are facing fiscal constraints at a level not experienced before, and at a time when resources for maintenance of even routine functions of the statistical systems are increasingly being threatened. The enthusiasm to expand the range of indicators and indices has not been met with an equally forceful movement for capacity building of statistical systems, nor have the requisite financial and human resources been devoted to the task.

Reporting processes that were initiated since the early 2000s in the context of the launch of the MDGs placed considerable emphasis on monitoring progress across various goals. The effectiveness of such monitoring was nonetheless limited by non-availability of data on crucial dimensions across countries. Chen et al.[32] point out that the data for nearly one-third of the MDG indicators were absent for almost half of the countries. It was also observed that the 1990 baseline data for several indicators were not available, indicators were not comparable across certain countries due to differing methodologies and definitions adopted for compilation, and certain indicators were not comparable across time due to different data source and absence of data at the disaggregated level.[33] These concerns assume particular global importance as the fervour for expanding the range of measures to assess development progress gains momentum in the SDG era. The SDG framework involves addressing several structural barriers to sustainable development such as inequality, environmental degradation, and unsustainable consumption patterns; their very inclusion poses challenges in terms of measurement. Most national data systems have largely been geared towards capturing data on key economic parameters with limited coverage of social indicators that represent key capabilities. They are neither designed nor prepared to meet the sudden surge in demand for new indicators that are qualitative in nature, and for which methodologies are not fully established.

The International Council for Science (ICSU) 2015 report states that only 29 per cent of the 169 SDG targets are well-developed, more than half of the targets need to be further specified, and 17 per cent require significant work.[34] The problem is particularly acute in the new dimensions, which are the hallmark of the SDGs. For example, environmental sustainability targets such as *ensure sustainable food production system* are much vaguer than other indicators. Reducing inequality, introduced as a goal for the first time at the global level, has targets addressing numerous dimensions but is termed by ICSU 2015 as being 'inadequately developed'. Further new measures are required to be specified in the areas of domains of human well-being, discrimination, and life expectancy inequalities.

As of April 2017, eighty-two SDG indicators were classified as belonging to Tier I. When an indicator belongs to Tier I, it implies that the indicator is conceptually clear and has an intentionally established methodology, that standards are available, and that data are regularly produced by countries for at least 50 per cent of the countries or populations in each region where the indicator is relevant. As many as sixty-one indicators belong to Tier II, which implies that the indicator is conceptually clear, has an internationally established methodology and standards are available but data not regularly produced by countries. Additionally, a large number of indicators (eighty-four) belong to Tier III, which implies that no internationally established methodology or standards are as yet available for the indicator, but methodology and standards are being (or will be) developed or tested.[35] Figure 4.1 illustrates this.

To cite a country as an example, in the case of Bangladesh, where data systems are relatively better developed, the Planning Commission

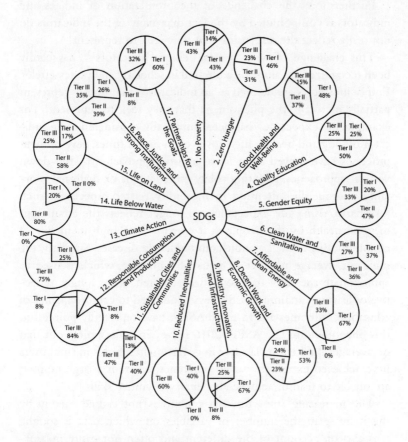

FIGURE 4.1 Tier-Wise Disaggregation of SDG Indicators

Source: Formulated by authors from United Nations. n.d. 'IAEG-SDGs: Tier Classification for Global SDG Indicators'. *Sustainable Development Goals*. Accessible at https://unstats.un.org/sdgs/iaeg-sdgs/tier-classification/; 20 April 2017.

reported that data were readily available for only seventy out of 230 indicators, and was partially available for another 108 indicators, whereas it was not available for sixty-three indicators. Data challenges are much more severe for goals 12, 13, and 14, where 57–69 per cent of the required data for these goals were not available (SDG data gap 2017 Planning Commission, Government of Bangladesh).[36] These goals relate to sustainable consumption and production patterns, climate change and conservation, and sustainability of oceans, seas, and marine resources, all of which are crucially important for a coastal country like Bangladesh.

Furthermore, the challenge of the proliferation of indices and indicators is compounded by the fact that many of the indicators do not really reflect the dimension that they seek to represent.

This challenge of what we call 'empty indicators'[37] has hardly been recognized, let alone be addressed in scholarly and policy circles. Empty indicators are defined as 'an indicator(s) that do not represent partially or totally the phenomena that they seek to represent'. For example, life expectancy has been universally considered as an indicator of long and healthy life. However, in recent times, development processes have moved from more holistic approaches to top-down vertical approaches, targeting solely either infant or maternal mortality without due attention to morbidity related aspects. In such a scenario, rising life expectancy no longer reflects the attainment of good health by the people as it coexists with high incidence of communicable as well as non-communicable diseases. Similarly, the indicator, average number of years of schooling, which is used to approximate the level of knowledge acquired, is no longer reflective of learning attainments. Surveys conducted to capture quality of education outcomes as PISA and ASER have repeatedly pointed to this phenomenon. The ASER-2016 survey in India points out that on average, children in class five in government schools in rural India have achieved extremely varied outcomes, wherein a large number are unable to read or achieve elementary cognitive skills.

The increasing stress on data systems is not caused merely by the increase in the number of variables on which data is sought; it is also on account of the different and often not easily measurable aspects on which data are demanded. The reporting on newly devised indicators is more intensive in terms of time and resources. In fact, underlying this entire exercise of measuring human progress is the fundamental question of how effectively quantitative indicators capture dimensions of quality of life.

4.3 QUALITY OF DATA SYSTEMS

Apart from non-existing data on crucial dimensions, even those that exist are challenged for their inaccuracy and unreliability. They are much more daunting and troublesome than mere lack of data. In most developing countries the problem is quite severe, and spans across a range of indicators. Non-standardized data collection methods, lack of clear understanding on the definitions to be used, and overlapping departmental jurisdictions often give rise to the compilation of similar data by multiple agencies using non-uniform methodologies.[38] These practises in turn severely affect the policy inferences that can be drawn from the analysis of such data.

Even where data are available for some indicators, they are compiled for several purposes, and do not have an equity lens embedded into them. Data disaggregated by region—that is, national, provincial, and/or locational (rural/urban)—along with social group and gender disaggregation is required for effective monitoring and reducing vulnerabilities. However, in many instances, such disaggregated data are just not available. It is surprising that even though data are collected from individuals and are amenable to such disaggregated compiling, they are often aggregated while reporting, as the ground level staff is not sensitized about the importance of maintaining such disaggregated data. For example, in the case of health-sector data emerging from Health Management Information System (HMIS) facility-based reports, although data are disaggregated at the point of collection, they are aggregated before being compiled into monthly reporting forms or databases.

Data sourced from census or periodic sample surveys pose the challenge of generating annual values from decennial or five/three-yearly surveys. Very often, data are interpolated or extrapolated to arrive at yearly values. When different agencies use varying assumptions and methodologies for such interpolation/extrapolation, the results obtained with the use of the same base data set can vary widely. A dramatic example of such inconsistencies in published reports is with respect to Fiji.[39]

The 1998 HDR had ranked Fiji forty-four with an HDI value of 0.869, making Fiji the only country to be included in the high human development category. However, during the same year, the Pacific Regional HDR, relying on updated data, ranked the country 102 with an HDI value of 0.667. The discrepancy was traced back to the estimates of life expectancy data used by the two reports. The global HDR used the 1986 census data and extrapolated from them, assuming that longevity would continuously improve. The Pacific HDR used the 1996 census which indicated that the progress in life expectancy was much lower than assumed. In addition, the per capita GDP estimates were also different with the global HDR using adjusted real GDP per capita, whereas the Pacific HDR used estimates of GDP per capita. This also contributed to the discrepancy between the two estimates leading to radically different policy implications for the national government.

Next, the data that are collected across countries or even provinces/districts could have varying methodologies for indicators leading to huge challenges of comparability. Moreover, even for the same indicator, the continuous quest to improve methodology for estimation leads to refinements in measurement, which could in turn render comparability of data on the same indicator difficult. The differing definitions and varying understanding of broad categories of indicators pose additional challenges. For example, in the case of the MDGs, the indicator 'proportion of births attended by skilled birth attendants' and 'proportion of population with sustainable access to an improved water source' could lead to differing interpretations as each country may have a different definition of what constitutes 'skilled' attendants and what can be categorized as 'improved' water source.

The SDGs also leave much ambiguity in the framing of targets and indicators which could potentially lead to a repetition of similar phenomena unless proactive measures are taken for harmonization of methodologies and definitions used. Some such efforts are already ongoing at the level of global data sets generated by the World Bank and UN agencies. In addition, efforts at regional levels are worthy of attention and emulation. For example, the MECOVI surveys[40] harmonize data on poverty and inequality for twenty-four countries in Latin America and the Caribbean, and also provide support to national governments in preparation of a database using such harmonized procedures.[41] The forty-eighth session of the UN Statistical Commission held in March 2017 suggested enhanced harmonization and national ownership of global household and thematic surveys in the light of the need to ensure monitoring of the SDGs.

Furthermore, the difference in the estimates of the same phenomenon using national definitions and data *vs.* international definitions, and data continues to be highly contentious. For example, in many countries poverty estimates are made using national sample surveys whereas the more widely used norm for international comparisons is the USD 1.25 a day poverty norm used by the World Bank and other international agencies. The differing national methodologies pose a challenge, and it is inevitable that a number of estimates for the same phenomenon will coexist till national governments agree to use uniform methodologies for estimating key indicators.

Lastly, despite huge strides made by statistical systems across nations in building respective databases, the situation with respect to gender disaggregated data continues to be poor particularly with respect to consumption, income, wealth, and assets. The UN's Statistical Commission has identified a set of gender indicators that encompass women's participation in economic and political activities, access to resources, education, health, and human rights, but much of the data on these aspects is not universally available at the level of disaggregation that is required to enable local action. One of the key limitations in gender studies is the lack of data on intra household distribution as much of the data on consumption and standard of living are available only at the household level. Moreover, much of women's work is not counted and accounted for, resulting in undervaluation of such work. Time use surveys in several countries have pointed to the severe underestimation of women's contribution to national income. The introduction of gender-related measures in the HDRs has provided an impetus to data collection efforts in relation to specific indicators, but it has not yet gathered the requisite momentum.[42] However, given that such surveys are expensive and time consuming, they are not conducted as frequently or in sufficient numbers across countries to enable a thorough understanding of the issues concerning gender inequalities.

4.4 HUMAN DEVELOPMENT APPROACH TO DATA GENERATION

The frontiers of measuring human progress have arrived at a stage today when there has been an intermeshing of quantitative and qualitative parameters. Though the expansion of methodologies to assess human progress cannot be attributed centrally to the human development paradigm, the paradigm has certainly provided avenues to transcend the rigidities of quantitative and qualitative approaches. In a workshop on Q^2 approach, poverty analysts argued that there is a blurring of *qualitative and quantitative* approaches to data collection. Though the quantitative approach epistemologically dwells on positivist methodologies, the possibility of deriving numerical explanations from qualitative approaches is equally possible. Similarly, there are possibilities of triangulating data to build quantitative estimates using qualitative data sets. The differences underlie types of data and its collection. The data can be of numerical or non-numerical forms, while methods would be relevant mainly from the perspective of how widespread and representative they are. Stark examples of the relevance of both methodologies are reflected the increasing reliance on participatory methods in poverty analysis and evolving large data sets to capture human development progress.

Various methodologies have been employed using the capability approach to measure well-being of an individual or a group. For instance, McGregor[43] elaborates on the methodology used by the ESRC research group, which included both subjective and objective measures of well-being in developing countries while conducting empirical research relating to social and cultural well-being in Bangladesh, Ethiopia, Peru, and Thailand. The emphasis is on the use of outcomes, structures, and processes to gather data on aspects of well-being. The tools included community profiling, resources and needs profiling, quality of life, income and expenditure survey and diaries, process research and structures, and regimes.

Further, as the understanding of well-being is essentially multi-dimensional and not confined uniquely to economic measures, several researchers have attempted to provide a holistic list of well-being dimensions and indicators. Chiapperò-Martinetti[44] measures five dimensions of well-being—housing, health conditions, education and knowledge, social interactions, and psychological conditions—using fuzzy sets theory. Fuzzy sets theory is used because achievement of certain functionings can be partial, and may not refer to either complete attainment or its absence as in the case of living a healthy life.[45]

Although a distinction is often made between objective and subjective indicators, the difference is not very rigid, as indicators are increasingly being derived from mixed methodologies using both objective and subjective indicators. Subjective indicators using qualitative data are often used to supplement statistical inferences drawn from objective criteria. This is especially the case in HDR analysis, where matters of dignity, self-esteem, attitudes, and opinions are vital. Mixed methodologies have been used in several country-level reports such as *balanced* focus groups in Argentina's 2005 HDR, perception study on inequality and intergenerational mobility in Honduras's 2011 report *Reducing Inequality*, and the original survey on citizens' perceptions on human security in Nigeria's *2016 HDR*.[46] Qualitative data include personal testimonies, interviews, case studies, focus group discussions, transcripts from community forums, and perception surveys. These are increasingly being used to provide a glimpse into, and cross check the quality of, services provided in various dimensions of interest in people's well-being, such as effectiveness of governance systems, and citizens' experience of various freedoms. Box 4.2 provides illustrative examples of such perception surveys.

Since qualitative data are not readily available in the form or level of disaggregation required, efforts to assess the levels of human progress across countries and regions have resorted to compile data using participatory techniques, which also enable such assessments to reflect people's voices. Although it is not much discussed, a question that needs to be raised is one of whether there is a specific human development approach to data generation. The human development approach has largely been perceived as applicable to analysis of data. However, it is also essential that the methods of data collection and their use be more democratic and open in the spirit of the human development approach. Moreover, the increasing power of democratic practice strengthened by the forces of decentralization and right to information involving people in gathering and analysing data could herald a transformation in unforeseen ways. This is particularly true in measuring human progress as the nature of such progress is also an arena where wide debate and discussion could lead to common elements of progress being identified in a participatory manner. It will enable people to function more as *agents* in determining their own well-being rather than as passive beneficiaries of *development*.

Participatory methods have been increasingly gathering data on improving the quality of life on a large enough scale to enable sound

BOX 4.2   Illustrative Examples of Perception Surveys

Perception surveys facilitate in capturing people's views and opinions on such issues as governance, quality of services, security, social norms, and inclusion. These surveys are based on asking people what matters to them.

Using a three-tiered system of scores, ratings, and status, the *2016 Freedom in the World* was a global survey of people's political rights and civil liberties across 195 countries and fifteen territories. The survey's premise was that liberal democratic societies were most conducive to achievement of freedom for all, and that the 1948 Universal Declaration of Human Rights applied to all territories notwithstanding geographical location, economic progress, or social composition.

The Turkish Human Development Index—Public Opinion (HDI-P) survey was undertaken to quantify public perception of the concept and criteria of human development. The 2016 survey was administered through sixty-one questions comprising examination of contributing factors of HDI such as shelter, human security, health, social life, personal finance, education, and social inclusion. Analyses of the indices for each of the components revealed that health, shelter, and human security contributed positively to HDI.

In addition to objective facts, the Delhi HDR 2013, structured around improving lives, promoting inclusion, took account of people's perceptions. The large perceptions survey enquired into a variety of developmental issues ranging from environmental challenges to quality of services, as well as citizen's aspirations with respect to education, employment, and prosperity.

Takeuchi and Hine make a case for perceptions data in the multiple roles they play in public policy and upholding answerability and enforceability, especially for the post-2015 agenda.

Source: Academic Foundation and Institute of Human Development. 2013. Delhi Human Development Report 2013: Improving Lives, Promoting Inclusion, New Delhi: Academic Foundation, Institute of Human Development; Accessible at http://ingev.org/en/library/ingev-reports/human-development-index-public-opinion-e-book-published/; Freedom House. 2016. *2016 Freedom in the World*. Washington, DC: Freedom House; Lengfelder and Cazabat, 'Review of Conceptual and Measurement Innovations in National and Regional Human Development Reports, 2010–2016'; Takeuchi, L. and Hine, S. 2015. 'Asking People What They Think', Working Paper 413, ODI, London; UNDP. 2007. *Measuring Human Development: A Primer*. New York: UNDP.

assessments to be made. It involves mixed methods to capture the both subjective and objective dimensions of deprivation. One such large-scale study that used such participatory processes on a large scale was that by Narayan-Parker's *Voices of the Poor*,[47] which encompassed 200 communities in twenty-three countries and provided insights on the importance and effectiveness of the institutions in the lives of the rural and urban poor.

Inspired by the HDRs, large-scale human development surveys have been initiated in a few countries to compile data on a variety of dimensions for which national statistical systems does not provide data. For example, the India Human Development Survey, designed and implemented jointly by the National Council of Applied Economic Research (NCAER) and the University of Maryland in 2004–5, covered 41,554 urban and rural households in all the states of India. The second round in 2011–12, covering the same households, created one of the largest panel data sets measuring various dimensions of human development. Availability of large-scale household-level data sets has facilitated innumerable smaller studies explaining the process of human development progress in India.

The Human Development Atlas in Brazil launched in 1998 compiled data on over 200 indicators for over 5,500 municipalities, enabling democratization of data. This Atlas serves as a guiding tool in resource allocation, and has been utilized in selecting beneficiaries at state, municipality, and household levels for improving the living conditions of needy people within a short time. In 2013, the analysis was extended to metropolitan regions, and a website was developed,[48] containing information relating to the municipal HDI and data on more than 200 indicators at the disaggregated level. In the 2004 Kosovo HDR, a survey covering 6,000 household across thirty municipalities was conducted as there was absence of census data for more than two decades.[49]

Alternate case studies of bridging the data divide are available at local and global levels. These initiatives have originated from the developing world where such initiatives have taken strong roots. For example, Chhattisgarh state in central India took the lead in preparing a provincial HDR which was built bottom-up from 17,000 villages that prepared their own report cards through a participatory method. Facilitated by the provincial government, which trained facilitators who went to the villages, conducted focus group discussions, and gathered data on amenities in the villages, the reports provided vital information with respect to the history of the village, the status of key human development indicators and the lacunae therein, and the aspirations of the people for the future. Each report also contained a section articulating what the people were prepared to contribute in order to make development happen in their village, and what support they expected from the government. The village report was ratified in the village assembly, and thereafter the reports were used by the stakeholders, working together, to compile sixteen district HDRs. After ratification by the district councils, the reports were used to compile the provincial HDR, released in 2005.

Another example that illustrates the power of people's participation in furthering the cause for people-centred development is from the Philippines, where a Human Development Network (HDN) was created with a group of development practitioners in 1994 to discuss how best to apply the major findings and conclusions of the HDR in a Philippine setting.[50] The HDN undertakes programmes and projects to further the cause of better reporting on human development, and undertakes advocacy to drive home the messages to a wider audience. Numerous such examples abound, making it necessary for analysts to take them seriously while recalibrating data systems at various levels.

The need for better data and their monitoring has been brought home starkly by the SDG agenda. Efforts to address the data challenges are ongoing in several countries. The United Nations Secretary-General's Independent Expert Advisory Group (IEAG) has emphasized the importance of strengthening and streaming the process and purpose of data, which is robust and promotes transparency and accountability to explain complex development agenda.[51]

The cost of such a revamping of data systems is huge. The IEAG report estimates that USD 1 billion per annum will be required to enable the world's seventy-seven lower income countries to catch up and put in place statistical systems to meet the data requirements of the SDG implementation. This excludes the cost of monitoring and evaluation which will be additional. About USD 100–200 million of overseas assistance may be required by lower income countries to further the building blocks of governance and service delivery.[52]

In this context, it may be useful to explore avenues for greater use of digital technology as it have the potential to revolutionise data systems.

For instance, use of smartphones, and satellite-based applications and imagery not only reduced the lag in data collection, but also contribute to improve the precision of data across time and space. The era of big data, including online searches, mobile banking transactions, and user-generated content such as blog posts and tweets, has led to newer computational techniques and creation of large data sets, which were hitherto not possible. In several cases, such big data has complemented official data and provided insights into behavioural patterns and trends in key indicators on a real time basis. Harnessing such data for enhancing human progress has immense value.[53] For instance, the Finance Ministry of India made use of satellite surveys for the first time in its 2017 series of annual economic survey. The digital images were used to compute the built-up area of structures, based on which the property tax to be paid was calculated. This demonstrates how the use of such technology could provide lucrative revenue collection options. Satellite images have also been used to argue the extent of urbanization is much more India than previously estimated.

★★★

The human development paradigm has revolutionized methodologies for measuring human progress in multiple ways. It has broken down the rigid separation between quantitative and qualitative methodologies, between subjective and objective modes of data compilation and analysis. It has provided a seamless linkage between micro and macro settings while popularizing participatory methods of data generation and analysis in numerous dimensions that have been constantly updated. This has led to extending the frontiers of development itself with several hitherto unmeasured aspects of well-being currently being measured, however imperfectly. It has made comparisons across countries possible on dimensions that matter for people's lives.

With the advent of the SDGs and the dramatic increase in the range of dimensions on which data is now sought to be monitored, strengthening of statistical capacity has assumed priority. The introduction of two specific targets in goal 17 in the SDGs on issues of data monitoring and accountability further lends a sense of urgency to this task. With the introduction of an over 230-indicator global monitoring system suggested by the SDSN, a thorough overhauling of the statistical systems is already underway in several countries. Though statistical systems are yet to gear up to equip themselves to provide the data on newer dimensions that are constantly brought under the fold of measurement, futuristic agenda demands that considerable investments of time and financial and human resources be made to strengthen them. While national statistical agencies are beginning to wake up to the challenge, it is necessary for scholars, too, to engage more deeply with measures of development. The preoccupation with defining and refining conceptual constructs will yield better results in terms of an altered development paradigm only when academics get their hands dirty with ground-level data, as well as with metadata. The future agenda would be to evolve a more integrated data system that is holistic and people-centred.

NOTES AND REFERENCES

1.   Stiglitz, J.E., Sen, A., and Fitoussi, J.P. 2010. *Report by the Commission on the Measurement of Economic Performance and Social Progress.* Paris: Commission on the Measurement of Economic Performance and Social Progress.
2.   The first National HDR was prepared in 1992 by Bangladesh. By 2016, more than 700 NHDRs had been published. Many countries also prepared sub-national HDRs. India has the most number of sub-national HDRs.
3.   Kuznets, S. 1934. *National Income 1929–1932.* A report to the US Senate, 73rd Congress, 2nd Session. Washington, DC: US Government Printing Office.
4.   Stiglitz, J.E. 2009. 'GDP Fetishism'. *The Economists' Voice* 6 (8). Article 5.
5.   For a detailed critique on the use of GDP as a well-being measure, refer to Cobb, C., Halstead, T., and Rowe, J. 1995. 'If the GDP Is Up, Why Is America Down?'. *The Atlantic Monthly* 276 (4): 59–78; Giannetti, B.F., Agostinho, F., Almeida, C.M.V.B., and Huisingh, D. 2015. 'A Review of Limitations of GDP and Alternative Indices to Monitor Human Well-Being and to Manage Eco-system Functionality'. *Journal of Cleaner Production* 87: 11–25; Henderson, H. 1996. 'Measuring Progress: Not by GNP Alone—New Economic Indicators Highlight Quality of Life'. *The Light Party.* Accessible at http://www.lightparty.com/Visionary/MeasuringProgress.html; 20 September 2017; Ivkovic, A.F. 2016. 'Limitations of the GDP as a Measure of Progress and Well-Being'. *Ekonomski Vjesnik* 29 (1): 257–72; Stiglitz, 'GDP Fetishism'.
6.   Concerns include non-inclusion of non-market production such as voluntary services, child care, and women's work at home. Crucial gaps comprise inability of national accounting systems to include ecosystem services, biodiversity, value of natural forests, and so on, in monetary terms.

7. For example, expenditure by individuals on drugs and alcohol, or expenditure on goods and services that are environmental *bads*, such as coal, petroleum products, and undesirable expenditure such as defence are computed in GDP, even when they do not contribute to net progress of a nation as we understand it.

8. Sen, A. 1999. *Development as Freedom*. New York: Oxford University Press.

9. For instance, while Repetto et al. suggested an adjustment using market value approach that includes depreciation of different forms of natural resources, El Serafy recommended including user costs of natural resource consumption. World Development Report 1997 introduced Genuine Savings that assesses the *level of savings in a country after depreciation of produced capital*. For details, see El Serafy, S. 1993. 'Country Macroeconomic Work and Natural Resources', Environment Working Paper No. 58, The World Bank, Washington, DC; 1996. 'Weak and Strong Sustainability: Natural Resources and National Accounting'. *Environmental Taxation Accounting* 1 (1): 27–48; Repetto, R., Magrath, W., Wells, M., Beer, C., and Rossino, F. 1989. *Wasting Assets: Natural Resources in the National Income Accounts*. Washington, DC: World Resources Institute; World Bank 1997. *World Development Report 1997: The State in a Changing World*. Oxford University Press: New York.

10. Nordhaus, W. and Tobin, J. 1972. 'Is Growth Obsolete?', in *Measurement of Economic and Social Performance,* ed. M. Moss, pp. 509–64. New York: NBER.

11. Ahluwalia, M. and Chenery, H. 1974. 'The Economic Framework', in *Redistribution with Growth,* ed. H. Chenery, M.S. Ahluwalia, C.L.G. Bell, J.H. Duloy, and R. Jolly, pp. 32–51. Oxford: Oxford University Press.

12. Stiglitz, J.E., Sen, A., and Fitoussi, J.-P., *Report by the Commission on the Measurement of Economic Performance and Social Progress.*

13. United Nations. 1961. *International Definition of Measurement of Levels of Living: An Interim Guide.* New York: UN Publication.

14. Drewnowski, J. and Scott, W. 1966. *The Level of Living Index.* Report No. 4. Geneva: United Nations Research Institute for Social Development.

15. Slottje constructed a composite index measuring quality of life, comprising twenty indicators across 130 countries drawing from the capabilities approach. For details, see Slottje, D.J. 1009. 'Measuring the Quality of Life across Countries'. *The Review of Economics and Statistics* 73 (4): 684–93.

16. Organisation for Economic Co-operation and Development (OECD). 2011. *How's Life?: Measuring Well-Being.* Paris: OECD Publishing.

17. For details, see Morris, M.D. 1979. *Measuring the Condition of the World's Poor: The Physical Quality of Life Index.* New York: Pergamon.

18. Camp, S.L. and Speidel, J.J. 1987. *The International Human Suffering Index.* Washington, DC: Population Crisis Committee; McGranahan, D.V., Richard-Proust, C., Sovani, N.V., and Subramanian, M. 1972. *Contents and Measurement*

of Socioeconomic Development: A Staff Study of the United Nations Research Institute for Social Development. New York: Praeger; United Nations Research Institute for Social Development (UNRISD). 1970. *Contents and Measurements of Socioeconomic Development*. Geneva: UNRISD.

19. For details, refer to McGillivray, M. and Noorbakhsh, F. 2007. 'Composite Indexes of Human Well-Being: Past, Present and Future', in *Human Well-Being: Concept and Measurement*, ed. M. McGillivray, pp. 113–34. Basingstoke: Palgrave Macmillan.

20. For details, refer to Dasgupta, P. 1990. 'Well-Being and the Extent of Its Realisation in Poor Countries'. *The Economic Journal* 100 (400): 1–32.

21. Political rights represent rights of citizens in determining who governs their country and what the laws are and will be. They show the level of liberties. Civil rights reflect the rights the individual has vis-à-vis the state. For details, see UNDP. 1992. *Human Development Report 1992: Global Dimensions of Human Development*. New York: Oxford University Press.

22. Dasgupta, 'Well-Being and the Extent of Its Realisation in Poor Countries'.

23. Dual Citizen LLC. 2016. The Global Green Economy Index: GGEI 2016—Measuring National Performance in the Green Economy (Fifth Edition). Accessible at https://dualcitizeninc.com/GGEI-2016.pdf; 20 November 2017.

24. Yang, L. 2014. 'An Inventory of Composite Measures of Human Progress', Occasional Paper on Methodology, UNDP Human Development Report Office, New York.

25. For details, see Gaye, A., Klugman, J., Kovacevic, M., Twigg, S., and Zambrano, E. 2010. 'Measuring Key Disparities in Human Development: The Gender Inequality Index', Human Development Research Paper 2010/46, UNDP, New York.

26. For details, see Gaye, A. and Jha, S. 2010. 'A Review of Conceptual and Measurement Innovations in National and Regional Human Development Reports 1998–2009', Human Development Research Paper 2010/21, UNDP, New York.

27. Lengfelder, C. and Cazabat, C. 2016. 'Review of Conceptual and Measurement Innovations in National and Regional Human Development Reports, 2010–2016', Background Paper for 2016 UNDP Human Development Report, United Nations, New York.

28. Sachs, J., Schmidt-Traub, G., Kroll, C., Durand-Delacre, D., and Teksoz, K. 2016. *SDG Index & Dashboards—A Global Report*. New York: Bertelsmann Stiftung and Sustainable Development Solutions Network (SDSN).

29. Ponzio, R. and Ghosh, A. 2016. *Human Development and Global Institutions: Evolution, Impact, Reform*. New York: Routledge.

30. For more, see Kelley, A. 1991. 'The Human Development Index: "Handle with Care"'. *Population and Development Review* 17 (2): 315–24; Ryten, J. 2000. 'Should There Be a Human Development Index?'. Paper presented at the International Association for Official Statistics meeting, Montreux, 5 September.

31. The 2007–8 crisis in financial markets illustrates this tellingly. The fact that US GDP growth was questionable, since almost 40 per cent of the GDP comprised financial savings, was typically ignored, and optimistic forecasts were made by the Federal Reserve as late as 2007, pointing to the hazard of using even traditional measures such as the GDP uncritically without examining its structure.

32. Chen, S., Francois, F., Johannes, J., and Klasen, S. 2013. 'Towards a Post-2015 Framework that Counts: Developing National Statistical Capacity', Discussion Paper (1), Paris 21, Paris.

33. Prabhu, K.S. 2005. 'Social Statistics for Human Development Reports and Millennium Development Goal Reports: Challenges and Constraints'. *Journal of Human Development* 6 (3): 375–97.

34. International Council for Science (ICSU). 2015. *Review of Targets for the Sustainable Development Goals: The Science Perspective*. Accessible at https://www.icsu.org/publications/review-of-targets-for-the-sustainable-development-goals-the-science-perspective-2015; 16 March 2017.

35. As per United Nations. n.d. 'IAEG-SDGs: Tier Classification for Global SDG Indicators'. *Sustainable Development Goals*. Accessible at https://unstats.un.org/sdgs/iaeg-sdgs/tier-classification/; 20 April 2017.

36. Government of People's Republic of Bangladesh. 2017. *Data Gap Analysis of Sustainable Development Goals (SDGs): Bangladesh Perspective*. Dhaka: Planning Commission.

37. Prabhu, 'Social Statistics for Human Development Reports and Millennium Development Goal Reports'.

38. For example, in India, female work force participation rate varies with the source of the data used, whether it is from the census or the National Sample Survey, both of which are official sources of data.

39. For details, see Prabhu, 'Social Statistics for Human Development Reports and Millennium Development Goal Reports'.

40. The Mecovi Program is the Spanish acronym for '*Programa Para El Mejoramiento De Las Encuestas De Hogares Y La Medicion De Condiciones De Vida*' or the Regional Programme for Improvement of the Surveys and Measurement of the Living Conditions in Latin America.

41. Alkire, S. and Samman, E. 2014. 'Mobilizing the Household Data Required to Progress toward the SDGs', OPHI Working Paper No 72, OPHI, Oxford.

42. For details, see Stotsky, J.G., Shibuya, S., Kolovich, L., and Kebhaj, S. 2016. 'Trends in Gender Equality and Women's Advancement', IMF Working Paper,

WP/16/21. Accessible at https://www.imf.org/external/pubs/ft/wp/2016/wp1621.pdf; 15 July 2017.

43.   McGregor, J.A. 2007. 'Researching Wellbeing: From Concepts to Methodology', in *Wellbeing in Developing Countries: From Theory to Research*, ed. I. Gough and J.A. McGregor. Cambridge; New York: Cambridge University Press.

44.   Chiapperò-Martinetti, E. 2000. 'A Multidimensional Assessment of Well-Being Based on Sen's Functioning Approach'. *Rivista Internazionale di Scienze Sociali* 108 (2): 207–39.

45.   In the fuzzy set theory, instead of denoting a value 0 or 1 to indicate a complete absence of presence of a particular functioning, any values between 0 and 1 are used to indicate the extent to which a particular functioning is attained, where a higher value represents higher attainment.

46.   Lengfelder and Cazabat, 'Review of Conceptual and Measurement Innovations in National and Regional Human Development Reports, 2010–2016'; UNDP. 2007. *Measuring Human Development: A Premier, Guidelines and Tools for Statistical Research, Analysis and Advocacy.* New York: UNDP.

47.   Narayan-Parker, D., Patel, R., Schafft, K., Rademacher, A., and Kara-Schulte, S. 2000. *Voices of the Poor: Can Anyone Hear Us?*, Volume 1. New York: Oxford University Press for the World Bank.

48.   Accessible at www.atlasbrasil.org.br; 23 July 2017.

49.   UNDP, *Measuring Human Development*.

50.   Human Development Network (HDN). 2005. 'Philippine Human Development Report 2005'. *HDN, UNDP, and New Zealand Agency for International Development (NZAID).* Accessible at http://hdr.undp.org/sites/default/files/philippines_2005_en.pdf; 18 March 2017.

51.   IEAG. 2014. 'A World That Counts: Mobilising the Data Revolution for Sustainable Development'. United Nations Independent Expert Advisory Group on a Data Revolution for Sustainable Development. Accessible at http://www.undatarevolution.org/wp-content/uploads/2014/12/A-World-That-Counts2.pdf; 17 January 2018.

52.   SDSN. 2015. *Indicators and a Monitoring Framework for Sustainable Development Goals–Launching a Data Revolution.* Sustainable Development Solutions Network, United Nations. Accessible at http://unsdsn.org/wp-content/uploads/2015/05/150612-FINAL-SDSN-Indicator-Report1.pdf.

53.   For example, the Finance Ministry of India made use of satellite surveys for the first time in its 2017 series of the Annual Economic Survey. The satellite images were used to compute the built-up area to estimate the potential property tax that could be collected in order to explain how urban India is missing out on a lucrative revenue source by computing. Satellite images have also been used to argue that the extent of urbanization is much more India than previously estimated.

5 Economic Growth and Human Development

Evidence of Muddled Pathways

Development dilemmas, such as the trade-off between equity and efficiency, which were earlier considered to be satisfactorily resolved, have sprung back to life with renewed vigour as challenges that seek immediate attention. The older understandings and theories are increasingly being reversed, making space for even more confusion in both analytical frames and empirical analyses. The fact that country typology is no longer along the traditional pathways adds yet another dimension to the overall fuzzy picture. For example, most recent evidence suggests that the bulk of poverty is now concentrated not only in the low-income countries, but in the middle-income countries as well.[1] This phenomenon, which affects a vast population across countries, has drawn global attention.

Untying the linkages between economic growth and human development has assumed urgency as current development processes no longer follow historical patterns. While countries can learn from one another, there are limitations as the developmental challenges are uniquely placed.[2] Though there is merit in engaging in cross-country comparison of development to learn of processes and trajectories, we need to be cautious as each country has pursued distinct pathways. The economic growth–human development mosaic is a puzzle that seeks critical reflection. The HDR 1996 highlighted that for more than a decade and a half since 1980, there has been a dramatic increase in economic growth in about fifteen countries that contain more than a quarter of the world's population. Despite this, the report of economic decline in around 100 countries that include another quarter of the world's population created turmoil among policymakers.[3]

Most countries have been experiencing dramatic transformation economically, politically, technologically, and socially. Globalization and its aftermath have challenged the role of economic growth and human development processes considerably. Issues of sustaining co-ordination and coherence among a wide variety of actors, such as politicians, corporations, civil society, and transnational organizations,[4] have become a crucial component of public debate.

The diversity of explanations of what, why, and how the relationship between economic growth and human development should be considered has been an area of serious scrutiny. The U-shaped analysis of economic growth and income inequality explains that distributional processes are largely automatic in a market-led economy. An equally pertinent variable for sustaining long term economic growth is the inclusion of the impact of economic growth on human wellbeing. The temporal effect of economic growth, therefore, largely represents the linkages between income inequalities and human development outcomes. Lastly, persistent income inequality could cripple sustainability of human development. A capability inequality trap may occur when countries experience high MPI as well as high levels of Inequality Adjusted Human Development Index (IHDI).

Against this backdrop, this chapter examines the nature and pattern of economic growth and human development processes across countries. It juxtaposes the relationship between them in the light of globalization and the varying outcomes of human development across countries. An analysis of linkages between GDP and HDI over the past three decades across countries indicates that the process is extremely dynamic in nature and that human development outcomes do not follow a defined trajectory.[5] This is particularly evident in the analysis of challenges facing human development, where we find the dominance of joblessness, impoverishment, displacement, and migration. The chapter concludes that economic growth and human development cannot be viewed as disconnected processes, since they influence each other in multiple ways. Literature on this subject has focused mostly on panel data analysis, trying to provide an explanation for the rate of change. Drawing on their inferences, the present chapter provides a cross-sectional analysis, as the data for most human development indicators are relatively limited. The argument here is that the pattern of economic growth and human development outcomes reflected across countries provides useful insights, forms, and reasons for variations in human development outcomes of countries.

The next section (5.1) discusses the context in which various countries embarked upon the process of economic growth and human development. Section 5.2 presents empirical evidence of linkages between economic growth and human development. This is followed by Section 5.3, which extends the discussion to income inequality. Section 5.4 presents an analysis on dynamic linkages of human development outcomes, while Section 5.5 raises concerns about human development in an era of goals and targets. Section 5.6 discusses the differential performance of some of the human development indicators. Section 5.7 concludes with a discussion on dwindling pathways of human development.

5.1 THE CONTEXT

A series of events that unfolded in the decades of 1970s and 1980s were momentous, pointing to the prevailing turmoil in both policy and government circles on the very notion of development and its implications for people in developing countries. During this period, as forces of globalization gathered strength, it deepened the sense of disquiet about the prevailing development paradigm. The debt crisis of the 1980s in countries of sub-Saharan Africa and the breakdown of the regime of fixed exchange rates, as well as the quadrupling of oil prices in 1973 by the Organization of the Petroleum Exporting Countries (OPEC), were shocks that considerably changed the power relations in the global arena.

The rising revenues of oil exporting countries were invested in commercial banks, which began to seek profitable avenues for investment. They found that the developing countries in sub-Saharan Africa and Latin America, with their seemingly insatiable appetite for funds, were an easy market. Funds were liberally lent to these countries without much verification of end use. The economies chugged along until OPEC raised the price of oil once again in 1979, which led the USA to pursue a tight monetary policy, triggering a rise in interest rates to rein in inflationary pressures in its wake. This single measure immediately hugely raised the debt burden of developing countries.[6] Simultaneously, terms of trade turned adverse for developing countries, owing to the recession in advanced market economies, and reduced the demand for primary commodities originating in these countries. This, in turn, affected GDP levels in countries where export earnings depended on one or two primary commodities, and that, too, exported mainly to markets in the industrialized countries. As stated earlier, increasing and unsustainable debt service obligations led the developing countries in Latin America and sub-Saharan Africa inexorably into a debt trap, compelling them to resort to financial support from the IMF and the World Bank through stabilization and structural adjustment packages.[7]

The impact of the structural adjustment package on countries has been rather complex and remains inconclusive, particularly for developing countries in sub-Saharan Africa, which already had high levels of poverty and inequality. Negative growth rates experienced by these countries resulted in deteriorated living conditions of the poor in the absence of adequate safeguards to protect the vulnerable sections.[8] Although there is lack of evidence that could highlight the extent to which economic growth failed to distribute benefits to the weaker sections of the population, the limited country-specific evidence that is available is convincing regarding the existence of the phenomenon. For example, Brazil was considered to be an 'economic miracle' experiencing an economic growth of nearly 10 per cent per year during late 1960s and early 1970s.[9] However, Fishlow pointed that this rapid growth resulted in an increase in income inequality, as the Gini Coefficient rose rapidly from 0.59 to 0.63 between 1960 and 1970.[10] During that period, the percentage income shares of the poorest 40 per cent declined from 10 to 8 per cent, and that of the rich 3.2 per cent increased from 27 to 33 per cent. In addition, a study by Weisskoff on Argentina, Mexico, and Puerto Rico confirmed that the situation of relative inequality had worsened during the 1960s in these countries.[11]

Fiscal stringency led to cuts in real per capita expenditure on social sectors in sub-Saharan Africa and Latin America. Real per capita government expenditure on social services in most countries of these two regions declined, as did the share of health and education in the total expenditure. Consequently, there was a decline of 26 per cent in social spending per head in sub-Saharan Africa, and a decline of 18 per cent in Latin America between 1980 and 1985.[12] Given that the expenditure in both regions was already skewed in favour of tertiary facilities, and that there was no restructuring of the pattern of expenditure during the reform period, cuts in expenditure meant a reduction in primary care facilities patronized by the poor. Its impact on social attainments is evident from the decline in enrolment rates, rise in drop-out rates, and increase in the extent of under-nutrition. The gross enrolment ratio in 25 intense adjusting countries, which rose sharply from 77.4 to 94.2 per cent between 1970 and 1980, fell in 1985 to 90.1 per cent. In Tanzania, gross enrolment ratio fell from 92.8 to 72.2 per cent between 1980 and 1985, in spite of high educational outcomes between 1960 and 1970. In a ten-country analysis, Cornia[13] observed that during the stabilization period, nutritional status declined or remained constant in all the countries except for South Korea. The declining trend in infant mortality rate and/or child death rate for two decades witnessed either slower rate of improvement or a reversal in the trend in all the countries.[14]

Although social sector policies were designed to be a part of the *adjustment package*, in reality, the focus was more on trade policies, public finance, public enterprises and the agriculture sector. Evidence from 1980 to 1993 indicated that less than 1 per cent of the 3,040 conditionalities imposed by the IMF and World Bank related to social sectors, and most of the provisions were add-ons and were trivial in magnitude to make any real difference to the situation on the ground.[15] These developments prompted further reassessment of the very notion of development by both scholars and practitioners.

The heightened debt burden on account of rise in global oil prices, coupled with stringent conditionalities associated with the stabilization and structural adjustment arrangements of the IMF and World Bank, wreaked havoc and undermined the performance on social attainments in most countries of the Third World. The crisis arising from the continued reliance on the mainstream paradigm was blatantly evident in its inability to address poverty, abjectness, disparities, and social cohesion. Disillusionment with the unidimensional focus on economic growth, along with the lack of control of developing countries over their own economies arising from the unleashing of the forces of globalization, led to intense international discussion on more humane ways of delivering development to people.

In the light of the huge human costs of adjustment, a demand for 'Adjustment with a Human Face'[16] was made in 1987, led by Cornia, Jolly, and Stewart, and supported by the United Nations Children's Fund (UNICEF). They demanded a more people-sensitive approach to adjustment, not only for social sectors, but for a whole range of policies that were expected to impact the human condition. The recommendations included expansionary macroeconomic policies, supported by meso-polices that addressed the needs of the vulnerable groups, restructured productive sectors, and enhanced equity and efficiency of the social sectors and compensatory programmes that protected basic living conditions of health and nutrition of low-income families. The acknowledgement that there was certainly a two-way linkage between economic growth-led processes with human development progress gained firm grounding. Further, it was believed that the process of human development progress could involve domestic and global factors.

The globalization process opened up a number of opportunities for the developing world. The interconnected financial markets enabled countries to access global resources for expansion and economic growth. The labour market processes globally started shaping local labour markets, as global value chains had their linkages with local enterprises. While globalization provided an enabling opportunity for global multinationals to seek newer markets, it also created a number of hurdles for developing countries for maximizing their terms of trade.

By the 1990s, it was clear that market forces cannot be depended upon to deliver on human development outcomes. The continued demand for reorienting development towards people's real requirements led to the formulation of the MDGs, that integrated global governance institutions such as the UN and the World Bank to nation-states.[17]

While the MDGs set the stage for global commitments on development, the quantification or objectification of development of select goals that can be monitored easily—substantive freedoms, rights, dignity, and empowerment—were missing from the global policy discourse. Evidence from developing countries was getting increasingly complex with the least developed economies visibly lagging in basic entitlements, while the middle-income groups faced fundamental transitional issues.

5.2 EXPLAINING THE LINKAGES BETWEEN ECONOMIC GROWTH AND HUMAN DEVELOPMENT

Typically, economic growth and human development cannot be seen occurring as independent processes. In a sixty-nine-country analysis, Ranis and Stewart estimated the relationship between economic growth and human development using a two-chain approach. In Chain I, the GNP path to human development was identified through household and government activity, community organizations and non-governmental organizations (NGOs). It assumed that the same level of GNP can lead to very different outcomes on human development performance, depending on the allocation of GNP to various groups and its distribution within each category. Chain II is the human development path to enhancing economic growth. Here, Ranis and Stewart argued that higher levels of human development affect the economy by enhancing people's capacities and, consequently, their creativity and productivity.[18]

The estimations, which spanned across four decades from 1960 to 2000, showed positive linkages between the two chains. Chain I was stronger when social expenditure ratio was high. The strength of Chain I was relatively weak in the low- and middle-income countries that had poor initial conditions. These countries were less likely to reap their full potential for economic growth if human development was not strengthened. Therefore, specific macroeconomic policies that enhance public spending relevant for human development and/or strengthening of social safety nets were needed.

Chain II was stronger in countries with strong state action on human development. For example, Sri Lanka and Costa Rica had created the necessary conditions through their strong human development policies for economic growth to take place. Adequate public expenditure to ensure that people have access to basic education and health was essential to ensure that the foundations of comprehensive development are strengthened and sustainable. Asian countries such as Indonesia,

Malaysia, and India recorded substantial improvements in their human development trajectories, including reduction in poverty rates despite relatively low economic growth.

Countries may be grouped into *four* categories depending on the nature and strength of linkages between economic growth and human development. If there are weak or broken links between economic growth and human development owing to leaning heavily on either one of them, a country is likely to experience *lopsided development*. Such development results in a failure to translate benefits of one chain to the other, depriving the country from getting optimal results. When the relationship between economic growth and human development is strong and balanced, and when growth and human development policies are mutually reinforcing, a country is likely to experience a *virtuous cycle of development*. An absence of policies directed towards both economic growth and human development can cause a country to be trapped in a *vicious cycle*.[19]

Against this conceptual background, a comparison of the 2015 human development index outcomes in terms of its economic (Gross National Income [GNI] per capita USD Purchasing Power Parity [PPP]) and non–economic components (comprising education and life expectancy indices) is meaningful (see Figure 5.1).

It can be observed that in most countries, life expectancy index seems better placed than the education index. At lower levels of GNI

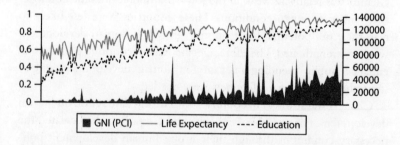

FIGURE **5.1**   Comparing GNIper capita (USD PPP) and Non–Economic Indices of Human Development Index: 2015
Source: UNDP. 2015. *Human Development Data (1990–2015)*. Accessible at hdr. undp.org/en/data; 28 April 2018.

(USD) per capita, the non-economic indices are at relatively low levels. Here, we find that the gap between life expectancy index and education index is wide. At higher levels of income, the gap between the life expectancy index and education index narrows down. The explanation becomes clearer when outcomes of non-economic indices are related with the GNIper capita (USD). Incidentally, countries with relatively high GNIper capita (USD) PPP have not been able to achieve corresponding expansions in non-economic dimensions of human development. On the other hand, there are over *seventy-five* countries in the low and lower-middle per capita group that are doing relatively well in the education and health-related indices, despite lower incomes. There are intra-country variations in outcomes and backlogs in human development progress. Several countries fall between *two* extremities: abjectness due to lack of income, and low capabilities achievements amidst high income.[20]

5.3 INCOME INEQUALITY AND ITS LINKAGE WITH HUMAN DEVELOPMENT

Inequality, traditionally considered an inevitable consequence of growth in its initial stage, is now considered harmful for growth. The nature of inequalities has emerged as a crucial point of debate. Global evidence indicates that since the year 2000, there has been a convergence in per capita income at the global levels, mainly attributed to the growth of middle-income countries like India and China. This debate throws some light on the direction of poverty reduction. The earliest evidence was in the works of Milanovic, who highlighted that global incomes were moving away from the classical income distribution paths and the convergence is occurring through rising middle-income shares.[21] The *Elephant Curve* examines income growth among countries from 1988 to 2008. Milanovic finds evidence of high improvements in living standards and reduction in headcount poverty in China, forming the hump of that curve. However, the trunk of the curve shows that the world's richest populations in advanced countries have become richer than before, while the tail shows that poorest in the world, particularly in Africa, have seen very little income growth. This data, represented by the Elephant Curve, gave a fillip to the inequality debate.[22]

The income inequality analysis was further deepened in the works of Chancel, Piketty, and others, who found that the trajectory shaping inequalities in income has been occurring over a longer duration. They reiterated that inequalities in income were caused by the nature of capitalist growth that gets reoriented and resurrected periodically. Thus, rising inequalities become an embedded characteristic of the capitalist growth process.[23]

Atkinson and Morelli also emphasize that inequalities are an outcome of systemic crises in market economies. They associate inequalities with growing forms of global crises, such as consumption crisis and financial crisis. Further, Alvaredo et. al (2016) too have corroborated that there has been a rise in income inequalities across countries. They pointed out that the decade-long global crisis since 2008 has increased global inequalities across top 0.01 per cent against the bottom 50 per cent. They find that although high growth rates in emerging countries have narrowed inter-country differences in inequalities, this phenomenon has not translated into intra-country reallocation of resources and wealth that eventually ensure social sustainability of the globalization process. Their research indicates that inequalities are not determined singularly by per capita incomes levels but also influenced by other factors.[24] Nayyar describes the policy lessons for countries that are trying to catch up with the developed countries, adopting a range of economic processes like economic integration with market systems through industrialization, financialization, and promotion of economic growth. However, he argues that the concentration, limited to select countries in Asia and Latin America, has failed to transform lives of people, as the per capita income levels have not improved in parallel.[25]

Even as we find that the linkages between economic and non-economic dimensions have broken down across countries, there are also additional interconnected issues that need closer scrutiny. Although much attention has been paid to explaining the effects of income inequality on economic growth, there seems to be complete neglect in explaining its relationship with human development. A perusal of the Gini–HDI relationship also shows a downward sloping curve only when the HDI reaches a value greater than 0.700 (Figure 5.2). There is a *fork-like* relationship between income inequality and human development. It reflects that while at lower levels of human development, income inequalities could either be high or low depending on the initial

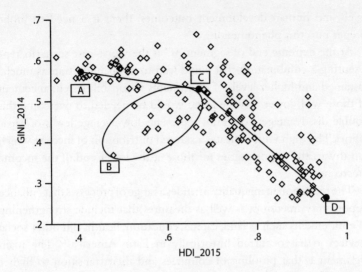

FIGURE 5.2   Scatter Plot between Gini Index of Consumption Expenditure and HDI: 2014–15
Source: Computed by authors from Human Development Data (1990–2015). Accessible at hdr.undp.org/en/data; 28 April 2018.

distribution of resources, countries with relatively high HDI achievements are associated with lower income inequalities. Using cross-section data for 2015–17, the Gini index of consumption expenditures and human development achievements are crucial, as the presence of income inequalities could reduce access and opportunities of households with relatively low levels of endowments, entitlements, and capabilities.

When we observe Figure 5.2 against this background, we find that a majority of the countries in the upper end of the fork (segment AC) have low levels of human development outcomes with relatively higher Gini index. At the lower end of the fork (cluster B) are countries with low human development and varying levels of income inequalities. At HDI of around 0.7 or more (segment CD), the associated Gini index is also lower. This tendency appears to continue with increasing values of HDI, and points to the need for continued commitment to human development, since it appears to be associated with lower levels of income inequalities. Even as the evidence presented here points to a crucial relationship between income inequality levels and human development outcomes, there is a need to probe deeper into this phenomenon.

At the extreme end of segment AC is the worst-case scenario, representing a combination that could lead to a capability trap, as much-sustained and higher levels of investments in capabilities enhancement of those with lower income levels would be needed to overcome this double disadvantage. Low HDI represents low average levels of capabilities. The high Gini indicates a skewed distribution of income which can thwart the opportunities for those at the lower end of the income spectrum.[26]

The reduction in inequality includes a range of processes that enhance opportunity freedoms, as well as measures that include strengthening of entitlements such as land, capital, education, health, and other social services as has occurred historically in Latin America.[27] The main argument is that profiling of countries and their transition to higher levels of incomes has its own costs. But these costs are largely capability enhancing in nature. While in the short run, it may curb improvements in per capita income levels, the achievement of higher levels of human development index up to point C, would place the countries at a juncture where there would be simultaneous improvements in human development outcomes and reduction of income inequalities. Thus, there seems to be linkages between capabilities and entitlements that have directly impacted the levels of income inequalities even in middle human development countries.

A classification of countries by GNI per capita (PPP) across ten percentile groups to compare the Gini index of consumption expenditure, IHDI, and HDI score point to distinct distributions across low-, middle-, and high-income countries (see Figure 5.3).

A classification of countries belonging to the bottom 20 per cent group indicates that they have Gini index that range between 10 and 30 per cent. Incidentally, at this group, the level of Gini index and IHDI overlap over one another and HDI values range between 0.45 and 0.55. In the middle 40 per cent group (that is, in the 20–60 per cent category), the HDI values are relatively higher and range between 0.60 and 0.75. But the effective values of HDI are lower as the IHDI values range between 0.40 and 0.60, and Gini index are also high, between 40 to 60 per cent. The point to be underscored is that though the Gini indexes are higher in the middle-income

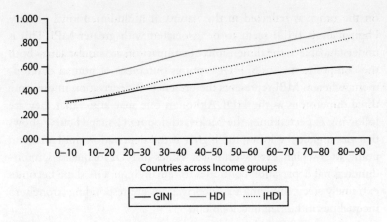

FIGURE 5.3 Percentile Analysis of Countries across HDI–IHDI–Gini: 2015–17
Source: Computed by Authors from Human Development Data (1990–2015). Accessible at hdr.undp.org/en/data; 28 April 2018.

group, the gap between HDI and IHDI is lower. It is only in the top 20 per cent category that the losses in HDI due to capabilities inequalities are the lowest and income inequalities are lower. There seems to be a cue here that human development progress could address both income inequalities and social inequalities.

5.4 DYNAMIC LINKAGES IN HUMAN DEVELOPMENT OUTCOMES

Evidently, the income inequality–human development linkage is critical in broadening the explanation of why a capability inequality trap persists. Capability inequality trap can be defined as a process in which countries experiencing high multidimensional poverty also experience high levels of IHDI, placing these countries at a dual disadvantage of poverty and loss of real choices, opportunities, and freedoms, arising from pervasive inequalities.[28] The difficulty in this exercise is the lack of data for both the parameters across several countries: while data sets are available for IHDI, corresponding data are not available for MPI.

The worsening of income inequality on the one hand, and the failure to provide equal freedoms for capability expansion for all individuals on the other, is reflected in the nature of multidimensional poverty. Higher levels IHDI seem to be associated with greater MPI. This is understandable as the dimensions of comparison are similar across both the composite measures: HDI captures outcomes of human development, whereas MPI represents the presence of deprivation in the same three dimensions as the HDI. Although one may argue that they are following expected lines, the backward sloping C-shaped curve shows that the higher the losses, the higher is the deprivation until a certain point, after which, even with lower values of HDI inequalities, multidimensional deprivation continues to remain high. The slope becomes extremely steep, implying that deprivations are responding strongly to inequalities in human development.

A comparison of the relationship across countries in presented in Figure 5.4. It is observed that the positive curve rises gradually when MPI is less than 0.2, and the loss in HDI is between 10 and 20 per cent. The positive slope of the MPI–IHDI distribution in the 20–30 percentage loss range in HDI—due to inequalities–becomes extremely steep subsequently, indicating a highly responsive distribution of deprivation. In an evaluation of Indian states, it was found that the HDI losses are mainly due to inequality in education and health attainment.[29] Furthermore, levels of MPI increase sharply when loss in inequalities in HDI range around 30–40 per cent, and the curve bends backwards. This clearly shows that linkages between *capability deprivation* and *capability inequalities* are extremely important.

This relationship can be further explained in *two* ways: the *population domination path* and *the income or GNI (PPP) path* (see Figure 5.4). The presence of low MPI and high IHDI raises the question whether highly populated regions have simultaneous presence of high inequality and deprivations. In this regard, a scrutiny of Figure 5.4(a) indicates that, in most cases, the losses in human development outcomes are weak. However, it is interesting to note the number of countries that are concentrated into groups. In the initial group, several countries with low levels of MPI and high levels of IHDI have relatively lower population shares. As MPI levels increase and the losses in IHDI are around 20–40 per cent, there is dominance of large and densely populated countries like India and Indonesia. They may be low on MPI, but the absolute number of people with capability deprivations continues to remain high. Countries with high

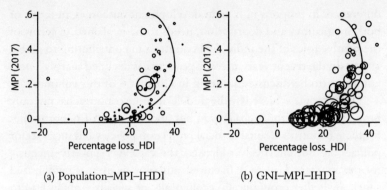

(a) Population–MPI–IHDI   (b) GNI–MPI–IHDI

FIGURE 5.4 Two-Way Linkage between MPI and IHDI
Source: Estimated by authors from Human Development Data (1990–2015).
Accessible at hdr.undp.org/en/data; 28 April 2018.

MPI and IHDI are visibly caught in the capability inequality trap. In contrast, the presence of large population in the countries with medium MPI and high IHDI shows that the aggregate population of these countries with extremely unequal human development outcomes is significantly higher.

Next, when we weigh the same relationship using GNI USD (PPP) dominance path, there are a large number of countries with higher incomes with significant levels of losses in IHDI. In several medium- and small-income countries, there is a simultaneous presence of losses in MPI and IHDI. Among the middle-income group, the MPI values of India and China are extremely low, while these are the most populous countries in the world. Between 2000 and 2015, most countries focused on the MDG 1 of halving income poverty. India and China were able to reduce the number of income poor from 1,650 million to 902 million, by adopting a range of policies and enhancement of economic growth rates. Therefore, although the standard of living of vast populations seems to have improved, the concerns of multidimensional poverty persists, so much so that the headcount value of the MPI poor in these two countries is equal to the number of poor in nearly sixty countries.

There is a larger presence of population in these countries that is simultaneously getting deprived of opportunities and has limited social service choices. These are serious points of concern. The differences in progress in human development outcomes, in terms of both inequalities and deprivation, needs to be explained in terms of the relative roles of the individual countries in contributing to global targets. In the recent years, income poverty has declined sharply across countries (to be discussed in detail in Chapter 6 of this volume).

The outcome achieved by the middle-income countries has not only brought out additional challenges, but also exceptional opportunities for these countries. If suitable social protection policies and social sector policies are not effectively addressed, the capability–poverty–inequality nexus might lead to a fractured outcome as even a randomized shock—whether economically, ecologically, or socially—might lead to cascading effects. While the reduction of income poverty is crucial to advance standards of living of individuals, challenges of sustaining these outcomes need closer scrutiny. Box 5.1 provides implications of poverty reduction in India and China on the global poverty level.

BOX 5.1　Poverty Reduction in Population Dominant Economies: Implications for Global Outcomes

The years 2000–14 have been critical. It was a period when most developing countries pursued implementation of target-driven policies on development. Reduction in income poverty was a crucial domain of this initiative. Global poverty reduction outcomes have largely been driven by reductions in India and China.

Though this outcome is worthy of reckoning, the achievement has brought forth additional challenges. Population living in Tier 1 and Tier 2 cities has increased in both the countries. In India, rural–urban and rural–rural migration has had its effects on labour market opportunities. A large number of migrants who are young and have elementary education seem to be getting absorbed as casual labour. As pointed by human geographers, the changing standard of living and education outcomes often changes aspirations of the population.

China, too, is facing pressures of migration and social exclusion in the urban areas. The presence of a strong social security system has made it amenable for workers with basic social protection. But in India, approximately 97 per cent population (economic census) does not have a safety net.

Thus, with the failure to understand dynamism in human development, both countries are experiencing problems of urban sustainability, urban poverty, and habitat.

Source: Ghosh, J. 2010. 'Poverty Reduction in China and India: Policy Implications of Recent Trends'. DESA Working Paper No. 92 ST/ESA/2010/DWP/92, United

Nations Department of Economic and Social Affairs, New York; Alkire, S. and Seth, S. 2013. 'Multidimensional Poverty Reduction in India between 1999 and 2006: Where and How?'. Oxford Poverty & Human Development Initiative (OPHI) Working Paper 60, Oxford Department of International Development Queen Elizabeth House (QEH), University of Oxford, Oxford. Recent estimates computed by authors using World Bank Poverty Data sets accessible at https://data.worldbank.org/topic/poverty; February 2017.

As we stated in Chapter 4 of this volume, human development is measured using medium-term and long-term indicators. But its evaluation often views it as a static cross-section phenomenon. Evidently, the complexity of relationship between capabilities and entitlements poses an additional challenge. The fundamentals of dynamism thereby imply that human development needs to be viewed (as discussed in Chapter 2 of this volume) as a combination of strengthening capabilities and maintaining entitlements. The globalization phenomenon and the ensuing patterns of development have made societies assetless, increased precarious forms of employment and jobless growth, reduced real wages, and pulled people repeatedly out of the workplace. The dynamism in human development is not only associated with intergenerational outcomes, but is also being determined by the contemporary process of development. It is in this regard that the Chronic Poverty Report[30] cautions us that vulnerable populations might be pulled back below the poverty line due to idiosyncratic risks like droughts, costly illness, or insecurity or conflict in the community.

5.5 DIFFERENTIAL PERFORMANCE OF HUMAN DEVELOPMENT INDICATORS

There has been an upsurge in a range of issues such as poverty amidst prosperity, persistent malnourishment despite zero hunger, and high enrolment in school with no learning. These problems represent the vicious trap of development. For example, a comparison of income poverty (measured by population living below income poverty line PPP USD 1.25 a day), and starvation (measured by Global Hunger Index [GHI]) shows that there is no definite association between the two indicators (Table 5.1). A comparison of the performance of select countries contributing to global hunger vis-à-vis their human development progress shows that global hunger is located disproportionately across middle and low human development countries. Most South Asian and African

TABLE 5.1 Profile of Income and Non–Income Poverty across Select Countries

HDI Rank 2015	Countries	HCR USD 1.25 2002–12	GHI 1990	GHI 2015	Per Cent Change in GHI	HDI 1990	HDI 2015	Per Cent Change in HDI
90	China	6.3	25.1	8.6	2.63	0.501	0.727	3.02
130	India	23.6	48.1	29.00	1.59	0.428	0.609	2.81
139	Zambia	74.3	47	41.10	0.50	0.403	0.586	3.02
147	Pakistan	12.7	43.6	33.90	0.89	0.399	0.538	2.32
154	Madagascar	87.7	44.8	36.30	0.76	NA	0.510	
163	Uganda	37.8	39.8	27.60	1.23	0.308	0.483	3.77
171	Afghanistan	NA	47.4	35.40	1.01	0.297	0.465	3.79
174	Ethiopia	36.8	71.7	33.90	2.11	NA	0.442	
178	Guinea Bissau	48.9	46.1	30.30	1.37	NA	0.411	
180	Mozambique	60.7	64.5	32.50	1.98	0.218	0.416	6.09
187	Central African Republic	62.8	51.9	46.90	0.39	0.314	0.350	0.77

Source: Global Hunger Report 2015 and Human Development Report 2015.[31]

countries report income poverty, though their scores are relatively lower in case of GHI. The presence of food security policies appears to have provided basic calorific food items to the population, yet there has been a failure to provide sustainable livelihoods to most people.

Though there has been a perceptible improvement in HDI values across countries, the GHI rates have been relatively low. This perhaps is also a reflection that capability losses due to distributional entitlements seem to be contributing to capability deprivation.

The current focus of global human development is towards achieving SDGs. Securing global public goods such as the SDGs need to include the economic growth and human development framework to encompass broader processes of equity, productivity, empowerment, and sustainability. Data challenges also cannot be ignored. Several countries continue to grapple with the problems of setting the stage for data systems, where only some of the available estimates of SDG index are useful in understanding the divergence in outcomes. Fully aware of the shortcomings of data and methodology, this section presents the preliminary explanations of the links between SDG performance of countries, using SDSN data sets.

The positive relationship between SDG index (2017) and GNIper capita USD PPP (2015) (presented in Figure 5.5) shows that countries

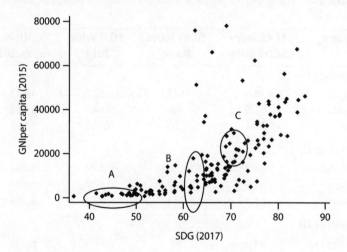

FIGURE 5.5 Relationship between SDGI and GNIper capita (PPP)
Source: Estimated by authors from Human Development Data (1990–2015). Accessible at hdr.undp.org/en/data; 28 April 2018.

seem to perform better as income levels progress. This cannot be oversimplified as there are a range of concentrations visible in the distribution, and can be further explained through a discussion of select country evidences.

The typology of countries can be identified on the basis of the levels of their GNIper capita and their HDI values. A sample of nine countries was selected on the basis of *three* broad categories: (*a*) similar GNIper capita but different HDI value; (*b*) similar GNIper capita income and similar HDI value; and (*c*) different GNIper capita and similar HDI outcomes. Outcomes of typology (*a*) and (*c*) show that countries seem to be pursing very different pathways for achieving SDGs. A perusal of evidence presented in Table 5.2 underscores that there are several countries that have been able to achieve similar SDG scores with the same levels of GNIper capita. Since SDG implementation is still in its initial years, the outcomes of these countries can be attributed to the initial human development investments, political commitment to social sector policies, and the desire to invest in basic capabilities.

TABLE 5.2 Typology Analysis of SDGs and Economic Growth of Select Countries

Country	SDG Index Score 2016	SDG Index Rank	HDI Value 2015	GNIper capita 2015
Typology I				
Nigeria	48.6	145	0.527	5,443
Vietnam	67.9	68	0.683	5,335
India	58.1	116	0.624	5,663
Typology II				
Bangladesh	56.2	120	0.579	3,341
Ghana	59.9	109	0.579	3,839
Zambia	51.1	134	0.579	3,464
Typology III				
Philippines	64.3	93	0.682	8,395
Egypt	64.9	87	0.691	10,064
Indonesia	62.9	100	0.689	10,053

Source: United Nations. 2017. *The Sustainable Goals Report*. New York: UNDESA.

The select countries in typology I belong to three regions: Africa, East Asia, and South Asia. We find that Nigeria, Vietnam, and India have similar GNIper capita but different HDI scores. Among them, although it has a low HDI score, Vietnam has performed better in the SDG index. Despite a higher GNIper capita, Nigeria seems to have lagged in terms of both HDI values and SDG index. Countries in the second group—Bangladesh, Ghana, and Zambia—belong to lower middle-income group and have identical HDI scores. Incidentally, they have also been able to achieve similar SDG scores. The third typology comprises Philippines, Egypt, and Indonesia. These countries have similar HDI scores despite varying GNIper capita. These countries have managed to also arrive at similar SDG values and belong to the better-performing developing country groups.

The point being highlighted is that countries that have been able to establish close linkages across GNIper capita and HDI levels have been able to achieve better SDG scores. In contrast, countries pursuing a piecemeal approach seem to have lost the relative advantage of human development outcomes. This approach reflects inadequate policy synergies and the secondary status accorded to social sector policies.[32] Therefore, even as the pathways seem to be extremely unclear, a country's ability to achieve complex development goals is driven by the country's own commitment to the well-being of its people.

5.6 CHALLENGES IN HUMAN DEVELOPMENT

The emerging outcomes of the complex confluence of inequalities in human development and economic growth have consequently created their own challenges to cope with growth and development. These challenges broadly include rising structural inequalities, coping with newer forms of vulnerabilities, dominance of multidimensional poverty, and worsening labour markets conditions.

Structural Inequalities

The increasing trade-off between economic growth and human development has deepened worries about the ability of countries to stabilize the development agenda, through both global and domestic policies. This assumes importance as a large proportion of the economic activities in the developing region continues to be dominated by agricultural activities and those in the urban informal sector, keeping total productivity at extremely low levels. As per the World of Work Report of ILO,[33] the output per worker ratio gap between the medium human development countries vis-à-vis high human development and very high human development is to the tune of 1:3:7. The estimates for low human development countries are about half of those in the medium human development countries. This structural economic composition of the developing countries crucially influences income levels and determines various forms of poverty. The dominance of low factor productivity, in turn, leads to low levels of wages and extremely high levels of underemployment.

The Oxfam Report 2016 estimates that in most of the rich countries and in most developing countries, the share of national income going to workers has been falling.[34] This decline, the report argues, is due to the unequal advantage of returns to capital through interest payments, dividends, or retained profits, as well as reducing taxes on capital gains. It has led to an unprecedented rise in the share of the top 1 per cent incomes and a rather sluggish improvement in the bottom 10 per cent of the global income. While the per capita income of the top 1 per cent increased from just over USD 38,000 in 2005 PPP to just over USD 49,800 (an increase of USD 11,800), that of the bottom 10 per cent increased from USD 196 to USD 261 (an increase of mere USD 65), leaving this group well below the extreme poverty line of USD 1.90 per day. Although both groups experienced roughly the same percentage of income growth over the period, the USD 65 per capita increase for the bottom 10 per cent was limited by the increase for the top 1 per cent, which was 182 times greater. The improvement of the lower income groups had limited effects on their standard of living as the global population distribution continues to be bottom heavy.

The structural conditions of most developing countries are dominated by agricultural systems driven by global trade practices and fragile climate conditions. The developed countries, on the other hand, have been experiencing extremely low rates of economic growth due to weakening of economic activities.

Many Forms of Vulnerabilities

The global financial crises have revealed a plethora of dimensions and patterns of an integrated global economy that can create collective economic opportunities but also instil stagnation across regions/countries. In two distinct perspectives, the fears raised by Rajan are echoed by Stiglitz.[35] They argue that inequality played an important role in triggering the 2007–8 crisis in the USA. The rapid spread of the crisis, initially to the developed countries and through trade and finance channels to the developing world, has had disastrous consequences for economic growth, from whose effects the world is yet to recover. As per World Bank estimates, an examination of poverty rates before and during selected periods of negative economic growth for a selection of countries indicates that poverty headcount rose during crisis episodes in Latin America during the 1980s and 1990s, and in Southeast Asia during the late 1990s.[36]

Another impact of the crisis-driven development and poverty is that it leads to unsustainable economic policies, often occurring through a reductionist fiscal framework that directly impacts policies and programmes that assist the poorest people. Evidently, poverty in the present time is not an outcome of only lowness of income or access to choices, but driven by diverse economic and social processes, both national and international.

Dominance of Multidimensional Poverty and Inequality

Central to most developing and developed economies is the coexistence of vulnerability, poverty, and inequality. From 1990 to 2010, after accounting for population size, the average income inequality in developing countries increased by 11 per cent.[37] A substantial majority of households in developing countries—more than 75 per cent of the population—live in societies where income is more unequally distributed than in the 1990s. In the same period, household income inequality increased by 9 per cent in high-income countries. Inequalities are pervasive not only in the economic dimensions. They have now permeated social dimensions as well. As per HDR 2016,[38] the Inequality-adjusted HDI value in sub-Saharan Africa is 32.2 per cent lower than the HDI value, and more than 25 per cent lower in South Asia and the Arab states. In four countries—Central African Republic, Comoros, Namibia, and Sierra Leone—the Inequality-adjusted HDI value is more than 40 per cent lower and in 35 other countries it is 30–40 per cent lower than the HDI value.

Role of Jobs, Employability, and Livelihoods

The process of economic growth in the era of neoliberalism and globalization has created opportunities for a few but has also left a vast proportion of individuals behind. ILO[39] reported in 2018 that although global economic growth rates have rebounded and remained stable in recent times, global unemployment is as high as 190 million. Even worse, vulnerable employment is gradually increasing across developing and emerging economies.

Productivity and prosperity are two key components of the SDGs, but at a time when employment opportunities are getting parched, the central focus both globally and nationally is on *jobs*. The 2017 OECD–ILO report,[40] which evaluated employability policies across eight countries, found that there are a variety of factors that determine skill utilization of workers and enterprises. Further, it recommended that policies aimed at improving skills utilization need to simultaneously evolve coherence across employment, skills, economic, and social policies.

A very interesting example cited in the OECD–ILO report is the one initiated in the Philippines, where the National Wages and Productivity Commission oversees the Productivity Olympics. As a part of the process, this commission awards micro, small, and medium enterprises for the best productivity practices nationwide. The Regional Tripartite Wages and Productivity Board identifies an enterprise based on scores in business excellence (total productivity, expansion and growth, and awards/recognition/certification) and resource management (people, and system, technology and green). Since 2006, the Commission has also implemented the Training for Work Scholarship Programme (TWSP) across private and public training institutions, benefiting over 2.4 million unemployed youth. In India, too, the challenge is to enhance employment opportunities, skills formation, and employability of workers.

The global quantum of jobs has seen a sharp decline in the recent years. Even among the shrinking employment shares, people are mainly getting concentrated in precarious jobs. The shifting of focus among global organizations, including ILO, from creation of jobs to issues of employment and employability has created further uncertainties. This trend has seen a huge upsurge in the quantum of migrants globally. However, a large proportion of migration is forced and conflict-affected.

5.7 MIXED OUTCOMES AND DWINDLING PATHWAYS

If economic growth alongside lopsided human development of the 1980s are seen as developmental issues, then they have become a trap in present times. Over the past two decades, global evidence shows that the relationship between economic growth and human development is subject to change, depending on the nature and strength of public policy on one hand, and the tenacity of structural constraints on the other. Country experiences indicate how a singular focus on economic growth is less than adequate for ensuring progress on human development outcomes, ultimately constraining the growth process itself. The reverse case—a uni-focal emphasis on human development without attention to capital investment and productivity—is also self-defeating in nature. Nonetheless, it cannot be denied that strong social indicators provide a sustained basis for enhancing economic growth in subsequent times.

This observation points to the fact that countries may not have the luxury of focusing on economic growth while neglecting social dimensions of development even in the initial stages of development. Moreover, in an era of participatory democratic systems and electoral politics, it may not even be feasible to neglect human dimensions for long period of times.[41] Furthermore, human development and economic growth processes seem to be getting extremely strained, since the pursuit of most countries is to first generate improved economic growth while neglecting human development. As it has been found empirically, such a pathway may not be sustainable.[42] There is substantive evidence that has shown that a one percentage point increase in the average growth rate of GDP per capita can reduce life expectancy shortfall by more than three percentage points over a period. Further, a more equal income distribution is associated with higher economic growth and determines the level of human development.[43]

Among the middle-income countries, a large absolute population with low capabilities near the poverty line has emerged as an opportunity for human development progress, but in the absence of effective, synergized policies to tackle capabilities–entitlement linkage, this potential remains unutilized.

The cross-country evidence on emerging issues and the two-way linkages for economic growth and human development point that the Chain 1 and Chain 2 issues—linking human development to economic growth through affirmative public policies—remain crucial. However, the complexity is that most countries have failed to translate growth processes into equitable opportunities. Moreover, the focus is narrowly on basic capabilities, as compared to aggregate capabilities, which can lead to substantive outcomes. Therefore, the fundamental underlying problem is to see issues of growth and prosperity on one hand, and poverty and inequality in human development on the other, as a part of a single process of development. The failure to explain these processes brings us to the discussion on why human development needs to be seen as a dynamic phenomenon.

Several developing countries have advanced to the middle-income category, and yet their performance on human development outcomes is mixed. The so-called *emerging economies* in Asia and Latin America (Brazil, China, India, Indonesia, Mexico, Russia, Turkey) have benefited from the globalization process, but developing countries, including those in sub-Saharan Africa, lag behind on most counts. The finding that the middle-income countries account for over 70 per cent of the world's poor where hunger, morbidity, and illiteracy are rampant, is a moot testimony to the pattern of growth that has been pursued. The evidence cited by an Oxfam Report points to the stark fact that the economic gap between the richest 20 per cent and the poorest 20 per cent population, globally, too, has widened, with the share of the poorest in global income declining from 2.3 to 1.4 per cent while that of the richest increasing from 70 to 85 per cent.[44]

In sum, as Nayyar[45] states, the links between macro-policies and human development attainments tend to be weakening over time. Most countries seem to depend on the trickle-down benefits of growth to tackle human development adversities. Though the SDGs sought to learn from the experiences of the MDGs and have broadened the concept and methodology of global policymaking, their implementation is clouded by the legacy of the past. An already truncated approach to human development is likely to also make the agenda of SDG piecemeal in nature.

The shared prosperity goal focuses on a combination of growth and greater equality, and, as such, is meant to complement the poverty mitigation target. Additionally, there is a need to acknowledge the fact that the twenty-first century discussion on poverty cannot occur within the narrow confines of objective estimations, as it ignores the interlinkages across the various dimensions, presented above. The processes that are pursued in evolving substantive linkages between economic growth and human development are as important as measuring the ends of such a process. The impact of the failure of effective policies in most of the SDGs can create a rippling effect on poverty reduction. Since poverty reduction continues to be the foremost goal of the SDGs (as of the MDGs), the focus needs to be on development policies that are egalitarian in nature that simultaneously address challenges of expanding human freedom amidst the fear of capability traps.

NOTES AND REFERENCES

1. A detailed discussion is available in Chapter 7 of this volume.

2. For Example, South Korea transformed itself from a developing country in 1960s to a high-income country in 2000s. China and other countries in East Asia have followed suit, indicating that it is indeed possible for a right mix of policies and conditions to achieve such a high rate of growth. Interestingly, all these countries have also scored high on social indicators such as education and health.

3. For more details, see UNDP. 1996. *Human Development Report: Economic Growth and Human Development*. New York: Oxford University Press.

4. For Details, see Pierre, J., ed. 2000. *Debating Governance: Authority, Steering, and Democracy*. Oxford: Oxford University Press.

5. Anand, S. and Ravallion, M. 1993. 'Human Development in Poor Countries: On the Role of Private Incomes and Public Services'. *Journal of Economic Perspectives* 7 (1, Winter): 133–50; Ghosh, M. 2006. 'Economic Growth and Human Development in Indian States'. *Economic and Political Weekly* 41 (30): 3321–7. doi: 10.2307/4418499; Ranis, G., Stewart, F., and Ramirez, A. 2000. 'Economic Growth and Human Development'. *World Development* 28 (2): 197–219; and Suri, T., Boozer, M.A., Ranis, G., and Stewart, F. 2011. 'Paths to Success: The Relationship between Human Development and Economic Growth'. *World Development* 39 (4): 506–22.

6. For example, the debt burden of countries in sub-Saharan Africa was estimated to have doubled between 1980s and 1990s.

7. Both sets of policies were based on a common logic steeped in the neo-classical paradigm with its naïve belief in the functioning of the market to ensure allocative efficiency, and in the belief that individual pursuit of self-interest maximizes social welfare. Since state intervention in the economic sphere is believed to be the root of all evils, the dominant recommendation of the two institutions was to roll back the involvement of the state to let markets function freely.

8. Cornia, G.A., Jolly, R., and Stewart, F., eds. 1987. *Adjustment with a Human Face Vol. I: Protecting the Vulnerable and Promoting Growth*. Oxford: Clarendon Press; Prabhu, K.S. 1994. 'The Budget and "Structural Adjustment with a Human Face"'. *Economic and Political Weekly* 29 (16–17): 1011–28.

9. Fields, G.S. 1980. *Poverty, Inequality, and Development*. Cambridge: Cambridge University Press.

10. Fishlow, A. 1972. 'Brazilian Size Distribution of Income'. *The American Economic Review* 62(1/2): 391–402.

11. Weisskoff, R. 1970. 'Income Distribution and Economic Growth in Puerto Rico, Argentina, and Mexico'. *Review of Income and Wealth* 16 (4): 303–32.

12. The World Bank study, which compared the social sector expenditures between 16 countries that received structural adjustment loans (SAL) during 1980–6 and 18 countries which did not, stated that more than 60 per cent of the SAL-borrowing countries showed a decline in per capita health and education expenditure, whereas a majority of the non-adjusting countries saw an increase in expenditure in health and education. Further, between 1980–6, the share of public expenditure in health and education of the total public expenditure declined from 21 per cent to 17 per cent in intense adjusting countries. For more details, see Kakwani, N., Makonnen, E., and Van der Gaag, J. 1990. *Adjustment and Living Conditions in Developing Countries (Vol. 467)*. Washington, DC: World Bank Publications; Stewart, F. 1991. 'Are Adjustment Policies in Africa Consistent with Long Run Development Needs?'. *Development Policy Review* 9 (4): 413–36.

13. The ten countries were Botswana, Brazil, Chile, Ghana, Jamaica, Peru, Philippines, South Korea, Sri Lanka, and Zimbabwe.

14. Cornia, G.A. 1987. 'Economic Decline and Human Welfare in the First Half of the 1980s', in *Adjustment with a Human Face (Vol. 1): Protecting the Vulnerable and Promoting Economic Growth,* ed. G.A. Cornia, R. Jolly, and F. Stewart, pp. 11–47. Oxford: Clarendon Press.

15. Jayarajah, C., Branson, W., and Sen, B. 1996, *Social Dimensions of Adjustment World Bank Experience, 1980–93*. Washington, DC: World Bank Operations Evaluation Department, p. 97.

16. The term *adjustment with a human face* was used for the first time in the public domain by Richard Jolly in the 18th World Conference of the Society

for International Development, Rome in 1985. The lecture was of particular importance, because it presented the issues of structural adjustment to hundreds of members from the international development community, including members from the World Bank. See Jolly, R. 1991. 'Adjustment with a Human Face: A UNICEF Record and Perspective on the 1980s'. *World Development* 19 (12): 1807–21.

17. Discussions on MDGs and SDGs as policy architecture are discussed in Chapter 6 of this volume.

18. Ranis, G. and Stewart, F. 2005. 'Dynamic Links between the Economy and Human Development'. New York: UN.

19. Ranis and Stewart, 'Dynamic Links between the Economy and Human Development'.

20. See Drèze, J. and Sen, A. 1999. *India: Economic Development and Social Opportunity*. Oxford: Oxford University Press.

21. Milanovic, B. 2016. *Global Inequality: A New Approach for the Age of Globalization*. Cambridge, Mass: Harvard University Press.

22. Kharas and Seidel challenge the Elephant Curve and find evidence towards global convergence. For more, see Kharas, H. and Seidel, B. 2018. 'What's Happening to the World Income Distribution? The Elephant Curve Revisited', Working Paper No. 114, Global Economy & Development, Washington, DC; Lakner, C. and Milanovic, B. 2016. 'Global Income Distribution: From the Fall of the Berlin Wall to the Great Recession'. *The World Bank Economic Review* 30 (2): 203–32.

23. Alvaredo, F., Chancel, L., Piketty, T., Saez, E., and Zucman, G. 2017. 'Global Inequality Dynamics: New Findings from WID. World'. *American Economic Review* 107 (5): 404–9. For more, see Piketty. T. 2015. 'Capital in the Twenty-First Century'. *The American Economic Review* 105 (5); Piketty, T. and Saez, E. 2006. 'The Evolution of Top Incomes: A Historical and International Perspective'. *The American Economic Review* 96 (2): 200–5; 2014. 'Inequality in the Long Run'. *Science* 344 (6186): 838.

24. Alvaredo, F., Atkinson, A.B., Chancel, L., Piketty, T., Saez, E., and Zucman, G. 2016. 'Distributional National Accounts Guidelines: Concepts and Methods Used on WID.world', Working Paper 2016/1, WID.world; Morelli, S. and Atkinson, A. 2015. 'Inequality and Crises Revisited', Working Paper No. 387, Centre for Studies in Economics and Finance, Naples.

25. Nayyar, D. 2013. *Catch Up: Developing Countries in the World Economy*. Oxford: Oxford University Press.

26. While Birdsall associated the notion of destructive inequality with economic inequality, the pattern that emerges from the fork-shaped inequalities also ascertains the simultaneous presence of economic and non-economic inequalities. See Birdsall, N. 2001. 'Why Inequality Matters: Some Economic Issues'. *Ethics & International Affairs* 15 (2): 3–28.

27.   Also see Birdsall, N. and Graham, C. 2000. 'Mobility and Markets: Conceptual Issues and Policy Questions', in *New Markets, New Opportunities? Economic and Social Mobility in a Changing World*, ed. N. Birdsall and C. Graham, pp. 3–21. Washington, DC: Brookings Institute Press.

28.   Detailed methodological aspects of deprivation and inequality indices are discussed in Chapter 7 of this volume.

29.   Suryanarayana, M.H., Agrawal, A., and Prabhu, K.S. 2011. *Inequality-Adjusted Human Development Index for India's States*. New Delhi: UNDP.

30.   Overseas Development Institute defines *chronic poverty* as the persistence of extreme poverty over years or a lifetime, and which can be transmitted intergenerationally. Shepherd, A., Scott, L., Mariotti. C., Kessy, F., Gaiha, R., da Corta, L., Hanifnia, K., Kaicker, N., Lenhardt, A., Lwanga-Ntale, C., Sen, B., Sijapati, B., Strawson, T., Thapa, G., Underhill, H., and Wild, L. 2014. *The Chronic Poverty Report 2014–2015: The Road to Zero Extreme Poverty*. London: Overseas Development Institute.

31.   UNDP. 2015. *Human Development Report: Work for Human Development*. UNDP; Von Grebmer, K., Bernstein, J., de Waal, A., Prasai, N., Yin, S., and Yohannes, Y. 2015. *Global Hunger Index: Armed Conflict and the Challenge of Hunger*. International Food Policy Research Institute.

32.   The importance of human development policymaking and the role of synergies in social sectors is discussed in Chapter 6 of this volume.

33.   ILO. 2014. *World of Work 2014: Developing with Jobs*. Geneva: ILO.

34.   OXFAM. 2016. 'An Economy for the 1%: How Privilege and Power in the Economy Drive Extreme Inequality and How This Can Be Stopped', Oxfam Briefing Paper 210, Oxfam.

35.   Rajan, R.G. 2011. *Fault Lines: How Hidden Fractures Still Threaten the World Economy*. Princeton: Princeton University Press; Stiglitz, J.E. 2012. 'Macroeconomic Fluctuations, Inequality, and Human Development'. *Journal of Human Development and Capabilities* 13 (1): 31–58.

36.   World Bank. 2015. *World Bank Databank*. Accessible at https://data.worldbank.org/topic/poverty; 31 March 2018.

37.   Seguino, S., Sumner, A., van der Hoeven, R., Sen, B., and Ahmed, M. 2013. *Humanity Divided: Confronting Inequality in Developing Countries*. New York: UNDP.

38.   UNDP. 2016. *Human Development Report: Human Development for Everyone*. New York: UNDP.

39.   ILO. 2018. 'World Employment and Social Outlook: Trends 2018'. Geneva. Accessible at http://www.ilo.org/global/research/global-reports/weso/2018/WCMS_615594/lang--en/index.htm; 31 March 2018.

40.   OECD–ILO. 2017. 'Better Use of Skills in the Workplace: Why It Matters for Productivity and Local Jobs'. Paris: OECD Publishing. doi: http://dx.doi.org/10.1787/9789264281394-en.

41. For a discussion on the relationship between economic growth, human development, and role of institutions, see Birdsall, N., Vanzetti, D., and de Córdoba, S.F. 2006. *The World is Not Flat: Inequality and Injustice in Our Global Economy.* Helsinki: World Institute for Development Economics Research.

42. Ranis and Stewart, *Dynamic Links Between the Economy and Human Development,* p. 13.

43. Also see Anand and Ravallion, 'Human Development in Poor Countries'; Aoki, M., Kim, H.K., and Okuno-Fujiwara, M., eds. 1997. *The Role of Government in East Asian Economic Development: Comparative Institutional Analysis.* Oxford: Clarendon Press; Burgess, R. and Stern, N. 1991. 'Social Security in Developing Countries: What, Why, Who and How?', in *Social Security in Developing Countries,* ed. E. Ahmad, J. Drèze, J. Hills, and A. Sen. Oxford: Clarendon Press; Drèze, J., and Sen, A. 1989. *Hunger and Public Action.* Oxford: Clarendon Press.

44. Hardoon, D. 2017. 'An Economy for the 99%', Oxfam Briefing Paper, Oxford.

45. Nayyar, D. 2013. *Catch Up: Developing Countries in the World Economy.* Oxford: Oxford University Press.

6 Social Sectors in Human Development

The preceding chapter discussed the challenges related to weak links between economic growth and human development. The growth-mediated strategy implemented since the late 1980s and the 1990s relied on increased affluence to enhance social attainments, assuming that the trickle-down mechanism would be effective and distributional errors would either be very low or absent. The empirical evidence over the years belies such hopes. Though there has been improvement in HDI values across countries, it is unclear whether these are equitably distributed across regions and social groups, and whether these levels are sustainable. This is particularly evident in the relationship between HDI and the SDGs, where most countries seem to remain concentrated in the low and middle levels of achievement—pointing to the complexities that characterize human development achievements.

The human development puzzle is simultaneously ensnared by multiple challenges. The presence of hunger despite drastic reduction in levels of income poverty, high mortality caused by communicable diseases despite universal immunization programmes, employability issues despite rise in literacy rates, clearly hints at the inability of social sector policymaking in tackling these challenges. It is imperative to identify alternatives that can address these conundrums.

Traditionally, welfare and distributional policies have been integral to government intervention as a means to address multiple challenges of development. The emergence of the welfare state[1] in Western Europe during the economic depression of the 1930s and World War II, with a firm belief in the Keynesian prescription of strong state intervention, led to a series of measures to ensure social security by national governments, particularly in Europe. The nature of the welfare state differed across countries with at least *four* different types of welfare state[2] regimes that reflected, among other things, varying responsibility for social sector provisioning. This paradigm received a setback during the 1960s and the 1970s owing to two parallel developments that had profound implications for the role of the state in social sector provisioning. The first development was in the theoretical realm, and related to the emergence of the notion of human capital and its importance in enhancing skills and productivity of labour.[3] The second was the emergence of the neoliberal paradigm consequent to the 1970s oil shock and the emerging rethink on the role of the state in development.

Human capital, defined as 'stock of skills and productive knowledge embedded in people',[4] was expected to be built largely through individual initiative. Individuals invest in themselves in education, health, medical care, on-the-job training, and migration, in the expectation of higher rates of return to such investment in the future, leading to accumulation of human capital. The nature of government policies is relatively limited—the state is a facilitator rather than a provider.[5]

The human capital framework was effectively nurtured during the 1970s with the rise of the neoliberal paradigm that emphasized the primacy of market forces and private sector initiatives over that of the state. These principles were also applied to social sectors where the *pay for services* principle operated just as in any other market. The debt-stricken developing countries adopted stabilization and structural adjustment policies, as well as the poverty reduction strategies of the IMF and the World Bank. Implementation of structural adjustment and stabilization policies led to a drastic reduction in public spending and implementation of fiscal prudence measures, which directly affected the quantum and quality of social sector provisioning. This was accompanied by the introduction of user charges and experimentation with public–private models in the social sectors.

The overwhelming impact of the globalization project was the achievement of economic prosperity at the cost of worsening inequalities within and across countries.[6] The entrenchment of neoliberalism in global policymaking has been countered through broadening the growth-led processes towards distribution, welfare, and involvement of people. Three main counter-global initiatives can be identified in this regard: the *first* one was at the time in the 1990s when the liberalization process was initiated in most developing countries. This was paralleled by global initiatives such as Education for All, which tried to push the agenda for ensuring a universal minimum level of basic capabilities. *Second*, in the early 2000s, when neoliberalism was entrenched globally, the MDGs defined substantive goals with individual targets that would accelerate the speed of social attainments in a mission mode. The partial success of MDGs led to the pursuit of SDGs since 2015. The SDGs highlighted the importance of pursuing a more holistic agenda that tackles several interrelated social sectors in an integrated manner. The importance of the human development approach arises in this context. *Lastly*, rise in the incidence of joblessness, vulnerabilities due to displacement, and uncertainties in employment conditions also led to a move towards a discussion on universal social protection policies. This encompasses a mix of contributory schemes (social insurance) and basic social security comprising non-contributory tax financed benefits for families and children. SDG 1.3 seeks to implement nationally appropriate social protection systems for all, including floors for reducing and preventing poverty. Although the terminology seems to have moved away from the ILO-type social security convention, the spirit continues to be protective rather than promotional in nature. The conceptual differences between protective and promotional are discussed in subsequent sections.[7]

It is against this background that the present chapter argues for a broadening of the role of the social sectors. It emphasizes the need to place social sectors on an equal footing with the economic sectors in defining human development policies. Traditionally, the economic sectors have been perceived as contributors to national income and economic growth. In contrast, social sector investment is perceived to be in the category of *welfare*. This limited orientation could be problematic as productive sectors take primacy in resource allocation, and social sectors face the brunt of any resource crunch.

The next section (6.1) delineates the distinctive features of the human development approach to social sectors. Section 6.2 presents some stylized facts relating to social sector policies. It is followed by Section 6.3, which discusses the role of state action. Section 6.4

highlights the global factors that govern social sector policy within the specific context of the MDGs and SDGs. Select innovative policies that have enabled national governments to accelerate social sector attainments are then outlined in Section 6.5. Finally, we make some concluding remarks.

6.1 HUMAN DEVELOPMENT APPROACH TO POLICYMAKING

Developing countries continue to be characterized by incomplete structural transformation, huge informal sectors, pervasive poverty, and multidimensional deprivation. Drèze and Sen suggested a reorientation of the concept of social security, requiring that it be viewed from a broader perspective and 'essentially as an *objective* to be *pursued through public means* rather than as a narrowly defined set of particular strategies'[8] (emphasis in the original). The crux of the argument of these scholars is that socio-security measures need to take the need for realizing a minimum level of income[9] into account, rather than address themselves only to instances when income falls below a prescribed minimum due to various contingencies.[10]

The International Labour Office and other international organizations have moved towards broadening the approach from social security to social protection. For instance, the ILO suggests that social protection should be approached in its various dimensions and through various phases. The dimensions include: access to essential goods and services; prevention of and protection against various risks; and promotion of potential and opportunities in order to break vicious cycles and pervasive tendencies. There now seem to be attempts to provide protective measures to all including those not in the workforce. Yet, for social protection to be effective in the true sense, it is necessary to strengthen the basic capabilities of vulnerable groups such that they are able to: (*a*) cope with contingencies; (*b*) escape structural traps that keep them entrenched in poverty, and (*c*) claim their rights and entitlements to take their place as citizens in society. To bridge the distance between capabilities, entitlements, and security, there is need to also guarantee promotional social security which is paradigmatically distinct from the ILO-type contingency measures.[11] Here, we argue that the social security approach to social sectors would include measures that improve endowments, exchange entitlements, real incomes, and social consumption. These have been referred to as *promotional social security measures*, thereby distinguishing them from the *protective social security measures* prescribed by the ILO.[12] The obvious advantage of this definition is that it links the concepts of social security and human development, providing a comprehensive framework for the analysis of social sectors. Within such a framework, social sectors include not only aspects of education, health and nutrition, and related sectors, but also those that contribute to augmenting incomes, such as rural development and employment programmes.

Traditionally, education and health have been treated as separate sectors, even though they have many common analytical elements, and despite their implications for equity and social justice being of a similar nature. Being constitutive parts of development, they are valuable for both *intrinsic* and *instrumental* reasons.[13] The narrow interpretation focuses solely on enhancing instrumental gains from social sector policies, whereas the broader connotation would connect the intrinsic and instrumental perspectives as a continuum.

The emphasis on effective social sector policies would remain in a conceptual vacuum as long as it is not placed within the larger discussion of the nature of *goods* themselves. Classically, goods have been classified into private and public goods.[14] While public goods represent commodities that have properties of non-rivalry and non-excludability, private goods essentially represent ownership and control by the individual. The neoclassical paradigm places consumption of commodities within these two categories to determine the nature of public policies. For them, *wants* are strictly individualistic and therefore warrant individual resource commitments. As argued in earlier chapters, the move away from the goods-based approach to the capability approach is by far more pragmatic as it represents the individual's own *doings and beings*. Therefore, it can be argued that social sectors that enhance basic capabilities of individuals should be considered public goods. Even within this, drawing from the Musgravian notion of merit goods, we can argue that goods or services that contribute to capability enhancement need to be treated as merit goods.[15] Thus, preventive social security measures such as basic social services, that seek to eliminate capability deprivation, should be treated as merit goods.

In societies with unequal capabilities, defining an ideal model of commodity sets can be challenging. For instance, prevalence of malnourishment and hunger as an epidemic would imply that provision of food to the poor should be treated as a public good. Similarly, if the aim is to achieve a transition from large-scale illiteracy to a literate employable population, then basic education should be treated as a public good. The prevalence of mortality from infectious diseases and high maternal mortality rate from poor maternal health would imply that preventive and promotional health care may need to be classified as a public good.

Similarly, promotional social security that seeks to enhance basic capabilities can be treated as Musgravian *public goods*. Services that contribute to improvements in human development such as basic/primary education, health and nutrition services are in the nature of public/merit goods and have the characteristics of non-excludability and non-rivalry. In the light of these services ensuring higher social rates of return, a strong case emerges for their public provisioning. An interesting dimension here is that as societies progress to higher levels of human development, these very categories of commodities could take the form of private goods, as some of the benefits accruing to individuals would be rival and excludable in nature. To give an example, the prevalence of malnourishment measured by obesity and lifestyle patterns would imply that food is a private good. Similarly, access to higher education and specialized skill sets would largely enhance private rates of return. These do not fall under strict categories, as the level of human development and per capita income need to be understood in tandem. In sum, an ideal human development-compatible social sector policy would include a greater dominance of public goods at low human development levels, while it will provide for a combination of public and private goods as human development processes advance. Thus, the constituents of merit goods could vary across societies and determined though public reasoning, and the role of public goods would be determined by the level and composition of capabilities.

Extending this perspective, fiscal efficiency norms have been discussed to reorient public expenditure framework in the 1990s. These discussions sought to capture human development enhancing expenditures to assess government's policies towards human well-being. The earliest fiscal efficiency norms were presented in HDR 1991, which emphasized the importance of strengthening public spending and enhancing finances for social sectors. It also argued that public expenditures to social sectors need not be defined solely by levels of per capita incomes.[16] The Report asserted that a critical role is played by the public sector, particularly in the case of low incomes and unmet basic human needs. It identified *four* efficiency parameters of public spending and provided broad norms for each of the ratios: (*a*) the public expenditure ratio; (*b*) the social allocation ratio; (*c*) the social priority ratio; and (*d*) human priority ratio.[17] Based on empirical evidence on expenditure patterns of countries and human development outcomes, the Report concluded that it may be necessary for the human expenditure ratio to be around 5 per cent if a country must do well in human development. Further, it suggested that it would be preferable to have a public expenditure ratio of 25 per cent and allocate around 40 per cent to social sectors and within this expenditure to allocate half towards social priority areas.

6.2 STYLIZED FACTS

The policies implemented under the neoliberal and human development frameworks differ considerably. In a detailed account, Jolly[18] states that the stark positions of the two approaches have influenced policy priorities at the national and international level and also determined poverty reduction strategies (see Table 6.1). He identifies *three* key requirements for social policies: (*a*) broader group of government and non-government actors in policymaking; (*b*) emphasis on human indicators rather than on economic and financial factors; and (*c*) democratization of global policymaking platforms. Table 6.1 provides some distinctions.

Understanding these differences is crucial, particularly when we analyse the cross-country variations in human development progress. The classic example of human development progress in the past decades is that of the Southeast Asian countries, which were able to attain high rates of economic growth alongside strong social sector attainments.[19] Contrasting this island of human development progress with the expansive arena of near-stagnant outcomes of several other countries raises questions about the contours of social sector policy in the fast growing economies. What is the role of the public sector in social sector provisioning? What is the time horizon over which the planning for social sectors needs to be pursued? Prabhu[20] identified key stylized facts that govern the success of social sector policies (see Box 6.1).

TABLE 6.1   Poverty Reduction: National Policy and International Priorities

Poverty Reduction	Growth
Key assumption: Growth must be consciously made pro-people and pro-poor	*Key assumption: Trickle-down can be expected*
Goal-Oriented Poverty Strategy	**Growth-Oriented Poverty Strategy**
• Empower the poor	• Ensure adequate economic growth
• Foster agency and empowerment especially of women	• Expand social sectors
• Ensure poor have access to assets	• Build in affordable safety nets
• Accelerate pro-poor growth	• Maintain open economy policies and international aid
• Mobilize international support for national action	
National Policies	
• Broaden choices and opportunities	• Enable free markets
• Strengthen human capabilities	• Get prices right
• Ensure participation	• Facilitate greater efficiency
• Moderate inequality	• Invest in human resource
• Enhance education and health attainments	• View education and health as important investments
• Restructure national budgets	• Control fiscal deficits
International Action and Support	
• Establish more democratic global governance to level the global playing field	• Remove trade barriers
• Strengthen bargaining power of poor countries	• Focus on economic co-operation
• Keep a positive attitude to international migration	• Provide humanitarian aid
• Enhance aid, especially to the least developed countries	• Ensure military security
• Ensure human security (reducing military expenditures)	

Source: Adapted from Jolly, R. 2003. 'Human Development and Neo-Liberalism: Paradigms Compared', in *Readings in Human Development: Concepts, Measures and Policy for a Development*, ed. S. Fukuda-Parr and A.K. Shiva Kumar, pp. 106–16. New Delhi: Oxford University Press.

BOX 6.1 Stylized Facts on Social Sector Policy in
Developing Countries

1. Social sector policy needs to be mindful of *initial conditions,* including structural constraints that limit access and availability of key social services to people.
2. Investment in social sectors yields better results when it is part of a *redistributive ethos* that permeates all public policies. The pursuit of inegalitarian policies in general and the subsequent implementation of social sector policies as add-on components could prove to be self-defeating.
3. Considering the long gestation period involved, *investment in social sectors must be sustained over decades* before the expected benefits can be realized. To ensure such investment, a national consensus needs to be built up, particularly in democratic countries, so that allocations to this sector do not vary with different political dispensations.
4. Various sectors that contribute to the enhancement of social opportunities and freedoms must be addressed in an integrated manner so as *to reap the benefits of synergies* generated. This implies that public investment must stress both promotional and protective social security simultaneously.

Source: Adapted from Prabhu, K.S. 1998. 'Social Sectors in Economic Development'. *Journal of Social and Economic Development* 1 (2): 268–87.

To elaborate, the initial conditions that ensure equitable distribution of productive assets go a long way in ensuring that the benefits of growth are also shared more equally. It was seen that in the two Southeast Asian countries of Indonesia and Malaysia, the emphasis during the 1970s was on raising incomes in the rural sector through measures such as land consolidation and investment in rural infrastructure, together with an emphasis on labour intensive manufacturing and shifting the composition of public expenditure towards sectors that benefit the poor. These measures ensured that the benefits of economic growth reached the vulnerable sections of the population.[21] Moreover, the broader educational attainment in Malaysia and the Republic of Korea that reported primary and secondary enrolment rates over 60 per cent as far back as 1970, provided a distinct edge in ensuring subsequent egalitarian growth.

The favourable initial conditions were accompanied by a redistributive ethos in overall policies and not just in policies relating to the social sectors. The East Asian countries implemented both land reform and employment intensive growth policies in the initial stages of development. This provided the requisite impetus for investment in education and health, which increased the income of the poor and improved schooling enrolments. Interestingly, the synergy achieved led to higher female literacy rates, too.[22] Thus, there is a need to develop synergies between policies for productive assets and capability enhancement for the poor and disadvantaged groups. It is not often realized that basic education can act as a redistributive measure.[23]

Data provided by the World Bank over the years have tried to trace the differences in the education and knowledge achievements among countries. These data sets compare achievements of countries across multiple categories such as basic education, investment in education, creation of knowledge, and investments in information technology. The data sets calculate composite indices across a range of sub-indicators.

A four-country comparison of India, China, Mexico, and South Korea from 1995 to 2012 (see Table 6.2) points out that each country has had a different outcome with regard to human development achievements. While some countries have invested heavily in sectors like education and health in the initial levels of development, others have followed an economic growth-led path of development. The thrust of the argument presented here is that redistributive policies have been achieved in either of two ways: countries have focused on income redistribution either through progressive taxation or through investment in social sectors.

In 1995, India and China had nearly similar levels of GNIper capita. However, social sector policies of China that prioritized public investments in education were reflected in a higher human development score for China. The inability of India to bolster education at the elementary level is also reflected in the overall knowledge transformation. Despite the information technology boom of the 1990s, India has seen an overall decline in the Knowledge Index from 3.570 in 1995 to 2.890 in 2012. During the same period, China managed to achieve steady growth in the Knowledge Index.

The importance of sustained investment in education is also evident in the differences in achievements between China and Mexico. While Mexico had almost ten times the GNIper capita income in 1995 as compared to China, the gap was considerably reduced by 2012. The stagnant

TABLE 6.2   Four-Country Comparison of Synergies in Development

Country	Year	GNIper capita income (in USD)	Life Expect-ancy	Human Develop-ment Index	Knowledge Index	Education Index
India	1995	2,035	60.4	0.460	3.570	2.510
	2000	2,495	62.6	0.494	3.000	2.300
	2012	4,776	67.3	0.599	2.890	2.260
China	1995	2,468	69.9	0.547	4.170	3.680
	2000	3,615	71.7	0.592	4.170	3.360
	2012	10,981	75.4	0.713	4.570	3.930
Mexico	1995	12,153	72.8	0.670	5.790	4.400
	2000	14,540	74.4	0.700	5.530	4.510
	2012	16,127	76.4	0.753	5.130	5.160
South Korea	1995	16,733	73.9	0.781	8.560	9.130
	2000	20,602	76.1	0.820	8.950	9.060
	2012	32,213	81.3	0.891	8.650	9.090

Source: Formulated by authors from KNOEMA. 2012. Accessible at knoema.com/
WBKEI2013/knowledge-economy-index-world-bank-2012, 10 March 2018;
United Nations. 2017. Accessible at hdr.undp.org/en/data#, 10 March
2018.; World Bank. 2017. Accessible at databank.worldbank.org/data/reports.
aspx?source=world-development-indicators, 10 March 2018.
Note: The Education Index is calculated using average years of schooling, secondary enrolment, and tertiary enrolment. The Knowledge Index is a composite
measure of the Education Index, Innovation Index (royalty payments and
receipts, patent count, and journal articles), and ICT Index (telephones, comput-
ers, and internet users).

economic growth and the failure of its trickle-down benefits have led to
lack of adequate progress in human development achievements in recent
years. As Sun and Young examined, the experience of South Korea has
shown that initial investments in education can foster income growth in
later periods. South Korea was able to surpass the income levels of Mexico
in the 1990s despite having started at a lower point in the 1960s. The
achievement of South Korea in terms of improving life expectancy was
also remarkable between 1995 and 2012. However, despite better initial

conditions in both education and life expectancy rates, Mexico could only achieve marginal improvements over this period. The initial conditions of South Korea's emphasis on mass education led to the benefits of more equitable distribution of education, and wage inequality decline between 1960 and 1985, as the premium enjoyed by people with higher education over those with primary education declined from an additional 100 per cent to 66 per cent.[24] South Korea's experience indicates that public investment in the education sector can contribute to people's well-being in the long run. In recent years, it has been able to achieve economic growth, near universal education, and high knowledge achievements.

This evidence lends credence to the theorizations of Alvaredo et al., who argue that income inequalities are not always an outcome of policies implemented today but are in fact a reflection of the policy regimes of the past.[25] It is argued that the levels of income inequalities across both developed and developing countries in the present times are alarming and harmful for growth.[26] The above example of Mexico shows that dependence on trickle-down policies is inadequate to achieve sustained equitable outcomes. The evidence for OECD countries during the period 1990–2010 shows that rising inequality led to a reduction of more than 10 percentage points of growth in Mexico and New Zealand. Even in the more advanced countries such as the USA, the UK, Sweden, Finland, and Norway, the growth rate would have been more than a fifth higher, had income disparities not widened.

Sustained public expenditure on social sectors with a focus on quantum and quality resources is essential for improved human development outcomes. Several developing countries have demonstrated the ability to achieve high rates of human development despite having low levels of per capita income. They have followed varied pathways,[27] but the cross-cutting factor is the proactive role of the state. Governments have played a key role in implementing people-centric policies. The emphasis was on universal access to social services that ensured well-being and capabilities.[28]

Moreover, an integrated approach is essential in the implementation of various components of social security in order to reap the benefits of synergies. Female literacy plays a key role in reducing infant mortality rate. It also improves nutrition and health levels in students thereby improving their school attainments. Similarly, programmes for poverty alleviation could also contribute to rise in income levels, which would in turn lead to better nutrition, health, and productivity levels.

Programmes that recognize and build on these interlinkages could be integrated for effective results. For example, improving the health conditions of people would require simultaneous investments in medical care, better water supply, sanitation, and nutrition. When programmes encompassing all these aspects are undertaken in an integrated manner, the results would ensue much faster than if only specific components are addressed in a sporadic and piecemeal manner.

6.3 ROLE OF STATE ACTION

The advent of the human development approach in 1990 provided a platform for a more holistic view of social sectors. The human development approach emphasized the need for *universal provisioning* of education, health, and other basic services that enhance capabilities. Through annual HDRs, the approach highlighted the ways in which countries could set about realizing this challenge. The emphasis on access to fundamental capability expansion as an entitlement and as an issue of ensuring equity ensured that the approach would go beyond the traditional view of considering education and health as merely *welfare sectors*. Consequently, the view of the state also changed from that of a paternalistic entity to one that was an enabler and initiator of people-centred development.

To provide a brief background, social security is embedded within the notion of the *welfare state* that came into prominence during the post–World War II period, although its origin can be traced back to the 1880s when Chancellor Bismarck initiated state provisioning of social security in Germany in the form of old age pensions, accident insurance, and medical care. The publication of the report *Social Insurance and Alliance Services* by the Beveridge Committee in 1942[29] was a landmark development that set a grand vision for social security by defining it as 'Freedom from Want'. This resonated with the demand of the Atlantic Charter on Social Security,[30] which considered social security as a means to 'relieve want and destitution'.

This powerful combination of forces led to the creation of a grand vision reflected in the Beveridge Committee Report. However, this vision was not supported adequately by operational measures that could translate it into reality, and even when such operationalization was attempted, it resulted in a dilution of the concept. Social security came to be identified largely with publicly provided contingency-related measures in the organized sector.[31]

As already discussed in Chapter 5 of this volume, the empirical points of connect and disconnect between the patterns of economic growth and social sector policies can be explained through the two-chain linkage between economic growth and human development outcomes. In *Chain I*, higher economic growth increases household income and enhances the revenue accruing to the government. This, in turn, improves the government's ability to increase public spending on education and health, thereby contributing to improved social attainments. Simultaneously, the increase in incomes of the households—the extent of which depends on the pattern of growth and distribution of resources—could lead to increased private spending on social services.

The extent to which the benefits of economic growth percolate down to the bottom of the pyramid depends on the institutional structure and the type of economic policies followed. Prabhu[32] points to the importance of monetary and fiscal policies in this regard, as they not only determine the general price level in the economy, but also have an impact on the relative prices of basic goods. This phenomenon indirectly influences expenditures of the poor on social sector services. The linkages between economic growth and human development are stronger when macroeconomic policies complement social policies, and when both are permeated by a redistributive ethos.

Chain II outlines the contribution of human development to economic growth. Higher levels of human development mean healthier, educated, and skilled population, which contributes to improvements in productivity and creativity. In turn, higher productivity attracts more foreign capital and higher exports, translating into higher income. Public policies to enhance people's capabilities play a crucial role in strengthening the linkages.[33] Jolly has explained that in the early stages of development, there is a strong case to accelerate action on education and health, to lay the foundation for later acceleration in economic growth rates.[34] He argues that at any given point, it is plausible to ensure adequate social expenditure and human development outcomes even in the absence of faster economic growth. In the neoliberal approach, improvements in social indicators are influenced only through an improvement in economic growth rates and rising per capita income levels. But in the case of the human development approach, he argues that well-being and capabilities can be improved by effective public spending and reallocating public resources to social sectors even when economic growth rates are relatively low.[35]

The human development approach lays considerable importance on the role of public action, which, following Drèze and Sen,[36] is defined as encompassing both state and people's action. State action is justified on the grounds that markets in developing economies are often inefficient. Egalitarian polices are a necessary condition to ensure that economic and social opportunities are available to all the sections of the population.[37] Additionally, the state is a facilitator which creates conditions for the development of private sector institutions that can overcome market failures. In a comparative analysis of Korea and India, Datta-Chaudhuri[38] indicates how an activist government could strengthen market-led institutions in such a way that it can influence the behaviour of economic agents effectively. Chen and Desai delineate three components to strengthen the route to improved social development, which includes governance, integration, and universality.[39] The fundamental complementarities between the state and the market have been harnessed to a large extent by the East Asian countries. The resultant reduction in education and health deprivation while maintaining high rates of economic growth have earned for these countries the sobriquet of *East Asian Miracle*.

6.4 SOCIAL SECTOR POLICYMAKING IN CONTEMPORARY TIMES

The ambitious vision put out in the Millennium Declaration, which resulted in the formulation of the MDGs, is the first such attempt in the world to consolidate numerous facets of development into a single comprehensive agenda for the countries of the world to be pursue. The MDGs also provided a framework within which the social sector policies in respective countries would be implemented. More importantly, the MDGs placed the onus of ensuring the well-being of people in all dimensions squarely on national governments, thereby stalling and reversing the ongoing attempts to pass on the responsibility of social sector development to the private realm.

The MDGs stimulated action on social sectors across countries. The necessity for them to report to the global UN forum led to enhanced accountability on national governments. However, the MDGs did not reflect the holistic and integrated vision of the Millennium Declaration, and had neither clear conceptual insight nor a specified methodology for achieving the goals. The MDGs spurred countries to adopt vertical targeted approaches to tackle specific indicators. The more holistic approach was given a go-by in most countries. Indeed, it may even be argued that the very indicators chosen for the MDGs were narrow and reflected more a mechanistic approach that measured progress in terms of inputs and outputs rather than in terms of processes, and quality of education and health.[40] For example, the indicators to track progress in education were net enrolment ratio in primary education, proportion of pupils starting grade one who reach grade five, and literacy rate among 15–24-year-olds. For health, they were the under-five mortality rate, infant mortality rate, and maternal mortality rate. Both dimensions reflect a truncated and narrow perspective of what constitutes *education* and *health*. The compulsions of reporting progress on MDGs periodically kept up the pressure to showcase specific initiatives.

Moreover, given their narrow focus on specific indicators, MDGs have been accused of derailing policy attention from core aspects of the human development agenda. The MDGs adopted a uniform approach irrespective of the initial conditions of countries, displayed low ambition in terms of targets set, and completely neglected both the distributional dimensions and the processes to be adopted to achieve the goals. In doing so, they inadvertently opened the doors for the existing dominant paradigm of globalization and liberalization, increasing existing gaps.[41] Overall, though, there has been much progress on specific goals and targets, the achievement, like the proverbial curate's egg, was only good in parts.

Much more damaging from the point of the global compact that the MDGs represented was the utter failure of the developed countries to contribute to the achievement of crucial goals through enhanced flow of financial resources. In keeping with the collective responsibility dimension articulated in the Millennium Declaration, MDG 8 was formulated, and included goals and targets for enhanced contribution of financial resources, along with technology transfers, increased access to affordable medicines, markets, and new technologies, as well as for ensuring debt sustainability.[42] However, in the absence of either a numerical target or timeline, the goal was not taken seriously by the developed countries, and the MDGs, in effect, became the responsibility of developing nations to fulfil. If Goal 8 was to be judged against the long-established UN target of 0.7 per cent of GNI as Overseas Development Assistance (ODA), although the flow of ODA from developed countries increased in absolute terms from USD 81 billion in the year 2000 to USD 135 billion in 2014, the progress in terms of percentage of GNI of the developed countries was only marginal, from 0.22 per cent in 2000 to 0.29 per cent in 2014.[43]

The SDGs sought to correct these anomalies and present a more integrated structure comprising seventeen goals and 169 targets. The goals include not only the traditional sectoral goals, but also recognize structural elements (Goal 10 on reducing inequality) and pay attention to the implementation mechanisms (Goal 17). They also recognize the interlinkages between goals that require coordinated and synergistic implementation. The goals also need processes that are more holistic in nature.

There has also been great vigour in engaging with a participatory process, so much so that the negotiations leading up to the SDGs, unlike the MDGs, are owned by national governments and civil societies. Moreover, since they are universally applicable to both developed and developing countries, they are no longer perceived as an imposition by the developed world on developing countries. The philosophy governing the SDGs of *leaving no one behind* and *reaching the farthest first* are also reflected in the articulation of the goals and targets, bringing up issues of distribution for nations to address.

6.5 INNOVATIVE POLICY EXPERIMENTS

Given the global consensus on the imperative to enhance social sector attainments, numerous policy initiatives to accelerate them have been taken at the national levels. Evidence across several developing countries shows that context-specific policies are better at achieving improvement in health and education outcomes, women's empowerment, environment, and community integration. The pathways combine the elements of human development approach through sectoral initiatives and rights-based approaches. Multi-sectoral approaches—such as conditional cash transfers, linking cash disbursements to specific conditionalities of behaviour in education and health realms—as well as other initiatives seeking to reap synergies across various sectors are important. In Table 6.3, we outline some of the innovative sector specific policies as well as inter-sectoral initiatives.

TABLE 6.3 Innovative Social Sector Policies

Country	Policy	Year	Details
		Enhancing Capabilities	
Thailand	30 Baht Scheme	2002	Universal access to registered health services for flat user fee of thirty baht per consultation
India, West Bengal	Reduction of out-of-pocket expenses	2011	Fair price shops, fair price diagnostic facilities, free drug policy at all government hospitals
Bangladesh	Monitoring by Bangladesh Rural Advancement Committee (BRAC)	2008	Monitor all the primary schools, including government-owned, private, and community schools, in thirty *upazilas* (subdistricts) across the country
Botswana	Botswana National Policy on HIV and AIDS (Revised)	2012	Multi-sectoral strategic framework guided by cultural values and historic principles
Sudan	Can't Wait to Learn	2013	Teach mathematics to out-of-school children through a self-paced, interactive, tablet-based system that children can access in community spaces
		Securing Entitlements	
India	Mahatma Gandhi National Rural Employment Guarantee Act (MGNREGA)	2005	Rights-based framework to provide rural employment with added focus on creation of 'durable assets'
		Agency and Empowerment	
Ethiopia	Education Sector Development Programs (ESDPs)	1997	Improve access to education for girls and reduce their levels of school dropout and repetition in order to close the gender gap
India, Kerala	Kudumbashree	1997	Three-tier women's community, democratic leadership support structure
Thailand	Bann Mankong Community Upgrade Program	2003	Focus on upgrading living conditions and engaging the poorest urban residents with other residents
Uzbekistan	Payments for Ecosystem Services (PES)	2010	Market-based tool for effective ecosystems management aimed at empowering local communities

(continued)

TABLE 6.3   (*Continued*)

Country	Policy	Year	Details
		Reaping Synergies	
Brazil	Bolsa Família Program (BF)	2003	Encourage families to invest in their children and thereby contribute to tackling the intergenerational transmission of poverty
Philippines	Pantawid Pamilyang Pilipino Program (4Ps)	2008	Cash grants to the poorest of the poor to improve health, nutrition, and education of age group 0–18
		Productivity	
India	Deen Dayal Upadhyaya Grameen Kaushalya Yojana	2014	Transform rural poor youth into economically independent and globally relevant workforce
Kenya	Agricultural Sector Development Strategy (ASDS)	2008	Transform agricultural sector into a profitable economic activity capable of attracting private investment and providing gainful employment to people

Source: Formulated by authors from DSD (Department of Social Development), SASSA (South African Social Security Agency), and United Nations Children's Fund (UNICEF). 2012. *The South African Child Support Grant Impact Assessment: Evidence from a Survey of Children, Adolescents and Their Households.* Pretoria: UNICEF South Africa; El Arifeen, S., Christou, A., Reichenbach, L., Osman, F.A., Azad, K., Islam, K.S., Ahmed, F., Perry, H.B., and Peters, D.H. 2013. 'Community-Based Approaches and Partnerships: Innovations in Health-Service Delivery in Bangladesh'. *The Lancet* 382 (9909): 2012–26; Kenya Agricultural Research Institute. 2012. *Policy Responses to Food Crisis in Kenya.* Washington, DC: IFPRI; KV, P.D. 2017. 'Women's Empowerment through Financial Inclusion: The Work of Kudumbashree'. *Imperial Journal of Interdisciplinary Research* 3 (2): 1023–30; Lasonen, J., Kemppainen, R., and Raheem, K. 2005. 'Education and Training in Ethiopia: An Evaluation of Approaching EFA Goals', Working Papers 23, Institute for Educational Research, Jyväskylä University Press, Finland; Paek, S.C., Meemon, N., and Wan, T.H. 2016. 'Thailand's Universal Coverage Scheme and Its Impact on Health-Seeking Behavior'. *Springer Plus* 5: 1952; Soares, F.V., Ribas, R.P., and Osório, R.G. 2010. 'Evaluating the Impact of Brazil's Bolsa Familia: Cash Transfer Programs in Comparative Perspective'. *Latin American Research Review* 45 (2): 173–90; Vij, N. 2011. 'Collaborative Governance: Analysing Social Audits in MGNREGA in India'. *IDS Bulletin* 42 (6): 28–34.

Sector-Specific Initiatives

The Child Support Grant (CSG) was introduced in the post–Apartheid South Africa in 1998. It provided cash grants to poor children, helping to improve their nutrition while reducing early pregnancy and sexually risky behaviour. When the CSG was first launched, the government set a household income threshold of ZAR 800 (USD 170) in rural areas and ZAR 1,100 (USD 234) in urban areas. In 2008, the government increased the threshold by about ten times the value of the grant. A large-impact assessment[44] conducted in 2012 concluded that early receipt of the CSG helped keep children healthy. Researchers found that for some children, the grant reduced the risk of common illnesses, such as the flu and stomach ache. Children who received the CSG early and had educated mothers reaped significant benefits. These children were less likely to face illness episodes and had overall improved health achievements.

Bangladesh is well-known in the sphere of public health for the development of oral rehydration therapy. Bangladesh Rural Advancement Committee (BRAC), an NGO, began in the 1980s by going door-to-door to generate awareness regarding Oral Rehydration Solution (ORS). Since 2008, BRAC has been tasked with monitoring all the primary schools, including government-owned, private, and community schools in thirty upazilas across the country.[45] Additionally, BRAC was also involved in poverty reduction activities through improving land resource base, improving agriculture extension services, aiding seed quality and procurement, improving agricultural marketing services, and mainstreaming women in agriculture.

The Indian state of West Bengal has adopted a three-pronged model of reducing out-of-pocket expenses of patients: by opening fair-price shops, by providing fair price diagnostic services, and by supplying free essential and life-saving drugs at all government hospitals.[46] The Ministry of Health, Government of India, has urged all the state governments to consider adopting the West Bengal model. Similarly, the Government of Botswana distributes anti-retroviral drugs free of cost; over the past decade, AIDS-related deaths have plummeted significantly there.[47] Although the scheme is not yet universal, the expansion of eligibility criteria over time has enabled more people to receive anti-retroviral treatment. These models emphasize that planned implementation and strict adherence to the guidelines are essential to ensure the programme's success.

The Ministry of Education in Sudan, along with UNICEF and other partners, developed an Accelerated Learning Program (ALP) to build basic competencies among the out-of-school children. Based on the ALP curriculum, the Can't Wait to Learn programme, launched in 2013, enables children in remote areas to complete Book 1, which covers the first three years' curriculum of traditional mathematics through digitized content on tablets. The larger aim of the programme is to cover all the subjects up to grade eight, providing certificates to children completing primary education, an essential prerequisite to enter secondary schooling or formal employment. Similarly, Ethiopia's success in raising access to primary education has been achieved mainly through supply-side measures. The number of primary schools increased from 16,000 in 2004–5, to more than 25,000 in 2008–9. During the same period, the national budget allocation for education increased to 5.5 per cent of the GDP. In 1997, the Ethiopian Ministry of Education launched the Education Sector Development Programs (ESDPs) with the aim of promoting equity by closing the gender gap in education. The improved access to education for girls reduced the rates of dropout and repetition by focusing on removal of obstacles to education access, on teacher training, and on technical and vocational training.[48] Aiming to put an end to child marriages and keeping girls in school, the *Berhane Hewan* (2004–6) pilot project provided support for girls to remain in school, and even granted a female sheep to each girl child on completion.[49]

The Kenyan Agricultural Sector Development Strategy (ASDS)[50] for achieving food security has been notable for enhancing productivity through a people-centric approach. In a two-pronged strategy, the government supported research and implementation of technology to increase agricultural productivity and extension services, and supported purchase and storage of Strategic Grain Reserves (SGRs). Additionally, the National Accelerated Agricultural Inputs Program provided inputs to small-scale farmers across the country. These examples suggest that well-designed and effectively implemented programmes can help achieve outcomes in poverty alleviation.

Women's empowerment is essential for enhancing gender equality and accord recognition to the value of women's labour. The success of

India's Kudumbashree as one of the largest women's networks in the world is an excellent example of poverty alleviation through enhancement of collective agency of women. Initially launched in 1998 as a micro-finance agency in the state of Kerala of India, this self-help organization has grown into a community-based organization. It has been an instrument of poverty alleviation, and has successfully promoted community counselling and microfinance through a democratic leadership support structure.[51] Several initiatives and programmes aimed at social and financial assistance have been supported under the umbrella of Kudumbashree. These include *Balasabhas*, Tribal Special Project, thrift and micro-credit societies, and interest subsidy scheme. As of September 2016, 89,752 neighbourhood groups have availed matching grant facilities, INR 31.7 billion (USD 460 million) worth thrift has been generated, and INR 9.89 billion (USD 150 million) worth interest subsidies have been disbursed through Kudumbashree.[52] These policies have gradually expanded their reach to multiple sectors, making the programme one of the most powerful to not only enhance women's incomes, but also raise their self-confidence and social status.

Rights-Based Policies

The process of economic growth in the era of neoliberalism and globalization has created opportunities for a few, but has also left vast proportion of the population behind. The ILO[53] reported in 2018 that though global economic growth rates have rebounded and remained stable in recent times, global unemployment is as high as 190 million. Even worse, vulnerable employment is gradually increasing across developing and emerging economies. Productivity and prosperity are two key components of the SDGs, but at a time when employment opportunities are getting parched, the central focus both globally and nationally is on *jobs*. The recent 2017 OECD–ILO[54] report evaluated employability policies across eight countries, and found that there are a variety of factors that determine skill utilization of workers and enterprises. Further, policies aimed at improving skills utilization need to evolve coherence across employment, skills, economic and social policies simultaneously.

The entitlement-based approach was applied in India to ensure rural employment under the Mahatma Gandhi National Rural

Employment Guarantee Act (MGNREGA). Launched in 2005, it makes a commitment to provide 100 days of employment per fiscal year for the rural poor households through self-selection processes. The ability to demand employment as a right has improved individual well-being. The MGNREGA has generated 19.8 billion person-days of employment in India. Positioned as an integrated social security programme, it also promotes rural development through its convergence with other sectors, particularly infrastructure, agriculture, and horticulture. In the process, the MGNREGA has facilitated creation of durable assets, and has helped generate additional employment and livelihood opportunities. By enabling individuals to demand employment as a right, it has contributed, in regions where its implementation has been effective, to improved individual well-being. It has also fostered collaborations between state and non-state actors—such as civil society organizations—through mandatory social audits to ensure transparency and accountability of the scheme. Social audits have played a transformative role in empowering the people and in promoting collective responsibility.[55]

The guarantee of employment as an entitlement under MGNREGA sought to expand capability sets to address multiple deprivations. However, its success was only seen in those areas which had favourable initial conditions. For instance, MGNREGA was successful in states like Tamil Nadu and Rajasthan because of strong political will towards pro-poor policies[56] in the former and the presence of community mobilization organizations in the latter.[57]On the other hand, its success was limited in states such as Jharkhand and Bihar because it has failed to meet the demand for work and remained largely supply driven.[58] This is more so because of the entrenched structural inequalities in these states manifested in weak mobilization of civil society and local governance institutions.

In recent years, the policy has evolved from being a demand-driven employment generation and asset creation programme, to ensuring integrated livelihood promotion through convergence with various other schemes in the areas of forest protection, horticulture promotion, road construction, sanitation, *Anganwadi* programme, and so on.[59] The success of MGNREGA was higher in states where the government structures already had an egalitarian approach. Targeted social welfare measures like *poor feeding* programme that provided free midday meals to school children began in Tamil Nadu as early as 1956.[60] The extension of food security through provision of subsidized food grains at 1–2 US cents per kilogram in states like Tamil Nadu and Andhra Pradesh also gave a fillip to rural food security along with employment generation.

Conditional Cash Transfer Schemes

Conditional Cash Transfers (CCTs) programmes, which originated in Latin American countries, have achieved significant popularity in recent times. CCTs provide direct benefits to people who are found eligible, but only after fulfilment of a certain set of conditions largely relating to school attendance health check-ups and the like. CCTs have become popular as they are seen to tackle multiple problems effectively and simultaneously, and with much better targeting at a reasonable cost. It is also recognized that they do not constitute a *silver bullet*, that they cannot work in isolation, and work best in the presence of other supportive policies. CCTs have today been adopted by several countries in various versions to address demand-side constraints in addressing poverty. The scope of the programmes has expanded beyond immunization and school enrolment, to engage with secondary school completion, adult education, housing, and microcredit.

The Bolsa Família Program of Brazil is the world's largest and most comprehensive CCT scheme. Initiated in 2003, it unified major programmes that had been working towards enhancing primary education and ensuring food security. Besides its immediate poverty impact, this programme also aimed to arrest intergenerational transmission of poverty through better education and health outcomes.[61] Its impact on poverty and inequality reduction, especially after the expansion of the programme to adolescents aged 16–17 in 2008, has been reported to have positive spill overs in significantly reducing crime.[62] Linking the CCT initiative with numerous social programmes and services, ensuring efficient administration, and good targeting have made this a model programme. In a municipality-level impact analysis, Rougier et al.[63] find a positive impact of the transfers on municipalities' local economic growth. Additionally, they make a case for linking social transfer schemes with promotion of local production and development.

The Pantawid Pamilyang Pilipino Program, administered by the Department of Social Welfare and Development (DSDW) of Philippines, is another CCT programme that has effectively targeted the poorest of the poor.[64] After bringing a million recipients above the poverty line, the programme is currently seeking to determine success factors, and identifying additional needs of these transiting households to keep them from returning to poverty.

The impacts of CCTs in the realms of poverty alleviation, education, health, social inclusion, and governance have been evaluated by several international agencies such as the World Bank, UNDP, Institute of Fiscal Studies, and International Food Policy Research Institute. The multiple objectives of CCTs may make impact assessments rather complex. However, their adoption across the globe shows that they have been well received.[65] CCTs have most often been linked to enhancing education, health, and nutrition outcomes. Sensitivity to marginalized communities and mindfulness of gender dimensions (for instance, Bolsa Familia cash transfers are made to the female head of household) make the programmes more inclusive. Their integrated nature is an advantage as it fosters inter-departmental co-ordination to deliver services in a synchronized manner.

Financial and administrative operational issues in the efficiency of targeting (minimizing errors of inclusion as well as exclusion) and capacity constraints present some impediments to the effective implication of CCTs. Further, easing of demand constraints does not guarantee enhancement of human capabilities, and provision of education cannot assure employment and a stable macro environment. Public oversight and audit tools, use of information technology for monitoring and evaluation, introduction of *complementary activities* to smoothen households' exit strategies from the programme (such as in Paraguay) show promise in helping overcome such obstacles.

Several innovative initiatives have been taken up in health and disease control in the Asian and Latin American countries—the 30 Baht Scheme of Thailand and Botswana's National Policy on HIV and AIDS,[66] for example—have attracted global attention. With the 30 Baht Scheme, Thailand became the first transition country in Asia to introduce a *universal coverage scheme* with the aim of ensuring equitable health care access for even the poorest citizens. The scheme was introduced in 2002 in the aftermath of the 1997 financial crisis, as part of a policy to substitute the erstwhile export-led growth strategy with one that included the goals of social protection and local level economic development. Its aim was to provide social protection, particularly to the poor and vulnerable sections of the population. The scheme was designed collectively by the government and civil society, and introduced as part of a comprehensive policy to augment incomes and improve health outcomes. The other components of this policy were the income-augmenting schemes of the Village and Urban Revolving Fund, and the One Tambon One Product scheme. Comprising both curative and select preventive/promotive health care services, the 30 Baht Scheme intended to provide health coverage for people belonging to the informal sector in order to enable lower absenteeism and enhance productivity. The Scheme's per capita spending was USD 79 in 2016, and various assessments indicate that the coverage of the scheme was substantial. In 2016, the Scheme was estimated to have covered 75 per cent of the population of Thailand and constituted 17 per cent of the total health expenditure of the country. Use of the designated health care facilities for care was higher in low-income areas and among the unemployed and chronic status groups. The impact of social policy through public action gained greater vigour when the government procured medicines and devices at the central level and leveraged the size of the scheme to negotiate lower prices.

Despite shortcomings such as a shift in health services towards more curative than preventive services, the 30 Baht Scheme enabled citizens to view health care as a right. The scheme succeeded in extending the coverage of health services to the poor and vulnerable in a focused manner,[67] and enabled the government to transcend the confines of focusing narrowly on economic growth. By recognizing that citizens' health is intrinsically valuable and crucial in improving productivity, the government was able to focus on a comprehensive menu of services to be offered at minimum cost to the citizens. By paying attention to not only the outcomes but the processes, actors, and institutions for delivery of health services, the scheme achieved integrated outcomes.

Further, Thailand's Bann Mankong community upgrade programme has been effective in bringing the poorest urban residents together through integration and imparting a sense of ownership among the slum dwellers. It has brought the group together financially and politically by enabling their participation through the creation of financial capacities and social support networks. Innovative policies in environment and ecosystems management are also yielding substantial improvements. With an aim to empower local communities, the Regional Environmental Centre for Central Asia (CAREC) has started a market-based tool—payment for ecosystem services (PES)—for effective ecosystems management.

6.6 CONTEMPORARY GLOBAL THRUST ON UNIVERSAL BASIC INCOME

In more recent times, there has been a thrust towards Universal Basic Income (UBI) as a mechanism to directly support every household with cash transfer of equal value.[68] This is tantamount to an admission that indirect methods of augmenting income have had limited success so far. The idea of unconditional grant or social assistance is not new—such forms of non-contributory policies have been a part of larger social security policies in various countries in the past. The difference with the demand for UBI currently pertains to the exigency arising out of the increasing use of artificial intelligence and robotics that is likely to lay off workers both in developing and developed countries in the future. In the former, poverty lines are so low that effectiveness of policies implemented therein seem to be limited in securing outcomes. In the latter case, regressive fiscal policies are not able to augment sovereign funds.[69] The UBI is generally calibrated at 25 per cent of net median market income per capita. Although no country has so far implemented it on a large scale, there are small case studies of twelve countries where the scheme has been implemented. There are vast variations in the set norms, ranging between a high value of USD 1,020 per month in Netherlands and as low as USD 1.5–USD 4.5 in India.

Further, the IMF argues that it is too early to explain the distributive impact of replacing existing transfers with a UBI, since it would depend on the coverage and progressivity of the existing transfer system. UBI is similar to some of the experiments of Social funds implemented in Latin America and social assistance programmes implemented in Asia, whereby the households receive direct cash benefits after means testing. The effectiveness of coverage would be different in case of UBI, as it is universal in nature and the policy would cover the entire vulnerable population.

The nature of implementation of UBI has had an impact in terms of reduction in income inequalities. The IMF evaluation reports that this reduction has also helped address intergenerational and health inequalities. However, UBI requires closer scrutiny. The problem is that most developing countries are dominated by the informal sector, and minimum wages are not determined. A reduction in income inequality through UBI would be possible only when there is sustained implementation of the policy, as the real disposable income of those who receive such transfers needs to be maintained. Therefore, the fiscal policy needs to garner support through the implementation of progressive taxes and introduction of consumption taxation to transfer of the resources and consolidating fiscal resources could bring in efficiency in public spending.[70] It also needs to encompass in-kind transfer subsidies of education and health. The debates are spread across two spectrums: (*a*) the view that assumes overtly that the UBI can enable achievement of equality; and (*b*) the view that points out the problems related to moral hazard and worsening of inequalities.

Those who argue in favour of UBI point out that it is a means to reduce inequalities as fiscal transfer will strengthen the income base of lower income households. Moreover, they contend that if it is accompanied by progressive taxation that impacts the higher income groups, inter-group inequalities will reduce. The contrary view is that while UBI may reduce income inequalities, it may not directly reduce gender and social inequalities. In most patriarchal societies, women continue to remain subordinated in the household and may not get the benefit of direct transfers. The problem of moral hazard is also higher, as the unemployed would be assured of subsistence income, and may not want to search for gainful employment.[71] Judgement on UBI is not yet out, as there is no clarity about the real benefits of the UBI yet.

The neoliberal orientation that monetary incomes can fix all problems seems to be the rationale for such programmes. Broadly speaking, proponents seem to argue for universal basic incomes for distinct reasons across developed and developing countries. UBI is being considered as a policy alternative that would help governments consolidate their fiscal resources from an array of policies such that their effectiveness is improved. But these alternatives cannot be considered in vacuum. Globally, most countries are facing fluctuating rates of economic growth, rising income inequalities, joblessness, and insecure employment opportunities. Though a money-metric approach like UBI can prevent the descent of the vulnerable families into destitution, it cannot ensure their ascent into better incomes and living conditions. Much more needs to be done to ensure better employment opportunities and living conditions.

Moreover, the UBI seems to be more in the nature of a superficial quick fix that does not address the underlying causes for the persistent deprivations. The neoliberal orientation that monetary incomes can fix all problems seems to be the rationale for such programmes.[72]

★★★

Evidence so far indicates that the policymakers' understanding of what constitutes social sectors is limited, and therefore, the policy orientation is largely paternalistic and focused rather narrowly on instrumental outcomes rather than on improving overall human well-being.

In the current state of development, where countries are grappling with inequalities, stagnant growth rates, and lack of progress on core human development indicators, the narrow interpretation of social sectors would imply that the outcomes would be achieved only in specific dimensions, yielding what Sen calls 'culmination outcomes' rather than 'comprehensive outcomes'.[73] On the other hand, successful experiences of most countries in the East Asian region, as well as in Latin America and sub-Saharan Africa indicate that cohesive social policies that are mindful of local-level specificities have been able to achieve more holistic progress in social indicators despite low growth rates. The dilemmas in social policy can only be resolved if there is a firm commitment towards enhancing the well-being of the people and is undertaken with strong political commitment and a long-enough time horizon.

The transformation of the policy regime in the twenty-first century in the form of the SDGs stands testimony to this fact. Given their ambitious agenda for 2030, do they imply a transformation of national social sector policies from piecemeal, sectoral approaches to more integrated and holistic approaches? It is too early to predict the way SDGs will be implemented and whether their spirit will be maintained. What is not in doubt, however, is that SDGs present a new framework within which to situate social sector policies. Moreover, the ethos of SDGs resonates with that of the human development approach, facilitating a more proactive role for the state in ensuring basic social sector attainments. Being a global, albeit voluntary, programme with periodic reporting requirements, the SDGs have the potential to ensure through peer pressure that the national governments take the responsibility for enhancing social sector attainments seriously.

As against this ambitious SDG agenda, the reality on the ground is somewhat grim in terms of the fiscal scenario that determines the ability of national governments to allocate resources to the social sectors. The social sector strategies of most countries during the past two decades have been influenced by the transition from an era of fiscal prudence norms to fiscal stimulus, and since 2008, to fiscal consolidation norms. Ortiz and Cummins observe that a growing number of countries have been undergoing cuts in public expenditure, and that the resource mobilization processes are moving more towards indirect taxes.[74] The tax base continues to be small and the brunt of the low level of resource mobilization is borne by social sectors and social protection policies.

There is growing concern of declining fiscal space[75] in fiscal policy as governments continue to be concerned about macroeconomic stability, even as they recognize the need to balance the requirements of debt servicing and funding short- and long-term expenditure requirements. Often, fiscal space is narrow, owing to low tax-GDP ratios. Spending patterns of low- and middle-income countries in Asia point to some encouraging trends.[76] The share of spending on *regrettable necessities* like defence is controlled in most cases. The emerging economies have deployed countercyclical fiscal policies tailored to individual country circumstances. They have been mindful of the country's prudential limitations, thereby alleviating the fear that persuing such policies would jeopardize fiscal prudence. However, while the goal-setting has broadened in the decades of the MDGs, and currently, the SDGs, lack of action on the part of developed countries to financially support developing countries in attaining the goals has meant that traditional public finance debates continue to dominate fiscal strategies for human development. The commitments, made by developed countries towards enhancing ODA to finance social sectors in developing countries, have not been fulfilled, leaving national governments largely responsible for funding their social sectors.

The outlook for the future, thus, needs to be moderated by the realities on the ground. The agenda for action on the SDGs must move beyond goal-setting to ensure that (*a*) developed countries contribute to what can best be termed *global public goods*, and (*b*) encourage a consensus on the nature of policies that need to accompany the achievement of SDGs at national levels. Monitoring outcomes without attention to processes would be an exercise in futility, and lead once again to a betrayal of the hopes and aspirations of the poor and vulnerable people of the world.

NOTES AND REFERENCES

1. The notion of a welfare state is one that mitigates 'the impact of the market, by providing some sort of minimum guarantee (mitigating poverty), covering a range of social risks (security) and providing certain services (health care, child and elder care, etc.) at the best standards available'. See Andersen, J.G. 2012. 'Welfare States and Welfare State Theory', Working Paper for Centre for Comparative Welfare Studies, Centre for Comparative Welfare Studies, Department of Economics, Politics and Public Administration, Aalborg University, Aalborg, p. 4.

2. These are Bismarkian welfare state, liberal welfare state, social democrat welfare state, and Mediterranean welfare state (Anderson, 'Welfare States and Welfare State Theory').

3. For instance, see Becker, G.S. 1964. *Human Capital: A Theoretical and Empirical Analysis, with Special Reference to Education.* Chicago: The University of Chicago Press; Mincer, J. 1974. *Schooling, Experience and Earnings.* New York: National Bureau of Economic Research; Schultz, T. 1961. 'Investment in Human Capital'. *American Economic Review* 51 (1): 1–17.

4. Rosen, S. 1989. 'Human Capital', in *The New Palgrave Dictionary of Economics, Vol. 2*, ed. J. Eatwell, M. Milgate, and P. Newman, pp. 681–90. London: Macmillan Press, p. 682.

5. A detailed discussion on the human capital/human resource development approach is presented in Annexure B.

6. Samir Amin called this as the project of globalization managed by global capitalism. As a staunch critic of imperialism and globalization, he argued extensively about North–South relations and cautioned about the dominance of crony capitalism from the North, which, according to him, led to the process of industrialization in emerging economies. For details, see Amin, S. 2014.

Capitalism in the Age of Globalization: The Management of Contemporary Society. London: Zed Books.

7. For more, see Prabhu, K.S. 2001. 'Socio-Economic Security in the Context of Pervasive Poverty: A Case Study of India', International Labour Office, Geneva; and Srivastava, R. 2008. 'Towards Universal Social Protection in India in a Rights-Based Paradigm'. *Indian Journal of Human Development* 2 (1): 111–32.

8. Drèze, J. and Sen, A. 1989. *Hunger and Public Action.* Oxford: Clarendon Press, p. 16.

9. Some scholars have reiterated that in the context of developing countries, tackling persistently low incomes ought to be an important objective of social security. For details, see Burgess, R. and Stern, N. 1991. 'Social Security in Developing Countries: What, Why, Who and How?', in *Social Security in Developing Countries,* ed. E. Ahmad, J. Drèze, J. Hills, and A. Sen, pp. 41–80, Oxford: Clarendon Press; Guhan, S. 1992. 'Social Security in India: Looking One Step Ahead', in *Poverty in India: Research and Policy,* ed. B. Harriss, S. Guhan, and R.H. Cassen, pp. 282–98. Oxford: Oxford University Press.

10. ILO introduced the concept of socio-economic security, which was similar in content to this broader notion of social security. See ILO. 1958. *Social Security: A Workers' Education Manual.* Geneva: ILO.

11. For more, see Burgess and Stern, 'Social Security in Developing Countries'; Prabhu, 'Socio-Economic Security in the Context of Pervasive Poverty'; and Srivastava, 'Towards Universal Social Protection in India in a Rights-Based Paradigm'.

12. Prabhu, K.S. 1996. 'Health Security for Indian Workers'. *Indian Journal of Labour Economics* 39 (4): 937–58.

13. The term *intrinsic* can be defined as opportunities viewed as ends in themselves, whereas *instrumental* view is when opportunities provide an enabling condition to enhance other forms of freedoms. While these terms may differ in their respective connotations, they are highly interlinked, and depend largely on the purpose for which they are sought.

14. For the sake of analytical simplicity, we are refraining from including common pool resources. Ostrom provides a detailed analysis of the classification of goods, as she argues that it affects the incentives that individuals face in defining their own consumer choices. For details, see Ostrom, E. 2005. *Understanding Institutional Diversity.* Princeton: Princeton University Press.

15. In 1956, Musgrave defined 'merit goods as some economic events such as free medical treatment for the poor and subsidies for low-priced housing'. Later, in 1969, he extended it as '[w]ants with regard to which consumer choice is abandoned and the satisfaction of which is imposed I have referred to as merit wants and have argued that they remain outside the normative

model'. For details, see Musgrave, R.A. 1956. 'A Multiple Theory of Budget Determination'. *FinanzArchiv/Public Finance Analysis* (H.3): 333–43; 1969. 'Provision for Social Goods', in *Public Economics*, by J. Margolis, pp. 124–44. p. 143.

16.   It further reiterated that 'the potential is enormous for restructuring national budgets and international aid in favour of human development'. See UNDP. 1991. *Human Development Report 1991*. New York: Oxford University Press.

17.   The public expenditure ratio was defined as the percentage of national income that goes into public expenditure; the social allocation ratio was the percentage of public expenditure that was earmarked for social services; the social priority ratio was the percentage of social expenditure devoted to human priority concerns; the human expenditure ratio was the percentage of national income devoted to human priority concerns. See UNDP, *Human Development Report 1991*, p. 39.

18.   Jolly, 'Human Development and Neo-Liberalism: Paradigms Compared'.

19.   For an interesting comparison of the human capital and human development approaches to policymaking in Mexico and South Korea respectively, see Suh, J. and Chen, D., eds. 2007. *Korea as a Knowledge Economy: Evolutionary Process and Lessons Learned.* Washington, DC: Korea Development Institute and The World Bank Institute.

20.   Prabhu, K.S. 1998. 'Social Sectors in Economic Development'. *Journal of Social and Economic Development* 1 (2): 268–87.

21.   Heller, P.S. 1988. 'The Implications of Fund Supported Adjustment Programs for Poverty: Experiences in Selected Countries—Occasional Paper 58' (Vol. 58), International Monetary Fund.

22.   Equity enhancing policy resulted in higher growth elasticity of poverty reduction in East Asian countries that ranged between 2.8 for Indonesia to 3.4 for Malaysia as compared to 0.2 for Zambia or 0.9 for Brazil. For details, see UNDP. 1997. *Human Development Report: Human Development to Eradicate Poverty*. New York: Oxford University Press, p. 74.

23.   A cross-sectional study of more than eighty countries indicates a strong negative relationship between basic education enrolment rates and the level of income inequality as measured by the Gini index. It also points out that income elasticity of enrolment ratio from education expenditure was between 0.31 and 0.43 at the primary and secondary levels respectively. This is an average for all income groups and the value for poor income groups may exceed 1.0. In the case of health, poverty reduction and government expenditure appeared to be more important than income growth for improving life expectancy. For details, see Barro, R.J. and Lee, J.W. 1993. 'International Comparisons of Educational Attainment'. *Journal of Monetary Economics* 32 (3): 363–94.

24. UNDP. 1996. *Human Development Report: Economic Growth and Human Development.* New York: Oxford University Press, p. 53.

25. Alvaredo, F., Chancel, L., Piketty, T., Saez, E., and Zucman, G. 2017. 'Global Inequality Dynamics: New Findings from WID World'. *American Economic Review* 107 (5): 404–9.

26. Bruno, M., Ravallion, M., and Squire, L. 1976. 'Equity and Growth in Developing Countries: Old and New Perspectives on the Policy Issues', Policy Research Working Paper No. 1563, World Bank, Washington, DC; Cingano, F. 2014. 'Trends in Income Inequality and Its Impact on Economic Growth', OECD Social, Employment and Migration Working Papers, No. 163, OECD Publishing, Paris; Presson, T. and Tabellini, G. 1994. 'Is Inequality Harmful for Growth?' *American Economic Review* 84 (3): 600–21.

27. Examples of Bangladesh, Chile, and Indonesia are noteworthy here. Bangladesh achieved egalitarian economic growth through an accelerated progress on female literacy, child immunization and mortality, as well as access to credit. A high social expenditure ratio, an important non-income factor in Chile, resulted in lower child mortality rates. In Indonesia, equitable distribution of social expenditures and radical decentralization of governance led to improving basic services and reducing poverty. For details, see Ranis, G. and Stewart, F. 2012. 'Success and Failure in Human Development: 1970–2007'. *Journal of Human Development and Capabilities* 13 (2): 167–95.

28. The role of the state in fostering human development was emphasized in several instances from South Asia in the last two centuries. Sri Lanka's government initiatives in health and education started in early 1900s with the passage of Education Ordinance No. 1. in 1939 and the establishment of first health unit in 1926 to provide primary health care and control infectious disease. Further, high public health spending between 1952 and 1981 significantly helped in reducing infant mortality rate during this period. Similarly, in the state of Kerala in India, the passing of a directive in the 1800s by Queen Gouri Parvathi of Travancore, calling for free and compulsory education, led to subsequent attainments in the sphere. For more, refer to Drèze, J. and Sen, A. 2002. *India: Development and Participation.* Oxford: Oxford University Press; Sen, A. and Drèze, J. 1999. 'The Amartya Sen and Jean Dreze Omnibus: (Comprising) Poverty and Famines; Hunger and Public Action; and India: Economic Development and Social Opportunity'. *OUP Catalogue*, Number 9780195648317, Oxford University Press.

29. Beveridge, W.H.B.B. 1942. *Social Insurance and Allied Services: Report of the Inter-Departmental Committee on Social Insurance and Allied Services.* London: HM Stationery Office.

30. Roosevelt, F.D. and Churchill, W.S. 1941. *Atlantic Charter.* London: John Wiley & Sons Ltd.

31.   Prabhu, K.S. 2001. *Economic Reform and Social Sector Development*. New Delhi: SAGE Publications.

32.   Prabhu, *Economic Reform and Social Sector Development*.

33.   Mehrotra and Jolly argue that there are two ways in which GNP influences human development attainments: one, by GNP's contribution, defined by levels of public spending; and two, by a focus on poverty alleviation programmes. The same level of GNP can bring about varying levels of advancements in human development, depending on the nature and distribution across different institutions. For details, see Mehrotra, S. and Jolly, R., eds. 1997. *Development with a Human Face: Experiences in Social Achievement and Economic Growth*. Oxford: Clarendon Press.

34.   Jolly, R. 1997. 'Profiles in Success: Reasons for Hope and Priorities for Action', in *Development with a Human Face: Experiences in Social Achievement and Economic Growth*, ed. S. Mehrotra and R. Jolly. Oxford: Clarendon Press.

35.   Jolly, 'Human Development and Neo-Liberalism'.

36.   Drèze, J. and Sen, A., eds. 1991. *The Political Economy of Hunger: Volume 1: Entitlement and Well-Being*. Oxford: Clarendon Press.

37.   Prabhu, *Economic Reform and Social Sector Development*.

38.   Datta-Chaudhuri, M. 1990. 'Market Failure and Government Failure'. *Journal of Economic Perspectives* 4 (3): 25–39.

39.   Governance includes having effective policy regimes that facilitate private action and social action. Integration would require strengthened coherence of policy to reap synergies of interrelated policies. Universality implies being applicable to all people without discrimination and ensuring democratic participation and rule of law. For details, see Chen, I. and Desai, M. 1997. 'Paths to Social Development: Lessons from Case Studies', in *Development with a Human Face: Experiences in Social Achievement and Economic Growth*, ed. S. Mehrotra and R. Jolly, pp. 421–34. Oxford: Clarendon Press.

40.   For a critique on the indicators used for MDGs, see Unterhalter, E. 2013. *Education Targets, Indicators and a Post–2015 Development Agenda: Education for All, the MDGs, and Human Development*. Cambridge, MA: School of Public Health, Harvard University.

41.   Fukuda-Parr, S., Yamin, A.E., and Greenstein, J. 2014. 'The Power of Numbers: A Critical Review of MDG Targets for Human Development and Human Rights'. *Journal of Human Development and Capabilities* 15 (2–3): 105–17; Nayyar, D. 2013. 'The Millennium Development Goals Beyond 2015: Old Frameworks and New Constructs'. *Journal of Human Development and Capabilities* 14 (3): 371–92; Saith, A. 2006. 'From Universal Values to Millennium Development Goals: Lost in Translation'. *Development and Change* 37 (6): 1167–99.

42.   Prabhu, K.S. 2016. 'Human Development: Changing Interpretations and Implications'. *Indian Journal of Economics* 96 (383): 769–82.

43.   United Nations. 2015. *Millennium Development Goal 8: Taking Stock of the Global Partnership for Development*. New York: MDG Gap Task Force Report.

44.   DSD (Department of Social Development), SASSA (South African Social Security Agency), and UNICEF, *The South African Child Support Grant Impact Assessment*.

45.   El Arifeen, S., Christou, A., Reichenbach, L., Osman, F.A., Azad, K., Islam, K.S., Ahmed, F., Perry, H.B., and Peters, D.H, 'Community-Based Approaches and Partnerships'.

46.   Government of West Bengal. 2013. Accessible at www.wbhealth.gov.in/nrhm/pdf/provision%20of%20%20free%20supply%20of%20vital%20and%20essential%20drugs.pdf; 10 March 2018.

47.   Glassman, A. and Temin, M. 2016. *Millions Saved: New Cases of Proven Success in Global Health*. Washington, DC: Brookings Institution Press.

48.   Lasonen, Kemppainen, and Raheem, 'Education and Training in Ethiopia'.

49.   Erulkar, A.S. and Muthengi, E. 2009. 'Evaluation of Berhane Hewan: A Program to Delay Child Marriage in Rural Ethiopia'. *International Perspectives on Sexual and Reproductive Health* 35 (1): 6–14.

50.   Kenya Agricultural Research Institute, *Policy Responses to Food Crisis in Kenya*.

51.   For more information, see http://www.kudumbashree.org; 10 October 2017.

52.   Praghabal Das, K.V. 'Women's Empowerment through Financial Inclusion'.

53.   ILO. 2018. *World Employment and Social Outlook: Trends 2018*. Geneva. Accessible at http://www.ilo.org/global/research/global-reports/weso/2018/WCMS_615594/lang--en/index.htm; 31 March 2018.

54.   OECD–ILO. 2017. *Better Use of Skills in the Workplace: Why It Matters for Productivity and Local Jobs*. Paris. doi: http://dx.doi.org/10.1787/9789264281394-en.

55.   Vij, N. 2011. 'Collaborative Governance'.

56.   For details, see Carswell, G. and Neve, G. 2014. 'MGNREGA in Tamil Nadu: A Story of Success and Transformation?'. *Journal of Agrarian Change* 14 (4): 564–85.

57.   For details, see Lakha, S. 2011. *Accountability from Below: The Experience of MGNREGA in Rajasthan (India)*. Asia Research Institute, National University of Singapore.

58.   For details, see Pankaj, A.K. 2008. 'Processes, Institutions and Mechanisms of Implementation of NREGA: Impact Assessment of Bihar and Jharkhand'. New Delhi: Ministry of Rural Development, GOI and UNDP, Institute for Human Development.

59.   For example, an impact assessment of convergence with horticulture and animal husbandry departments by the Sikkim State Rural Management and Development Department, see TISS. 2018. *A Report on Impact Assessment*

on *Technical Quality and Economic Assessment of the Category B (Individual Assets for Vulnerable Sections) Under MGNREGA and Their Impact on Improving the Income Status of the Beneficiary Household.*

60. Kattumuri, R. 2011. 'Food Security and the Targeted Public Distribution System in India', Asia Research Centre Working Paper 38, LSE, London.

61. For more details, see Soares, F.V., Ribas, R.P., and Osório, R.G., 'Evaluating the Impact of Brazil's Bolsa Familia'.

62. For more details, see Chioda, L., De Mello, J.M., and Soares, R.R. 2016. 'Spillovers from Conditional Cash Transfer Programs: Bolsa Família and Crime in Urban Brazil'. *Economics of Education Review* 54 (c): 306–20.

63. Rougier, E., Combarnous, F., and Faure, Y.A. 2017. 'The "Local Economy" Effect of Social Transfers: A Municipality-Level Analysis of the Local Growth Impact of the Bolsa Familia Programme in the Brazilian Nordeste'. Cahiers du GREThA 2017–09, Groupe de Recherche en Economie Théorique et Appliquée, Université de Bordeaux Avenue Léon Duguit, Pessac.

64. Fellizar, F.M.D.R., Geges, D.B., Faulmino, C., Pangilinan, M.M.Q., Ilagan, G.A.B., and Palis, C.S.J. 2017. 'Perceived Effects of Conditional Cash Transfer Program among Beneficiaries in Selected Barangays in Pila, Laguna, Philippines'. *Ritsumeikan Journal of Asia Pacific Studies* 35: 70–88.

65. For more details, see Prabhu, K.S. 2009. 'Conditional Cash Transfer Schemes for Alleviating Human Poverty: Relevance for India', Discussion Paper, UNDP India, New Delhi.

66. UNDP. 2012. *Botswana National Policy on HIV and AIDS*. Government of Botswana.

67. For more, see Mongkhonvanit, P.T. and Hanvoravongchai, P. 2017. 'The Impacts of Universalisation: A Case Study on Thailand's Social Protection and Universal Health Coverage', in *Towards Universal Health Care in Emerging Economies*, ed. I. Yi, pp. 119–54. London: Palgrave Macmillan; Paek, S.C., Meemon, N., and Wan, T.H., 'Thailand's Universal Coverage Scheme and Its Impact on Health Seeking Behavior'.

68. IMF and World Economic and Financial Surveys. 2017. Fiscal Monitor: Tackling Inequality, Washington, DC.

69. For more, see Bardhan, P. 2017. 'Universal Basic Income—Its Special Case for India'. *Indian Journal of Human Development* 11 (2): 141–3.

70. Mundle, S. and Sikdar, S. 2017. 'Budget Subsidies of the Central Government and 14 Major Indian States: 1987–88 and 2011–12'. *Ideas for India*. Accessible at http://ideasforindia.in/article.aspx?article_id=1776.

71. For a comparison analysis of the pros and cons of UBI, see Ministry of Finance, Government of India. 2018. 'Chapter 09', in *Economic Survey 2016–17*. New Delhi: Ministry of Finance, Government of India.

72. Saith, A. 2017. 'Universal Basic Income in India? A Conversation Without the Mahatma'. *Indian Journal of Human Development* 11 (2): 167–72. doi: 10.1177/0973703017733872.

73. Sen, A. 1997. 'Maximization and the Act of Choice'. *Econometrica* 65 (4): 745–79.

74. Ortiz, I. and Cummins, M. 2013. 'The Age of Austerity: a Review of Public Expenditures and Adjustment Measures in 181 Countries', Working Paper March 2013, Initiative for Policy Dialogue and the South Centre, New York.

75. Roy and Heuty define fiscal space more broadly as 'concrete policy actions for enhancing domestic resource mobilization, and the reforms necessary to secure the enabling governance, institutional and economic environment for these policy actions to be effective', and, therefore, call for a hierarchical approach to defining fiscal space in respect of the level of per capita income of countries. See Roy, R. and Heuty, A. 2005. 'Investing in Development: the Millennium Development Goals, Aid and Sustainable Capital Accumulation'. *Journal of International Affairs* 58 (2): 161–75.

76. Roy, R. 2015. 'Room at the Top: An Overview of Fiscal Space, Fiscal Policy, and Inclusive Growth in Developing Asia', in *Fiscal Policy, Inequality, and Inclusive Growth in Asia*, ed. D. Park, S-H. Lee and M. Lee, pp. 26–68. New York: Routledge.

7 Deprivation and Distribution

The inability of economic growth to reduce extreme poverty is evident from the numerous missed targets for the past five decades. The World Bank had set a target of eradicating absolute poverty in low- and middle-income countries by the year 2000. Despite this, in 2012, nearly 315 million people were extremely poor (living on less than USD 1.25 per day) and 2.78 billion were moderately poor (USD 1.25–USD 4.00 per day). Moreover, a vulnerable population of about 4.73 billion people (USD 4.00–USD 10.00 per day) was identified.[1] Poverty is no longer concentrated in low-income countries but exists in the middle-income countries as well.[2]

Debate about inequality and poverty has largely focused on income and economic deprivation, while there has been a complete neglect of the social and cultural aspects. In sharp contrast, the human development approach provides a multidimensional lens to poverty and inequality, as deprivations go beyond the income dimension and encompass non-income aspects such as basic capabilities. Further, poverty emanates from socio-cultural differentiations, and the resultant horizontal and vertical inequalities worsen capability losses. Policies to address such inequalities, therefore, need to pay heed to the differing initial conditions and recognize ethnicity, class, gender, and spatial concerns.

There is a wide chasm in the definition and understanding of poverty between the developing and the developed world. The developed countries largely relied on the monetary approach to define poverty, and were concerned with issues of social exclusion. Among the developing countries, there has been a natural affinity towards a more a participatory approach to define poverty.

Traditionally, classical economists had viewed poverty through a broader lens. Adam Smith emphasized that social achievements like being able to appear in public without shame and being able to take part in the life of the community are essential.[3] Marx attributed the existence of poverty to the very existence of capitalism. For him, poverty never existed naturally, but was artificially produced by the advent of mass production.[4] Subsequently, Lewis argued that the existence of poverty is due to a culture of poverty whereby low income households with relatively poor entitlements, human capital, and poor living conditions have a low self image due to their abjectness.[5] Subjective well-being literature further elaborates on some of these issues, and points out that continued exclusion, alienation, and discrimination of individuals on the basis of class, caste, religion, and ethnicity could stem from a range of processes that owe their origin to the individual, society, and even market-driven forces.

The inequality debate, on the other hand, has largely been concerned with problems related to distribution. In recent evaluations of rising income inequalities, Milanovic,[6] Wade,[7] and Piketty[8] have provided interesting evidence on growth and inequality in general and distribution outcomes in particular.[9] They have pointed to the inability of growth to provide equitable outcomes and opportunities for all. Further, Sen points out that 'an increasingly common tendency in public economics—to say that we should concentrate on removing poverty whereas inequality a quite different matter'.[10]

The separation of the poverty and inequality debates has only trivialized the larger question of the role of distribution in the growth process. As we have stated in Chapter 6 of this volume, redistribution is crucial in order to reduce deprivation and enhance equity. This chapter argues that the analysis of poverty and inequality cannot be conducted in independent silos as they have numerous interconnections, and that the importance of distribution needs to be highlighted as an integral part of ensuring equity and justice in development.

Capabilities are determinants of functionings and beings in the society. Initial capabilities like health, bodily integrity, education, and other such aspects of life are socially determined and restricted by an individual's social positioning.[11] Therefore, as Sen emphasized, even deprivation and inequalities need to be assessed on the basis of the people's capabilities.[12]

This chapter puts forth the viewpoint that poverty emanates from socio-cultural differentiations, and that the resultant horizontal and vertical inequalities could cause capability losses. The following section, 7.1, presents conventional perspectives on poverty and inequality with a discussion on global poverty measures. Section 7.2 elaborates on the global estimations of poverty–inequality traps. The following section, 7.3, examines the existing linkages in human development, poverty, and inequality, with a particular focus on the capabilities approach. Section 7.4 examines the various multidimensional indices of poverty and inequality. Section 7.5 dwells on aspects of discrimination, deprivation, and the concerns of voicelessness elaborated through the understanding of feminization of poverty. Section 7.6 continues the discussion by focusing on social exclusion, while highlighting the linkages between horizontal inequalities and capabilities. Section 7.7 provides an understanding of spatial issues and poverty. Concluding remarks follow.

7.1 CONVENTIONAL PERSPECTIVE ON POVERTY AND INEQUALITY

Poverty and inequality have been perceived as perpetuation of deprivation and multiple forms of disparities across various moral philosophies. In the eighteenth and nineteenth centuries, political economists considered inequality to be at the core of poverty and social harmony. Smith declared: 'Wherever there is great property, there is great inequality'. He further argued that for every rich person, there are at least five hundred poor who are 'driven by want and prompted by envy'. [13]

The traditional, unidimensional perspective explained poverty and inequality based purely on income dimensions, and anticipated their automatic reduction with rising GDP levels. However, asset, wealth, education, health, and social and gender relations have also emerged as dimensions that cause deprivation and disparities. As Thomas Paine commented, the inter-linkages between poverty and inequality-related dimensions of development have contradictions of simultaneous 'splendid appearances' and 'extreme wretchedness'. [14]

The conceptual understanding of poverty has undergone substantial change since the debate effectively came into focus in Rowntree's famous poverty studies of York in 1899 and Booth's studies in London in 1887. [15] The shift in understanding of poverty from an absolute concept towards one that also includes relative deprivation has led to questions of identifying *who is poor*, distinguishing the poor from the non-poor, and also deriving unique *poverty lines* that would help count the number of poor. While discussing this characteristic feature of poverty, Sen stated that the concept requires us to first identify 'who should be the focus of our concern'.[16] He believed that the 'focus of the concept of poverty has to be on the well-being of the poor as such, no matter what influences affect their well-being vis-à-vis the non-poor'.[17]

Unidimensional Approach

The monetary approach is one of the earliest and most commonly used frameworks to assess the extent of poverty. Based on the works of Rowntree and Booth, poverty is identified as a shortfall in consumption (or income) from some poverty line that is valuated at market prices. Dominated by positivist methodologies, the key assumption of this approach is that if there exist appropriately devised tools, then uniform monetary metrics that can take into account all the relevant heterogeneity across individuals and their situations can be derived.

However, the validity of the monetary approach depends on defining well-being, which is measured in terms of utility. Utility, in turn, is derived from either income or consumption expenditure, and poverty is then measured as a shortfall from a poverty line defined in terms of income or consumption expenditure. This distinguishes the poor from the non-poor, the assumption being that there is an inherent discontinuity between the two groups.

Over the years, the monetary approach has influenced the concept and measurement of poverty and inequality and has systematically helped the process of individual estimation and overall aggregation. This continues to be the dominant framework even in contemporary times because of the ease of estimation and the ability to evaluate change over a period of time. This framework has guided the orientation of estimating poverty at the national and international levels. In order to overcome the limitation posed by differing income/consumption expenditure levels chosen for cut-off points to identify the poor that make international comparisons difficult, efforts have been made to arrive at a unified poverty line estimated globally. Box 7.1 presents the debates on the global poverty line measure.

BOX 7.1   Overview of Global Poverty Estimates

Most countries have evolved methods to reasonably estimate local poverty lines, largely using monetarist methods. Ravallion, Datt, and Walle[18] measured the magnitude and severity of absolute poverty across thirty-three developing countries and clustered together their poverty lines to arrive at international poverty lines. International poverty line estimates have always been expressed in US dollars. However, for the purpose of measuring poverty, the line is converted into local currencies through purchasing power parity (PPP) exchange rates. The estimates, based on the poverty line of the poorest countries, indicated that about one in five persons lived in poverty. When the poverty line is more generous, estimates indicate that globally one in three persons lives below the poverty line.

Since 1990, the World Bank has published comprehensive estimates of extreme poverty using USD 1 a day parameter, which are now widely accepted by the international community. Subsequently, poverty lines were updated to USD 1.08 per day in 2001 and USD 1.25 per day in 2005. This norm was adopted to monitor progress against the MDG of reducing extreme poverty in low- and middle-income countries.

The World Bank's work has been ground-breaking, but critics point out that its estimates are flawed. Gordon[19] argues that the World Bank's poverty line of USD 1 a day is meaningless, as it does not capture whether a household with an income below that threshold has sufficient money to live decently. Similarly, there is no clarity whether revision of international poverty lines represents comparative levels of basic standards or merely a revision for time. Gordon argues in favour of lower income thresholds and for using a budget standards approach to measurement, as statistics should measure adequacy and not arbitrary thresholds. A budget standard is a specified basket of goods and services which, when priced, can represent a particular standard of living. It has been argued that the World Bank's poverty line appears arbitrary, indicating that the calculations underpinning it are not sufficiently anchored to specific human requirements The bias in the Bank's calculations may be substantial. and therefore the extent of global poverty may well be understated.

Source: Chen, S. and Ravallion, M. 2012. *An Update to the World Bank's Estimates of Consumption Poverty in the Developing World*. Washington, DC: World Bank; Gordon, D. 2002. 'The International Measurement of Poverty and Anti-Poverty Policies', in *World Poverty: New Policies to Defeat Old Enemies*, ed. P. Townsend and D. Gordon, pp. 53–80. Bristol: The Policy Press; Ravallion, M., Datt, G., and Walle, D.V. 1991. 'Quantifying Absolute Poverty in the Developing World'. *Review of Income and Wealth* 37 (4): 345–61; Reddy, S.G. and Pogge, T. 2010. 'How Not to Count the Poor', in *Debates on the Measurement of Global Poverty*, ed. S. Anand, P. Segal and J.E. Stiglitz, pp. 42–85. New York: Oxford University Press.

It has been argued that the determination of poverty and identification of the poor hinges on setting the ceiling and identifying a reference group. There is considerable agreement that, although driven by substantive methodologies such as surveys and standard-of-living assessments, these definitions are largely arbitrary in nature, rendering global comparisons rather uncertain. For example, the World Bank estimates released in 2008 identified sample countries with per capita consumption expenditure of less than USD 60 per month.[20] The concerns raised were that the reference group in the existing methodology could be contracted to a degree without any appreciable change to the mean.[21] The other point that is equally contentious is that the national poverty line methodologies do not conform to the global level estimates, and remain incomparable. A large proportion of the world's poor who may be located in other regions, regardless of the international poverty line, may fail to get accounted for (see Figures 7.1a and 7.1b).

Despite these challenges, a mere comparison of the World Bank estimations indicate a high incidence of poverty among central and southern African countries (50 per cent and above). This is followed by a large proportion of population in 20–30 per cent share; this group is dominated by India and a significant number of countries with about 0–10 per cent poor population. However, this needs to be interpreted

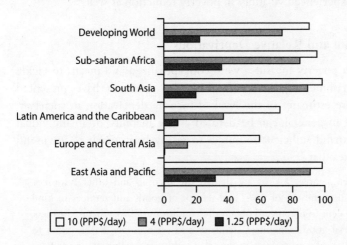

FIGURE 7.1a Head Count Ratio of Regions across Different Poverty Lines: 1990

Source: Authors' analysis from World Bank Databank. 2015. Accessible at http://databank.worldbank.org/; 22 April 2018.

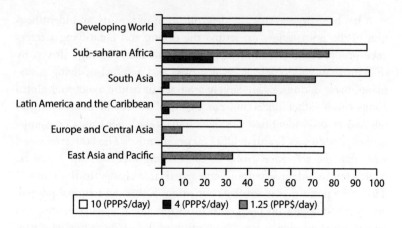

FIGURE 7.1b   Head Count Ratio of Regions across Different Poverty Lines: 2012

Source: Authors' analysis from World Bank Databank. 2015. Accessible at http://databank.worldbank.org/; 22 April 2018.

with caution: while the linear decline for select countries was linked with improvements in overall rate of economic growth (such as in China) on one hand, India, Nigeria, Bangladesh, and Brazil, on the other, experienced volatility in poverty reduction as well.[22]

Absolute and Relative Deprivations

Though poverty measures were conceptualized as a means to tackle impoverishment, poverty line estimates seem to have presented moderate estimates of the level of income deprivation in society.[23] Poverty, in general, can be defined as the inability of an individual to command sufficient resources to satisfy basic needs.[24] Townsend elaborates that

> [w]hen people lack or are denied the income and other resources, including the use of assets and receipt of goods and services in kind equivalent to income, to obtain the conditions of life—that is, the diets, material goods, amenities, standards and services—to enable them to play the roles, participate in the relationships and follow the customary behavior which is expected of them by the virtue of their membership in society, they are said to be in poverty.[25]

Sen[26] defines the poor as 'those people whose consumption standards fall short of the norms, or whose incomes lie below that (consumption norms) line'. Over the years, both social exclusion and participatory approaches to poverty have evolved to capture the presence of absolute and relative deprivation across material and non-material sources, using a variety of methodologies and tools.[27]

A lively debate between Sen and Townsend[28] on poverty not only brings out interesting perspectives on the notion of expanding the domain of poverty as encompassing both *absolute* and *relative poverty*, but also helps us look at the challenges that both economic and sociological perspectives provide in theorizing human deprivation. The sociological aspect of poverty draws on the relativist notion—poverty is viewed as a state of being worse off than others in society. The narrower connotation of absolute poverty would pertain to the number of poor who fall below the normative poverty line. A broader connotation was proposed by Sen, whereby poverty is viewed as a condition of not having some basic opportunities of material well-being or the failure to have certain minimum 'capabilities'.[29] Around the same time, Townsend advanced the concept of relative poverty, wherein two individuals with equally low levels of income experience different levels of deprivation. He points to the presence of local variations in social integration, association, and exchange, as well as in prices, especially costs of housing, in relation to facilities gained, including locational facilities, which can alter the overall vulnerabilities of individuals.

Inequalities of What?

Following Sen, we can argue that inequality reduction is crucial both intrinsically and functionally. Intrinsically, inequality reduction is an objective for its own sake as a part of ensuring justice. It is important functionally as it has an impact on the economy and is interlinked to other dimensions. In the preliminary phases, inequality indicates that something is askew with the growth process.

The conventional notion regarding inequalities is that they are inevitable as distribution to factors of production is relative to the value they earn. In the production process, the classical Kuznets hypothesis[30] of development reflects this viewpoint. The hypothesis states that economic progress (measured by per capita income) is initially accompanied by rising inequality, but that these disparities get reduced at a later stage as the benefits of development permeate more widely. When the relationship between per capita income and Gini index is plotted, it takes the shape of an inverted U. It is assumed that economic growth reduces income inequality, and that all individuals would equally benefit from poverty reduction.

Nancy Birdsall[31] distinguishes between *two* kinds of inequalities: constructive and destructive inequalities. Constructive inequality is good for the economy, wherein it 'reflects differences in individuals' responses to equal opportunities and is therefore consistent with efficient allocation of resources in an economy'. Destructive inequality underlines the 'privileges for the already rich and blocks potential for productive contributions of the currently less rich, and therefore contributes to economic inefficiency reducing rather than enhancing the potential for growth'. Birdsall adds that the inequality is more likely to be destructive in developing countries, whereas it is more likely to be constructive in the developed countries, since markets and institutions in developing countries are weak and fragile. While these distinctions help to explain the negative effects of inequalities on growth and development, the conceptual clarity provided by Birdsall does not represent any sacrosanct levels or categories.

The poverty measures in the monetary approach also use two other aspects of income distribution for assessment purposes: inequality measures like Gini index to measure spread, and *income standard* such as mean or median income to measure size. Inequality dimensions have also been extended to understand poverty better. The classical head count ratio and poverty gap measure, when estimated on the basis of distribution among the poor, indicates the severity of poverty. Further, applying income distribution methods to below the poverty line helps in estimating the depth and severity of poverty. Sen[32] presented the inequality-adjusted poverty index (also called the Sen's Index), and argues that, given the same level of poverty gap and head count among the population, a rise in the Gini index among the poor widens relative income deprivation or the severity of poverty.

Critique of Unidimensional Approaches

There are interconnections between income inequality, poverty, and income standards. For instance, there is a tendency for inequality and poverty to move together, particularly when growth in the distribution is small and its size relatively unchanged. The different and often contesting definitions of poverty open up a gamut of issues that must be addressed before arriving at the definition or measurement of poverty, as Laderchi, Saith and Stewart argue.[33] The monetary approach suffers from three major lacunae making them the Achilles' heel of estimation. *First*, it ignores several variations relating to physical features, climatic conditions, and work habits across geographical spaces. *Second*, it does not take into consideration the subjective factors relating to choices and customary consumption habits in translating the minimum dietary requirement into minimum food requirement. *Lastly*, it becomes difficult to specify the non-food minimum requirements. To address this challenge, the monetary approach assumes a certain relative share of food in total average consumption expenditure in the sample population and then estimates minimum income requirements for other household/individual expenditure. However, in practice, the actual amount spent on food varies according to habits and culture, and is a function of relative prices across regions.[34] There is a problem in providing a *universal* definition of poverty. The concerns about transferability of definitions of poverty from one society to another cannot be addressed without modification of poverty lines.

Another issue pertains to whether poverty and inequality are *objective* or *subjective measures*. Most statements about poverty suggest objectivity, implying that the measures reflect a certain reality in the poverty statistics. However, measurements are affected by value judgements, calling into question the possibility of objectivity in the measurement of poverty. Further, the monetary approach strictly focuses on the income dimension of poverty and inequality. The non-economic factors present in poverty, such as access to education, health, public spaces, and so on, are considered to be dimensions that can be automatically addressed when economic growth is achieved. The emerging core issue is to delineate the boundaries through which deprivation and poverty are seen, and how these indicators could be captured in understanding issues related to deprivation.

The basal *unit* over which poverty and inequality are measured is another issue requiring attention. In most instances, inequality and poverty measures reflect aggregate levels of deprivation and disparities.[35] For instance, poverty is defined at the level of the *household/family*, since income and consumption data cannot be disaggregated to the individual level. In the monetarist approach, well-being is an aggregate measure that does not take into account heterogeneities in the society. Therefore, intra-household allocation of resources becomes irrelevant in this approach. There are also *geographical considerations* in identifying relative poverty as regions with visible income poor tend to be identified for targeting poverty policies.

Stewart classifies inequalities into vertical and horizontal inequalities. She defines horizontal inequalities (HIs) as 'inequalities among groups of people who share a common identity'. Such inequalities have economic, social, political, and cultural status dimensions. 'Horizontal inequality differs from vertical inequality (VI) in that the latter is a measure of inequality among *individuals* or *households*, not *groups*-furthermore, measurement of VI is often confined to income or consumption'.[36] Stewart affirms that HIs often are a contributory element to conflict. This is based on the hypothesis that violent mobilization is often triggered when different kinds of perverse inequalities are faced by a group with salient identity. She adds that these inequalities can take the form of economic, social, political, or cultural inequalities.[37]

The empirical study by CRISE research programme reveals that the probability of conflict increases in places where economic and social HIs are high. Further, high HIs have strong positive relationship with incidence and intensity of conflict. In an inter-country analysis of districts in Indonesia, Stewart, Brown, and Mancini[38] estimated that changes in child mortality rates over a period of time have significant positive relationship with episodes of deadly ethno-communal violence after controlling intervening factors such as population size, ethnic diversity, and economic development. Other forms of HIs, including education, employment, landless agricultural labour, and civil service employment, also induce conflict, but their incidence is less than that of child mortality. Moreover, the income measure of VI and greater religious population did not show any significant relationship with onset of communal violence. Further, the CRISE study affirms that consistent political, economic, and social HIs are more likely to trigger conflict. In such a case, both the leaders and the population of the deprived group seek to mobilize people to fight against the perceived injustice.

7.2 GLOBAL ESTIMATES OF POVERTY–INEQUALITY TRAPS

The global poverty estimates as discussed above have played a crucial role in comparing levels achieved by countries.[39] Setting a poverty line is as central as strategizing policy to eliminate poverty.[40] Trends in global poverty have changed considerably. Based on the estimates, *three* broad categories are seen here: (*a*) global poverty levels have come down considerably since the initiation of MDGs, but over 900 million people continue to live below the poverty line; (*b*) the low-income countries have experienced low economic growth and performed badly in reducing income poverty. Among these, the proportionate population below the poverty line is as high as 47 per cent; (*c*) the lower middle-income countries with high economic growth but average MDG performance have over 530 million people below poverty line. They face problems of multidimensional poverty and inequality. On the contrary, middle-income countries seem to have progressed faster in terms of both growth rate and MDG achievements (see Table 7.1).

The complex reality of global inequality is its conjoint linkage with poverty. The inequality trap is a reflection of the lack of opportunities among generations of the poor to education, thereby restricting their participation in the labour market. In turn, this reduces their ability to make free and informed choices that enable them to realize their potential as individuals. Unequal distribution of power between the rich and the poor—between dominant and subordinate groups—helps the rich maintain control over resources. Unequal social networks imply that a poor person's social network may be geared primarily towards survival, with limited access to networks that would link him or her to better jobs and opportunities. The rich, by contrast, are bequeathed with much more economically productive social networks that maintain economic rank.

TABLE 7.1 Trends in Poverty Reduction across Countries: 1999–2012

Country Name	1999	2002	2005	2008	2010	2011	2012
Low-Income	280	295	289	298	293	287	278
	67.61	*65.51*	*59.16*	*56.23*	*52.44*	*49.99*	*47.23*
Low- and Middle-Income	1,751	1,645	1,401	1,254	1,120	983	897
	34.34	*30.96*	*24.74*	*21.87*	*19.05*	*16.52*	*14.88*
Lower-Middle-Income	862	858	771	742	661	579	522
	38.08	*35.99*	*30.79*	*28.24*	*24.4*	*21.03*	*18.68*
Upper-Middle-Income	602	499	316	241	194	147	126
	28.95	*23.3*	*14.35*	*10.69*	*8.48*	*6.38*	*5.42*
Middle-Income	1,464	1,355	1,082	977	850	719	641
	33.71	*29.94*	*23*	*20.03*	*17*	*14.22*	*12.53*
World	1,755	1,650	1,406	1,260	1,126	989	902
	29.08	*26.29*	*21.59*	*18.65*	*16.27*	*14.12*	*12.73*

Source: World Bank Databank. 2015. Accessible at http://databank.worldbank. org/; 22 April 2018.

Notes: (1) Number of poor at USD 1.90 a day (in millions)

(2) Figures in italics are poverty headcount ratios at USD 1.90 a day (per cent of population)

7.3 LINKAGES BETWEEN HUMAN DEVELOPMENT–POVERTY–INEQUALITY (HDPI)

Deprivation and unfreedoms in any society have social and economic dimensions that not only overlap but also reinforce one another. Such deprivations often lead to capability losses and hinder overall human development. With the onslaught of globalization, the proliferation of policies for inclusion of the excluded ethnic and indigenous groups may be subverted. The loss of indigenous cultures and traditional occupations poses the risk of their extinction or the peril of their being sacrificed at the altar of development. These social divisions in their severe form lay the groundwork for extreme poverty, deprivation, and conflict. It is pertinent to unravel the myriad ways through which social institutions, social norms, and social competencies direct the process through which individuals interact and integrate within a society.

The manifestation of poverty in individuals often translates into issues of well-being or its lack, encompassing multiple dimensions. The question, then, would be how to aggregate deprivation across multiple dimensions. Undoubtedly, there are problems with the method of aggregation, as it could lead to loss of information—a concern that must be tested for in the final results. There have been several other concepts and methodologies that have either extended the discourse to encapsulate the multidimensionality of deprivation, or have sought to challenge the monetarist framework.

Drawing from the framework in Chapter 2 of this volume, the process of capability deprivation can be explained through (*a*) individuals' own endowments and initial entitlements, which are heterogeneously distributed and contribute to unfreedoms of individuals with relatively low entitlements; (*b*) the further reinforcement of capability deprivation when we place the individual within the prevalent social systems, where the unfreedoms are determined by the nature of social practices, norms, and values that can constrain choices, voices, and agency. They determine the adaptive preferences that perpetuate deprivation, particularly of individuals belonging to vulnerable and marginalized groups; (*c*) inequalities in capabilities of individuals, which also shape their access to markets. The exchange entitlements of individuals with better capability sets help them access market-led opportunities, whereas those with capability deprivation are either rejected or discriminated by the markets (see Figure 7.2). Note that market imperfections are more challenging in case of labour who are employed in the unorganized sector, in precarious jobs, or are migrant labour

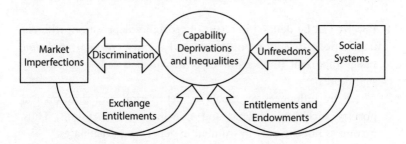

FIGURE 7.2 Explaining the Continuum of Human Development Framework for Poverty and Inequality
Source: Formulated by authors.

and/or are casually employed. There is ample literature available on discrimination in labour markets across classes, castes, and genders. This has been explained in detail by Marxist theorists, who have pointed to the vulnerabilities of the proletariat in demanding equal opportunities at the hands of the bourgeoisie. While critical reflections of capitalist hegemony are crucial and need to be included in explaining pervasive inequality, one needs to be mindful of individuals' capability deprivation, which limits their participation in market and non-market realms.

The Capabilities Approach to Poverty

The understanding of poverty is significantly advanced when it is viewed through the capability lens. It is based on the premise that capability is substantive freedoms that a person enjoys to lead the kind of life he or she has reason to value. The substantive freedoms include opportunity freedom and process freedom. The absence of the former would determine the level of poverty, whereas the latter contributes to the pattern of poverty.[41]

Sen formalized the capability approach in his book *Commodities and Capabilities*,[42] where he argued that poverty ought to be perceived more as deprivation of basic capabilities rather than as lowness of income. This approach rejects the neoclassical premise that development could be solely measured through utility maximization or by its proxy of monetary incomes, and instead, focuses on indicators that reflect freedom to live a valued life.[43] Sen's contribution to welfare and poverty analysis provided the foundation for subsequent conceptualization of capability deprivation and, further, to reconceptualize poverty as capability deprivation.[44] Sen's main arguments are as follows:

1. Poverty can be defined in terms of capability deprivation, wherein deprivations in education, health, and dignity are seen an *intrinsically* important (unlike low income, which is only *instrumentally* significant).
2. There are influences on capability deprivation, and thus, on real poverty including income and non-income dimensions. Thus, income is not the only instrument in generating capabilities.
3. There is acknowledgement of variations in the income–capability relationship across individuals, groups, and communities. Thus, the

instrumental relationship between low income and low capability is more nuanced rather than the aggregate. Further details are available in Box 7.2.

BOX 7.2   Relevant Pointers for Capability Deprivation

Poverty can be understood as one of the worst forms of human deprivation. It is manifested in people's lives in multiple ways, including lack of basic necessities of material well-being and other opportunities for living a tolerable life. The facets of identification and aggregation of capability deprivation are rooted in the premise of explaining human deprivation with a set of achieved functionings.

There is a need to identify breaks in distribution of capabilities between poor and non-poor, but these capabilities are context-dependent and arbitrary. The UNDP concept of human poverty referred to deprivation in three essential elements of human life—longevity, knowledge, and a decent standard of living. The HPI was one of the earliest attempts at multidimensional poverty measurement. The HPI, established on the lines of HDI, aimed to arrive at an aggregate measure of overall deprivation of the poor, encompassing differentiated forms of deprivations. This measure was to be a weighted index as it included multiple dimensions of deprivation, which were then reduced to a numeric value.

The commonly used strategies for reducing dimensions include factor analysis, fuzzy set applications, broader rankings or averages such as those used in HDI or HPI, or even the MPI. The Oxford Poverty and Human Development Initiative tried to gauge the value judgements in the measurement of multidimensional poverty and divided the existing approaches to poverty measurement into five categories:

1. *Non-normative approaches* that seek to bypass normative judgements altogether: Statistical and stochastic dominance are the tools used.
2. *Approaches deriving normative judgements from individual preferences*: Hedonic, most favourable and participatory approach.
3. *Approaches deriving normative judgements from behavioural preferences*: Survey-based, market prices-based estimation.
4. *Approaches basing normative judgements on the views of qualified decision makers*: Expert-based, policymaker-based perception.
5. *Approaches that seek to avoid the pitfalls of paternalism and adaptive preferences* and adaptive preferences associated with the above approaches: Shadow prices-based and rights-based approaches are the methods used.

Interestingly, the emphasis on multidimensionality in the capability framework makes aggregation issues important. Since each of the different capabilities is *intrinsically* valuable, no trade-offs between achievements can be introduced. This limits the scope of aggregation, but is desirable for political purposes and reducing manageable information.

Source: Anand, S. and Sen, A. 1997. 'Concepts of Human Development and Poverty: A Multidimensional Perspective', Human Development Papers, pp. 1–20. New York: UNDP; Foster, J. and Sen, A. 1997. 'On Economic Inequality After a Quarter Century'. Annexure to the enlarged edition, in *On Economic Inequality*, ed. A. Sen. Oxford: Clarendon Press.

Within the capability approach, poverty can be defined as failure to achieve certain minimal or basic capabilities. Basic capabilities can be defined as 'the ability to satisfy certain crucially important functionings up to certain minimally adequate levels'.[45] Income poverty often coexists with acute malnourishment, morbidity, and mortality, particularly among children and women in low-income households, resulting in capability deprivation. The ability to conceptualize and measure absolute poverty in basal capability relative deprivation would have to be based on a comparison of the characteristics of commodities and formation of differentiated functionings.

Capability Approach to Inequality

The foremost departure of the capabilities approach with respect to inequalities is in drawing the distinction between equity and equality. Equity is about understanding and providing people what they require to enjoy full and healthy lives. However, since the original position of each individual could vary, fairness and justice to achieve equity would imply greater efforts to promote those lagging behind. Equality, or equality of opportunities (as presented in the Rawlsian framework), aims to ensure that everyone gets the same things in order to enjoy full and healthy lives. In a society, there are individuals with differing functionings. They may have varying access, process, and opportunity freedoms. They could also have differing initial conditions: while some individuals may have experiences of historical alienation, there could be others facing discrimination in the present times. Thus, anticipating that equality of opportunity would help achieve equality of outcome is contentious.

The question of inequalities and the interlinkages with growth and capability expansion have frequently been debated. In the classic Tanner Lectures, Sen stated that '[t]he powerful rhetoric of "equality of man" often tends to deflect attention from these differences'.[46] Entrenched inequality may also erode social cohesion, and some types of inequalities can make it difficult to achieve even efficiency thereby, causing what is called destructive inequality.[47]

Equity entails going beyond distribution of rights and material choices, but encompasses bridging gaps in capabilities, endowments, exchange entitlements, productive opportunities, and empowerment. A focus on equity, therefore, enables tackling inequalities as a sustainable process. There are a range of extensions of the capabilities approach in explaining inequalities, presented below in Table 7.2.

TABLE 7.2 Capabilities and Equality of What?

Equality in	Characteristics	Impact on Entitlements/ Capabilities	Constraints
Diverse Humanity	External characteristics	Inherited fortunes in the natural and social environment	Natural and social milieu
	Personal	Age, gender, physical and mental health, and other capabilities	
Diversity of Foots	Material (Income–Economic)	Opportunity freedom	Household-level rather than individual-based
	Non-material (happiness, liberty, opportunities, rights, or need-fulfilments)	Availability of conversion factors	Subjectivity in interpretation
Diverse Egalitarianism	Disharmonies in scale of equality	Equality in income dimension but inequality in other non-income dimensions	Rights may not translate into capabilities due to endowment heterogeneities

(*continued*)

TABLE 7.2   (*Continued*)

Equality in	Characteristics	Impact on Entitlements/ Capabilities	Constraints
Achievement and Freedom	Transition of focal variable from entitlements to capabilities	Distinction between achievement and the freedom to achieve	Individual and collective forces
Functionings and Capability	Freedom to choose capability and functionings	Similar capabilities may yield differing functionings	Individual interpretation of capability sets

Source: Adapted from Sen, A. 1992. *Inequality Reexamined*. Oxford: Oxford University Press.

There are *five* areas to equality that are highlighted in the capabilities evaluation framework. *First*, it acknowledges diversity of humanity as the possibility of unique positions of each individual that contributes to his or her freedom and to collective freedoms. *Second*, this comparison is not confined singularly to income or economic categories, but is extended to various intrinsic freedoms that are valued by individuals. The choice of equality analysis ranges across income, wealth, happiness, and participation. *Third* is the presence of diverse egalitarianism so that while a society could have achieved equality in select variables, there could not be other inequities coexisting. It becomes convenient to believe that all the major ethical theories of social arrangements—the utilitarian, libertarian, or Rawlsian approaches—tend to evaluate equality only on a set of focal variables . The capabilities approach enables comparison of inequalities across multiple focal variables. It argues that the level and nature of inequality would differ across variables, and that an inequality measure should be amenable to such comparisons as well. The capabilities approach acknowledges linkages across multiple forms of inequities in capabilities that determine the nature of egalitarian outcomes.[48] *Fourth*, the distinction between *achievement* and *freedom to achieve* is important. For example, the reduction in education inequality is not only based on equal access to education, but also on the access and the opportunity freedom to benefit from education. Significant variations across gender, race, and class play a crucial role in enhancing the freedom to achieve education in a society. Diversity goes beyond identification of the focal variable to also include the nature of how the variable is utilized. *Fifth*, the role of moving away from material indicators like income to non-material parameters like functionings and capabilities provides a unique base for comparison. The focal variable or choice of space in terms of freedom to achieve functionings that he or she has reason to value provides a general approach to the evaluation of social arrangements. This yields a specific way of viewing the assessment of equality and inequality.

The capabilities approach to inequality broadens the framework to include material and non-material inequities. The unidimensional approach to inequalities may contribute to the reduction of income inequality, but the presence of inequalities in education, health, or nutrition could lead to rise in both inter- and intra-generational inequalities.

Distributional inequalities of power create hierarchies across groups—rich and poor, dominant and subordinate—that further strengthen groups that control resources. Additionally, in many countries, poor individuals in geographically isolated regions, and racial and ethnic minorities have less political power and less voice. The social setting of poor persons may be geared primarily towards survival, with limited access to networks that would link them to better jobs and opportunities. The rich, in contrast, have much more economically productive social networks that maintain their economic supremacy.

There are close linkages between entitlements and capabilities that determine the level of equity in a society. The demands of substantive equality may require greater attention when inequality becomes pervasive. For example, consider two girls in rural areas in the age group of 8–14 years who would like to access education. The conventional approach would view this access in physical terms, and thus, focus on improving the provision of the education services. The capability approach expands the evaluative lens to encompass capabilities of the girls and entitlements as well, and thus, evaluates the access freedom of girls to education, the constraints on health and nutritional status, and entitlements of households—elements that play a crucial role in determining opportunity freedoms too.

When thinking about equity, it is necessary to see how opportunities and barriers are not influenced only by personal circumstances and within households, but also by systems, policies, and societies. The girls not only face personal barriers to education, such as lack of ready access to transport or poor schooling infrastructure, but they also experience social barriers, which will determine their choice of continuation of education. These issues suggest that every initiative to enhance equality of opportunities need not ensure equity in outcomes.

7.4 ESTIMATION OF MULTIDIMENSIONAL OUTCOMES

As discussed in Chapter 4 of this volume, measurement of development and deprivation as multidimensional phenomena has gained momentum. This involved measuring both economic and non-economic dimensions of deprivation and inequality. HDR 1996 introduced Capability Poverty Measure (CPM)[49] in assessing deprivation in health and nutrition, reproduction, and female literacy. The measure focused exclusively on capability deprivation amongst women, with the rationale that such deprivation is high in developing countries, and that such deprivation has implications for the development of society and family. HDR 1997 made further refinements and proposed a Human Poverty Index (HPI–1), focusing specifically on developing countries. HPI–1 served as a complementary measure to income poverty by assessing the most basic dimensions of deprivation, namely, a short life, lack of basic education, and lack of access to public and private resources (HDR 1997). However, since the nature of deprivation in developed countries necessitates a separate analysis, a Human Poverty Index (HPI–2) relevant to industrialized countries was proposed in HDR 1998. The HPI–2 assesses capability deprivation in the same three dimensions of HPI–1 with an additional component of social exclusion.

Measuring Multidimensional Poverty

Yielding to the demand for a multidimensional measure of poverty that included many more aspects of deprivation, HPI was replaced by MPI, which was introduced in 2010. The distinctive characteristic of MPI was that, unlike UNDP's human development measure, it captured deprivation at the household level. Furthermore, MPI estimations are based on micro-data at the household level. This enabled the inclusion of overlapping deprivations. It was also amenable to disaggregation by dimension, region, and ethnic groups. Further, it measures not only the level of deprivation but also its intensity. The index comprises the same dimensions of the HDI, with ten indicators.[50] Each individual is assigned a deprivation score according to his or her deprivations at the household level. The maximum deprivation score is 100 per cent with each dimension equally weighted; thus, the maximum deprivation score in each dimension is 33.3 per cent. The education and health dimensions have two indicators each, so each indicator is worth half of 33.3 per cent, which is 16.7 per cent. The standard of living dimension has six indicators, so each indicator is worth one-sixth of 33.3 per cent, which amounts to 5.6 per cent.

Like the unidimensional income poverty measure, headcount ratio, H, is the proportion of the multidimensionally poor in the population:

$$H = \frac{q}{n} \tag{7.1}$$

where q is the number of people who are multidimensionally poor, and n is the total population.

The intensity of poverty, A, reflects the proportion of the weighted component indicators in which, on average, poor people are deprived. For poor households, only (deprivation score c greater than or equal to 33.3 per cent), the deprivation scores are summed and divided by the total number of poor people.

$$A = \frac{q_i c_i}{q} \tag{7.2}$$

where c_i is the deprivation score that the ith poor individual experiences. MPI is the product of H and A.

Apart from the UNDP measures on deprivation, the International Food Policy Research Institute, in 2006, proposed a GHI for 120 countries, measuring poverty using three indicators: undernourishment, child mortality, and child underweight.

Estimation of Inequalities in Human Development Outcomes

The expansion of multidimensional measurement of development and deprivation also led to demands to understand complex forms of inequalities in the realm of human development. The transition from unidimensional measures of income inequality to measurement of education- and health-related inequalities failed to capture the losses due to inequalities in human development outcomes. The IHDI adjusts the HDI for inequality in the distribution of each dimension across the population. It is based on a distribution-sensitive class of composite indices proposed by Foster, Lopez–Calva, and Szekely,[51] which draws on the Atkinson[52] family of inequality measures. It is computed as a geometric mean of inequality-adjusted dimension indices. The IHDI in its current form was inspired by a similar index produced by Mexico's national HDR. The IHDI can be adapted to compare the inequalities in different subpopulations within a country, provided that the appropriate data are available. National teams can use proxy distributions for indicators, which may be more available in their data sets.

The IHDI accounts for inequalities in HDI dimensions by discounting each dimension's average value according to its level of inequality. The IHDI equals the HDI when there is no inequality across people, but falls below the HDI as inequality rises. In this sense, the IHDI measures the level of human development when inequality is accounted for. The inequality-adjusted dimension indices are obtained from the HDI dimension indices, I_x, by multiplying them by $(1 - A_x)$, where A_x, defined by Equation 7.3, is the corresponding Atkinson measure:

$$I_x^* = (1 - Ax) \times I_x \qquad (7.3)$$

The IHDI is based on the Atkinson Index, which satisfies subgroup consistency. This ensures that improvements (or deteriorations) in the distribution of human development within only a certain group of the society imply improvements (deteriorations) in the distribution across the entire society. The IHDI is the geometric mean of the three-dimension indices adjusted for inequality.

The IHDI, Gender Inequality Index (GII),[53] and MPI represent advancement in terms of the dimensions measured as well as the methodologies used. These indices provide insights that are more useful than various unidimensional measures of development for policy advocacy. The new indices introduced in more recent HDRs are on technically firmer ground, and have included newer dimensions that are integral to the human development paradigm. They are also more technically sophisticated and follow more rigorous methodologies. In that process, however, the simplicity of the indices, which was the core strength of the earlier human development measures, has been lost, thereby restricting their reach. The trade-off between somewhat crude and yet readily computable indices verses more technically sound and rigorous measures has been a contentious issue, with movement in either direction attracting both votaries and critics.

Efforts to simplify multidimensional poverty measurement continues to be a global agenda. In 2018, Iyer and Prabhu[54] presented the Integrated Poverty Index (IPI), providing a summary measure of poverty/deprivation measure that includes the *poor* across economic, education, and health-nutrition related dimensions. Since cohorts for each of the measures are in different dimensions, the IPI enables the researchers to estimate a composite score rather than a head count based on indicator intersections. Based on similar characteristics of the HDI, the IPI is the geometric mean of normalized indices measuring deprivation in each dimension. Additionally, the authors have highlighted the importance of estimating poverty using macro data systems to facilitate periodic evaluations. The advantage of this exercise has been its easy replicability and conformity with the fundamental properties of poverty indicators.

7.5 DISCRIMINATION, DEPRIVATION, AND VOICELESSNESS: FEMINIZATION OF POVERTY

Interestingly, the interaction between capability deprivation, inequality, voicelessness, and subordination is reflected starkly in what Pearce[55] called 'feminization of poverty'. This term was used to indicate the manifestation of poverty among female-headed households and their economic repercussions. The debate on feminization of poverty draws attention to the fact that women constitute a disproportionate share in the world's poor. This is particularly evident among female-headed households.[56]

The generalized idea of *feminization of poverty* simplistically measures 'the proportion of female-headed households whose incomes fall below the poverty line'.[57] As Chant[58] points out in the present context, the usage of this term 'is often in a cursory and unsubstantiated manner and does not necessarily highlight aspects of poverty that are most relevant to women at the grassroots'. The universal validity of *feminization of poverty* is increasingly being empirically challenged.[59] However, with the focus on *human poverty*, it is essential to move away from the income aspect of feminization of poverty debate to incorporate a multidimensional measure of overall deprivations faced by women. The sociology of poverty aspires to study both poverty as an experience of men and women situated in the lowest rungs of the social ladder, as well as a situation whose existence plagues the conscience of modern societies, and that they hence seek to fight.[60] Although the causes and consequences of poverty are heavily gendered, the standard conceptualization of poverty fails to consider the gender dimension, resulting in gendered losses in policymaking.[61] The multiple deprivations faced by women are reflected in the policy discourse on poverty, where capability deprivation or capability poverty is observed to vary both in absolute and relative terms across girls and boys, and across women and men in the same household. The challenges are especially severe for those with other gender identities as they suffer not only from capability deprivation but also discrimination and social stigma. The coping mechanisms may also vary, based on the agency and empowerment of an individual. Equally crucial are relative differences in response, and impact of implementation of anti-poverty policies and programmes.[62]

Poor households resolve the internal crisis arising from poverty in multiple ways. A large burden of the solutions is shouldered by women who then become involved in various processes such as allocating greater time to care work (such as, in rural areas, collection of water and fuel, taking care of livestock, kitchen gardens, and fodder collection), engaging actively in the workforce, or taking up home-based work. It may also involve greater sacrifices from women with respect to their needs related to nutrition, food, health care, or leisure. It may also entail selectively pulling girl students out of schools and making them shoulder the responsibilities of the earning adult female. In contrast, men resolve poverty mainly by strategies such as increasing the time spent on work, enhancing debt-peonage, migration, taking up multiple jobs, or even desertion or abandonment of family.[63]

In view of the above, it is imperative to discard the *statistical purdah* that continues to obscure women's work. The inadequate methods of measuring labour or of accounting the value of women's contribution renders much of women's work invisible. It is also essential to understand the undercurrents that drive women into the workforce and the implications thereof. For example, the sixty-first round of National Sample Survey (NSS) data in India (2004–5) showed a 'revival' in women's work participation primarily driven by an increase in 'self-employment'.[64] Further analysis highlighted the sharp increase in unpaid labour by women as a sub-category of the self-employed. There was a fall in the number of female casual workers by 6 per cent, which was mirrored by a rise in the number of self-employed women that touched 61 per cent in 2004–5, within which the sub-category of unpaid women workers rose to 72.5 per cent. This rise in female labour force participation (FLFP) occurred due to jobless growth in India. Evidently, the rise in FLFP rates was mainly in the informal sector as self-employed and casual workers. It has been argued that women's contribution (particularly in homebased enterprises) as unpaid labour increases at times of distress and economic crises. In fact, the surge in female participation in the informal economy is often associated with an employment environment characterized by extraordinary insecurity and volatility.[65]

Recognition of women's agency remains central to understanding its relation to poverty. The positive role played by women in the process of development leads to their being considered *active agents of change*. Koggel[66] argues that there needs to be a distinction in promoting women well-being and women's agency. Whereas the well-being strategies are cast in the welfarist mode, with women being treated as passive recipients of measures, the agency approach perceives women to be active agents who themselves promote and achieve social and political transformations that can then better the lives of both men and women.[67]

7.6 SOCIAL EXCLUSION: LINKAGES BETWEEN CAPABILITIES AND HORIZONTAL INEQUALITIES

The term 'social exclusion' was originally used in France in 1974[68] to refer to the various categories of people who were unprotected by social insurance at the time but labelled as *social problems*. Some of the categories of exclusion identified were mentally and physically handicapped persons, suicidal people, aged invalids, abused children, substance abusers, delinquents, single parents, multi-problem households, marginal, asocial persons, among others. Within European social policy, the issue of poverty and social exclusion has been a social misfit in the larger growth paradigm.[69] Though a subject of recurrent interest, it received widespread political attention when the Lisbon Council of March 2000 adopted strategic goals and political processes, aiming to counter the risk of poverty and social exclusion. The activities of the UN agencies like ILO and the Social Summit lent further visibility to these issues. The Commission on European Communities explained social exclusion as referring to the 'inability to enjoy social rights without help, suffering from low self-esteem, inadequacy in their capacity to meet their obligations, the risk of long term relegation to the ranks of those on social benefits, and stigmatization'.[70] The European Foundation for the Improvement of Living and Working Conditions defined social exclusion as 'a process through which individuals or groups are wholly or partially excluded from full participation in the societies in which they live'.[71]

This connotation of social exclusion also reflects some of the facets of relative deprivation emphasized by Townsend in his explanation of the linkages between the unprivileged poor and society. There have been several other clarifications to the connotation as well. Le Grand[72] defined social exclusion as occurring when a person is excluded if he or she is a resident in society, but for reasons beyond his or her control, cannot participate in normal activities of citizens in that society, despite his willingness to be part of the mentioned activities. Atkinson[73] identified three characteristics of social exclusion: (*a*) *relativity*, which states that as a definition. exclusion is a relative concept (specific to the society); (*b*) *agency*, wherein the process of exclusion occurs due to the action of agents; and (*c*) *dynamics*, focusing on the relevance of future prospects and current circumstances. While Room[74] argued that social exclusion can occur with relational and dynamic aspects, and added three more factors: *multidimensionality, neighbourhood dimension* (that deficient or absent communal facilities are in question), and major *discontinuities* that are involved. Dynamic focus and emphasis on process are its distinguishing features. The study of social exclusion involves understanding of the process of becoming poor and some of the outcomes of such deprivation. It moves well beyond articulation of exclusion as an economic phenomenon, and integrates the perspective in a socio-economic and cultural framework.

Interestingly, while lowness of income can be considered to be the barometer to explain poor living conditions among groups of individuals, it may not be the only factor causing collective unfreedoms. Sen calls for the need to reposition the notion of social exclusion away from income poverty to encompass the broader Aristotelian perspective of an *impoverished life*. In doing so, he argues that social exclusion occurs through a process of alienation from economic, social, cultural, and political processes among a group of individuals as it pervades a range of social relations. In the Aristotelian understanding, social exclusion through the capabilities lens relates to the inability to interact with others elements (people and institutions) and partake in the life of the community. Collective capability failures, in turn, also tend to limit living opportunities.[75] The problem of social exclusion can thus be seen as one of capability failure. The lexicon of social exclusion helps foster hybrid forms of injustice which give rise to what Fraser[76] calls 'bivalent collectivities'. The intersectional effect of social and economic disadvantage leads to perpetuation of cultural-valuational disadvantage.[77] For example, the tendency to consider girls coming from rural or hinterland as communicating only in the regional dialect would lead to a predisposed understanding of their capabilities. Thus, exchange entitlements of women in this milieu would continue to encounter discrimination on the basis of gender and region. It is not surprising, therefore, that women often continue to face challenges in the distribution of labour, property, and other valued resources in a society.[78] The basic features of social exclusion and its indicators also throw light on the ways in which there is 'denial of equal access to opportunities imposed by certain groups of society upon others'.[79] The process through which individuals and groups are wholly or partially excluded from full participation in the society in which they live has led to embedded social relations.[80] Box 7.3 elaborates the policies and outcomes of social exclusion and socio-cultural identities in India.

Various studies globally have reported that the condition of the indigenous people is seldom at par with the rest of population in any country. Studies in Latin America by Psacharopoulos and Patrinos[81] first provided a regional assessment of the miserable living standards among the indigenous people, and found systematic evidence of socio-economic conditions that reflected levels far below the national average. They also reported strikingly lower levels of human capital formation

BOX 7.3   Socio-Cultural Identities and Social Exclusion in India:
Policies and Outcome

In India, the dynamics of poverty and inequality have been attributed to caste and the position of an individual therein. Caste stratification impedes social mobility, hindering vertical and horizontal integration. Caste-based segregation of deprivation and inequities is often manifested in the capabilities deprivation though incomplete citizenship or denial of civil rights. Further, the pervasiveness of vast socio-cultural inequalities in freedom of expression and access to rule of law and justice is perpetuated with challenges to secure political rights and means to participate in the exercise of political power. The intersectionalities of all forms of social exclusion have led to inequities in access to property, employment, and education. These denials are the key dimensions of an impoverished life.

Banerjee et al. find evidence of strong preference for in-caste marriages among middle-class Bengali arranged marriages (using the Indian Human Development Survey [IHDS] 2004–5) and 95 per cent of marriages annually are recorded as intra-caste. Guru points to a wave of *Sankritization* among Dalit households with respect to their dietary habits, dressing, and other social interactions. However, the initial level of resource constraints that determine the social relations for most excluded communities fail to translate the mere copying of the upper-caste practices into functionings, and do not expand the capability set of individuals. The process of improving capabilities requires that multiple deprivations that SCs have inherited due to the exclusions of the past be addressed, and protection against exclusion and discrimination in the present be provided, encouraging their effective participation in the social, economic, and political processes of the country.

Among the minority communities, the Muslims emerge as the main religious group. The Sachar Committee Report identified Muslims as standing on the fringe of the socio-economic life of the country. It stressed on the low proportion of representation of Muslims in education and employment. It is also necessary to view the condition of the Muslim population with regard to other indicators of deprivation that reiterate their marginalized status, such as health, economic participation, and political representation. Their status further depreciates in light of caste-like structures within the minority religions like the Muslims and the Christians. The lower castes among these religions often bear the maximum brunt of the lack of affirmative action that is extended to their Hindu counterparts, and leave them further deprived.

Thorat and Newman highlight discrimination against low caste and Muslim job applicants in India. Even in jobs with high qualifications, the

SCs and STs are given lower wages than their upper-caste colleagues, despite positive changes vis-à-vis traditional caste rules of discrimination in labour, land, inputs, and consumer goods markets. These social groups also indicate the worst human development indicators with respect to education, health, political participation, and so on. De Haan analyses the incidence of poverty in India among the STs across the indicators of education, health, landlessness and employment status, wage relations, and other indicators including access to agricultural inputs and consumer goods, to find that they come worse off in most spheres.[82] Furthermore, it is interesting to note that these wide disparities persist despite the array of affirmative measures taken by the Government of India. De Haan asserts the need for rescuing the term *exclusion* from the poverty debate so as to correct the deeply entrenched social, economic, and political inequalities.

Source: Banerjee, A., Duflo, E., Ghatak, M., and Lafortune, J. 2013. 'Marry for What? Caste and Mate Selection in Modern India'. *American Economic Journal: Microeconomics* 5 (2): 33–72; De Haan, A. 2011. 'Rescuing Exclusion from the Poverty Debate: Group Disparities and Social Transformation in India', Working Paper No. 517, International Institute of Social Studies, The Hague; Guru, G. 2009. 'Food as a Metaphor for Cultural Hierarchies', Working Paper 10/2009, Center for the Advanced Study of India, University of Pennsylvania, Philadelphia; Sachar Committee. 2006. *Social, Economic and Education Status of the Muslim Community in India*. New Delhi: Government of India; Thorat, S. and Newman, K. 2010. *Blocked by Caste—Economic Discrimination in Modern India*. New Delhi: Oxford University Press.

in terms of education and health, persistence of poverty, and social exclusion through labour market discrimination and limited access to public education and health.[83] De Alba[84] also discusses the indigenous versus non-indigenous divide in Mexico, and finds that the former are poorer than the latter, particularly in the rural areas of Mexico.

In conclusion, it is pertinent to understand that social institutions and social competencies are critically important in determining individual capabilities. It can be argued that the societal institutions along with social norms affect choices that people make within any capability set. It cannot be ignored that social institutions and competencies impact the functioning of all other institutions (state and the market). For instance, the District Level Household and Facility Surveys over the years have indicated that most developing countries are struggling with home-based child deliveries for several decades.

Lack of acceptance of modern forms of medicines in local communities and lack of perceived benefits of local forms of treatment continue to lead to underutilization of public services. The interaction between formation of capabilities and social institutions affects the power and influence of particular groups over policy choices at all levels, thereby affecting the level of distribution of capabilities.[85] Poverty, thus, seems to emanate from a string of socio-cultural relations in society between unequal individuals.

7.7 POVERTY AND SPATIALITY

Most of the empirical studies that set out to explain spatial inequality in a country end up with differing levels of public infrastructure as a key explanatory factor. Spatial inequality is defined as inequality in economic and social indicators of well-being spread across varied geographical units within a country. Spatial inequality is a dimension of equality, but it has added significance when spatial and regional divisions and differences align with political and ethnic tensions and undermine social and political stability, further deepening spatial inequality.

Inter- and intra-regional disparities are crucial in explaining varying capability deprivations. Inter-regional inequality may be of concern in itself, especially when the geographical regions align with political, ethnic, language, or religious divisions. Every country has its *poor areas*—places where the incidence of poverty is unusually high by national standards. The questions that arise are: why are certain regions poorer than others? Why are there sharp regional disparities?

A *spatial poverty trap* can be said to exist if the household living in the better endowed area sees its standard of living rising over time, while the others in that same area see no difference in their standard. In a panel analysis of China over 1985–90, Jalan and Ravallion[86] estimated spatial inequalities in poorer rural areas. They found that more remote inland provinces have shared rather little in the country's overall economic growth since reforms began. They found that areas in southern rural China were so poor that the consumption levels of some households living in them have been falling even while identical households living in better off areas enjoy rising consumption levels. In an analysis for Bangladesh, Ravallion and Wodon[87] found that poor areas are not poor only because households with readily observable attributes that foster poverty are geographically concentrated. There appear to be sizeable spatial differences in the terms of given household characteristics. Further, also present are independent spatial differences that are not accountable to any obvious differences in observable household characteristics, or to differences in the returns to those characteristics. The specific characteristics of these spaces affect mobility of population groups too.

Capability poverty in the inland regions is often distinct from those that are close to growth areas. The coexistence of spatial effects with social dynamics, inadequate public provisioning, and poor quality of access to growth sector continues to hinder their progress in human development. An analysis by Kundu, Mohanan, and Varghese[88] for Indian states found that spatial inequalities measured by weighted coefficient of variation (CV) was higher and was rising faster than the unweighted CV in all the years as more populous states had not improved their per capita income levels as much as the less populated states. They argued that the population effect in low-income states (such as Bihar and Uttar Pradesh) further pulls down their per capita income levels.

The impact of spatial deprivation drives migration patterns as well as access to opportunities for human progress. Some of the arguments of understanding spatial differences in human development outcomes include strong geographic effects on living standards for similar households may exist and persist over (possibly considerable) time. There may be also be limitations to policymakers as standards of living may be completely determined by mobile, non-geographic characteristics of households. However, a significant subset of these characteristics is unobserved by policymakers and is spatially auto-correlated as a result of a sorting process through migration. The case for targeting poor areas is not obvious in a setting in which there are no evident barriers to migration. The discussion on free migration as capability has been central to this perspective. Certain geographies can affect formation of capabilities. Regions with high poverty rates would also have spatial concentration of households with poor characteristics. Through free migration, households seek to expand freedoms in regions with positive geographies.

Publicly provided goods in this setting, such as rural roads, generate non-negligible gains in improving living standards. The prospects for growth in poor areas will then depend on the ability of governments and community organizations to overcome the tendency for under-investment that such geographic externalities are likely to generate. Aspects of geographic capital relevant to consumption growth embrace both private and publicly provided goods and services. Private invest-ments in agriculture, for example, entail external benefits within an area, as do *mixed* goods (involving both private and public provision-ing) such as health care.

Often, discussions on relative poverty and horizontal inequalities shift away from the field of economics to a broader domain of under-standing of the social dimensions of poverty. One of the earliest works in this field is found in the works of George Simmel, where he tried to analyse, within the social framework in 1907, what makes a person poor. For him, 'it is the assistance a person publicly receives from the community that determines her status of 'impoverished'.[89] At the same time, openness to the outside world, which is well recognized as a long-term source of efficiency and growth, can also lead to spatial concentration. There is a case for policy initiatives to ensure a more spatially equitable allocation of infrastructure and public services, and for policies to ensure freer migration.

Lastly, drawing from the poor-areas programme, it can be argued that some areas have both seasonal and chronic poverty. *Lifetime poverty*—how many individuals remain chronically poor throughout their lives—is important to recognize, and the *time horizon* for the identification needs to be defined. Chronic poverty is measured mainly as the presence of impoverishment over a period of time and counts the number of people who have moved in and out of poverty over seasons and years. Therefore, the longer the time perspective, the less poverty will appear.

***

This chapter started with an overview of global poverty and failure of economic growth to reduce inequalities and extreme poverty. It has illustrated the presence of numerous dimensions and processes that overlap and intersect with one another to render large sections of population to be deprived and subject to high inequality. While this phenomenon has been studied and measured, parallel policies to address it in a multidimensional way are in a nascent stage. Even theorizations of poverty and inequality have occurred in silos.

A multidimensional phenomenon cannot be dealt with unidimensional policy measures such as reducing income poverty. The illustrative examples of innovative measures in the previous chapter of this volume point to the synergies among the several dimensions that are being tackled. These, in tandem with an overall redistributive ethos of governments, along with political will, are fundamentally necessary to tackle the complex phenomena of *poverty amidst inequality* and *inequality amidst poverty*.

The human development and capability approach reinforces the fact that deprivation and distributional failures occur due to individuals' own initial endowments and entitlements, market-led discrimination and social systems that perpetuate marginalization, vulnerabilities, and alienation of individuals across a range of identities. Under these circumstances, any anticipation that public policy alone would serve a tool to address all forms of maladies could be extremely far-fetched. The moral value of human development involves justice and flourishing. Hence, the process of simultaneously tackling poverty and inequality calls for strengthening human agency, empowerment, and fostering public reasoning, apart from regulating markets and implementing effective policies.

NOTES AND REFERENCES

1. World Bank. 2012. 'World Development Indicators'. Accessible at databank.worldbank.org/data/reports.aspx?source=world-development-indicators; 10 March 2018.

2. Sumner, A. 2012. 'Where Do the Poor Live?' *World Development* 40 (5): 865–77.

3. Smith, A. [1776] 1976. *An Inquiry in the Nature and Causes of the Wealth of Nations*. New York: Oxford University Press.

4. Trucker, R. 1972. *Marx-Engels Reader*. London: W.W. Norton and Company.

5. Lewis, O. 1969. 'The Culture of Poverty'. *American* 215 (4): 19–25.

6. Milanovic, B. 2016. *Global Inequality: A New Approach for the Age of Globalization*. Cambridge, Mass: Harvard University Press.

7. Wade, R.H. 2014. 'The Piketty Phenomenon and The Future of Inequality'. *Real-World Economics Review* 69 (4): 2–17.

8.   Piketty, T. 2011. 'On the Long-Run Evolution of Inheritance: France 1820–2050'. *Quarterly Journal of Economics* 126 (3): 1071–131.

9.   These perspectives consider human beings as instrumental to development. They fail to consider losses in individual well-being due to lack of resources, as well as loss of dignity and respect due to socio-economic and cultural inequalities.

10.   Sen, A. 2010. 'Adam Smith and the Contemporary World'. *Erasmus Journal for Philosophy and Economics* 3 (1): 50–67, 53.

11.   Nussbaum, M. 2011. *Creating Capabilities: The Human Development Approach.* Cambridge, MA: Harvard University Press, p. 18.

12.   Korsgaard, C.M. 1993. 'A Commentary on G.A. Cohen, "Equality of What? On Welfare, Goods and Capabilities" and Sen, A. "Capability and Well-Being"', in *The Quality of Life,* ed. M. Nussbaum and A. Sen, pp. 54–61. Oxford: Oxford University Press, p. 550.

13.   Smith, *An Inquiry in the Nature and Causes of the Wealth of Nations*, p. 550.

14.   Paine, T. 1995. 'Agrarian Justice', in *Collected Writings (Vol. 76)*, ed. E. Foner, pp. 396–413. New York: Library of America, p. 397.

15.   As early as in the nineteenth century, the pioneering efforts of Booth (1887 Study of East End London) and Rowntree (First Scientific Study of Poverty in 1902) estimated the quantum of monetary resources necessary to attain nutritional adequacy, adequate clothing, shelter, and diet, together with estimated needs for clothing and rent, with those failing to meet these standards were identified as living in *primary poverty*, as they fell below the poverty line. Since then, there have been substantive advances and acceptance of the monetary approach to poverty estimation. For details, see Booth, C. 1887. 'The Inhabitants of Tower Hamlets (School Board Division), Their Condition and Occupations'. *Journal of the Royal Statistical Society* 50: 326–40; Rowntree, B.S. 1902. *Poverty. A Study of Town Life.* London: MacMillan.

16.   Sen, A. 1981. *Poverty and Famines: An Essay on Entitlement and Deprivation.* Oxford: Oxford University Press, pp. 9–10.

17.   Sen, *Poverty and Famines.*

18.   Ravallion, Datt, and Walle, 'Quantifying Absolute Poverty in the Developing World'.

19.   Gordon, 'The International Measurement of Poverty and Anti-Poverty Policies'.

20.   Among the seventy-five countries included for purpose of the estimation were Malawi, Mali, Ethiopia, Sierra Leone, Niger, Uganda, Gambia, Rwanda, Guinea-Bissau, Tanzania, Kazakhstan, Mozambique, Chad, Nepal, and Ghana.

21.   Reddy, S.G. 2009. 'The Emperor's New Suit: Global Poverty Estimates Reappraised', UN-DESA Working Paper 79, New York.

22. Basu, K. 2013. 'Shared Prosperity and the Mitigation of Poverty: In Practice and in Precept', Policy Research Working Paper, Working Paper Series 6700, The World Bank, Washington, DC.

23. For more about unidimensional measures of poverty and inequality see Ray, D. 1998. *Development Economics*. Princeton: Princeton University Press; Sen, *Poverty and Famines: An Essay on Entitlement and Deprivation*.

24. Fields, G.S. 2002. *Distribution and Development: A New Look at the Developing World*. Cambridge, MA: MIT Press.

25. Townsend, P. 2006. *Introduction: Compendium of Best Practices in Poverty Measurement*. Rio de Janeiro: Rio Group, p. 16.

26. Sen, *Poverty and Famines*, p. 9.

27. Measurement issues related to gender, sustainability, human progress, and human development have been discussed in Chapters 4, 8, and 9, respectively.

28. For details, see Sen, A. 1987. *Commodities and Capabilities*. Oxford University Press; 1985. 'A Sociological Approach to the Measurement of Poverty: A Reply to Professor Peter Townsend'. *Oxford Economic Papers* 37 (4): 669–76; Townsend, P. 1985. 'A Sociological Approach to the Measurement of Poverty—A Rejoinder to Professor Amartya Sen'. *Oxford Economic Papers* 37 (4): 659–68.

29. Sen, 'A Sociological Approach to the Measurement of Poverty', p. 669.

30. Kuznets, S. 1955. 'Economic Growth and Income Inequality'. *American Economic Review* 49 (1): 1–28; 1963. 'Quantitative Aspects of the Economic Growth of Nations, VIII: The Distribution of Income by Size'. *Economic Development and Cultural Change* 11 (2): 1–92.

31. Birdsall, N. 2006. 'Stormy Days on an Open Field: Asymmetries in the Global Economy', WIDER Working Paper Series 031, World Institute for Development Economic Research (UNU-WIDER), Helsinki, p. 7.

32. Sen, A. 1973. *On Economic Inequality*. Oxford: Clarendon Press; 1976. 'Poverty: An Ordinal Approach to Measurement'. *Econometrica* 44 (2): 219–31.

33. Laderchi, C.R., Saith, R., and Stewart, F. 2003. 'Does It Matter That We Do Not Agree on the Definition of Poverty? A Comparison of Four Approaches'. *Oxford Development Studies* 31 (3): 243–74.

34. Sen, *Poverty and Famines*.

35. Sen, *Inequality Reexamined*.

36. Stewart, F. 2010. 'Horizontal Inequalities as a Cause of Conflict: A Review of CRISE Findings', Background Paper, World Development Report 2011, World Bank, Washington, DC, p. 6, 2.

37. Economic inequalities encompass unequal access to ownership of assets. Social HIs consist of unequal access to a range of services, such as education, health care and housing, as well as education and health status. Political HIs include unequal power among groups, distribution of political opportunities and unequal opportunities for political participation to voice their needs.

Lastly, cultural HIs are associated to disparities in the identity and status of varied groups such as language, norms and practices, customs, and religion. See Stewart, 'Horizontal Inequalities as a Cause of Conflict', pp. 1–2.

38. Stewart, F., Brown, G.K., and Mancini, L. 2005. 'Why Horizontal Inequalities Matter: Some Implications for Measurement', Working Paper 19, Centre for Research on Inequality, Human Security and Ethnicity (CRISE), University of Oxford, Oxford.

39. Since the USD 1.25 poverty line was seen as abysmally low, the global poverty line was redefined at USD 1.90 a day. The World Bank defined extreme poverty as living on less than USD 1.25 (PPP-adjusted) per person per day. It is equally pertinent to see that the trend in poverty reduction at USD 1.90 has been similar. Although over years, there have been revisions to global poverty lines (from USD 1.25 to USD 1.90), the approaches have been similar in methodology and scope.

40. Basu, K. 2015. *The Poverty Line's Battle Lines*. Accessible at http://www. eco-business.com/opinion/the-poverty-lines-battle-lines/; 10 March 2018.

41. Sen, A. 1999. *Development as Freedom*. New York: Oxford University Press, p. 87.

42. Sen, *Commodities and Capabilities*.

43. Laderchi, Saith, and Stewart, 'Does It Matter That We Do Not Agree on the Definition of Poverty?'.

44. Sen, *Development as Freedom*, pp. 87–8.

45. Capability poverty could include a number of functionings/deprivations that include inadequacy of clothing, lack of nourishment and shelter, avoidance of preventable morbidity, and so on. It also captures complex social deprivations such as not being able to take part in the life of the community and public life. For details, see Sen, A. 1993. 'Capability and Well-Being', in *The Quality of Life*, ed. M. Nussbaum and A. Sen, pp. 30–53. Oxford: Clarendon Press, p. 34.

46. Sen, 'Equality for What?', pp. 215–16.

47. Sen, *Development as Freedom*.

48. As explained in Annexure A in this volume, it is argued that the capabilities approach sensitizes the analysis to encompass multidimensional inequalities. The libertarian approach of Robert Nozick emphasized the transfer of liberties by completely rejecting the demands of equality of end states—for example, equal entitlements for income or happiness.

49. CPM measures deprivation using three indicators: (*a*) percentage of underweight children under age five; (*b*) percentage of births unattended by trained health personnel; and (*c*) female illiteracy.

50. These are health (child mortality, child malnourishment), education (school attendance—minimum of years 1–8—and years of

schooling—absence of any household member who has completed five years of schooling), and standard of living (lack of access to safe drinking water, sanitation, electricity, cooking fuel, type of flooring, and assets). For details, see Alkire, S. and Santos, M.E. 2010. 'Acute Multidimensional Poverty: A New Index for Developing Countries', Background Paper No. 2010/11, Human Development Report Office, UNDP, New York; Dotter, C. and Klasen, S. 2014. 'The Multidimensional Poverty Index: Achievements, Conceptual and Empirical Issues', Human Development Report Office Occasional Papers, UNDP, New York; Kovacevic, M. and Calderon, M. 2014. 'UNDP's Multidimensional Poverty Index: 2014 Specifications', Human Development Report Office Occasional Paper, UNDP, New York.

51. Foster, J.E., López–Calva, L.F., and Szekely, M. 2005. 'Measuring the Distribution of Human Development: Methodology and an Application to Mexico'. *Journal of Human Development* 6 (1): 5–25.

52. Atkinson, A.B. 1970. 'On the Measurement of Inequality'. *Journal of Economic Theory* 2 (3): 244–63.

53. Details on GII, Gender Equity Index (GEI,) and Social Institutions and Gender Index (SIGI) are in Chapter 8 of this volume.

54. Iyer, S.S. and Prabhu, K.S. 2018. 'Economic Growth and Integrated Poverty Index: An Estimate Using Macro-Level Aggregates at Subnational Levels in India'. *Indian Journal of Human Development* 11 (3): 289–312.

55. Pearce, D. 1978. 'The Feminization of Poverty: Women, Work, and Welfare'. *Urban and Social Change* Review 11 (1–2): 28–36.

56. Pearce, 'The Feminization of Poverty'.

57. Fukuda-Parr, S. 1999. 'What Does Feminization of Poverty Mean? It Isn't Just Lack of Income'. *Feminist Economics* 5 (2): 99–103, 99.

58. Chant, S. 2006. 'Re-Visiting the "Feminisation of Poverty" and the UNDP Gender Indices: What Case for a Gendered Poverty Index?', Working Paper Issue 18, Gender Institute, London School of Economics, London, p. 211.

59. Cagatay, N. 1998. 'Gender and Poverty', UNDP Working Paper Series WP5, Social Development and Poverty Elimination Division, UNDP, New York.

60. New economic geographers have emphasized that there are powerful forces of agglomeration that tend to lead to a concentration of economic activity, magnifying natural geographical advantages that a region may enjoy. Thus, spatial agglomeration brings the benefits of returns to scale, and hence helps efficiency and growth. For details, see Paugam, S. 2009. 'What Forms Does Poverty Take in European Societies at the Beginning of the Twenty-First Century?', in *Between the Social and the Spatial Exploring the Multiple Dimensions of Poverty and Social Exclusion*, ed. K. De Boyser, C. Dewilde, D. Dierckx, and J. Friedrichs, pp. 3–19. Farnham: Ashgate Publishing.

61. For more, see Benería, L. and Bisnath, S. 1996. *Gender and Poverty: An Analysis for Action*. New York: UNDP.

62. For more, see Sen, G. 2008. 'Poverty as a Gendered Experience: The Policy Implications'. *Poverty in Focus* 13: 6–7.

63. Sen, 'Poverty as a Gendered Experience'.

64. National Sample Survey Organisation (NSSO). 2005. 'India— Employment and Unemployment July 2004–June 2005', NSS 61st Round, Ministry of Statistics and Programme Implementation, New Delhi.

65. Mazumdar, I. and Neetha, N. 2011. 'Gender Dimensions: Employment Trends in India, 1993–94 to 2009–10'. *Economic and Political Weekly* 46 (43): 118–26.

66. Koggel, C.M. 2013. 'A Critical Analysis of Recent Work on Empowerment: Implications for Gender'. *Journal of Global Ethics* 9 (3): 263–75.

67. Koggel, 'A Critical Analysis of Recent Work on Empowerment', p. 183.

68. Historically, René Lenoir, as Secrétaire D'etat a L'action Sociale of the French Government, who wrote about it a quarter of a century ago, is given credit of authorship of the expression. For details, see Sen, A. 2000. 'Social Exclusion: Concept, Application, and Scrutiny', Social Development Papers No. 1, Office of the Environment and Social Development, Asian Development Bank, Manila.

69. Rodgers, G., Gore, C., and Figueiredo, J.B., eds. 1995. 'Social Exclusion: Rhetoric Reality Responses'. Contribution to the World Summit for Social Development, International Institute for Labour Studies, International Labour Organization, Geneva.

70. Commission of the European Communities. 1992. 'Towards a Europe of Solidarity: Intensifying the Fight Against Social Exclusion'. *Fostering Integration* COM (92) 542 Final, Brussels, 23 December, p. 10.

71. European Foundation for the Improvement of Living and Working Conditions. 1995. *Public Welfare Services and Social Exclusion: The Development of Consumer-Oriented Initiatives in the European Union*. Dublin: European Foundation for the Improvement of Living and Working Conditions.

72. Le Grand, J. 2003. 'Individual Choice and Social Exclusion', CASE paper 75, Centre for Analysis of Social Exclusion, London School of Economics, London.

73. Atkinson, T. 1998, 'Social Exclusion, Poverty and Unemployment', CASE paper 4, in *Exclusion, Employment and Opportunity*, ed. A.B. Atkinson and J. Hills, pp. 1–20, London: Centre for Analysis of Social Exclusion, London School of Economics and Political Science.

74. Room, G.J. 1999. 'Social Exclusion, Solidarity and the Challenge of Globalization'. *International Journal of Social Welfare* 8 (3): 166–74.

75. Sen, *Development as Freedom*.

76. Fraser, N. 1997. 'From Redistribution to Recognition? Dilemmas of Justice in a "Post Socialist" Age', in *Justice Interruptus: Reflections of Post Socialist Condition*, ed. N. Fraser, pp. 68–149. New York: Routledge.

77. Fraser, 'From Redistribution to Recognition?'.

78. Kabeer, N. 2000. 'Social Exclusion, Poverty and Discrimination: Towards and Analytical Framework'. *IDS Bulletin* 31 (4): 83–97.

79. Thorat, S. 2008. 'Labour Market Discrimination: Concept, Forms and Remedies in the Indian Situation'. *The Indian Journal of Labour Economics* 51 (1): 31–52.

80. Thorat and Newman, *Blocked by Caste*.

81. Psacharopoulos, G. and Patrinos, H.A., eds. 1994. *Indigenous Peoples and Poverty in Latin America: An Empirical Analysis.* Washington, DC: World Bank.

82. The NSS Survey 2004–5 has shown that the average level of consumption for the *adivasi*s (tribals) stands at 70 per cent of the total average. This figure was lower for the adivasis than any other national group from the mid-1990s to mid-2005.

83. Hall, G., Layton, H.M., and Shapiro, J. 2006. 'Introduction: The Indigenous Peoples' Decade in Latin America', in *Indigenous Peoples, Poverty and Human Development in Latin America*, ed. G. Hall and H.A. Patrinos. pp. 40–66, New York: Palgrave Macmillan.

84. De Alba, I.G.G. 2010. 'Poverty in Mexico from an Ethnic Perspective'. *Journal of Human Development and Capabilities* 11 (3): 449–65.

85. For details, see Paugam, S. 2012. 'Rereads of Raymond Aron, Disillusions of Progress (1969)'. *Sociology* 3 (4): 413–20; Stewart, F. 2013. 'Capabilities and Human Development: Beyond the Individual—The Critical Role of Social Institutions and Social Competencies', Occasional Paper 2013/03, UNDP, New York.

86. Jalan, J. and Ravallion, M. 2001. 'Household Income Dynamics in Rural China', UNU-WIDER Discussion Paper 2002/10, United Nations University World Institute for Development Economics, Helsinki.

87. Ravallion, M. and Wodon, Q. 1997. *Banking on the Poor? Branch Placement and Non-Farm Rural Development in Bangladesh.* Washington, DC: World Bank.

88. Kundu, A., Mohanan, P.C., and Varghese, K. 2013. *Spatial and Social Inequalities in Human Development: India in the Global Context.* New Delhi: UNDP.

89. Paugam, 'Rereads of Raymond Aron', p. 4.

8   Gender and Human Development

Women's marginalization and vulnerabilities continue to remain key constituents within the human development debate. There are critical gaps in the formation of basic capabilities across men and women in society, which need substantive focus as the processes that occur are markedly different from one another. Gender-based differences in human development outcomes are not only due to differences in access and opportunity freedoms, but also on account of differences in endowments and entitlements. The real concerns about women's human development achievements are regarding capability deprivation and inequalities in access to labour markets, access to social opportunities, political participation, and access to social protection.

We argue that entitlement transfers through state policy alone will not be able to resolve the issue as capability losses also impinge on women's freedom in making choices. The human development approach helps to capture a range of complexities concerning the role of women in development. The intersectionalities that engulf women's choices are rooted within the larger question of gender-based equity, justice, and freedom. Numerous struggles and movements have provided greater clarity about the notion of gender. They have also led to recognition of space for people with all gender identities (not just women and men) to interact without any form of bias in exercising choices and utilizing opportunities to lead a life they have reason to value.[1] Further, there is a need to distinguish between gender equality and gender equity. Gender equity encompasses equality in access to capabilities and entitlements for men and women, at the same time being sensitive to the historical and contemporary disadvantages that women face in a society. For example, it could be assumed that rise in education levels would automatically lead to improvements in labour force participation rates, but in the case of women, this may not always be so. Numerous socio-cultural norms tend to override women's decision to participate in the labour market.[2]

The Women in Development[3] (WID) school of thought argued that women's rights need to be addressed in both economic and political spheres. Its efforts were towards integrating women within the development paradigm by addressing issues of equality of rights,[4] establishment of *women-only* projects and organizations, and addressing the efficiency based *practical* rather than *strategic* needs[5] and interests of women.[6] Next, the Women and Development (WAD) school provided a critique of the capitalist relations between patriarchy and development. Their arguments, rooted in neo-Marxist feminism, extends the dependency theory to point out that women have always been a part of the development process, and that their inclusion is not a sudden occurrence.[7] Placing women's agency at the core, the WAD approach sought to underline the structural basis of exploitation based on differences in gender, class, and nations. Since WID and WAD shared a static conceptualization of women as a homogenous undifferentiated group whose condition was predetermined by their sex, there was a need to reincorporate distinctions by placing a value on gender needs and interests in both strategic and practical terms. In recognition of the fact that the organization of kinship and family relations is a central aspect of the gendered structures of constraints faced in most societies, the Gender and Development (GAD) paradigm came into being. It represented the intersectional analysis between gender and other dimensions of identity like social class, race, ethnicity, and sexual identities, and emerged as a conceptual framework in the early 1980s. This approach emphasized that policies and initiatives could modify socially constructed gender roles and relations by addressing strategic gender needs and interests. Thus, GAD focused on the examination of not only gender relations and sexual division of labour, but also sexual division of responsibility.

Over the years, women's movements have contributed to repositioning the archaic notions and presumptions of development that laid bare women's invisibility in society. Sen's contributions have been particularly significant in this regard. His focus on women's marginal status in society draws from the notion of 'adaptive preferences'—preferences that adjust to women's *second-class status*.[8] From the outset, he refrained from explaining categories of capabilities, fundamentally because there are different ways in which individuals may be located in the state of poverty, abjectness, and vulnerability. For Sen, the presence of vast numbers of missing women due to sex-selective birth controls, as well as lack of livelihood opportunities, are *equal concerns* that indicate losses in primary capabilities. Indeed, in *Poverty and Famines*, while discussing the presence of hunger and starvation, he eloquently points to instances when women tend to place themselves in a subordinate position while consuming food items. While proteins are fed to male members, women often forgo basic calorific intakes, sodium, and nutritional components of staple food.[9] This is a classic enunciation of how gender inequalities in ensuring food entitlements continue to be a practice among a number of households, especially in the developing countries. Therefore, the average progress on the poverty front, measured by the utilitarian construction, may estimate an overall reduction in hunger, but women may continue to be a larger constituent of the malnourished and undernourished component in society. Nussbaum considers these and similar constraints that women face as the cause of capability failure.[10]

Moreover, the prevalent public budgeting fails to take into account the full economic benefits of women's development and gender equality for multiple reasons.[11] In realization of the importance of gender equality and empowerment in development, several governments have used gender budgeting in fiscal policy and administration as an important tool to achieve gender mainstreaming. It is argued that gender-budgeting leads to a focus on women–related issues, and in general to positive externalities that need to be factored in when budget decisions are made. For example, investment in girls' and women's education can entail private gains for the education of girls, improve health and education levels of children, and also lead to a reduction in fertility rates, thereby leading to a positive impact on economic growth. The multiple benefits that such education can yield can be used as an argument to secure higher allocations in the budget.

The birth of the human development paradigm coincided with global debates on inclusion of women in development and the policies that enable such inclusion. The approach examined more deeply the complexities that revolve around the phenomena of missing women, feminization of poverty, and women's agency. It also provided newer tools of assessment such as GEM (Gender Empowerment Measure), GDI, and GII. It argued that the persistence of sharp gender inequalities in many forms is a reflection of the lower status that is attributed to women globally.

Against this background, this chapter explores the capability approach as an alternative framework for inclusion of gender into the development discourse. It explains concepts such as choice, opportunities, and freedoms that have eluded women for centuries and raises the following questions: how do various pathways of human development explain gendered outcomes? What are the interlinkages between capabilities and entitlements processes in explaining the varying outcomes for women and men in a society? We examine some of these questions in detail.

The next section (8.1) elaborates the role of capabilities in securing gender outcomes. Section 8.2 focuses on gendered entitlements and how they facilitate women's well-being. In Section 8.3, an elaborate discussion on the four core processes of human development—equity, sustainability, productivity, and empowerment—are investigated through a gender lens to unravel their implications for gender and human development. Section 8.4 reflects on the role of equality in securing gender inclusive human development outcomes and processes. Section 8.5 deliberates on the questions of agency and empowerment, while Section 8.6 looks at the debates around women's productivity by inculcating newer methodologies like time-use statistics. This is followed by Section 8.7, where women's contribution to environment and sustainability is explored. Section 8.8 argues in favour of newer methodologies to understand the gendered process of development. The concluding section summarizes the debate.

8.1 GENDER AND CAPABILITIES

Examining women's capabilities brings in a range of interesting explanations. Capabilities assume importance since they help to look at 'what people are actually able to do and to be—in a way informed by an intuitive idea of a life that is worthy of dignity of the human being ... for each and every person'.[12] The process of expansion of human capabilities is relatively distinct across females and males in terms access freedom, opportunity freedom, and achieved functionings. Globally, women have faced greater disadvantages than men, both at the societal and household levels. Drèze and Sen point out that economic development does not automatically result in improving conditions for women.[13] In relative terms, women are subjected to restrictive choices and lower freedoms, and often face greater vulnerabilities than men in elementary fields like education, nutrition, health, and survival.[14] The capability losses that women endure translate into a loss of valuable *functionings* for them. Some of the issues that determine outcomes for women are the forms of inheritance laws and social systems, prevailing gender norms, and socio-economic hierarchies.

A perusal of the level of human development indices of females and males indicates that in most countries female outcomes are relatively lower than those of their male counterparts (see Figure 8.1 comparing gender-wise HDI and aggregate GDI scores).

We find that the gap between the HDIs of females and males is relatively lower in the low- and the middle-income group. This is also directly reflected in the low GDI scores.[15] Needless to say, the presence of low GDI reflects the presence of greater unfreedoms among females as compared to males. The higher HDI countries have GDI values

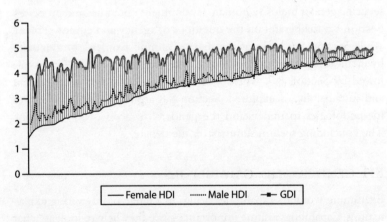

FIGURE 8.1   Comparing Gender-Wise HDI and Aggregate GDI Scores (2015)
Source: Estimated by authors from Human Development Data (1990–2015). Accessible at hdr.undp.org/en/data; 22 April 2018.

closer to 1, indicating greater gender equality. But these aggregates do not capture the processes that define human development outcomes for female and males.

The debate between Sen and Nussbaum provides clarity on this issue. They point to three aspects that require attention: (*a*) comparison of functionings and capabilities as intrinsic dimensions of progress, helping to understand gender inequality far better than the means to achieve them; (*b*) addressing constraints to achieve threshold-level capabilities of life, liberties, and opportunities that are crucial to secure gender equality; and (*c*) unjust background conditions that marginalize women in society and lead to greater gender inequality.[16]

While Sen did not provide a detailed list of capabilities to capture women's development, Nussbaum extends her list with threshold-level capability to encompass basic political principles of life, liberties, and opportunities that each individual deserves and secures.[17] She argues that in the absence of the threshold levels of each capability, human functioning is not available to individuals. Individual threshold-level capabilities of women emerge as a *necessary condition* to prevent any kind of subsequent vulnerabilities, deprivations, and/or unfreedoms in achieving primary capabilities.

Drawing from the Rawlsian theory of justice, Sen extended the notion to elaborate on the idea of basic capabilities: the ability of a person to do certain basic things.[18] For Sen, there are certain capabilities like health, education, political and civil liberties, and choice of occupation invariably are the primary/basic capabilities.[19] Interestingly, this progression seems to be occurring through the simultaneous interplay of economic, social and cultural factors that operate differentially to augment men's position in society and circumvent women's choices. Clark cautions that local values and practices often cannot be compared with one another as there are vast socio-cultural and geographical heterogeneities in the population that are shaped historically over years. Robeyns, on the other hand, looks at the differences within the genders as a manifestation of group inequalities that are also perpetrated along the lines of race, caste, or nationality. These result in inequality in achieved functionings that implies inequalities in capabilities, leading to the conclusion that women and men start at differential levels of opportunity sets in the first place.[20]

Links between basic capabilities and complex capabilities have been explained in Chapter 2 in this volume. The ability of capabilities to contribute to overall gender equality is based on the notion of collective freedom. A few components suggested in the Sen's 1980 debate, 'Equality for What?', demystify this process and point out that gender equality is, in fact, extremely dynamic in nature, as societies are at unequal starting points and there is vast heterogeneity amongst population groups.

8.2 STRENGTHENING GENDERED ENTITLEMENTS

To understand the role of entitlements for women's well-being, the prevailing nature of gender relations and importance of social milieu need to be explained. If women are seen as *agents* within the household, then equality of entitlements further contributes to equality among social arrangements or social institutions. Household-level gender relations in entitlements are a reflection of the dominant social system, and therefore, a candid representation of women's position at the household level, which determines gender equality. For example, the right to reproductive health is fundamental to women's well-being. Pre-birth elimination of girls and sex determination in developing countries is in gross violation of girls' *right to life*. In patriarchal societies, these practices further subordinate women's position and reflect themselves in a secular decline in the share of women in aggregate societal positions.

Women have remained at the margins of social, political, and economic spaces for long. Societies have been divided along gender lines. Securing rights and entitlements of women to build resources for greater independence and fulfilment of women's rights needs to be located as a crucial concern within the existing structures.[21] An example of this can be found in the unequal inheritance patterns among women globally (see Table 8.1 for a South Asian example). Although most South Asian countries have accepted the idea of women holding independent property rights, including land rights, and although this acceptance is reflected in the inheritance laws of the 1950s, such laws remained largely confined to issues that affect private land alone. Even until the late 1980s, property rights did not form a part of the development discourse in distribution of land rights.

TABLE 8.1 Gender-Sensitive Entitlements in Property Rights in South Asia

Country	HDI	Inheritance Law	Source	Jurisdiction	Rights of Wives and Daughters on Intestate Succession
Afghanistan	0.468	Afghan Civil Code sections 289–342 and 1993–2267	Islamic Law (Hanafi)	All Afghans	Women sharers (as wives, sisters, grandmothers, or daughters) inherit but not equally to their male counterparts.
Bangladesh	0.558	Muslim Personal Law and Administration of Justice (Shariat) application Act of 1937	Islamic Law	Muslims	Women sharers (as wives, sisters, grandmothers, or daughters) inherit but not equally to their male counterparts.
		Hindu Inheritance (removal of disabilities) Act of 1928; Hindu law of inheritance (Amendment) Act of 1929	Hindu Dayabhaga system	Hindus	Widow receives life estate; unmarried daughter and daughters with sons inherit; married daughters with daughters and childless daughters do not.
		Succession Act of 1925	Common Law	Christians	Widow receives one-third; lineal descendants (sons and daughters) receive two-thirds divided among them.

(continued)

TABLE 8.1 (*Continued*)

Country	HDI	Inheritance Law	Source	Jurisdiction	Rights of Wives and Daughters on Intestate Succession
India	0.586	Hindu Succession Act of 1956	Hindu religion	All Hindus	Estate divided into shares: widows receive one share; sons, daughters, and mother of the deceased receive one share each; heirs of predeceased sons and daughters receive one share between them.
		Muslim Personal Law (Shariat) Application Act of 1937	Islamic Law	Muslim Community	Generally women (as wives, daughters, sisters, or grandmothers) inherit half of the share of their male counterpart.
		Indian Succession Act of 1925 (portions)	English Common Law	Christian Community	Widow receives one-third; lineal descendants (sons and daughters) receive two-thirds divided among them.
		Indian Succession Act of 1925 (portions)			
		Indian Succession Act of 1925 (portions)	Parsi Custom	Parsi Community	Widows and children (sons and daughters) inherit equal shares among them.
Nepal	0.540	Country Code of Nepal (Muluki Ain) (1963) Eleventh Amendment (2002)	Hinduism	All Nepalese	Unmarried daughters and sons inherit ancestral property equally. If daughter inherits and then marries, she must return her share of ancestral property to the heirs (brothers). Widows inherit from deceased husbands.

Pakistan	0.537	Muslim Personal Law (Shariat) Application Act of 1962 (MPLA)	Islamic Law	All Muslims (presumed to be Hanafi unless proved otherwise)	Women (as wives or daughters) shar-ers receive half as much as their male counterparts.
		Customary law (via the MPLA)	Custom	For inheritance of agricultural land	Inheritance decided by the personal law of the citizen.
Sri Lanka	0.750	Muslim Intestate Succession Ordinance No. 10 of 1931	Muslim Intestate Succession Ordinance No. 10 of 1931	Muslims in Sri Lanka, no opt out option	Women (as wives, daughters, sisters, and grandmothers) inherit but not equally to their male counterpart.
		Matrimonial rights and inheritance (Jaffna), aka Thesawalamai	Tamil custom from the Jaffna region	Tamil inhabitants of the Jaffna peninsula and Jaffna Tamils no longer residing in the Jaffna peninsula, and their property no matter where it is located; no opt-out option	Widow keeps separate property; widow receives half the property acquired during marriage, and half shared equally amongst children (sons and daughters); widow has no right to ancestral property and children (sons and daughters) inherit equally.
		Kandyan Law (1939)	Law and custom of Kandyan monarchy (ended in 1815)	All Sinhalese who can trace their lineage back to the north-central province of Kandy during the period of the Kandyan monarchy	Widows receive life estate of non-ancestral property (maintenance from ancestral property if non-ancestral is insufficient), then devolves to descendants.

(continued)

TABLE 8.1 (Continued)

Country	HDI	Inheritance Law	Source	Jurisdiction	Rights of Wives and Daughters on Intestate Succession
				Does not apply to Sinhalese without this heritage now living in the Kandyan provinces	For the descendants, inheritance of ancestral land depends on marriage type (*binna* or *diga*) and origin of ancestral land (paternal or maternal).
		Matrimonial Rights and Inheritance Ordinance	Roman–Dutch Law as adopted and interpreted by judicial decision	Sinhalese who are not Kandyan or who opt out of the Kandyan Act; and non-Muslims others when statutes and codified customary laws do not apply	Paternal ancestral land and binna (groom moves to bride's home), then daughter inherits equally with brothers and unmarried sisters.
					Paternal ancestral land and diga (bride moves to groom's home), then daughter does not inherit.
					All children inherit maternal ancestral land equally provided that mother had not married in binna on her father's property (where paternal ancestral land inheritance rules apply).
					Widow inherits one half share; one half shared among descendants (sons and daughters).

Source: Formulated by authors from Scalise, E. 2009. *Women's Inheritance Rights to Land and Property in South Asia: A Study of Afghanistan, Bangladesh, India, Nepal, Pakistan, and Sri Lanka*. Brandon: Rural Development Institute.

The distributive land reform programmes of the 1950s and 1960s in India, Pakistan, and Sri Lanka, and of the 1970s in Bangladesh, continued to be modelled upon the notion of a unitary male-headed household, with titles being granted to men alone, except in cases where there was no adult male in the household. This bias has been replicated in the resettlement schemes in Sri Lanka, even though customary inheritance systems there have been bilateral or matrilineal.[22] Women's lack of control over land in South Asia, where land is the source of both economic and social significance, translates into a weakening of their position in case of male migration, divorce, abandonment, or death.[23] However, since there is a plurality of legal arrangements in this region and customary laws often override formal legislations, the issue of protection of land rights of women and their interpretations for her well-being and agency pan out to form distinct pockets of vulnerabilities. In sum, in most developing countries even today, land rights are not extended to women and state-led policies determine the extent to which women have a voice in decision-making.

8.3 WOMEN AND PATHWAYS OF HUMAN DEVELOPMENT

This section provides a detailed evaluation of the core concepts discussed thus far within the human development framework. There are *two* constituents in the human development approach: capabilities and entitlements (as discussed in Chapter 2 of this volume). These, when applied through the four processes (also discussed in Chapter 2 of this volume) of human development (equity, sustainability, productivity, and empowerment) provide a unique understanding of how these intersections can determine differing gender outcomes, and points to the pathways that can be adopted.

The processes of expansion of human development are traced in Figure 8.2. Their intersections indicate the possibly constrained outcomes of women's capabilities and entitlements. The capability losses and unfreedoms are depicted in the darker section to represent the losses that women perceive in the course of their interface with each of these distinct categories. The pathways to gender and development are discussed in the following paragraphs.

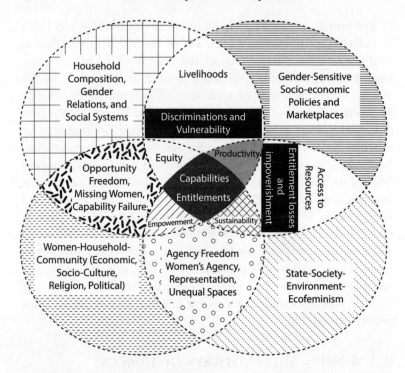

FIGURE 8.2 Constituents and Process of Women and Human Development
Source: Authors' analysis.

The application of gender-based outcomes indicates the intersectionality of each process. For example, gender equality and gender productivity contribute to building basic capabilities as well as expanding opportunities for economic participation for women. However, this expansion would be built on equity-based constraints at the household level (gender relations, social milieu, household structure, and such) and productivity-based constraints (absence of affirmative gender policies to sensitize markets for women's participation). Dominance of either of the constraints would lead to both labour market discrimination and vulnerabilities for women.

Similarly, gender productivity and sustainability processes would have to be seen in the context of rising women's labour force participation rates. Since women's contribution to environment is well recognized, policies that are sensitive to ecofeminism need to be implemented. Policies that enhance private property regimes without a women-inclusive perspective would only perpetuate entitlement losses and impoverishment. Further, the integrated understanding of sustainability and empowerment involves comprehending the institutional context of the state and society on the one hand, and women's own position in the socio-economic, cultural, and political context, on the other.

Agarwal argues that women's overt compliance with social norms does not necessarily mean that they have accepted the legitimacy of intra-household inequality—it might be a reflection of a lack of options for them. Thus, constraints to capability expansion and lack of entitlements can limit both access and opportunity freedoms thereby restricting women's agency significantly.[24] Also, the mere involvement of women in various activities that continue to subordinate them to men does not lead to formation of women's agency. Lastly, gender empowerment and gender equality are closely linked both in terms of improvements in functionings and capabilities. The formation of agency freedom and opportunity freedom is defined both by expansion of individual freedoms as well as collective freedoms. The presence of low sex ratios and capability failures among women reflects the weak link between empowerment and equality in achieving egalitarian outcomes.

8.4 ON GENDER EQUALITY

Gender inequities manifest themselves through discrimination against women in a wide-ranging gamut of socio-economic indicators. Women's secondary status in society is universal, cutting across all contexts, and can be interpreted as violence against women. Since gender relations constitute a social phenomenon, their ramifications are primarily played out in the arena of interpersonal relationships, with both social and economic implications.[25] Additionally, research by Klasen and Wink established that unequal access to health care, differential access to nutrition, comparative neglect of girls, and pre-birth elimination of girl foetuses contribute to the wider phenomena of missing women. Moreover, they called for an ethical distinction between the other causal factors and pre-birth elimination of girl foetuses.[26]

Even today, most developing countries, typically with patriarchal structures, grapple with pre-birth elimination of girls that are causing deaths (or prevention of life of girls and women) with certainty.[27] Simultaneously, the socio-cultural practices in such societies also lead to neglecting women, thereby increasing their vulnerabilities to poor health and nutritional outcomes. Neglect of girls and women further perpetuates chances of higher mortality among women and girls. Often, pre-birth elimination of girls is associated with late-term elimination of pregnancy, which poses other health hazards to women. This is perpetuated with pre-birth and post-birth interventions that inherently favour boys over girls. It is noteworthy that several countries—such as Singapore and those in East Asia (specifically, China, South Korea, and Taiwan)—that have better health care systems than others have also experienced worsening gender equality. Sen terms this phenomenon 'high-tech sexism'.[28] Box 8.1 provides further details in the issue of *missing women*.

The human development approach has expanded its analytical sphere to include questions of women's agency, at both household and societal levels.[29] One basic measure of women's agency globally is with regard to political participation of women. We can argue that improvement in women's participation translates directly into political power, and results in resource access and policy outputs. Unequal participation rates imply less representative and lowered legitimacy of governments.[30] A criticism of Sen's framework for women's agency is that it focuses largely on issues of low well-being and restricted agency of women as compared to the agenda of contemporary women's movements and gender theory.

Global evidence indicates that there is a significant *gender gap* in political participation among women and men. This is reflected in multiple dimensions like their voting behaviour, partisan attitudes and opinions, civic engagement, and non-conventional political participation. For instance, Inglehart and Norris found that there are gender gaps in the voting behaviour in the USA, Sweden, Germany, and the Netherlands. They found that this occurs due to cultural factors, differences in value orientations between women and men, and attitudes towards post-materialism and nature of women's movements.[31] Similar results were observed by Desposato and Norrander in Latin America.[32] They found that gender gap in political participation diminishes

BOX 8.1 Why Being Aware of and Sensitive to Women's Agency Matters

The concept of *missing women* has gained prominence ever since the issue was flagged by Sen as a way of assessing the cumulative impact of gender bias on mortality. This trend is particularly notable among women in large parts of Asia and North Africa, and is a result of sex bias in care as compared to the corresponding ratios in Europe, North America, and sub-Saharan Africa. The phenomenon of missing women reflects the presence of unequal access to medical care in society, where men have a relative advantage over women. The result is women tend to have lower age-specific mortality rates than men. It also occurs due to *natality inequality*.

Researchers in Europe and North America found that women tend to outnumber men to the average ratio of 1.05 in Europe and North America even though males outnumber females at birth. This stands in sharp contrast to male-to-female ratios in many parts of the developing world, for example, 0.98 in North Africa, 0.95 in West Asia, 0.95 in Bangladesh, 0.94 in China, and 0.93 in India and Pakistan. The estimation of missing women varies according to different studies. For instance, Sen used the benchmark of sex ratio of 1,022 girls per 1,000 males as observed in sub-Saharan Africa to arrive at the figure of approximately 100 million missing women globally in the early 1990s. Coale pegged this number at sixty million, based on Model Life Tables;[33] Klasen and Wink re-estimated this number at eighty-nine million in 1994 and revised it to 101 million in 2003. However, all of them estimate that the number is extremely high, making it an issue of marked concern for development in general, and for gender and development in particular.

Had gender biases for mortality remained constant in relative terms, we would expect that all regions in the world, except Republic of Korea, would experience a rising sex ratio. It is estimated that the sudden rise in the number of missing women is mainly because of the increase in total population in China, India, Pakistan, South Korea, Afghanistan, Egypt, and sub-Saharan Africa. Thus, it becomes imperative to understand from a development perspective the factors that lead to the unevenness in mortality rates for women.

Source: Coale, A.J. 1991. 'Excess Female Mortality and the Balance of the Sexes in the Population: An Estimate of the Number of "Missing Females"'. *The Population and Development Review* 17 (3): 517–23; Drèze, J. and Sen, A. 2002. *India: Development and Participation*. New Delhi: Oxford University Press; Klasen, S. 2006. 'UNDP's Gender-Related Measures: Some Conceptual Problems and Possible Solutions'. *Journal of Human Development* 7 (2): 243–74; Sen, A. 2003. 'Missing Women—Revisited: Reduction in Female Mortality Has Been Counterbalanced by Sex Selective Abortions'. *British Medical Journal* 327 (7427): 1297–8.

significantly among the educated and employed younger women. Also, representation of women in electoral politics helps reduce gender gaps and equalize participation rates. Moreover, while men tended to participate in unconventional, protest-based movements in societies with higher political freedoms, women were more active in such political movements largely in authoritarian regimes.

As per a UNESCO report, of the 775 million adults worldwide in 2010 without basic literacy skills in the sub-Saharan African countries, nearly 64 per cent were women. It has also been argued that entitlements can be strengthened by addressing gender-based literacy deficits, poverty, socio-economic status, cultural attitudes and expectations, social norms, ethnicity, and geographical locations.[34] Thus, women's empowerment can occur only when developing countries address multiple layers of disadvantages they face in society.

Reducing gender inequalities in participation results in rapid economic growth, improved labour productivity, and healthier children. As Figure 8.3 indicates clearly, a low MPI level does not necessarily imply that countries have achieved lower levels of gender inequalities. The huge variations in GII across countries situated at similar levels of MPI point to the need for specific measures to address gender inequality. General policies adopted to reduce economic and social inequalities do not automatically lead to reduction in gender inequalities. This is illustrated clearly in the case of three South Asian countries—Bangladesh, India, and Pakistan—that share a similar

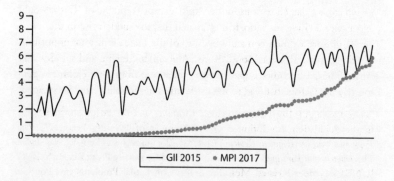

FIGURE 8.3　Comparing MPI with GII across Countries: 2015–17
Source: Estimated by authors from Human Development Data (1990–2015). Accessible at hdr.undp.org/en/data; 22 April 2018.

socio-cultural milieu and norms that govern women's freedom. Of the three countries that are at similar levels of MPI, Bangladesh has a lower GII score as compared to India and Pakistan. Gender-specific assessments of progress are, therefore, imperative. This can be facilitated only when gender-disaggregated data are periodically available.

8.5 GENDER EMPOWERMENT PATHWAYS AND WOMEN'S AGENCY

Empowerment can be broadly understood as the process of awareness and capacity building that increases participation and decision-making power. The transformational power of empowerment leads to changes in opportunity structures in an equalizing and inclusive direction.[35] Global evidence often suggests that the anti-female bias prevailing across multiple dimensions gets substantially reduced when women have greater voice, representation, and agency within the family.[36] Women's empowerment is reflected in improved democratic participation not only within the household structures, but also at the larger socio-political level.

We emphasize that women's political participation is not merely based on whether she is allowed greater access to political opportunities, but is also a reflection of associated capabilities like better education and employment opportunities, political freedoms, and availability of democratic social spaces. The agency role for women is often overshadowed by social rules and conventional perceptions about legitimacy.[37]

Agency as a conceptual construct is complex, with shades of meaning that need to be grasped before its application, particularly to women. For example, often it is presumed that the *act of participation* promotes *agency,* without the realization that the question of women's agency is inextricably tied to her role within the household. Two distinct tendencies may be identified: one of co-operation that 'adding to total availabilities'; and the other of conflict emerging from the division of 'total availabilities among the members of the household'.[38] Therefore, women's well-being at the household level tends to be associated and interconnected with that of her family. Many a times, she tends to relegate her well-being below that of her own family members.[39]

Further, the importance of differing forms of freedom across genders needs to be recognized. Kabeer asserts that the predisposed ethical frameworks determine gender relations in a society, which, in turn, influence the formation of gender-based capabilities and functionings. She suggests that whenever gender differentials in functionings exist, it is necessary to distinguish between variations that arise from (*a*) differences in preferences; and (*b*) those that embody a denial of choice.[40] While explanations for differential gender outcomes vary, there is agreement that these are due to a combination of levels of development, choices in access, opportunities freedom, and entrenchment of gender-based discrimination across economic, social, cultural, and political institutions.[41]

Further, the abilities of women and girls, such as levels of education and independent source of income through paid employment, are factors leading to their greater voice and visibility within the family. In turn, these translate into agency that influences male and female mortality rates and gender biases of survival. Murthi, Guio, and Drèze use district level estimates in India to argue that factors enhancing agency of girls and women, such as female literacy rate and women's labour force participation, contribute more positively to enhancing women's survival. In contrast, reduction of poverty, level of urbanization, availability of medical facilities, among other factors, decrease male child mortality.[42]

When affirmative policies of the state lead to greater inclusion and reduction of historical alienation, *good freedoms* ensue. *Bad freedoms* occur when capabilities and entitlements of individual are safeguarded solely through the narrow interpretation of liberties. Rights and entitlements are often invoked in defence of the right to private property. Strengthening empowerment—both as a means of social protection and as an enabler for expansion of human capabilities—has evolved both theoretically and empirically, and needs acceptance and acknowledgement as being integral to women's well-being.

8.6 GENDER–BASED EXPLANATION OF PRODUCTIVITY: LIVELIHOODS, TIME–USE, AND WOMEN

Defining women's productivity is equally a challenge as it is a complex issue, intertwined with economic and non-economic roles of women. It has been widely reported that globally women are more likely to be poorer than men. The intra-household distribution of resources, both economic and non-economic, tends to have a strong androcentric bias. There are sharp differences in the opportunity structures for men and women to access basic and threshold capabilities like nutrition, education, and survival.[43] The differentials in the basic and threshold capabilities often translate into inability of women to access higher forms of functionings and beings.

The gender-based inequalities at the household level also intersect with inequalities in the purportedly gender-neutral institutions of markets, state, and community, making gender inequality a society-wide phenomenon.[44] Therefore, gender inequalities in participation in the growth led processes must be seen as a constituent with other dimensions like poverty, health, and nutrition. They need to be tackled at the societal level as well as through explicit interventions tailored to addressing specific forms of disadvantages that women face in the course of their lives.[45]

The distribution of women across various labour markets has also varied sharply (see Figure 8.4). The labour force participation of women is closely linked with the levels of income. Women belonging to low income countries have the highest labour force participation reflecting their need rather than their choice.

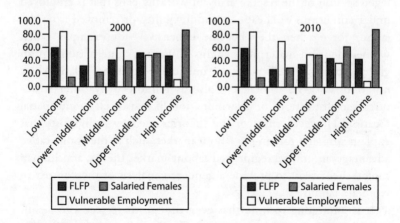

FIGURE 8.4 Income Group-Wise Women's Labour Issues of Countries across Various Income Groups (2000–10)

Source: ILO. 2018. Accessible at www.ilo.org/ilostat/faces/ilostat-home; 20 April 2018.

The SDG framework under Goal 5 recognizes the canvas of gendered capability comparisons of well-being and achievements, and draws particular attention to the need for ending social, cultural, institutional, and structural disadvantages against women to empower and incorporate them as stakeholders in the development process under Goal 5.[46] When women seek to enter labour market institutions with their weak capabilities, they invariably get located in dirty, dangerous, and demeaning jobs. A holistic social protection policy needs to address such systemic and multidimensional deprivations in capabilities for women.

Women's contribution to livelihoods has remained constrained on account of exclusionary definitions of what is considered economically productive. Indeed, women's contribution to economic development was included within the developmental agenda only through the work of Boserup in the 1970s.[47] Despite the groundbreaking contribution, the incorporation of women within the livelihood framework continues to remain on an unequal footing. For example, in agriculture, while men take charge of economic affairs, small scale and limited management of agricultural land remains in women's hands.[48]

Under capitalism, women have always formed the underprivileged section of the reserve army of working class that is employed under conditions of cheapness and flexibility, or removed from the labour force when they became expensive—for example, when women demand maternity benefits.[49] Women's integration within globalization is predicated on unequal bargaining relationships not only vis-à-vis capital, but also as reinforced by other structures and institutions of discrimination like caste, class, and spatial location. However, most of the theories used by economists that explain women's role in the labour market, such as the comparative advantage argument, segmented labour market theory, and human capital theory, fail to provide a gendered analysis of the context of women's labour.[50]

It is interesting to note that even though there seems to a shift towards greater capital-intensive production processes and flexible labour market processes, women seem to face the brunt of informalization. The rise in women's labour force participation rates in several developing countries has been associated with worsening income poverty levels. Women have largely been absorbed in casual and informal conditions of work that are often demeaning, dirty, and dangerous.[51] Global evidence points to the overwhelming representation of women in the informal workforce, particularly in parts of Africa, Latin America, and Asia. ILO data point that in countries like Uganda, Guatemala, Honduras, and Peru, more than two-thirds of women's labour is concentrated in non-agricultural informal workforce.

The human development framework engages with livelihood issues from the perspective of the interconnectedness of various kinds of freedoms available to women. It incorporates the flow of productive resources, creation of capabilities, inclusion of care and non-care work, gender mainstreaming within national income accounts, and gender budgeting. The productivity pathways of human development for women would, thus, include participating in the labour market not only in paid activities, but also in those that increase their freedom at home and while seeking health care, education, reproductive decisions, and social and political life. Productivity is not solely defined as a ratio of marginal output and wage relations, but is in fact extended to capture the non-material contributions too. The example of Deccan Development Society (see Box 8.2) reflects how enhanced of productivity also led to empowerment, agency, and sovereignty of participants over a period of time.

The question is whether, in the era of globalization, women's participation in the workforce on unequal terms represents any kind of positive freedom and agency, or whether it means an addition to the unfreedoms and vulnerabilities that women face. The negative effects affecting their agency and well-being need to be recognized and resolved through 'strategies that make use of the resources of national and international bodies to counteract disempowerment and exploitation'.[52] These vulnerabilities manifest themselves in the form of skewed time-use patterns, non-inclusion of sectors that employ women predominantly in national income statistics, and the absence of gender budgeting. For example, a World Bank study in 1992 pointed that while women's labour force participation (LFP) rate globally was barely 16 per cent as compared to 53 per cent for males, the inclusion of jobs such as collecting fuel and fodder, working on dairy, poultry, or

BOX 8.2   Integrating Productivity and Empowerment Processes

The Deccan Development Society (DDS) was established in 1983 in Medak district, a drought prone area of Andhra Pradesh, India. Through community-based institutions, DDS sought to effectively address the issue of rural livelihoods, food security, health, biodiversity, child education, local knowledge systems, and so on. It organized Dalit women into *sanghams* (grassroots associations of the poor) across seventy-five villages. The organization, with 5,000 Dalit women members, envisions the consolidation of these village groups, who would actively participate in local governance and federate them into a strong pressure lobby for women, the poor, and Dalits.

DDS facilitates women belonging to poor households to lease or purchase lands through a variety of government schemes. The *sangham* network brought over 1,000 hectares of fallow land under cultivation and produced an extra 800,000 kilograms of sorghum in the very first year of the programme. DDS was a means to encourage women producers of traditional crops access a markets. It eliminated the presence of middlemen. Further, it also enabled producers' access to fair prices.

Over the years, DDS has diversified considerably to encompass food distribution systems, watershed management, seed modification of traditional crops, and so on, transforming the lives of poor Dalit women in the state. Expansion of triadic capabilities of empowerment, sovereignty, and autonomy over local resources and socio-political institutions, has enabled women to enhance their economic productivity, as well as strengthen their voices against self-regulating market and the state.

Source: Agarwal, B. 2003. 'Gender and Land Rights Revisited: Exploring New Prospects via the State, Family and Market'. *Journal of Agrarian Change* 3 (1–2): 184–224; Kumbamu, A. 2009. 'Subaltern Strategies and Autonomous Community Building: A Critical Analysis of the Network Organisation of Sustainable Agriculture Initiatives in Andhra Pradesh'. *Community Development Journal* 44 (3): 336–50.

kitchen garden production for the family, improved this ratio to 51 per cent for females, as compared to 64 per cent for males.[53]

This brings within itself another issue of contrasting time-use and leisure patterns among women and men. Offer and Schneider[54] find that married women spent about ten hours more per week on multi-tasking as compared to men. These additional hours were spent mainly on housework and childcare as pointed by Hirway in time-use studies in India.[55] The human development and capabilities approach takes cognizance of such differentials in time-use and productivity among women and men.[56] It also incorporates the differentials among women even at different levels of capabilities, associated rights, and freedoms.

8.7 SUSTAINABILITY: ENVIRONMENT AND DIFFERENTIATED GENDERED OUTCOMES

Sustainability includes economic, environment, and social dimensions.[57] We focus on the environmental and institutional dimensions owing to their special significance for women both as contributors to sustainability and as those who bear the brunt of environmentally and institutionally unsustainable patterns.

The growing environmental movement worldwide points to a greater participation of women than men. This linkage between women and environment is attributed to the secondary status of women and the gendered division of labour within the household, where women are 'encouraged to be ecologically benign, while making males ecologically destructive'.[58] Agarwal provides a strong reflection on this issue, and states that the relationship of a community to its local forest can be characterized by multiple interests, which differ not only by socio-economic class, but also by the intersectionality of gender and class. She argues that unequal positioning of women within the economic, social, and political spheres also dictates women's contribution within the environmental sphere, where they have greater dependence on natural resources than men do. For example, the burden of procuring firewood and fodder is borne mostly by women. Thus, the gendered division among economic resources and labour determines the nature and extent of women's dependence on environmental resources over that on men.[59]

The environment challenge plays a crucial role both intrinsically and instrumentally. It has a crucial role in addressing intergenerational and intragenerational equity. In understanding women's relationship with the environment, it is necessary to combine the diverse considerations of equality and efficiency. Thus, putting women at the forefront of such a debate would entail that we understand environmental concerns from the viewpoint of unequal spaces that women occupy and the 'cooperative conflicts'[60] within these gender relations. It is pertinent in this context to understand the presence of cooperative conflicts in society.

There is scope for both co-operation and conflict between women and men, and between women of different socio-economic groups, in the pursuit of asserting rights on the environment. Thus, even though there are various benefits of co-operation, the availability of many different arrangements superimposes conflicts in a general background of cooperative gains. This must be contextualized further in the wake of the efficiency arguments along with issues of inequality and injustice. Box 8.3 provides insights from Uganda on this aspect.

BOX 8.3 Cooperative Conflicts and Household-Level Resource
Allocation in South Uganda

An experimental study on pooling and sharing of household resources in the Gisu area of Uganda in 2005, studies the evidence of gender and cooperative conflicts. It studied the sharing of monetary resources between couples in four stages: *first,* in secrecy; *second,* where each spouse was allowed to withhold a certain amount in secret while contributing the rest to a common pool; *third,* where the pool was increased by 50 per cent; and *fourth,* allocation of pooled resources.

The main finding of the study was that although, normatively, men were in control of household finances, women did better for themselves. However, in reality this was not a reflection of the normal patterns of sharing resources. While a large number of wives readily accepted that husbands controlled and allocated monetary resources within the household, husbands, on the contrary, were reluctant to admit that. The differentials in sharing and retaining resources within the household provide evidence on how well-being and ill-being preferences vary for women and men when they are seen through livelihood strategies, resource allocations, and well-being outcomes.

The absence of pooling of household resources highlights the position that households are not unitary structures but have gender-divided interests and decision-making processes. There are contrasting evidences of sacrifice of resources by women in favour of their husbands and children. The research also highlights the complexities of associating women with altruism and men with self-interest. Researchers find that marriage is a co-operation, but has larger connotations than mere material exchange among poorer communities in the Global South. There is greater evidence of a co-dependent relation, wherein men also need women to maintain gender identities and as character referees within the society.

Source: Jackson, C. 2013. 'Cooperative Conflicts and Gender Relations: Experimental Evidence from Southeast Uganda'. *Feminist Economics* 19 (4): 25–47.

Global processes of production, consumption, and distribution have increasingly become dominated by unsustainable patterns that result in overexploitation of natural resources, loss of key habitats and biodiversity, and pollution of land, seas, and atmosphere.[61] Viewed from the experiences of women from developing countries, this means additional burdens imposed on them by the indiscriminate global development trajectories that compound their everyday miseries. The development trajectory to replace women from the traditional productive activities, along with appropriation and destruction of the base of natural resources, has removed land, water, and forests beyond women's management and control. Their condition has further worsened because of indiscriminate ecological destruction of soil, water, and vegetation systems, impairing productivity and renewability. Shiva raises an alarm at this developmental model and its perpetration of violence against women. She labels this process 'maldevelopment', which reinforces the male–female inequities and inequalities. Destruction of natural habitations (forests, water, and land) has alienated societies and support systems. The violence against the environment has its reflections in the rise of violence against women. Shiva argues that women who depend on nature for drawing sustenance for themselves, their families, and their societies have been adversely affected by the rise in the control of natural resources, which affects gender relations as males continue to dominate the market economy.[62]

Research has established that women's access to environment is governed by their control over assets. Since most of women's workload is predicated on the gendered division of labour, the use and access to the common property resources (CPRs) also distinctly varies between women and men. For example, Agarwal observes that in rural South Asia, not only do women and girls have typically longer workdays than men and boys, but they also bear responsibilities that link them to the forests and village commons in particular ways. They are mostly responsible for cooking and cattle care, making them responsible for firewood and fodder collection. Similarly, men are affected by timber scarcities that are associated with making and repairing of agricultural implements and household repairs. In addition, in most poor rural households, the dependence of women on the non-wood forest products (NWFPs) as a supplementary source of income is exceedingly high, and is threatened by privatization of the commons and other 'developmental' activities that cut off women from accessing the commons. This dependence arises from lower access to paid employment opportunities and sources of incomes that might allow them to purchase this firewood and fodder, lower occupational mobility for women, lower levels of training, and wage differentials for the same level of work between women and men. Due to the greater task-specificity of the nature of work, women often find it more difficult than men to find employment during the slack season (see Box 8.4).

BOX 8.4   Vulnerability of Women to Disaster Risks and Climate Change

Globally, various studies have indicated that women and children are more likely than men to be at risk during natural disasters. These idiosyncratic risks emerge both from customary practices and societal norms that differ between genders. For instance, Alam and Collins find that during cyclones in the Asian sub-continent, women found it more difficult to escape due to factors like social norms about representation of women in terms of clothing, length of hair, and promotion of maternal values like sacrifice. Even in the case of earthquakes, female mortality was found to be significantly higher than of males in Latur, Maharashtra. It was observed by WHO that women were more likely to die because they were sleeping inside houses, while men escaped because they were sleeping in the open fields during harvest season. Young boys who were away at school and men who had out migrated for work also escaped the disaster.

Women are not only at high risk during sudden natural disasters like floods and cyclones, but they are also disproportionately affected in long drawn disasters like droughts and climate change. In Burkina Faso, the gendered roles in livelihoods activities like agriculture and care responsibilities are higher for women. Despite their significant contribution to family labour, women have less access to information regarding droughts and weather forecasts. Since these are dispensed through radios or disseminated at workshops and training which women were restricted to attend, access to information about any disasters eludes them.

Gendered asymmetry of information also impacts women's resilience and disaster preparedness. In Cambodia, the changing weather cycles have increased the seasonal variations like high temperatures, unseasonal rainfall, and frequency of floods. According to World Bank data, 75 per cent of Cambodian women are engaged in agricultural activities. Thus, women and female headed households are more likely to be burdened by crop failures and agrarian distress. Though ethnographic evidences have repeatedly pointed out that women are more likely to be affected during disasters, there is lack of gender-disaggregated disaster data to corroborate this.

Source: Alam, E. and Collins, A.E. 2010. 'Cyclone Disaster Vulnerability and Response Experiences in Coastal Bangladesh'. *Disasters* 34 (4): 931–54; Asia Foundation. 2018. *Cambodia Atlas of Gender and Environment*. Phnom Penh: The Asia Foundation; Ritchie, A., McOmber, C., Pelling, M., Audia, C., Crowley, F., and Visman, E. 2017. 'Building Resilience by Challenging Social Norms: Towards a Gender Transformative Approach in BRACED', Learning Paper #5; World Health Organization (WHO). 2002. *Gender and Health in Disasters*. Geneva: World Health Organization.

To remedy the situation, institutions engaged in sustainability need to place greater importance on achieving gender equity, as it has larger cultural and social impacts. For example, religion as an institution has characteristically been male-dominated. It has embedded biases towards women who have been attributed secondary status in almost all walks of life. Although institutions are designed to settle disputes, establish and enforce rules, and prevent abuse of power, the presence of customary laws and ideologies justifies women's subordinate position through socially embedded convictions about honour and propriety.[63] There is a strong preference for male children in several East and South Asian countries such as India, China, and the Republic of Korea. In India, the main cause is the need to pay dowry, while in China, it is because of stringent fertility regulations. In the Republic of Korea, the presence of a strong patriarchal family system, with little autonomy for women, has heightened gender discrimination against girls.[64] Although such discrimination has legal restrictions, it often finds sanction through customary practices. Another example is the practice of triple *talaq* (unilateral divorce or repudiation), which has been problematic in several Islamic countries. These countries apply a portion of religious family law instead of legislations based on liberal values.[65] However, many of these countries have sought to create sustainable and gender inclusive spaces by overriding such customary religious laws.

8.8 MEASURING GENDER AND DEVELOPMENT

Issues related to women's freedom and empowerment were in the limelight in 1995, the year when the Fourth World Conference on Women was organized in Beijing. The Beijing Declaration and

Platform for Action reiterated a global commitment to achieving equality, development, and peace for women worldwide. Box 8.5 provides the trajectory of UN conferences on discrimination against women.

For more details regarding various UN initiatives in setting the agenda and bringing global attention on sensitive issues to the forefront see Annexure D. In response to the need to measure gender-sensitive development and empowerment, the HDR 1995 presented two new indices, GDI and GEM. GDI was derived directly from the HDI using the same three dimensions and indicators relating to knowledge, long and healthy life, and command over resources. The implication was that it is the deprivation in these three components that causes gender disparities. GEM was computed from three indicators: (*a*) percentage of seats occupied by women in the national parliament; (*b*) percentage

---

BOX 8.5   Trajectory of UN Conferences on Discrimination
against Women

1. The first Conference, held in Mexico City in 1975, highlighted the 'double burden of exploitation' that underdevelopment placed on women, and called for the removal of obstacles that hindered the full integration of women into national development.
2. The second Conference, held in Copenhagen in 1980, called upon governments to initiate direct commitments to 'equal and full participation of women in economic and social development', including a more direct effort to integrate women within the national planning process.
3. The third Conference, held in Nairobi in 1985, further reoriented national governments to include women's issues to end discrimination. The assertion of this conference was that without the advancement of women, development itself was not possible.
4. The 1995 Conference produced the Beijing Declaration and Platform for Action (PfA), which recognized that a number of issues that women faced like poverty could be eradicated by addressing the structural inequalities of the process of economic growth. It culminated in the adoption of the Declaration by 189 countries, who committed to ensure equality of women with men both in law and practice.

Source: Jain, D. 2005. *Women, Development, and the UN: A Sixty-Year Quest for Equality and Justice*. Bloomberg: Indiana University Press; UN Women. n.d. *Short History of the Commission on the Status of Women.* Accessible at http://www. un.org/womenwatch/daw/CSW60YRS/CSWbriefhistory.pdf; 11 March 2018.

of women in economic decision making positions; and (*c*) women's share of income. It was specifically formulated to focus on aspects of women's participation and decision-making. It reflects the ability of women to exercise agency in economic and political realms of life. Thus, while GDI captures inequalities in expansion of capabilities, the ability to use these capabilities and take advantage of the opportunities offered is reflected in GEM.[66]

Like the HDI, the GDI measured gender inequalities in achievement in three basic dimensions of human development, but the methodology captured inequalities across male and female groups.[67] The health-related dimension measured female and male life expectancy at birth. The education dimension measured as expected years of schooling for children and mean years for adults aged twenty-five and above, for female and male groups. Lastly, command over economic resources was measured for female and male groups, based on estimated earned income. However, unlike the dimension index estimation, capturing command over economic resources involved estimations of relative female-to-male ratios. The female share of the wage bill (S_f) was calculated as follows:

$$S_f = \frac{\dfrac{w_f}{w_m} \times EA_f}{\dfrac{W_f}{W_m} \times EA_f + EA_m} \tag{8.1}$$

where W_f / W_m is the ratio of female to male wage, EA_f is the female share of the economically active population and EA_m is the male share of the economically active population.

The male share of the wage bill was calculated as:

$$S_m = 1 - S_f \tag{8.2}$$

Estimated female earned income per capita (GNI_{pcf}) is obtained from GNI_{pc} first by multiplying it by the female share of the wage bill, S_f, and then rescaling it by the female share of the population, $P_f = N_f/N$:

$$\text{GNI}_{pcf} = \text{GNI}_{pc} \cdot S_f / P_f \tag{8.3}$$

The subsequent estimation of the GDI follows the dimension estimation procedure, which provides female dimension scores and male dimension scores across income education and health capabilities. GDI is then obtained as the ratio of the female HDI and male HDI. Several scholars have pointed that the GDI is inadequate to depict the multifarious discrimination faced by women more so in developing countries. The interplay of caste, class, and gender relations is prominent among South Asian countries like India; important issues of access to fuel and water, property rights, and violence against women were completely ignored.[68]

The HDR 2010 points to three main points of criticisms levied against the twin gender-related measures.[69] Since the GDI is nothing but HDI adjusted for gender inequalities, it combines in itself both the level of achievements and disparities therein, though the common understanding is that it reflects only gender disparities. Secondly, the GEM was criticized for reflecting a strong developed country and urban elite bias as the indicators chosen are largely relevant only for these countries. Finally, the challenges of data used for the construction of the indices, particularly the income indicator, were huge: nearly three-fourths of the country estimates of relative share of women and men in income were based on imputations.

Over the years, methodologies to capture women's role in human development have advanced considerably (see Figure 8.5 for a menu of the available measures for estimating gender in human development). There have been extensive empirical works capturing quantitative, unidimensional indicators across longevity, knowledge, and income. As part of the inequality indices introduced in the twentieth anniversary report, GII was computed as a composite measure. Using three dimensions—reproductive health, employment, and labour market participation—the composite index captures loss of achievement in key dimensions due to gender inequality. The GII is able to capture the overlapping disadvantage. The GII is computed using the association-sensitive inequality measure suggested by Seth.[70] This implies that the index is based on the general mean of general means of different orders—the first aggregation is by a geometric mean across dimensions; these means, calculated separately for women and men, are then aggregated using a harmonic mean across genders. The achievement matrix is represented as:

$$\begin{pmatrix} MMR & AFR & SE_w & PR_w & LFP_w \\ 1 & 1 & SE_m & PR_m & LFP_m \end{pmatrix} \qquad (8.4)$$

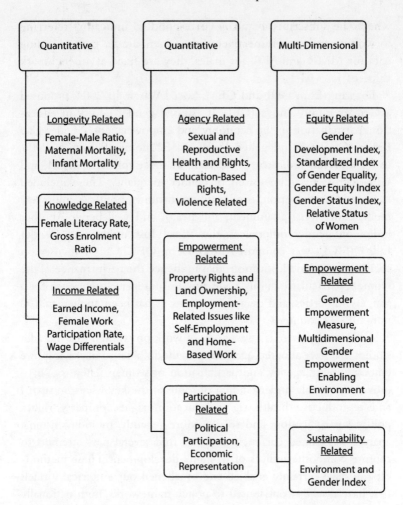

FIGURE 8.5 Menu of the Available Measures for Estimating Gender in Human Development

Source: Adapted by authors from Klasen, S. 2006. 'UNDP's Gender-Related Measures: Some Conceptual Problems and Possible Solutions', *Journal of Human Development* 7 (2): 243–74; Chant, S. 2006. 'Re-Thinking the "Feminization of Poverty" in Relation to Aggregate Gender Indices'. *Journal of Human Development* 7 (2):201–20; Cueva Beteta, H. 2006. 'What Is Missing in Measures of Women's Empowerment?'. *Journal of Human Development* 7 (2):221–41; IUCN. 2013. *The Environment and Gender Index (EGI) 2013 Pilot*. Washington, DC: IUCN.

where the subscripts *w* and *m* correspond to indicators referring to women and men respectively. Since there are no corresponding data for MMR and AFR for males, they are fixed at a benchmark value of 1.

Drawing from GDI and GEM, Social Watch, in 2004, proposed a Gender Equity Index (GEI). It assessed gender equity in education, participation in the economy, and empowerment. Gender Gap Index (GGI) was calculated by World Economic Forum in 2006, using fourteen indicators—the same as those for GDI, GEM, and GEI—across five dimensions of gender inequality. These included economic participation, economic opportunity, political empowerment, educational attainment, and health and well-being. Another index on gender differences, the Social Institutions and Gender Index (SIGI), was computed in 2009 by OECD. SIGI focuses on societal norms and institutions that influence the performance of the women, particularly family code, physical integrity, preference for a son, civil liberties, and ownership rights. It has been applied to 102 non-OECD countries.

Additionally, there is a vast body of work on women that includes studies that have adopted qualitative methodologies to mainly capture empowerment, agency, and participation of women. They, too, have provided valuable understanding of some of the key issues on sexual and reproductive health rights, education rights, property rights, political participation, and so on. More recently, multidimensional analysis has gained currency. In it, we find several new attempts to capture composite indices of women's development. These methodologies have certainly enabled and broadened our empirical models that have directly contributed to policy frameworks, both nationally and internationally.

★★★

For decades, feminist movements have challenged the ascribed roles for women and men. The tendency to view men as productive agents and household heads, while perceiving women primarily as housewives, mothers and *at-risk reproducers*,[71] severely constrained the imagination of policymakers and development practitioners, and created a chasm between economic growth and realization of social human rights.[72]

That narrow understanding of socio-economic factors also contributed to the failure to translate them into social justice perspectives.[73] The ideas of liberalism, in both political and economic spaces, have resulted in exclusion of women, particularly in the context of developing countries. The absence of accountability for women within the development paradigm was the starting point of understanding the role of WID.

The feminist movement critiqued the long-held beliefs of the monetarist approach as an insufficient indicator of measuring progress. It highlighted the hierarchies within the social order that are a result of the failure of the 'trickle down' process.[74] The human development approach reaffirmed the importance of the nature and extent of disparities in access, opportunity, and outcome freedoms of women in development. We argue that the human development approach gains considerable conceptual rigour with the contribution by Sen–Nussbaum, whose analysis increased our comprehension of the multilayered structures of capabilities. Sen–Nussbaum analysis itself has considerably enhanced understanding of the presence of these structures. However, Nussbaum's analysis has also faced criticism. Clark points out that Nussbaum's move towards a shared account of core human capabilities runs the risk of 'internal criticism' of the local values and practices by external standards, thereby setting up potential for abuse.[75] Further, it has been argued by some commentators that 'it is paternalistic for a middle class North American philosopher to determine capabilities for other cultures and societies', advocating more participatory approaches instead.[76] Robeyns, on the other hand, looks at the differences within genders as a manifestation of group inequalities that are also perpetrated along the lines of race, caste, gender, and nationality. These result in inequality in achieved functionings, implying inequalities in capabilities, and leading to the conclusion that women and men start at differential levels of opportunity sets in the first place.

The non-binding nature of gender related commitments regarding women's equality continues to persist in the MDG and SDG era. While there have been several targets that seek to ensure women's equality and improve their economic, educational and political participation, the results have been modest at best. We need to reflect on caution raised by Kabeer. Although global understanding of gender discrimination needs attention from global policy frameworks, given the vast intersectionality issues, we cannot assume that a single set of universally agreed upon priorities will be able to reduce prevailing gender-based inequities. She also argues that unless women are allowed to participate and make policy decisions for themselves, there is always an unrealized potential for improving gender dichotomies.[77] The current policy frameworks to building human development are considerably fragmented across multiple categories that seem to be perpetuating historical alienation and vulnerabilities of women in society. The various pathways of human progress, therefore, need to be placed within the understanding of principles, pillars, and processes of human development. These intertwined within capabilities and entitlements would lead to a more gender-just society.

NOTES AND REFERENCES

1.   While we recognize the need to go beyond the two-way categorization of gender, the chapter examines the role of women in greater detail than the other categories.

2.   Nussbaum stated that '[w]omen in much of the work lack support for the most central human functions, and this denial of support is frequently caused by their being women. But women ... have the potential to become capable of these human functions, given sufficient nutrition, education, and other support'. See Nussbaum, M.C. 1995. 'Human Capabilities, Female Human Beings', in *Women, Culture, and Development: A Study of Human Capabilities*, ed. M. Nussbaum and J. Glover, pp. 61–104. New York: Oxford University Press, p. 114.

3.   See Annexure B for more discussion on various schools of thought.

4.   For further elaboration see Razavi, S. and Miller, C. 1995. *From WID to GAD: Conceptual Shifts in the Women and Development Discourse* (Vol. 1). Geneva: United Nations Research Institute for Social Development.

5.   For more on this, see Kabeer, N. 1994. *Reversed Realities: Gender Hierarchies in Development Thought*. London: Verso; Moser, C.O. 1989. 'Gender Planning in the Third World: Meeting Practical and Strategic Gender Needs'. *World Development* 17 (11):1799–825.

6.   Women's interests are based not only on the basis of biological factors, but one that is shaped by gender, class, and ethnicity positions. Hence, gender sensitivity in policymaking, it was argued, required not only awareness of gender issues but also including particular requirements of women. For details, see McIlwaine, C. and Datta, K. 2003. 'From Feminising to Engendering Development'. *Gender, Place and Culture* 10 (4): 369–82. Molyneux emphasized

that strategic needs are formulated on the basis of the women's subordination to men—for example, sexual division of labour, burden of domestic labour and children, lack of political equality, and so on—which necessitate the establishment of gender equal alternatives economically, socially, and politically. For details, see Molyneux, M. 1985. 'Mobilization without Emancipation? Women's Interests, the State, and Revolution in Nicaragua'. *Feminist studies* 11 (2): 227–54.

7.   For more, see Benería, L., Berik, G., and Floro, M. 2015. *Gender, Development and Globalization: Economics As If All People Mattered.* New York: Routledge; Kabeer, *Reversed Realities: Gender Hierarchies in Development Thought;* Rathgeber, E.M. 1990. 'WID, WAD, GAD: Trends in Research and Practice'. *The Journal of Developing Areas* 24 (4): 489–502.

8.   Sen, A. 1987. 'Gender and Cooperative Conflict', Working Paper No. 18, World Institute of Development Economics Research, Helsinki.

9.   Sen, A. 1981. *Poverty and Famines: An Essay on Entitlement and Deprivation.* New Delhi: Oxford University Press.

10.   Nussbaum, 'Human Capabilities, Female Human-Beings'.

11.   Seguino, S. 2000. 'Gender Inequality and Economic Growth: A Cross-Country Analysis'. *World Development* 28 (7): 1211–30; Stotsky, M.J.G. 2016. *Gender Budgeting: Fiscal Context and Current Outcomes.* Washington, DC: International Monetary Fund.

12.   Nussbaum, M.C. 2001. *Women and Human Development: The Capabilities Approach* (Vol. 3). Cambridge: Cambridge University Press, p. 5.

13.   Drèze, J. and Sen, A.K. 1995. *Economic Development and Social Opportunities.* New Delhi: Oxford University Press; 2002. *India: Development and Participation.* New Delhi: Oxford University Press.

14.   This is equally true for people with other gender identities.

15.   Details regarding measuring of GDI are discussed in Section 8.8 of this chapter.

16.   Sen calls it the phenomenon of 'adaptive preferences'; that is, preferences that adjust to women's second-class status. For details, see Sen, 'Gender and Cooperative Conflict'.

17.   Nussbaum's list of central human capabilities includes life, bodily health, bodily integrity, senses, imagination and thoughts, emotions, practical reason, affiliation, concern for other species, play, and control over one's environment. For details, see Nussbaum, *Women and Human Development;* 2003. 'Capabilities as Fundamental Entitlements: Sen and Social Justice'. *Feminist Economics* 9 (2–3): 33–59.

18.   Sen, 'Equality of What?'

19.   The primary capabilities have been alternatively termed as elementary capabilities. For further reference, see Sen, 'Capabilities, Lists, and Public Reason'.

20. Clearly, the moral ethics of societal well-being may define gender justice as an aggregate connotation and may fail to engage with diverse socio-cultural praxis that are located at the individual levels. For details, see Clark, D.A. 2006. 'Capability Approach', in *The Elgar Companion to Development Studies*, ed. D.A. Clark, pp. 32–45. Cheltenham: Edward Elgar; Richardson, H.S. 2000. 'Some Limitations of Nussbaum's Capabilities'. *Quinnipiac College Law Review* 19 (2): 309–32; Robeyns, I. 2010. 'Gender and the Metric of Justice', in *Measuring Justice: Primary Goods and Capabilities*, ed. H. Brighouse, and I. Robeyns, pp. 215–35. Cambridge: Cambridge University Press.

21. The capability framework provides an explanation that the inequalities in capabilities and entitlements are fundamental cause for inequalities of achieved functionings among women and men in the society. For details, see Nussbaum, 'Human Capabilities, Female Human-Beings'; Robeyns, I. 2003. 'Sen's Capability Approach and Gender Inequality: Selecting Relevant Capabilities'. *Feminist Economics* 9 (2–3): 61–92.

22. Agarwal, B. 1995. *A Field of One's Own*. New Delhi: Cambridge University Press.

23. Scalise, E. 2009. *Women's Inheritance Rights to Land and Property in South Asia: A Study of Afghanistan, Bangladesh, India, Nepal, Pakistan, and Sri Lanka*. Brandon: Rural Development Institute.

24. Agarwal, B. 1997. '"Bargaining" and Gender Relations: Within and Beyond the Household'. *Feminist Economics* 3 (1): 1–51, p. 24.

25. Mukhopadhyay, M. 2003. 'Creating Citizens Who Demand Just Governance: Gender and Development in the Twenty-First Century'. *Gender and Development* 11 (3): 45–56.

26. Klasen, S. and Wink, C. 2003. '"Missing Women": Revisiting the Debate'. *Feminist Economics* 9 (2–3): 263–99, pp. 280–1.

27. See Drèze and Sen, *India: Development and Participation*.

28. Sen, 'Missing Women'.

29. For some details, see Peter, F. 2003. 'Gender and the Foundations of Social Choice: the Role of Situated Agency'. *Feminist Economics* 9 (2–3): 13–32.

30. Desposato, S. and Norrander, B. 2009. 'The Gender Gap in Latin America: Contextual and Individual Influences on Gender and Political Participation'. *British Journal of Political Science* 39 (1): 141–62.

31. Inglehart, R. and Norris, P. 2000. 'The Developmental Theory of the Gender Gap: Women's and Men's Voting Behavior in Global Perspective'. *International Political Science Review* 21 (4): 441–63.

32. Desposato and Norrander, 'The Gender Gap in Latin America'.

33. Coale, A.J. 1991. 'Excess Female Mortality and the Balance of the Sexes in the Population: An Estimate of the Number of "Missing Females"'. *The Population and Development Review* 17 (3): 517–23.

34. UNESCO reports that capabilities in most development countries are extremely gender-unequal. The presence of vast gender-based literacy deficits is found in most countries in the world (eighty-one of 146 countries), especially countries in South and West Asia. Estimates indicate that it would take another fifty-six years for these countries to tackle gender inequality. See UNESCO. 2012. *From Access to Equality: Empowering Girls and Women through Literacy and Secondary Education*. Paris: UNESCO.

35. Andersen, J. and Siim, B., eds. 2004. *The Politics of Inclusion and Empowerment: Gender, Class and Citizenship*. Basingston: Palgrave Macmillan.

36. Drèze and Sen, *India: Development and Participation*.

37. Sen, 'Gender and Cooperative Conflict'.

38. Sen, 'Gender and Cooperative Conflict'.

39. Agarwal, '"Bargaining" and Gender Relations'.

40. Kabeer, N. 1999. 'Resources, Agency, Achievements: Reflections on the Measurement of Women's Empowerment'. *Development and Change* 30 (3): 435–64.

41. For evidence of inequalities in labour market, see the case of MGNREGA in India in Khera, R. and Nayak, N. 2009. 'Women Workers and Perceptions of the National Rural Employment Guarantee Act'. *Economic and Political Weekly* 43 (44): 49–57.

42. Murthi, M., Guio, A.C., and Drèze, J. 1995. 'Mortality, Fertility, and Gender Bias in India: A District-Level Analysis'. *Population and Development Review* 21 (4): 745–82.

43. Drèze and Sen, *India: Development and Participation*.

44. Chant, S. 2006. 'Re-Visiting the "Feminisation of Poverty" and the UNDP Gender Indices: What Case for a Gendered Poverty Index?', Working Paper Issue 18, Gender Institute, London School of Economics, London.

45. Kabeer, N. 2003. *Gender Mainstreaming in Poverty Eradication and the Millennium Development Goals: A Handbook for Policy-Makers and Other Stakeholders*. London: Commonwealth Secretariat.

46. United Nations. 2017. *Progress towards Sustainable Development Goals*. Accessible at http://undocs.org/E/2017/66; 15 March 2018.

47. Boserup, E. 1970. *Woman's Role in Economic Development*. London: George Allen & Unwin.

48. Kelkar, G. and Krishnaraj, M., eds. 2013. *Women, Land and Power in Asia*. New Delhi: Routledge.

49. Hensman, R. 2011. *Workers, Unions, and Global Capitalism: Lessons from India*. New York: Columbia University Press.

50. Fine, B. 1992. *Women's Employment and the Capitalist Family: Towards a Political Economy of Gender and Labour-Markets*. London: Routledge.

51. Kabeer, N. 2007. 'Footloose Female Labour: Transnational Migration, Social Protection and Citizenship in the Asia Region', Working Paper,

IDRC–WRC, Ottawa; Standing, G. 1999. 'Global Feminization through Flexible Labor: A Theme Revisited'. *World Development* 27 (3): 583–602.

52. Koggel, C.M. 2007. 'Empowerment and the Role of Advocacy in a Globalized World'. *Ethics and Social Welfare* 1 (1): 8–21.

53. Bennett, L. 1992. *Women, Poverty, and Productivity in India.* Washington, DC: World Bank. For a more recent analysis on women's labour force participation rate, see Razavi, S.S. and Staab, S. 2008. 'The Social and Political Economy of Care: Contesting Gender and Class Inequalities'. Working Paper presented at Expert Group Meeting organized by the Division for the Advancement of Women (DAW), Geneva.

54. Offer, S. and Schneider, B. 2011. 'Revisiting the Gender Gap in Time-Use Patterns: Multitasking and Well-Being among Mothers and Fathers in Dual-Earner Families'. *American Sociological Review* 76 (6): 809–33.

55. Hirway, I. 1999, December. 'Time Use Studies: Conceptual and Methodological Issues with Reference to the Indian Time Use Survey'. Paper presented at International Seminar on Time Use Studies, Ahmedabad.

56. Also see Dixon, R.B. 1982. 'Women in Agriculture: Counting the Labor Force in Developing Countries'. *Population and Development Review* 8 (3): 539–66.

57. See Chapter 9 in this volume for a detailed discussion on the more comprehensive notion of sustainability.

58. Tindall, D.B., Davies, S., and Mauboules, C. 2003. 'Activism and Conservation Behaviour in an Environmental Movement: The Contradictory Effects of Gender'. *Society & Natural Resources* 16 (10): 909–32.

59. Agarwal, B. 2010. *Gender and Green Governance: The Political Economy of Women's Presence Within and Beyond Community Forestry.* New Delhi: Oxford University Press.

60. Co-operative conflicts have been understood by Sen as pertaining to the social arrangements regarding who does what, who consumes what, and who takes decisions, emanating from the combined problems of cooperation and conflict between the two sexes. For details, see Sen, 'Gender and Cooperative Conflict'.

61. U.N. Women. 2014. *World Survey on the Role of Women in Development A/69/156.* New York: United Nations, p. 11.

62. Shiva, V. 1995. *Staying Alive: Women, Ecology, and Survival in India.* New Delhi: Kali for Women.

63. Goetz, A.M. 2007. 'Gender Justice, Citizenship and Entitlements: Core Concepts, Central Debates and New Directions for Research', in *Gender Justice, Citizenship and Development,* ed. M. Mukhopadhyay and N. Singh, pp. 15–57. New Delhi: Zubaan.

64. Das Gupta, M., Zhenghua, J., Bohua, L., Zhenming, X., Chung, W., and Hwa-Ok, B. 2003. 'Why Is Son Preference So Persistent in East and South Asia? A Cross-Country Study of China, India and the Republic of Korea'. *The Journal of Development Studies* 40 (2): 153–87.

65. Shmueli, B. 2016. 'Tax, Don't Ban: A Comparative Look at Harmful but Legitimate Islamic Family Practices Actionable under Tort Law'. *Vanderbilt Journal of Transnational Law* 49 (4): 989–1043.

66. United Nations Development Programme (UNDP). 1995. *Human Development Report: Gender and Human Development.* New York: Human Development Report Office, UNDP.

67. UNDP. 2015. *Human Development Reports.* Accessible at http://www.hdr. undp.org/en/content/gender-development-index-gdi; 15 March 2018.

68. Prabhu, K.S., Sarker, P.C., and Radha, A. 1996. 'Gender-Related Development Index for Indian States: Methodological Issues'. *Economic and Political Weekly* 31 (43): WS72–WS79.

69. UNDP. 2010. *The Real Wealth of Nations: Pathways to Human Development.* New York: Oxford University Press.

70. Seth, S. 2009. Inequality, Interactions, and Human Development. *Journal of Human Development and Capabilities* 10 (3): 375–96.

71. As explained in Kabeer, *Reversed Realities*. For more, see Jaquette, J.S. and Staudt, K.A. 1988. 'Politics Population and Gender: A Feminist Analysis of US Population Policy in the Third World', in *The Political Interests of Gender: Developing Theory and Research with a Feminist Face,* ed. K.B. Jones and A.G. Jonasdottir, pp. 214–34. London: SAGE Publications.

72. Elson, D. 2002. 'Gender Justice, Human Rights and Neo-Liberal Economic Policies', in *Gender Justice, Development and Rights,* ed. M. Molyneux and S. Razavi, pp. 78–114. Geneva: UNRISD.

73. For further readings, see Kabeer, *Reversed Realities*; Molyneux, M. and Razavi, S., eds. 2002. *Gender Justice, Development, and Rights.* New York: Oxford University Press.

74. Kabeer, *Reversed Realities*.

75. Clark, 'Capability Approach'.

76. Stewart, F. 2001. 'Women and Human Development: The Capabilities Approach by Martha Nussbaum'. *Journal of International Development* 13 (8): 1191–2.

77. Kabeer, N. 2010. 'Women's Empowerment, Development Interventions and the Management of Information Flows'. *IDS Bulletin* 41(6): 105–13.

9 Sustainability

Securing the Present and the Future

Sustainability as a concept has lent itself to varied connotations over time. Nonetheless, its application is dominated by climate- and environment-related issues. Indeed, as far back as 1987, the World Commission on Environment and Development (WCED) Report, popularly known as the Brundtland Commission Report, defined sustainable development[1] as 'development that meets the needs of the present without compromising the ability of future generations to meet their own needs'.[2] Two essential elements of the definition were (a) the focus on human needs; and (b) integration of environmental, economic, and social dimensions of sustainability. WCED pointed to the need for paying attention to the content of growth, to make growth less material- and energy-intensive, and the impact of growth more equitable. It argued that these measures were required to be taken along with the preservation of ecological capital, improving the distribution of income, and reducing vulnerability to economic crises.

In the early 1990s, there was considerable debate around Brundtland's definition that led to three prominent reflections. Solow defined sustainability as 'whatever it takes to achieve a standard of living at least as good as our own and to look after their next generation similarly',[3] and emphasized intergenerational dimensions through sustainability of living standards, taking a broader view than that of sustainability of needs alone. Anand and Sen[4] viewed sustainable development as an issue of distributional equity and of 'sharing the capacity of well-being between present people and future people in an acceptable way—that is in a way which neither the present nor the future generations can readily *reject*'.

Furthering this line of reasoning, Haq argued that sustainable development demands 'a balance between the compulsions of today and the needs of tomorrow, between private initiative and public action, between individual greed and social compassion'.[5] Countering this perspective, Sen pointed out that 'people do have "needs", but they also have values, and in particular, cherish their ability to reason, appraise, act and participate'.[6] Applying the same yardstick to Solow's approach, Sen comments that 'sustaining living standards is not the same thing as sustaining people's freedom to have—or safeguard—what they value and to which they have reason to attach importance'. The IPCC Report (2018) recognizes that the United Nations SDGs, adopted in 2015, provides an established framework for assessing the links between global warming of 1.5 degree Celsius or 2 degree Celsius and development goals that include poverty eradication, reducing inequalities, and climate action. It argues that the mitigation options on pathways are associated with multiple synergies and trade-offs across the SDGs. The processes are complex, yet the total number of possible synergies exceeds the number of trade-offs, and their net effect will depend on the pace and magnitude of changes, the composition of the mitigation portfolio, and the management of the transition.[7] For example, breathing clean and fresh air, the ability to seek happiness from nature such as walking in forests, viewing rare species plants, animals and birds, and other valuable *doings* and *beings* appeared to be missing from both Brundtland's and Solow's definition of sustainability. Repositioning sustainability as an issue of intergenerational equity, the 2030 Agenda for Sustainable Development is a plan of action for People, Planet, Prosperity and Peace. It echoes and widens the threefold classification of the Brundtland Commission of environmental, economic, and social sustainability to the global compact to evolve linkages across economic and human progress both for the present and the future.

Against this backdrop, this chapter further explores the evolution of the concept of sustainability and traces its implications. Section 9.1 sets out the core issue that sustainable development seeks to address—vulnerability in all its dimensions. Section 9.2 presents a discussion on weak and strong sustainability. This is followed by Section 9.3, which presents the human development approach to sustainability and its three pillars, namely, environmental sustainability (Section 9.4), economic sustainability (Section 9.5), and social sustainability

(Section 9.6), and brings to the fore the implications of both the neoclassical and the human development approaches. The last section presents the way forward, and addresses issues of resilience and policies to ensure sustainability in its true sense.

9.1 THE ISSUE

The application of the notion of sustainability revolves around reducing vulnerability and building people's resilience. Vulnerability,[8] a concept most closely associated with disaster risks, is often perceived as being determined by both susceptibility and coping/adaptive capacity. While vulnerabilities due to disasters are important, it is necessary to adopt a much broader perspective that encompasses, at the very least, economic, social, and environmental dimensions. Many vulnerabilities that people face are caused by macroeconomic shocks that could result in job losses, and illness episodes that drain a family's economic resources. Riots and political turmoil can also contribute to an individual's vulnerability. However, attention by both scholars and practitioners has largely been focused on contextual or outcome[9] vulnerability on account of climate change—a rather narrow view of the issue.

When viewed from a multidimensional lens, vulnerability is often assessed as being external or idiosyncratic in relation to the characteristics of a household. Vulnerability stems from multiple sources and varies according to household status and region. For example, people who live in coastal regions are more vulnerable to environmental risks such as flooding, whereas those in hilly regions are exposed to risks due to landslides and glacial melting. Similarly, during a recession, a casual worker in the informal sector would be affected much more than a white-collared worker with social security benefits in the organized sector. Within these settings, vulnerability is highest among the poor, socially excluded, minority groups, differently abled people, women, children, elderly people, and migrants, since it leads to an erosion in the person's or household's standard of living, and could even be responsible for their slipping into poverty. While often vulnerability emanates from economic processes, social dimensions such as race, identity, low income, and physical and mental challenges can aggravate the situation. Moreover, some of the vulnerabilities can interact with one another and reinforce the situation, such as that of marginalized groups whose low social status leads to denial of several opportunities.

Expansion of basic capabilities and access to legitimate entitlements and endowments enhance people's adaptive capacities and make them less vulnerable to hazards. Since both risks and capability levels of individuals affect the extent of vulnerability faced, efforts to reduce vulnerability and build resilience[10] will have to work on both these aspects.

A commonly prevalent viewpoint is that poor people are agents of environmental damage. The human development approach rejects this proposition and argues that the poor are, in fact, victims of environmental degradation. The contribution of the poor to environmental pollution or damage is appreciably lower than that of the rich because their livelihoods depend on natural resources to a much greater extent than that of the rich. This gives them a vested interest in preserving natural resources. Moreover, the cascading impacts of the environment on the poor manifest themselves in lack of access to improved cooking fuel, drinking water, and sanitation, with severe consequences for their health, education, and livelihoods. Empirical evidence from Malawi suggests that an increase in the time spent on collecting firewood and other resources reduces the likelihood of children attending school. A similar trend is observed in rural Ethiopia, where schooling is unlikely to be regarded as a primary activity for children, particularly boys, because most of their prime time is spent on collecting water.[11] This situation is seen across most developing economies, where human development achievements are extremely poor.

Environmental degradation can jeopardize the livelihoods of millions of people. Nearly 40 per cent of the economically deprived people worldwide draw their income largely from agriculture, fishing, and forestry activities like hunting and gathering. A review of case studies of rural communities living in or on the fringes of tropical forests highlighted that forests determine nearly 40 per cent of the income of poor households as against 17 per cent for non-poor households.[12] Yet, the role of community (especially women) cannot be forgotten in securing lives, livelihoods, and environment (see Box 9.1).

Apart from environmental factors, economic crises contribute to vulnerability, particularly that of the poor. Even if people are not actually pushed into extreme poverty due to austerity policies, they could continue to be vulnerable as risk from unforeseen contingencies like economic crises, natural disasters, illness, and such others erode their incomes further.[13] The gravity of the situation of vulnerable popula-

> **BOX 9.1** Poor Women in India Assume Responsibility for the Environment
>
> The *Chipko* movement (*chipko* is a Hindi word meaning to embrace, hug, or stick) started in the mid-1970s in Reni village in the state of Uttarakhand, India. It illustrates the role of responsibility and collective action in ensuring the preservation of critical natural capital.
>
> The movement dates back to March 1974, when a group of Uttarakhandi women were mobilized under the leadership of Gauri Devi to prevent cutting of trees. A company had been contracted by the State Forest Department to cut 2,500 trees for commercial purposes in the Reni forest near the ecologically fragile Himalayan region. The river Alaknanda was prone to frequent floods, and the villagers were worried that cutting trees would worsen the situation. In an effort to prevent this from happening, the women embraced or hugged a tree that was identified to be cut down. This collective action sent a strong message against the destruction of natural resources and the resultant disturbance of ecological balance. Seeing the movement gather momentum, state government was forced to investigate. Thereafter, in 1976, the government imposed a ten-year ban on cutting trees in the region. The message spread, and similar, large protests took place in other parts of the country. The Indian prime minister, Indira Gandhi, imposed a ban in other states as well. The Chipko movement has also set up a cooperative to safeguard local forests and manage fodder production that would not damage trees.
>
> *Source*: Compiled by authors from www.apnauttarakhand.com/chipko-movement; 15 March 2018.

tions in the developing world can be understood from the fact that it constituted roughly three-fifths of its population in the 1990s and half of its population in 2000. It is this group that needs to be economically stable for the economy to be sustainable in the long run. Most of the workers in this group are also likely to be in what ILO calls 'vulnerable employment'.[14] ILO estimates that more than half of the developing countries' workers—about 1.45 billion—are in 'vulnerable employment', and are less likely than wage earners to either have formal working arrangements or social protection covering health care and pensions. Their incomes and standards of living are vulnerable to any contingency that may arise in the household (for example, illness), regional (flood or drought), or macroeconomic levels (recession or inflation). Any adverse contingency, therefore, affects them. This phenomenon has exhibited no signs of declining; indeed, vulnerability has actually been on the rise since the 2007–8 global financial and economic crisis.

9.2 WEAK AND STRONG SUSTAINABILITY

The debates on sustainability have been dominated by the notions of weak and strong sustainability. The weak sustainability proposition assumes that natural and man-made capital are substitutable, which means that the sustainability requirement of maintaining the total value of capital could be achieved by depleting natural capital and replacing it with manufactured and human capital.[15] This follows the fundamental proposition in the neoclassical analysis that assumes that natural capital and manmade capital are substitutable. A pareto-optimum distribution of economic resources and natural resources ensures efficient allocation and utilization of resources, such that it is impossible to make anyone economically better off without making someone else economically worse off. But this process of pareto-optimality is independent of income distribution as well as the physical scale of natural resources.[16] Note that the aim of neoclassical economics is stimulation of the economic growth process, and this also includes ensuring that the total value of manufactured and natural capital remains constant over time. The challenge here is that in order to maintain steady state in growth rates, and since there would be exploitation of resources, particularly depletion of natural capital, it would need to be substituted by investment capital. This belief furthered the unbridled use of natural resources, with devastating implications for the environment and ecology that the current generation is experiencing.[17] Though there have been efforts to nullify the burden of environmental degradation through introduction of carbon taxes and such measures, the task of securing lives of the future generations has become weaker due to ever increasing exploitation of natural resources to satiate economic growth-led demands.

The weak sustainability paradigm gained support from another theoretical construct, the Environmental Kuznets Curve (EKC), which came into prominence during the 1990s. The EKC hypothesis proposes an inverted U-shaped relationship between per capita income and environmental pollution. It presents an optimistic picture of the future by claiming that, in the long run, there will be a downward trend in environmental pollution. This effectively means that economic growth contributes to improved environmental quality instead of unsustainability of the environment. Overall, the EKC hypothesis does not seem convincing, because improvement in environment quality resumes at income levels that are *too high to be realized at the global level,* and the stable ecosystem would collapse well before such *a turning point is reached.*[18]

As opposed to the view of weak sustainability, the human development approach subscribes to the notion of strong sustainability, and perceives sustainable development as encompassing sustainability across economic, environmental, and social dimensions.[19] Strong sustainability rejects the notion that natural capital be substituted by other forms of capital such as manmade capital or human capital.[20] It affirms that there exists 'critical natural capital', which cannot be substituted by other forms of capital such as manufactured capital and human capital. Including strong sustainability in the human development approach requires a further exploration of the relationship between the intrinsic and instrumental value of nature, and the notion of responsibility that takes into account this relationship.

The premise of strong sustainability has an emphasis on sustaining the ecosystems and their services, and ensuring environmental rights for present and future generations. Adopting a broader view of the environment and going beyond greenhouse gas (GHG) emissions, the human development approach encompasses a variety of dimensions such as preserving biodiversity, and considers impacts on aspects such as health, water and sanitation, ecology, and climate change, and improving resilience in the light of greater frequency of natural disasters. What distinguishes this approach as against the geocentric focus of conventional approaches is its people-centric focus, which results in greater discussion and debate on vulnerability, adaptive capacity, and resilience, particularly for those belonging to vulnerable groups and those residing in vulnerable locations. There are certain key aspects to strong sustainability that need to be explained.

First, the *non-substitutability* clause of strong sustainability calls for preservation of natural capital, which requires policy interventions in both renewable and non-renewable resources. In the case of the former, the goal is to limit the consumption to sustainable levels, while for the latter, the rule is to develop alternatives using renewable substitutes to minimize non-renewable resource exploitation. These policy interventions, in addition to stable population growth levels, will ensure a constant stock of critical natural capital.[21] In terms of maintaining biodiversity, the interpretation of strong sustainability would imply efforts to deal with its losses.[22]

Second, strong sustainability uses the tool of ecological footprint, which relates human activity to the carrying capacity of the earth in terms of the maximum population size that can be supported by a given amount of resources.[23] It has also been argued that the preservation of critical natural capital does not mean that nature should be preserved as it is, or that non-renewable resources should not be used at all. What it does require is that receipts from the use of natural resources such as coal should be invested in the development of renewable energy sources so that the *aggregate value of the total natural resource stock remains constant.*

Third, the preservation of natural capital is also important from the point of view of the low-income rural population, which is most often concentrated in the fragile and less environmentally friendly regions. As per UNEP's[24] global estimates, more than 600 million rural poor live on land prone to degradation and water stress, and in upland areas, forest systems and dry lands that are subject to climatic and ecological disruptions. The bulk of this population depends on natural resources for its livelihood and sustenance. The productive capacity of the environment and the ability of the population to avail of it is of fundamental importance to their capability to survive.

Lastly, a lack of development or misdirected development increases the risk of environmental disasters. The possibility of a natural event leading to a disaster depends on two aspects—intensity of the hazard, and the extent of vulnerability of the people.[25] Individuals, groups, or regions are vulnerable due to their high susceptibility, and low coping and adaptive capacities. For example, natural disasters like cyclones cause extensive environmental loss. Destruction of ecosystems that can increase coping and adaptive capacity of the habitants in case of a risk and/or disaster has also led to an erosion of the adaptive capacities of people.

Sustainability is an integral process of the human development approach.[26] The HDR 2011 defined it as 'the expansion of the substantive freedoms of people today while making reasonable efforts to avoid seriously compromising those of future generations'.[27]

The role of collective agency and capabilities in social interactions and management of natural capital require further elaboration.[28] The notion of responsibility is key to understanding collective capability. Responsibility implies not only exercising self-restraint voluntarily so that the obligation towards others is satisfied, but also switching from individual choice to a more responsible way of acting while taking other people into consideration. Since freedoms of the current generations cannot jeopardize the freedoms of the future generations, debates on this issue have veered around whether there needs to be a threshold beyond which the freedoms of the individuals need to be circumscribed. This includes not only an intergenerational dimension, but also individual freedoms within a generation that need to be subsumed in the interest of the collective freedoms of the society.

9.3 SUSTAINABILITY IN HUMAN DEVELOPMENT

Sustainability is an inalienable process of human development and can also be considered as an end in itself. Haq clarifies that the terms sustainable *human development, sustainable development,* and *human development* can be used interchangeably. He explains that the emerging concept of sustainable human development as one 'based on equal access to development opportunities, for present and for future generations. The heart of this concept is equity—in access to opportunities, not necessarily in results'.[29] An elaboration of this broader connotation of sustainable development is to recognize that equity and sustainability are two sides of the same coin. Following from the above reasoning, we outline the analytical pathway to sustainable development in Figure 9.1.

Sustainable development is intrinsically linked to equity, which is perceived in terms of *capability equality* of people. We argue that equity in capability is achieved when equity in opportunity freedom and process freedom is achieved in society. Freedoms include not only those relating to the environment, but also freedoms in the economic, social, political, and cultural realms. As stated in Chapter 4 of this volume, equity in capability is ensured when each individual in society enjoys a

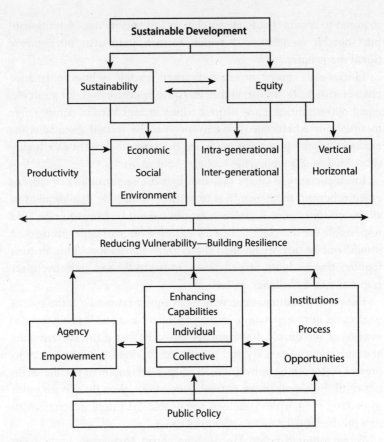

FIGURE 9.1 Analytical Pathways to Sustainable Development
Source: Authors' analysis.

full and healthy life. There could be variations in the original position, but suitable affirmative policies from the state could create an enabling environment of opportunity freedom, so that people enjoy equality of opportunity. However, whether such freedom leads to equality in outcomes is contentious.

Ensuring equity in the capability realm is an extremely dynamic process and can be secured (*a*) in vertical and horizontal dimensions, and (*b*) in terms of intergenerational and intra-generational freedoms. Failure to capture these linkages will lead to a *capability inequality trap* (to be discussed in Section 9.5). Vertical and horizontal equity are required to ensure that intra-generational inequality does not translate into 'durable inequalities',[30] which, in turn, perpetuate intergenerational inequalities.

Horizontal equity is ensured when people whose normative characteristics are similar, and have equal opportunities, for example, equal opportunities across various ethnic groups. Vertical equity refers to situations where unequals may need to be treated unequally; for example, special provisions made for the poor, such as free or highly subsidized food supplies, medical care, and so on.

Intergenerational equity demands that the responsibility of citizens extends beyond their own lives to further sustainable development in all dimensions. Since future generations cannot be blamed or be held responsible for the conditions they inherit from past generations, they should not be any worse than the current generations. This, in turn requires that each country's citizens, individually and collectively, act responsibly—a challenge in itself.[31]

However, pursuing intergenerational equity cannot be at the cost of neglecting intra-generational equity.[32] Anand and Sen[33] assert that the essence of sustainable development would be lost if the current generation's issues of poverty and misery are overlooked in an anxiety to protect forthcoming generations. If today's development paradigms do not fulfil the claims of the current generations, then there is no point in making the current paradigm sustainable for future generations to pass on the same or more aggravated issues.

When intergenerational inequalities persist, particularly in the form of horizontal inequalities, they could be a potent force that fosters conflict. Therefore, sustainable development should focus attention not only on the future, but also on the present. As Haq commented, there is something distinctly odd about worrying about unborn generations if the present generations are poor and miserable, and development patterns that 'perpetuate today's inequities are neither sustainable nor worth sustaining'.[34] Several proposals have emerged in the recent past on the way in which the issue can be addressed. Nussbaum[35] argues in favour of 'limits to freedoms' since freedoms that some people possess could limit the freedom of others.[36] Nussbaum cites an example that supports this argument: freedom of landowners to keep their land limits attempts at land reforms, which could be central for securing freedoms for a large number of the poor. Thus, addressing asset/wealth inequalities is equally crucial in securing sustainable human development, both in the short term and as a long-term phenomenon.

In an attempt to incorporate sustainability into the capability approach, Peeters, Dirix, and Sterckx have suggested that 'the goals of sustainable development should be informed by a framework that consists of enhancing capabilities up to a threshold level, as well as constraining the functioning combinations beyond this threshold in terms of their greenhouse gas emissions'.[37] They argue that sustainable human development can neither ignore inequitable deprivation in the developing countries nor unsustainable consumption levels in the developed ones. In their view, sustainable human development should include constraining human activities in order to prevent losses in future citizens' well-being due to the magnified adverse effects of climate change.[38]

Emerging literature in recent times has acknowledged that strengthening linkages between equity and sustainability can expand human freedoms and capabilities of individuals across generations. Summing up succinctly, Sachs argues that 'a good society is not only an economically prosperous society (with high per capita income) but also one that is also socially inclusive, environmentally sustainable, and well governed'.[39]

9.4 ENVIRONMENTAL SUSTAINABILITY: ISSUES AND CHALLENGES

Achieving environmental sustainability is influenced both by the understanding of what it means but also by the tools and mechanisms adopted in the policy arena. The responsibility for today's development conundrums and unsustainable development rests squarely on the development approach followed thus far. Select tools emerging from the neoclassical paradigm, namely, the concept of weak sustainability, environmental Kuznets Curve, and genuine savings,[40] have been part of the toolkit of economists and policymakers while taking important decisions on the environment, resulting in misplaced priorities and misguided policies.

Countries all over the world are facing the challenge of environmental degradation adversely affecting people's well-being. Between 1970 and 2008, carbon emissions in low-, medium-, and high-HDI countries are estimated to have increased by 248 per cent, and countries reporting the fastest increase in the HDI value were associated with rapid increase in emissions. Rising population and increasing consumption have also been identified as factors contributing to rising emissions, though it is the high consumption levels that seem to have a more devastating impact. For example, it is estimated that the carbon emissions of a person in the UK for two months equal the carbon emissions of a person in a low-HDI country for a year.[41] Despite the numerous international conventions and resolutions that have been passed by the comity of nations, there has not been much concrete action on the ground among developed countries in reducing emissions. Box 9.2 illustrates one such failed international legislation.

Similar to the Kyoto protocol, the influential (though not legally binding) Agenda 21[42] has not been effective as its very format seems to have worked against integration. Segmentation of the Agenda into sectoral issues led to them being pursued in silos, and worse still, interconnected issues being posed as 'trade-offs' between various components. In aspects that are crucial for the achievement of sustainable development, there was virtually no progress.[43] The Paris Agreement of 2015 is another historic agreement, bringing together 195 UNFCC members to commit to *low carbon, resilient, and sustainable future*. The main aim of this universal agreement is to cap the rise in global temperatures in this millennium to below 2 degrees Celsius and to further decrease it to 1.5 degrees Celsius above pre-industrial levels. There are no predefined targets for this: instead, each country regularly plans and reports its strategy, such that each target is beyond the previous target. Discussion in various UN conferences related to the environment and their role in advancing the notion of sustainable development are discussed in Annexure D in this volume.

The rapid depletion of resources and the consequent adverse impact in terms of faltering growth rates was raised more than four decades ago by the study on 'Limits to Growth' by Meadows et al.,[44] published by the Club of Rome.[45] The study argued that high rates of growth fuelled by high consumption levels and extensive use of natural resources are not sustainable in the long-run.[46] Though its predictions have been strongly contested, the study continues to cast its shadow on current debates on environment and economic growth.

BOX 9.2   Kyoto Protocol: A Weak Legislation That Failed to Meet Its Desired Goals?

The Kyoto protocol, a legally binding agreement, emphasizes the concept of *common but differentiated responsibility,* which places greater responsibility on the developed countries—owing to their long history of dangerous levels of GHG emissions—and obligates them to curb their emissions rates given their long history of dangerous levels of GHG emissions. It defined the first period of commitment from 2008 to 2012, which required the developed countries to reduce their GHG emissions to *at least 5 per cent below their 1990 levels.* During the second commitment period from 2013 to 2020, countries are to commit to cap GHG emission to at least *18 per cent below 1990 levels.* The developing countries were not legally bound by any ceilings, but were to benefit, through financial aid from developed countries, from green projects undertaken.

Implementation of the Kyoto Protocol has been tardy, as is evident from the fact that despite its formulation in 1997, it could get off the ground only in February 2005. Implementation is also seriously hampered as large countries such as the USA, India, and China have not signed the agreement. This has which in turn has influenced other countries like Canada, Russia, and Japan to opt out of the agreement. The protocol is currently led by the European Union and Australia, which cover only 15 per cent of the global emissions, seriously undermining its efficacy. The efficacy of the protocol is thus seriously undermined. Consequently, although the countries that are party to the protocol (thirty-seven industrialized countries) have successfully reduced their total GHG emissions during their first phase to 22 per cent—well beyond the agreed 5 per cent— lower than the 1990 levels, global carbon emissions have increased at an alarming rate of 49 per cent, as estimated by the Global Carbon Project. This is because other major polluter countries are not party to the treaty.

Source: UNFCC. 2015. *Kyoto Protocol 10th Anniversary: Timely Reminder Climate Agreements Work.* Press release, UN Climate Change Newsroom. Accessible at http://newsroom.unfccc.int/unfccc-newsroom/kyoto-protocol-10th-anniversary-timely-reminder-climate-agreements-work/#downloads; Hamid, A. 2012. 'Durban's Lifeline to Kyoto'. *New Straits Times,* January 10.

It is clear that economic growth will enhance the levels of waste generation and hence have a negative impact on the ecology. Measures to mitigate the impacts of climate change also have costs which need to be factored into policy. Ackerman et al.[47] estimate that if 2.5 per cent of GDP is used on safeguarding climate change when the growth of the nation is at 2.5 per cent per annum, this cost would correspond to missing out on one year's growth of the nation. It would also mean that it would take one additional year for average incomes to double, given the climate cost incurred. Stern[48] estimates that the cost of reducing GHG emissions can limit world economic growth by 1 per cent GDP each year. However, he also cautions that the cost of not protecting the climate is much more massive, leading to a loss of nearly 5 per cent of global GDP per year, and if worse conditions are considered, the loss can shoot up to 20 per cent of GDP each year.

The growing challenges of transforming technologies to reduce emissions at the cost of limiting growth processes continue to be inconclusive. The environmental debate is also set within a forceful perspective of rights and obligations of nations, and has acquired a strong North–South dimension, with the developing countries arguing that whereas the developed countries have been responsible for much of the past emissions, the cost of adjustment falls disproportionately on the developing countries whose pollution levels are likely to rise as they take to a higher growth path.[49] The issue of *who is responsible* and *who pays* has acquired political overtones, thus rendering the resolution of the roles and responsibilities of countries towards global sustainability that much more complex.

Environmental degradation is a serious challenge to livelihoods of the poor, as nearly 40 per cent of the world's land is of poor quality. Similarly, as forest resources are depleted, the livelihoods of an estimated 350 million people in the world who live in forests and dependent on forest produce for income generation are being affected. Indoor and outdoor pollution, lack of sanitation, and unclean drinking water have increased the risk of disease burden, particularly in urban areas, demonstrating a strong link between environmental health risk and environmental degradation. Unplanned and rapid demographic and spatial expansions can jeopardize the government's capacity to provide universal basic amenities such as water sanitation and housing. UN-Habitat[50] estimates that nearly a quarter of the world's population in urban areas lives in slums in developing countries. Poor living conditions—lack of sanitation and hygiene, and inadequate drinking water—risk lives of 7.4 per cent of the children in the world due to severe wasting. They are also an underlying cause of 45 per cent of child mortality cases globally.[51]

Some of the important solutions, highlighted to abate climate change challenges in a scenario of resource depletion, have prompted a demand for adopting sustainable consumption and production patterns. It has been argued that rising population, apart from adopted lifestyles, contributes to increasing consumption. Even if the rate of consumption of energy and goods and emissions of carbon dioxide (CO_2) is reduced in absolute terms, the total energy consumption will still not decline, given the rising population.[52] According to a study by UN-DESA,[53] human interventions have led to the degradation of 60 per CENT of the world's ecosystem services in the last fifty years, placing enormous strain on the natural functions of the earth. Cities account for 2 per cent of the planet's land, but consume 75 per cent of earth's natural resources for goods and services and emit nearly 80 per cent of global CO_2.[54] Thus, the ability of the planet's ecosystems to sustain future generations can no longer be taken for granted.

Several recommendations have called for a change in the systems of production and consumption, including reduction in dependency on fossil fuels and improved use of renewable energy. Similarly, the need for reduction in material and energy intensity of ongoing economic activities as well as reducing emissions and wastes in all processes such as extraction, production, consumption, and disposure is acknowledged and discussed at length in the Conference of Parties (COP) discussions as well (see Box 9.3 for details).

Overconsumption is a phenomenon that is observed more in advanced countries, whereas hazardous and environmentally polluting production processes are largely found in developing countries. Moreover, developed countries—where more stringent environmental norms have been put in place—have often transferred *unclean* or *dirty* technologies to developing countries where regulatory systems are weak or non-existent. Sustainable production also includes within its ambit resource use efficiency, so that input use is minimized per unit of production; sustainable consumption relates to the creation of a demand for less resource-intensive and sustainable products. These two processes help poverty alleviation, enhance health and well-being, and reduce environmental degradation. Sustainable production also entails revamping the overall production processes that not only improve production efficiency but also moderate the pace of climate change.[55]

BOX 9.3   Pathways to Sustainable Consumption and Production

'TRANSMILENIO' SYSTEM IN BOGOTÁ, COLUMBIA

Bogotá, the capital city of Columbia, has dramatically improved the quality of life of its residents owing to substantial improvement in scale and use of public transport. In 2000, the city established one of the most advanced Bus Rapid Transit Systems (BRTs) in the world. The Transmilenio, as it is called, includes more than 1,300 large buses with a capacity of 160 passengers each. The BRT also runs a feeder system to the outskirts of the city in order to provide easy accessibility to public transport to people living in low-income areas. In addition, in order to further promote sustainable means of transport in the city, separate bicycle paths and pedestrian zones of more 300 kilometres were demarcated. The city has also been observing a car-free day each year since February 2000. These initiatives have reduced the use of private vehicles in Bogotá, facilitated a reduction in GHG emissions SO_2 by 43 per cent, NO_x by 28 per cent and particulate matter by 12 per cent, helped citizens save average commuting time by nearly twenty minutes (~32 per cent), and caused a decline in the number of traffic fatalities and collisions.

SUSTAINABLE RURAL ENERGY PRODUCTION IN NEPAL

In 2010, a quarter of Nepal's population lived in poverty, and only 15 per cent of the country was urbanized. Because of its geographic location, Nepal has substantial hydropower potential. Despite this natural advantage, the country barely meets 2 per cent of its total energy requirement. The Rural Energy Development Programme brought catalytic change in the economy growth and development of the country. With the aid of the local government and community mobilization, the programme initiated decentralized renewable energy services in the isolated parts of the country. The programme enabled the provision of reliable electricity to the poor, vulnerable, female, and rural communities at large by constructing micro-hydropower systems and making improved cooking stoves available. This move empowered the citizens by providing new sources of income and employment opportunities (an increase of nearly 8 per cent) and led to increased incomes. With every micro-hydropower plant, nearly forty new business opportunities are created. The programme also led to an improvement in health, sanitation, and environmental conditions in the regions where it was implemented, and improved educational outcomes of children. The programme thus brought about an equitable and sustainable change in economic, environmental, and social spheres.

SOLID WASTE MANAGEMENT IN BAGO, PHILIPPINES

Bago was tagged as one of the dirtiest cities in the region because of an absence of efficient mechanism for solid waste management. Social impacts of loopholes in city management were also evident, with the city grappling with poverty, malnutrition and other associated health problems. In 2007, Kabahin Ka Project (for Solid Waste Management as a Social Enterprise) was initiated that uses *takakura* method of composting. It uses native organisms that are fermented through plant and vegetable waste. Households use the compost produced for backyard gardening, while the city government uses it for beautification of the city and landscaping buildings. The remainder is distributed amongst farmers for free. This initiative has led to a 50 per cent decline in the waste generated in the city.

Source: IGES. 2010. *Kitakyushu Initiative for a Clean Environment: Final Report.* Kitakyushu: IGES. Accessible at https://kitakyushu.iges.or.jp/publication/KI_FinalReport_2010.05.19.pdf; 15 November 2017; Turner, M., Kooshian, C., and Winkelman, S. 2012. *Case Study: Columbia's Bus Rapid Transit Development and Expansion.* Washington, DC: Centre for Clean Air Policy; UNDP. 2012. *Case Studies for Sustainable Development in Practice: Triple Wins for Sustainable Development.* New York: United Nations.

9.5 ECONOMIC SUSTAINABILITY: WHY DOES IT MATTER?

The notion of economic sustainability refers to sustainability of the systems of production that are able to satisfy current and future consumption levels. It ensures that the economic systems (both macroeconomic and financial) are viable and sustainable in the long run. From the human development perspective, it also implies that interaction between these economic systems and human institutions is just and enhances people's freedoms and capabilities.

Economic sustainability in the sense described above seems to elude the world today as macroeconomic systems are not stable, the links between economic growth and human development are weak and faltering, and inter- and intra-generational justice seems a distant mirage. The responsibility for this state of affairs rests, at least partly, in the trust that policymakers and economists have had on mainstream economic theories, particularly the unflinching faith in the Kuznets Curve and trickle-down hypotheses, to deliver the benefits of growth to the poor. These two forces together have led to policy complacency and neglect of the pattern and content of growth. Such a half-hearted approach has resulted in a rise in inter- and intra-generational inequalities and led to redistributive measures being considered purely as palliative measures in public policy.[56]

Ironically, despite the single-minded focus on ensuring a high rate of growth, the global record on ensuring macroeconomic sustainability has not been satisfactory, barring a few exceptions.[57] Two features are prominent here: (*a*) low and declining growth in a majority of countries; coupled with (*b*) periodic crises that have been increasingly devastating in their impact on economies. The hope that middle-income countries (MICs)—which have exhibited some dynamism—will lead the way has also been dashed thanks to the inability of these countries to transcend their middle-income status and move to the high-income category, warranting the description of their being in a 'middle-income trap'.[58]

Global growth, which was around 3.5 per cent in 1960s, dropped to 2.4 per cent during the 1970s, a decade of economic turbulence. It deteriorated further to 1.4 per cent in 1980s and 1.1 per cent in 1990s, the decade when liberalization gathered considerable strength.[59] The World Commission on Fair Globalisation[60] arrived at similar conclusions, stating that in terms of per capita income growth, only sixteen developing countries grew at more than 3 per cent per annum between 1985 and 2000. In contrast, fifty-five developing countries grew at less than 2 per cent per annum and twenty-three suffered negative growth. Figure 9.2 indicates the highly volatile global growth along a steadily downward trend over the past five decades.

Apart from low growth, countries have been roiled by repeated crises. Atkinson and Morelli[61] point out in an analysis of twenty-five countries that between 1911 and 2010, there occurred as many as 100 systemic banking crises and 101 consumption crises across those countries, with both the crises often overlapping each other. The 2007–8 global financial and economic crisis has been described as the largest in terms of impact since World War II: the GDP of the USA

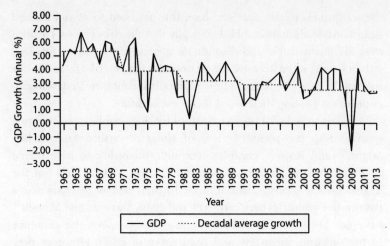

FIGURE 9.2 World GDP Growth (Annual %) over Past Five Decades
Source: Authors' calculations. Accessible at databank.worldbank.org/data/home;
15 March 2018.

declined by over 7 per cent in the last quarter of 2008, while the overall global output declined by 1 per cent and markets around the world
experienced colossal disruptions in asset and credit markets, massive
erosions of wealth, and unprecedented numbers of bankruptcies.[62]
The IMF initially estimated in mid-2007 that the actual and potential
write-offs of assets originating from the USA would be to the tune of
USD 50 billion.[63]

These developments have considerably undermined public confi-
dence in the ability of the economics profession to provide meaningful
policy prescriptions that would enable the world to scramble out of
the current dismal situation. Economists, in turn, have discovered, to
their dismay, that the existing toolkit that they possess is no longer
adequate to analyse the world economy. Incidentally, the present-day
economists seem to have joined, albeit belatedly and rather reluctantly,
Haq's clarion call way back in 1971 to 'stand economic theory on its
head'.[64] The 2007–8 crisis typifies the maladies of the overreliance on
markets, especially financial markets, weak regulatory mechanisms of
national governments, and the monitoring of wrong indicators.

While the crisis has been devastating for economies of the developed
countries, the measures to address the crisis do not seem to recognize

the seriousness of the issue and have thus far been short-sighted and unsustainable. Ellmers and Hulova argue that the debt crisis is far from over as 'unsustainable and illegitimate debt is still a risk to financial stability and, ultimately to the economic and social fabric of our nations'.[65] Box 9.4 illustrates how high public debt level in developing countries is eroding their social sector expenditure.

Another strand of thought questions the sustainability of economic growth from the point of view of rising inequality. Analysts like Stiglitz[66] and Rajan[67] consider economic inequality to have played an important role in the US financial crisis of 2008, which was the trigger for the global financial crisis. In their review of crises across twenty-five countries between 1911 and 2010, Atkinson and Morelli[68] have not been able to establish a causal link between the existence of high-income inequality and occurrence of crises. However, they

---

BOX 9.4   Unsustainable Debt Levels

Economic imbalances often trigger external debt. In 2012, global current account divergences accounted for 2 per cent of world GDP, which is only slightly lower than the 2006 level of 3 per cent that triggered the world's worst financial crisis. Between 1985 and 2010, it is estimated that net public debt (difference between debt inflows and debt payments) flows to developing countries were as high as USD 530 billion, which is equal in size to five Marshall Plans. The high debt levels in developing countries have compelled these countries to distort priorities, according more importance to public debt servicing than to investment in social sectors. For example, World Bank data for 2010 indicate that the developing countries as a whole paid out USD 184 billion towards debt service, which is about three times the annual resources required for fulfilling the MDGs. In Brazil, public debt servicing as percentage of GDP was 24.5 per cent of GDP as against a meagre 1.7 and 2.1 per cent of the GDP that accounts for public spending on education and health sectors, respectively.

Source: Millet, D., Munevar, D., and Toussaint, E. 2012. *World Debt Figures*. Committee for the Abolition of Third World Debt; Munevar, D. and Toussaint, E. 2013. 'The Debt of Developing Countries: The Devastating Impacts of IMF–World Bank "Economic Medicine"'. Global Research, October 11, CADTM. Accessible at http://www.globalresearch.ca/the-debt-of-developing-countries-the-devastating-impacts-of-imf-world-bank-economic-medicine/5354027; 15 November 2017.

do point out that there is no doubt that the levels of inequality have become starker and deeper in the post-crisis scenario.

Further, austerity policies to correct for imbalances following a debt crisis also disturb the social fibre and affect the freedoms and choices of the current and future generations.[69] These policies reduce public spending on social sectors such as health, education, and social security, thereby limiting the capability stock to a low level. Further, they also restrict a country from investing and implementing technologies to reduce environmental degradation from current economic activities, and this has its repercussions on intergenerational justice. The prevailing low public and private sentiment—induced by high levels of unemployment, lack of adequate safety nets, low levels of human capital, poverty, and inequality—causes a country to be stuck in the vicious cycle of low-level equilibrium where each condition feeds on the other, thereby making it all the more difficult to manage future shocks and crises.

A phenomenon in recent times, currently outside policy attention, is the stagnation in several of the MICs. It is emerging that several countries in the middle-income group are unable to graduate to the high-income category, leading to what some analysts describe as the 'middle-income trap'.[70] In a study covering 124 countries between 1950 and 2010, Felipe found that thirty-nine countries were categorized as middle-income in 1950s. This grew slightly to about fifty in the 1990s, and the number has hovered around this magical figure[71] since then, as very few countries transited from low-income to middle-income category and from lower-middle-income to upper-middle-income category. Egawa describes the middle-income trap as 'a situation in which an MIC falls into economic stagnation and becomes unable to advance its economy to a high-income level for certain reasons specific to MICs'.[72] While there are varied explanations for this phenomenon, all of them point to failures on the human development front as the principal reason for this situation.

Income inequality is offered as an important explanation for the middle-income trap. Inequality reflects lack of distributional equity, where the bottom of the pyramid has least access to education and health services. This further aggravates the issue by limiting the expansion of human capabilities, and thereby lowers the levels of human capital. These factors breed on each other to produce a vicious cycle of low level of equilibrium in the economy.

The root cause of the middle-income trap lies in the failure of countries that grew in terms of per capita income to resolve developmental challenges of poverty, under-nutrition, education, access to clean drinking water, sanitation, and the like. Consequently and ironically, poverty is now essentially considered a middle-income phenomenon as the bulk of the poor live in MICs. More than half of the world's poor are in lower-middle-income countries (LMICs) like China, India, Indonesia, Pakistan, and Nigeria—poverty is no longer a phenomenon of low-income countries. Although there has been drastic reduction in income poverty in China, in 2010, India had an estimated 384 million poor, that is, about 31 per cent of the world's extreme poor (USD 1.25 definition) and 224 million, that is, about 30 per cent of the world's population, that lived below the poverty line (USD 1.90 definition).[73]

The lack of adequate focus on enhancing people's capabilities has resulted in the ironical situation of the countries graduating to a middle-income status but forced to carry their basket of woes into this category. The need to pay attention to people's issues of education, health, water and sanitation, and the environment is now compelling, as it is only enhanced capabilities of people that will enable countries to lift themselves out of the middle-income trap. Moreover, the acute income inequality in some of the MICs is also a threat to social cohesion.

9.6 SOCIAL SUSTAINABILITY

Social sustainability is one of the most underspecified aspects of sustainability. It is particularly prone to varied interpretations depending on the disciplinary approach of the concerned researcher or policymaker. At one end, social sustainability could be conceived as combining environmental protection and economic growth with social equity. At the other end, it could be interpreted as relating to social institutions and processes. Part of the challenge emerges from the fact the word *social*, which has both analytical and normative meanings, with the analytical aspect requiring a theory on the relationship between society and nature.[74]

There are numerous ways in which social sustainability has been interpreted. The connotation of social sustainability to the *needs* mentioned in the Brundtland Commission's definition visualizes not only basic material needs such as food, clothing, and housing, but other social needs such as education, social relationships, and self-fulfilment.[75] Extending this to include *work* as well as *justice*, Litting and Griessler[76] define social sustainability as one that satisfies 'an extended set of human needs and are shaped in a way that nature and its reproductive capabilities are preserved over a long period of time and the normative chains of social justice, human dignity and participation are fulfilled'. Osti[77] reinforces the notion of work beyond income to include human dignity as a source of freedom and personal expression, social recovery and employment, recognition, and social integration. Following Robert Putnam, social sustainability could also be defined as maintaining of social capital at a sustainable level for future generations.

Why should we consider *social* sustainability? Viewed from the lens of distributional justice, lack of social unsustainability manifests itself in the social arena as inequalities, and Nancy Birdsall distinguishes between *two* kinds of inequalities, which have been elaborated in Chapter 7.

Moreover, governments in developing countries face challenges while taking corrective measures to address inequalities. This is because of unequal distribution of power and the fact that governments at the local levels are vulnerable to pressure from local elites or local interest groups. Evidence shows that there is an element of ineffective public delivery, where a part of the local government is dominated by elite groups. This enhances the possibilities that such groups would usurp public resources.[78] This can be explained further when we look at how elite capture affects the acquisition and enhancement of human capabilities. In a study of sixty-three countries, Akçay[79] found an inverse relationship between corruption and levels of human development. The elite capture political power and formulate social, economic, and political policies that perpetuate such inequalities, thereby adversely affecting not only the effective freedoms of people of the current generation, but also those of the future generations.

One of the most common symptoms of rising horizontal inequality (discussed in Chapter 4 in this volume) is also associated with social sustainability. The breakdown of social cohesion with rising horizontal inequality often has a history of being a colonized country or region. As colonial powers favoured or privileged certain groups and/or regions of the society, they have sown the seeds of inequality that later grow as other factors strengthen it. Colonial leaders keep the best resources for themselves and develop systems that lead to discrimination and unequal access to all sorts of capital, including social capital, in order to sustain power. As evident from the studies done by CRISE,[80] postcolonial leaders are unable to correct this problem.

To illustrate, political inequalities in Sudan and South Sudan, where a centrally controlled state has added to the extreme marginalization of the country's periphery, have been the driving cause for forty years of civil war that trailed after Sudanese independence.[81] Indeed, it still contributes to violence in Sudan and South Sudan. The deepened feeling of marginalization, or actual marginalization itself, has fuelled other economic and social problems, given the lack of state presence and interest particularly in three regions: Warrap, Jonglei, and Unity. Cattle raiding has been the most common cause of conflict—itself a product of gender, ethnic identities, as well as social hierarchies that thrive on political, social, and economic factors such as competition over ownership and access for water, grazing land, and cattle, which often serves as bride price.[82] For example, in December 2011, inter-ethnic violence in Jonglei killed hundreds of people. These grievances over unequal governance have stimulated an atmosphere of uncertainty in all the three regions, making people engage in violent conflict.

Another example is unequal access to social services that have other political and economic factors interlinked as major drivers of conflict. Saferworld conducted a participatory conflict analysis in Kosovo, highlighting that inequalities in provision of electricity are a major cause of conflict. People tend to develop resentment and frustration over Serbian communities instead of over Kosovo Energy Corporation (KEK) due to 'scheduled and unscheduled power cuts, uneven distribution of electricity throughout Kosovo and difficulties paying electricity bills'. This is mainly because financial institutions function largely within Serbian communities, thereby separating them from the rest of Kosovo. Thus, northern Kosovo has comparatively better provision of electricity due to continuous support from Belgrade.[83]

Persistent social inequality, which in recent years has taken the form of inequality in multiple dimensions, could lead to *capability inequality trap* and *capability poverty trap*.[84] This was discussed in Chapter 4 in the context of the inter-linkages between the two types of traps. Stewart argues that, 'the capabilities trap leads to low human capital and probably cultural and social capital, while the asset trap reinforces the situation of low incomes and poor capabilities generally'.[85] In an estimate of capability inequalities across social groups in India, it was found that the relative status of human development outcomes of belonging to scheduled tribes remain poor.[86] Most critically, there was vertical inequality in income distribution. Even with respect to the access to affirmative policies that have been implemented in India since 1990s, we found that relatively few people belonging to the SCs and STs seemed to get the benefits. Interestingly, capability inequality is the lowest in case of education- and health-related outcomes, indicating clearly that in contemporary times, these dimensions could be pathways to tackle vertical and horizontal inequalities in India. In another study, Baulch et al.[87] reported similar results and highlighted that the ethnic minorities in Vietnam are characterized by poor schooling as well as lack of access to credit and lower receipts of remittances.

9.7 WAY FORWARD

The long-term objectives that respect planetary boundaries and ensure sustainable modes of consumption and production would require immediate measures including lower carbon modes of production and consumption, such as adaptive agricultural practices that reduce emissions and protect natural environment, improved waste management techniques, enforcement of laws and regulations on pollution, provision of incentives that promote efficient, cleaner, and diversified energy sources, and better account of environmental risks and costs at project and national levels. It is also necessary to put in place policies that reduce risk and vulnerability through risk mitigation insurance mechanisms, such as crop and livestock insurance, and health insurance. In addition, improving capacities of people to tackle risks and disasters in order to reduce their vulnerability of the population against climate change is of utmost importance.

Besides, economic sustainability—expressed in terms of inclusive growth, poverty eradication, and creating green jobs—would require short- to medium-term measures such as maintaining public and private debt at sustainable levels, creating employment opportunities, enforcing labour market regulation for decent work and policies that encourage green consumption, ensuring access to assets (land, credit, and information), reducing volatility by controlling portfolio flows and harnessing their sectoral allocations to promote fixed investment, and promoting an exchange rate that reduces currency crisis and supports growth.

It needs to be recognized that gainful employment is essential for a human being's self-respect and dignity, opening up of opportunities, and enabling greater choices for the individual in the realms of education, health, and nutrition, whose benefits go far beyond mere survival. Decent jobs also empower people, giving them voice and a social network, which are important objectives in themselves during the process of development.

Similarly, in the social realm, short-term measures to ensure social inclusion and movement from limited focus of safety nets towards social policies that provide universal social protection and redistribution in the long run would entail securing rights that protect minorities, diversity and culture; improved social integration through education and quality employment, decentralized governance; and improved stock of social competence and social cohesion.

That said, there is a growing demand/plea to arrive at an *institutionally integrated view* for a freedom-centred approach wherein the role of promoting basic capabilities, increasing kinship ties, and collective freedom are extremely useful in building sustainable human development. To conclude, while either perspective is equally crucial, it is evident that deepening vulnerabilities over time can best be addressed when the current institutional structure enables the enlargement of choices that can be sustained in the future.

NOTES AND REFERENCES

1. The term *sustainable development* was used for the first time in International Union for Conservation of Nature, Natural Resources and World Wildlife Fund. 1980. *World Conservation Strategy: Living Resource Conservation for Sustainable Development*. Gland, Switzerland: IUCN.

2. WCED. 1987. *Our Common Future (Brundtland Report)*. Oxford: Oxford University Press.

3. Solow, R.M. 1993. 'An Almost Practical Step Towards Sustainability'. *Resources and Policy* 19 (3): 162–72, p. 168.

4. Anand, S. and Sen, A. 1994. 'Sustainable Development: Concepts and Priorities', Occasional Paper 8, Human Development Report Office, UNDP, New York, p. 31.

5. Haq, M. ul. 1995. *Reflections on Human Development*. Oxford: Oxford University Press, p. 77.

6. Sen, A. 2010. 'Sustainable Development and Our Responsibilities'. *Notizie di Politeia* 25 (98): 129–37, p. 135.

7. Sen, 'Sustainable Development and Our Responsibilities', p. 136. Also see IPCC. 2018. 'Summary for Policymakers', in *Global Warming of 1.5°C: An IPCC Special Report on the Impacts of Global Warming of 1.5°C above Pre-industrial Levels and Related Global Greenhouse Gas Emission Pathways, in the Context of Strengthening the Global Response to the Threat of Climate Change, Sustainable Development, and Efforts to Eradicate Poverty*, ed. V. Masson-Delmotte, P. Zhai, H.O. Pörtner, D. Roberts, J. Skea, P.R. Shukla, A. Pirani, W. Moufouma-Okia, C. Péan, R. Pidcock, S. Connors, J.B.R. Matthews, Y. Chen, X. Zhou, M.I. Gomis, E. Lonnoy, T. Maycock, M. Tignor, and T. Waterfield. In Press.

8. Vulnerability is determined by the risks that people face and their coping capacity, which depends crucially on their capabilities. Dubois and Rousseau give an equational definition: Vulnerability = Risk/Capability. Vulnerability increases when the intensity and exposure to risk is high, but declines if the person possesses the capabilities to cope with the risk exposed. For details, see Dubois, J.-L. and Rousseau, S. 2008. 'Reinforcing Household's Capabilities as a Way to Reduce Vulnerability and Prevent Poverty in Equitable Terms', in *The Capability Approach: Concepts, Measures and Applications*, ed. F. Comim, M. Qizilbash, and S. Alkire, pp. 421–36. Cambridge: Cambridge University Press.

9. Outcome vulnerability is referred to as 'a linear result of the projected impacts of climate change on a particular exposure unit (which can be either biophysical or social), offset by adaptation measures'. Contextual vulnerability takes 'a processual and multidimensional view of climate–society interactions. Both climate variability and change are considered to occur in the context of political, institutional, economic and social structures and changes, which interact dynamically with contextual conditions associated with a particular 'exposure unit'. For details, see O'Brien, K., Eriksen, S., Nygaard, L.P., and Schjolden, A. 2007. 'Why Different Interpretations of Vulnerability Matter in Climate Change Discourses'. *Climate Policy* 7 (1): 73–88, pp. 75–6.

10. Resilience refers to the 'person's capability to resist a downward movement of well-being by mobilising her potentiality'. Disaster risk management and building resilience is an essential area often referred to in public and policy discourse; however, a detailed study on it is beyond the scope of this chapter. See Dubois and Rousseau, 'Reinforcing Household's Capabilities as a Way to Reduce Vulnerability and Prevent Poverty in Equitable Terms', p. 428.

11. UNDP. 2011. *Human Development Report 2011: Sustainability and Equity: A Better Future for All*. New York: Palgrave.

12. For a more detailed understanding on the adverse impact of environment on the poor and vulnerable refer to UNDP, *Human Development Report 2011*.

13. Nayyar underscores the real picture of the extent of poverty in the developing world. He estimates that between 1993 and 2008, the number of people living below USD 1.25 per day declined from 1.9 billion to 1.3 billion. However, the number of people living below USD 2 per day remained nearly the same at 2.5 billion between 1991 and 2008, with a spike close to 3 billion in 1990s. See Nayyar, D. 2013. *Catch Up: Developing Countries in the World Economy.* Oxford: Oxford University Press.

14. ILO uses the term vulnerable employment to refer to all those engaged in either own account work or contributing as unpaid workers to a family enterprise. For details, see ILO. 2004. *A Fair Globalization: Creating Opportunities for All.* Report of the World Commission on the Social Dimension of Globalization. Geneva: ILO, p. 9.

15. Natural capital refers to 'everything in nature that provides human beings with well-being, from natural resources to environmental amenities and the pollution absorptive capacity of the environment'. Manmade capital refers to 'the physical means of production (factories, machineries etc.) and infrastructure'. Human capital refers to 'knowledge and skills'. For details, see Neumayer, E. 2012. 'Human Development and Sustainability'. *Journal of Human Development and Capabilities* 13 (4): 561–79, p. 577.

16. See Pearce, D.W. 1976. *Environmental Economics.* London: Longman.

17. When public policy relies on market criteria for maximizing present value of resources, it helps achieve short-term efficiency, but not factors such as income distribution, intangible environmental goods, and safer future, which determine human welfare in the long run. See Daly, H.E. 1977. *Steady State Economics.* San Francisco: W.H. Freeman and Co., p. 185; Hueting, R. 1984, 'Economic Aspects of Environmental Accounting'. UNEP, First Environmental Accounting Workshop, 5–8 November, World Bank, Washington, DC, p. 24.

18. For example, Selden and Song found that the turning point for SO_2 was USD 10,391, and that for SPM was USD 12,275. Much damage to the ecology would occur before such high levels of income are reached. For more details see Selden, T.M. and Song, D. 1994. 'Environmental Quality and Development: Is There a Kuznets Curve for Air Pollution'? *Journal of Environmental Economics and Management* 27 (2): 147–62.

19. While we recognize that cultural and political sustainability are important, they are not within the scope of this work.

20. See Hinterberger, F., Luks, F., and Stewen, M. 2004. 'Economic Growth and Sustainable Development', in *Knowledge for Sustainable Development: An Insight into the Encyclopedia of Life Support Systems (EOLSS).* Oxford: UNESCO, EOLSS Publishers.

21. For details, see Harris, J., Wise, T., Gallagher, K., and Goodwin, N.R., eds. 2001. *A Survey of Sustainable Development: Social and Economic Dimensions* (Vol. 6). Washington, DC: Island Press.

22. Rockström et al. elaborate that the depletion of biodiversity can lead to increase in vulnerability of terrestrial and aquatic ecosystems to climate change, thereby lowering safe boundary levels for these processes. They found that the rate of depletion of groundwater should at least be equal to the rate of its replenishment. It is this second interpretation of the strong sustainability that is more in vogue. For details, see Rockström, J., Steffen, W.L., Noone, K., Persson, Å., Chapin, F.S., III, Lambin, E., Lenton, T.M., Scheffer, M., Folke, C., Schellnhuber, H.J., Nykvist, B., de Wit, C.A., Hughes, T., van der Leeuw, S., Rodhe, H., Sörlin, S., Snyder, P.K., Costanza, R., Svedin, U., Falkenmark, M., Karlberg, L., Corell, R.W., Fabry, V.J., Hansen, J., Walker, B., Liverman, D., Richardson, K., Crutzen, P., and Foley, J. 2009. 'Planetary Boundaries: Exploring the Safe Operating Space for Humanity'. *Ecology and Society* 14 (2): 32.

23. For details, see Dietz, S. and Neumayer, E. 2006. 'A Critical Appraisal of Genuine Savings as an Indicator of Sustainability', in *Sustainable Development Indicators in Ecological Economics: Current Issues in Ecological Economics*, ed. P. Lawn, pp. 117–35. Cheltenham: Edward Elgar; Neumayer, E. 1999. *Weak versus Strong Sustainability: Exploring the Limits of Two Opposing Paradigms*. Cheltenham: Edward Elgar.

24. UNEP. 2012. *Sustainable Consumption and Production for Poverty Eradication*. Nairobi: United Nations Environment Programme.

25. Alliance Development Works. 2012. *World Risk Report 2012: Environmental Degradation and Disasters*. Institute for Environment and Human Security, UNU–EHS.

26. See Chapter 2 for details on the processes of human development.

27. UNDP, *Human Development Report 2011*.

28. Pelenc, J., Lompo, M.K., Ballet, J., and Dubois, J.-L. 2013. 'Sustainable Human Development and the Capability Approach: Integrating Environment, Responsibility and Collective Agency'. *Journal of Human Development and Capabilities* 14 (1): 77–94.

29. Haq, *Reflections on Human Development*, pp. 40–1.

30. Durable inequalities is a concept articulated by Naila Kabeer. For details, see Kabeer, N. 2009. 'Poverty, Social Exclusion and the MDGS: The Challenge of "Durable Inequalities" in the Asian Context'. *IDS Bulletin* 37 (3): 64–78.

31. For example, adhering to the pillar of intergenerational equity would require that the developed countries accept the responsibility for much of the emissions already in the atmosphere, and work towards a solution for developing countries. This acknowledges the unfairness of the situation that such countries are placed in. See Lele, S. and Jayaraman, T. 2011. 'Equity in the Context of Sustainable Development', Background Paper submitted to Ministry of Environment and Forests, Government of India, for presentation at the UN High-Level Panel on Global Sustainability, New Delhi.

32.   Sustainable development should thus focus attention not only on the future but also on the present. See Haq, *Reflections on Human Development*, p. 79.

33.   Anand and Sen, *Sustainable Development*; Anand, S., and Sen, A. 2000. 'Human Development and Economic Sustainability'. *World Development* 28 (12): 2029–49.

34.   Haq, *Reflections on Human Development*, p. 79.

35.   Nussbaum, M. 2003. 'Capabilities as Fundamental Entitlements: Sen and Social Justice'. *Feminist Economics* 9 (2–3): 33–59.

36.   Also see Crabtree, A. 2013. 'Sustainable Development: Does the Capability Approach Have Anything to Offer? Outlining a Legitimate Freedom Approach'. *Journal of Human Development and Capabilities* 14 (1): 40–57.

37.   Peeters, W., Dirix, J., and Sterckx, S. 2013. 'Putting Sustainability into Sustainable Human Development'. *Journal of Human Development and Capabilities* 14 (1): 58–76, 58.

38.   Capability ceilings have been proposed in Holland, B. 2008. 'Ecology and the Limits of Justice: Establishing Capability Ceilings in Nussbaum's Capabilities Approach'. *Journal of Human Development* 9 (3): 401–25.

39.   Sachs, J. 2015. *The Age of Sustainable Development*. New York: Cambridge University Press, p. 25.

40.   Genuine savings, as per World Bank methodology, refers to 'net savings minus depreciation of natural capital from the depletion of natural resources minus damage caused by carbon dioxide emissions minus, for a few mostly developed countries and more recent years, damage caused by suspended particulate matter emissions'. This methodology has an inherent bias towards underestimating environmental pollution, since the measure is generally computed for only one or two pollutants. For example, it often includes only CO_2 emissions and not SO_2 or NO_x, which are perhaps more relevant in the current context. Also, the measure does not include natural resources like water, biodiversity and likes. Further, see Neumayer, *Weak versus Strong Sustainability*, p. 566.

41.   UNDP, *Human Development Report 2011*.

42.   Agenda 21, which mapped the plan of action essentially for ecological sustainability along with socio-economic dimensions of sustainability, subsumes forty chapters on challenges to the three pillars of sustainable development, the role of chief groups, and lays out ways of implementation. As a response to the recommendations of Agenda 21, the Commission on Sustainable Development was established by the UN General Assembly in order to ensure effective implementation and follow up of United Nations convention on environment and development. For details, see Drexhage, J. and Murphy, D. 2010. 'Sustainable Development: From Brundtland to Rio 2012', Background Paper for the High-Level Panel on Global Sustainability, United Nations, New York.

43. For example, though resource use per unit of global output declined significantly over the past twenty-five years by about 30 per cent, the overall use of resources is 50 per cent more than a quarter of a century ago.

44. Meadows, D.H., Meadows, D.L., Randers, J., and Behrens, W.W. 1972. *The Limits to Growth*. New York: Universe Books.

45. Club of Rome was established in 1968 by eminent thinkers to identify, evaluate, develop, and communicate common concerns over the future of humanity and the planet. It has published thirty-three reports on issues relating to the future of humanity.

46. Meadows et al. arrived at their controversial conclusions based on a model that assumed ever-expanding population and mounting demands that this would entail on the finite resource base of economies. Their recommendation was to give urgent attention to conservation measures including population control, particularly in the developing world, and *zero growth* in countries of the developed world. For details, see Elliott, J. 2006. *An Introduction to Sustainable Development* (Third Edition). London: Routledge.

47. Ackerman, F., DeCanio, S.J., Howarth, R.B., and Sheeran, K. 2009. 'Limitations of Integrated Assessment Models of Climate Change'. *Climatic Change* 95 (3–4): 297–315.

48. Stern, N. 2008. 'The Economics of Climate Change'. *American Economic Review* 98 (2): 1–37.

49. The USA alone is responsible for 4 per cent of all global emissions, whereas 136 developing countries together are responsible for only 24 per cent of global emissions.

50. UN-Habitat. 2013. *State of the World's Cities 2012/13: Prosperity of Cities*. London: Earthscan.

51. USAID. 2015. 'Water and Development Strategy and Multi-Sectoral Nutrition Strategy'. Implementation Brief July 2015. Accessible at https://www.usaid.gov/sites/default/files/documents/1865/USAID_WASH_Nutrition_Brief_2015.pdf; 8 October 2016.

52. The Earth Summit in 1992 defined sustainable consumption and production as 'the use of services and related products which responds to basic needs and bring a better quality of life while minimising the use of natural resources and toxic materials as well as the emissions of waste and pollutants over the life cycle of the service or product so as not to jeopardise the needs of future generations' (Oslo Symposium. 1994. *Roundtable on Sustainable Production and Consumption*. Accessible at http://www.iisd.ca/consume/oslo004.html#top, 10 April 2017). This was later redefined as 'a holistic approach to minimising the negative environmental impacts from consumption and production systems while promoting quality of life for all', a value that the human development approach endorses (UNEP. 2015. *Sustainable Consumption and Production: A Handbook for Policymakers*. Nairobi: United Nations Environment

Programme, p. 10). Attaining sustainable consumption requires a shift in the current patterns of consumption towards types of goods and services that have lower energy or material intensity without compromising on quality of life.

53.   UN–DESA. 2010. *Trends in Sustainable Development: Towards Sustainable Consumption and Production*. New York: United Nations, p. 4.

54.   Sustainable Development Solutions Network Thematic Group on Sustainable Cities. 2010. 'The Urban Opportunity: Enabling Transformative and Sustainable Development', Background Paper for the High-Level Panel of Eminent Persons on the Post–2015 Development Agenda, SDSN, New York.

55.   UNEP, *Sustainable Consumption and Production*.

56.   An ardent critic of the neoclassical paradigm, Haq argued that growth led orientation of development is neither respectful of the physical environment nor has it been able to address satisfactorily issues of poverty, deprivation and vulnerability. Haq, *Reflections on Human Development*, p. 78.

57.   For example, China and South Korea, whose average GDP growth (annual per cent) between 1965 and 2014 has been 9.06 per cent and 7.47 per cent, respectively (World Bank Data Sets).

58.   See Egawa, A. 2013. 'Will Income Inequality Cause a Middle-Income Trap in Asia?', Bruegel Working Paper 2013/06, Bruegel, Brussels; Felipe, J. 2012a. 'Tracking the Middle-Income Trap: What Is It, Who Is in It, and Why? Part 1', ADB Economics Working Paper Series, No. 306, Asian Development Bank, Manila; 2012b. 'Tracking the Middle-Income Trap: What Is It, Who Is in It, and Why? Part 2', ADB Economics Working Paper Series, No. 307, Asian Development Bank, Manila.

59.   Harvey, D. 2005. *A Brief History of Neoliberalism*. Oxford: Oxford University Press.

60.   ILO, *A Fair Globalization*.

61.   Atkinson, A.B. and Morelli, S. 2011. 'Economic Crises and Inequality', Human Development Research Paper 2011/06, UNDP, New York.

62.   IMF. 2009. *World Economic Outlook: Crisis and Recovery*. Washington, DC: IMF.

63.   While the scale of the crisis is distressing, what is puzzling is the spectacular failure of the majority of economists around the world in anticipating and predicting the crisis, with a few exceptions. Indeed, as Silver pointed out, economists of the Wall Street Journal Forecasting Panel predicted only a 38 per cent likelihood of a recession in the USA in 2008 even as the recession had already begun to make its impact. See Silver, N. 2012. *The Signal and the Noise: Why So Many Predictions Fail—But Some Don't*. New York: Penguin Press.

64.   Rajan, R.G. 2010. 'Introduction', in *Fault Lines: How Hidden Fractures Still Threaten the World Economy*. Princeton: Princeton University Press; Haq, M. ul. 1971. 'Employment in The 1970's: A New Perspective,

Society for International Development'. Paper presented at 12th World Conference, WBG, Ottawa, 16–19 May 1971. Accessible at http://pubdocs.worldbank.org/en/526641398285893357/wbg-archives-1651847.pdf; 2 February 2018.

65. Ellmers, B. and Hulova, D. 2013. *The New Debt Vulnerabilities: 10 Reasons Why the Debt Crisis Is Not Over.* Brussels: EURODAD, p. 4.

66. Stiglitz, J.E. 2012. *The Price of Inequality: How Today's Divided Society Endangers Our Future.* New York: W.W. Norton and Company.

67. Rajan, *Fault Lines.*

68. Atkinson and Morelli, *Economic Crises and Inequality.*

69. Khalid, M. 2014. 'Advancing, Sustaining Human Progress: From Concepts to Policies'. Inaugural Mahbub ul Haq–Amartya Sen Lecture, University of Geneva.

70. For details, see Egawa, 'Will Income Inequality Cause a Middle-Income Trap in Asia?'; Felipe, 'Tracking the Middle-Income Trap: What Is It, Who Is in It, and Why? Part 1'.

71. The study estimated that there are thirty-five countries that can be stated as caught in the middle-income trap, and the phenomenon is extensively found in Latin America, Middle East, African countries, and a few Asian countries. In 2010, only fifty-two countries have been classified as *middle-income,* indicating hardly any movement either into or out of this group. For more details, see Felipe, 'Tracking the Middle-Income Trap: What Is It, Who Is in It, and Why? Part 1'.

72. Egawa, 'Will Income Inequality cause a Middle-Income Trap in Asia?', p. 2.

73. Olinto, P., Beegle, K., Sobrado, C., and H. Uematsu. 2013. *The State of the Poor: Where Are The Poor, Where Is Extreme Poverty Harder to End, and What Is the Current Profile of the World's Poor?* Poverty Reduction and Economic Management (PREM) Network, number 125, The World Bank, October 2013. Accessible at http://documents.worldbank.org/curated/en/311511468326955970/pdf/818010BRI0EP120Box0379844B00PUBLIC0.pdf; 20 April 2018; The World Bank. 2016. Poverty and Shared Prosperity: Taking on Inequality. Washington, DC: World Bank Group. Accessible at https://openknowledge.worldbank.org/bitstream/handle/10986/25078/9781464809583.pdf; 10 December 2016.

74. Litting, B., and Griessler, E. 2005. 'Social Sustainability: A Catchword between Political Pragmatism and Social Theory'. *International Journal for Sustainable Development* 8 (1–2): 65–79.

75. Using a broader framework within the three pillars defined by the Brundtland Commission, the social aspect of sustainability can be defined as including 'processes that generate social health and well-being now and, in the

future, and those social institutions that facilitate environment and economic sustainability now and, in the future'. See Dillard, J., Dujon, V., and King, M. 2008. 'Introduction', in *Understanding the Social Dimension of Sustainability*, ed. J. Dillard, V. Dujon, and M. King, pp. 1–12. New York: Routledge, p. 4.

76.   Litting and Griessler, 'Social Sustainability', p. 72.

77.   Osti, G. 2012. 'Green Social Cooperatives in Italy: A Practical Way to Cover the Three Pillars of Sustainability?'. *Sustainability: Science, Practice and Policy* 8 (1): 82–93.

78.   Acemoglu, D. and Robinson, J.A. 2008. 'Persistence of Power, Elites, and Institutions'. *American Economic Review* 98 (1): 267–93; Bardhan, P.K. and Mookherjee, D. 2000. 'Capture and Governance at Local and National Levels'. *American Economic Review* 90 (2): 135–9; Dasgupta, A. and Beard, V.A. 2007. 'Community Driven Development, Collective Action and Elite Capture in Indonesia'. *Development and Change* 38 (2): 229–49.

79.   Akçay, S. 2006. 'Corruption and Human Development'. *Cato Journal* 26 (1): 29–48.

80.   Stewart, F. 2010. 'Horizontal Inequalities as a Cause of Conflict: A Review of CRISE Finding', Background Paper for World Development Report 2011, Centre for Research on Inequality, Human Security and Ethnicity, Queen Elizabeth House, University of Oxford, Oxford.

81.   Brinkman, H-J., Attree, L., and Hezir, S. 2013. *Addressing Horizontal Inequalities as Drivers of Conflict in the Post-2015 Development Agenda*. Geneva: Saferworld, UN Peacebuilding Support Office.

82.   Saferworld. 2012. *People's Peacemaking Perspectives in South Sudan*. Accessible at http://www.saferworld.org.uk/downloads/pubdocs/South%20 Sudan%20Brief.pdf; 7 April 2015.

83.   Saferworld. 2007. *Kosovo at the Crossroads: Perceptions of Conflict, Access to Justice and Opportunities for Peace in Kosovo*. Accessible at http://www.safer-world.org.uk/images/pubdocs/SafePlace%20Conflict%20Analysis%202%20 Report%2020071202%20English.pdf; 7 April 2015.

84.   Stewart, F. 2009. 'Horizontal Inequality: Two Types of Trap'. *Journal of Human Development and Capabilities* 10 (3): 315–40.

85.   Stewart, 'Horizontal Inequality', p. 324.

86.   Iyer, S. and Chawla, P. 2017. 'Entangled Basic Capabilities & Social Cohesion in India: Measuring Exclusions, Impoverishments and Distances'. Paper presented at IARIW-ICRIER Conference on Experiences and Challenges in Measuring Income, Inequality, and Poverty in South Asia, Delhi, 23–5 November.

87.   Baulch, B., Chuyen, T.T.K., Haughton, D., and Haughton, J. 2007. 'Ethnic Minority Development in Vietnam'. *Journal of Development Studies* 43 (7): 1151–76.

10 Epilogue

The genesis of the human development paradigm was at a time when there was considerable vigour among the countries of the Global North and South to find an alternative path for development. The series of intensive dialogues that took place in the 1970s and 1980s provided the much-needed platform for the developing countries to shape their destiny. In the 2010s, has this agenda been fulfilled? What has been achieved? Has people-centric development remained only in the realm of rhetoric? To what extent can developing countries cope with the current adversities of capitalist development in its present form? Can the inter- and intra-generation inequalities be bridged adequately?

In the 2010s, when the global society is situated at the cusp of change, two options present themselves. One is a movement towards further individualization of development trajectories in the spirit of the utilitarian logic. The other is a move towards a more universal vision that values equity, justice, and peoples' agency. The quest in this book has been to revive the debate about the meta-question of human flourishing and its pathways that enables people to live a life that they value and have reason to value. This has indeed been the essence of the human development paradigm since its inception, and needs urgent revival in the present times.

The journey of the human development paradigm with its integral processes has left its own imprints—some firm, some still nebulous. If the expectation has been to advocate for a people-centred paradigm, its success has been rather impressive, as within a period of less than three decades, human development has become an integral part of the lexicon of development. However, if its evaluation were to be from the deeper perspective of Mahbub Haq's original objective of bringing about a change in the development paradigm itself, that seems to be a distant reality. The rise of HDI as an alternate to GNP has certainly been an achievement to reckon with, but the typically restrictive focus of the market-oriented approach has reinterpreted human development as being synonymous with education, health, and nutrition, thereby undermining the very paradigm from within.

The value of liberal spaces for all, as propagated by Amartya Sen, seems to be captive to liberalism and neoliberalism. The ethos of neoliberalism that favours only a select few who have the purchasing power is diametrically opposite to the spirit of universalism and human freedom that is advocated by the human development paradigm. Numerous concerns have been raised about the siege of the concepts of choices, freedoms, and agency, which constitute the core elements of the human development approach, within the larger project of global capitalism. Even today, equity and justice—dimensions that are enshrined as values of the human development paradigm—have not been recognized, let alone integrated into development policies.

Social sectors continue to be oriented as those constituting welfare, rather than being recognized for their intrinsic value of enhancing capabilities. Poverty and deprivation are most commonly viewed from the monetary lens even as efforts to assess and address multidimensional poverty are slowly gaining credence. The employment scenario in most countries remains fragile, with social protection being trimmed and truncated in the name of fiscal stringency. The world continues to be an unequal arena for women, restricting their choices and freedoms, and not taking into account their substantial contributions both in monetary and non-monetary spheres. Crises of environmental degradation and climate change have evoked animated responses from countries, although not backed up adequately by effective action.

The co-opting of the human development phenomenon by the neoliberal paradigm has led to a widespread use of its vocabulary of agency, participation, and the like, without imbibing its spirit. In the struggle between two opposite ways of viewing the world, the neoliberal paradigm, rather than the human development approach, seems to be gaining in strength as the concepts and lexicon are usurped by the mainstream paradigm. Consequently, the policy regime fails to recognize the diversity of individuals and their needs, leading to the measurement of human progress to the narrow confines of averages. Data systems of the world continue to fail in adequately capturing differences across social groups, genders, and ethnic minorities. Vulnerability of individuals has not yet been mapped adequately, nor have policies to address them gained prominence.

Consistent advocacy by numerous stakeholders has yielded some results, one outstanding example being the formulation and implementation of MDGs, and subsequently, the SDGs. Though the global agenda-setting has been in the spirit of fostering equity and justice, its translation is in the hands of agencies that are steeped in the neoliberal paradigm. Consequently, piecemeal interpretation and subsequent implementation weaken the spirit of the agenda. The only way to counter these tendencies is for people to find a place within *people-centred development*, so that the term does not become empty rhetoric at the hands of bureaucrats and the select few who are influential in the global policy arena.

The global policy architecture has significantly influenced the human development paradigm. Any discussion about the future path of human development without being mindful of the global policy imperatives that enable or hinder it is an exercise in futility. Over the years, global systems have played a very important role in nudging the increasingly *unequal world* towards equity and justice. The rejuvenation of this architecture is imperative as the onslaught of economic crisis, environmental fragility, and worsening social inequities cut across economies in both the developed and the developing world. Increasingly, the *agency* of countries in shaping national policies is being undermined by widespread globalization and increasing strength of neoliberal forces. In order to counter these tendencies in the developmental realm, numerous global dialogues have been organized by international agencies on issues that matter to people. At the political level, the rise of the G-20 after 2007 is a demonstration of the resolve of countries to provide an alternate platform for dialogue on contentious issues.

Interestingly, for all the attention bestowed upon maintaining and boosting economic growth, the world continues to be volatile, with decelerating and fluctuating growth rates. The fact that the world is much more interconnected now than ever before in terms of finance, trade, and immigration flows renders the situation even more challenging. The fluid geopolitical situation, with the reshaping of global power relations and the emergence of newer coalitions of countries, adds an additional dimension and points to a search to find alternative pathways out of this complex situation.

The development scenario of the 2010s is at one stroke different and yet similar to the situation of crisis that prevailed globally in the 1980s. While the 1980s were riddled with financial crises, in the 2010s, several ills emerging from the long-time neglect of core developmental issues have resurfaced to the forefront. The financial crisis of 2007–8 that shocked developed countries out of a false sense of complacency not only affected growth rates but also had a severe impact on employment, which continues to linger almost a decade after the initial shock. The hazards of an increasingly globalized world are also being more manifest as a ripple in one country cascades into shock waves in others through trade and financial flows. The environmental crisis has also assumed alarming proportions as increasing incidence of so-called natural disasters wreak havoc across coastal, hilly, and upland regions alike. While the nature of the crisis in the 2010s differs from that in the 1980s, the complexity of the triple crisis—financial, economic, and environmental—calls for a complete break from the dominant development paradigm in order to ensure more humane and just development outcomes. Given the world's unflattering record on both economic growth and environmental fronts while relentlessly pursuing the growth-oriented policy, the time is now ripe for revisiting the development paradigm on values of human flourishing and freedom.

Fundamental to this policy paralysis is the fact that the values on which the development paradigm is based have not yet changed. Moreover, progress cannot be achieved or sustained amid conflicts and violence, which are often rooted in social and economic deprivations. It is, in fact, quite a challenge to visualize sustainable development in a globalized world when respect for *global commons* is minimal and a large number of countries relentlessly follow paths that typically lead to unsustainable development. The need is for sufficiently nuanced and differentiated policies that fit the local conditions of each country, since global prescriptions will not work and policies need to be tailored and adapted to local situations. In turn, this requires public debate and engagement to shape feasible alternatives pathways that gain widespread acceptance and result in a new social compact.

The global agenda setting is no longer confined to national, regional, international, or supranational narratives but is decided by the interconnections between these levels. But the fears of the rising protectionist tendencies and deepening right-wing political narratives can be addressed proactively only when there is an affirmation to retain the coherence of the global society. The growth–development dilemma in the global arena seems to be groping in the dark to address issues of forced migration and emerging displacement of people because of technology, digitization, and environmental disasters. Further, financing for human development has always remained on the sidelines of the debate, and has not been taken up the vigour with which it ought to be pursued. With shrinking resources and multiplying responsibilities, including national and global commitments, national governments are neither able to meet the rising aspirations of people, nor able to garner sufficient political will to ensure adherence to global policies that they have ratified.

At a time when countries from the South are gaining global dominance in policymaking, several alternative regional platforms seem to have arisen to seek solutions only for their collective challenges. These outcomes are extremely crucial, but the perpetuation of regionalism would only compromise achieving the *global whole*. In the multipolar world, regional co-operation and informal networks seem to be coming up with solutions to key global issues. They seem to have provided space, opportunities, and participation, and have been mediating across governments, markets, and civil society, mainly through informal processes. The invigoration of this process would now have to culminate in a formal process, when the global governance systems are reformed to a larger democratic identity. It was precisely a decade ago that the demand for reforming global governance institutions had gained momentum, but did not gain traction for several reasons. For the human development paradigm to succeed, it would be necessary for a social compact based not merely on goals, targets, and indicators, but on the *values* that govern them. This has been a long standing demand yet to be fulfilled.

Finding answers to these questions needs yet another round of global dialogues on peoples' choices, well-being, and freedom, which are imperative for both the developed and the developing world. Human development advocated for a just world rooted in the dignity of the human being and one wherein the entitlements of people are ensured. This rights-based approach, combined with a concern for the core values of *humanness* as reiterated by Aristotle, seems to be moving farther and farther away from the horizon of global actors. The world continues to grapple with the overwhelming concern of ensuring self-interest, whether it is at the level of the individual, community, or nation-state.

We end with a few questions: can the twenty-first century afford to continue with this attitude and approach? Can global governance continue to be held captive in the hands of a few powerful nations? Should the voices of the poor and disadvantaged across all countries not find a rightful place in shaping policies for a better world? Human development must succeed in this effort if the twenty-first century is to usher in a more humane development that focuses on the *humanness* of human beings.

Annexure A

*Critical Reflections on Values That Shaped
Contemporary Approaches to Development*

The theoretical paradigms influencing economics have undergone
several shifts since the time of Adam Smith. Common to these changes
has been a quest for values that ensure equity and justice. These
issues acquired relevance during the eighteenth and nineteenth
centuries even as tumultuous developments such as the Industrial
Revolution (1760–1820/1840), the French Revolution (1789–99),
and American Independence (1776) took place, and the demand for
freedom and liberty became vociferous. The advent of the Industrial
Revolution led to the fading away of the feudal order and rise in the
importance of the individual as an entity. The individual's worth, it was
asserted, emerged more from his or her contribution to production
rather than from belonging to a particular group or community. The
French Revolution reinforced this change in perception and brought
to the fore the notion of an individual's liberties. These developments
contributed to the rise of capitalism and the philosophy of *laissez-faire*,
which advocated the primacy of an individual's natural rights with the
pursuit of his/her self interest as its natural corollary.

These processes inadvertently brought to the forefront issues such
as the relationship between economics and ethics, and thereby, issues
of equity and justice. To a modern twenty-first-century economist,
trained in the precise tools and techniques that the discipline has
come to acquire and advocate, it may not be very apparent that in the

early times of the development of the discipline, issues of ethics were
the core concerns of economists. Economics and ethics came from
common moorings of the intertwining of the disciplines of philosophy and economics. Issues of morality were intertwined with theories
of public choice, and ethical norms to regulate private conduct were
stipulated routinely by economists.

The preoccupation of thinkers with ethics and public policy in the
early years of the formation of the discipline of economics yielded rich
dividends and opened up streams of thought that continue to influence
present day analysis. Two important philosopher–economists who were
influential in this context were Jeremy Bentham, whose 1781 publication, *Morals and Legislation*,[1] formed the nucleus of what emerged as the
utilitarian school of thought, and Immanuel Kant, whose 1788 *Critique
of Practical Reason*[2] formed the basis for the principle of *Categorical
Imperative* and for the theory of social contract that ensued. Ironically,
though these two were contemporaries and had put forth their ideas
around the common theme of equity and justice during the same time,
the paths they followed were completely different.

It is a mark of the intellectual distance between the early philosopher–economists and the modern-day intellectuals that economics,
once considered a branch of ethics, has attained such dominance that it
has maintained only a nebulous relationship with ethics. The influence
of ethics has been contained within the confines of *welfare economics*,
implying thereby indirectly that human welfare is not necessarily the
concern of other branches of economics. The disjuncture between
economics and ethics occurred largely because the engineering branch
of economics overtook the normative side of economics.[3] This resulted
in a deep and disturbing change in the view of a human being from an
ethical individual, whose own values are shaped and modified in the
light of the values that govern society, to one who is primarily self-
seeking and whose primary goal is of self-interest. The synchronization
of individual needs with those of the collective remained an enigma
that continues to intrigue and engage theoreticians and philosophers
to the current day.

This view of a self-seeking individual has been questioned time and
again by prominent economists and thinkers. John Rawls highlighted
that individual accounting based on self-interest could deviate from
social accounting and emphasized the role of institutions to ensure

distributional justice. Sen pointed out that an individual is not always self-seeking and the family as a social unit or a firm as an economic unit cannot operate entirely on the basis of only such behaviour of individuals. His Nobel Prize-winning work highlights the difficulties in arriving at social choice from individual decisions.[4]

Equity is most commonly understood as *impartial justice* or *fairness*. It is considered to be achieved when everyone is treated fairly and equally. Equity has the notion of justice embedded in it, but this raises more questions such as how is fairness judged? Fairness in what? What is the process by which fairness is ensured and what are its dimensions? As evident, the questions for which answers are needed straddle the realms of both philosophy and economics and are rich and varied in nature.

THE UTILITARIAN APPROACH

The utilitarian approach owes its origin to Jeremy Bentham,[5] an early student of Adam Smith, though the concept of utility is of much earlier vintage dating back to the Epicurean thought in the seventeenth and eighteenth centuries. Bentham,[6] following Hume, presented the principle of utility as the 'test and measure of all virtue' replacing thereby the idea of the 'original contract' based on the supremacy of natural rights, the state and the church.

Utility was defined by Bentham as 'that property in an object whereby it tends to produce benefit, advantage, pleasure, good or happiness'.[7] It is obtained when 'we contemplate an action impersonally and discover the action actually possesses certain identifiable characteristic'. The *Happiness Principle* was at the core of the utilitarian logic. A lawmaker was expected to frame laws that were in conformity with happiness. 'Pleasures then, and the avoidance of pains, are the *ends* that the legislator has in view'.[8]

An action was viewed as right if it promoted utility and as wrong if it promoted disutility, the reverse of happiness.[9] 'An action then may be said to be conformable to the principle of utility, or, for shortness sake, to utility, (meaning with respect to the community at large) when the tendency it has to augment the happiness of the community is greater than any it has to diminish it.'[10] The interests of the community were nothing but the 'sum of the interests of the members who compose it'.

Accordingly, *good* laws were those that yielded 'the greatest good for the greatest number', wherein each person accounted for one in making that number.[11] As Mill commented, 'the happiness which forms the utilitarian standard of what is right in conduct, is not the agent's own happiness, but that of all concerned. As between his own happiness and that of others, utilitarianism required him to be as strictly impartial as a disinterested and benevolent spectator'.[12]

Two implications are important to note here: (*a*) pleasure and pain are ascertained by the *consequences* they produce and *not by intent*, a phenomenon known as *consequentialism;* and (*b*) total pleasure or pain is nothing but an aggregation of the pains and pleasures of individuals who constitute the community—or *sum ranking procedure*. It was considered possible to calculate, compare, and measure pleasure and pain using felicific calculus.

The Happiness Principle, along with the sum ranking procedure, led to the *Principle of Impartiality*, wherein one person's happiness is counted for exactly as much as another's. For the utilitarians, maximizing welfare would mean maximizing utility, which would ensure equal treatment of everybody's interests and avoid *unfair discrimination*. Utility is maximized when incremental utility from an additional unit of good or service is equal across people in cases where resource base is independent of its distribution. In instances when the resource base is not independent of its distribution, fairness requires that the marginal utility gain of gainers equals marginal utility loss of losers. The famous dictum (attributed to Bentham by J.S. Mill), 'everybody to count for one, nobody for more than one',[13] sums up the utilitarian logic, and it is this dictum that has been the subject of much discussion. Subsequent critiques of the utilitarian paradigm dwell on the shortcomings of this summary statement. It is not as if Bentham was unaware of the fact that all individuals do not have equal capacity for pleasure and pain. However, he assumed that the law of large numbers would balance out interpersonal qualitative differences, so that the average intensity would be the same for individuals taken together as a community.

Another important aspect is to recognize that the notion of utility embedded within itself the notion of liberty. Utility represented the 'fullest satisfaction of the purely subjective desires of individuals and society'.[14] Implied in this choice was the notion that individuals were free to make their choices and were also free to evaluate and estimate their own experiences of pleasure and pain. By ingeniously combining the notion of liberty with hedonistic calculations and were they pre-empted questions about the motives of an individual. As Rosen[15] comments, '[b]y incorporating liberty into their hedonism, many of the problems developed within contemporary utilitarianism regarding quantities and qualities of pleasure simply disappear. So long as each person counts for no more than any other, it is up to each to choose which pleasures to value most and which pains to avoid'.

The utilitarian paradigm was further deepened and expanded by J.S. Mill, a student of Bentham. It is often claimed that Mill rejected the utilitarian logic of Bentham. This does not seem to be the case, although he was distinctly uncomfortable with two main propositions of Bentham: the equation of an individual's utility with his or her own pleasure, and the assumption that the individual will act in the general interest of society. The first proposition seemed to imply that the goal of human beings was only to maximize pleasure, which did not seem very different from the pursuits of animals. Mill sought a way out by bringing in a distinction between lower and higher pleasures, with the latter including mental, physical, aesthetic, and moral pleasures.

With regard to the second proposition, Mill's contention was that individuals act in order to promote private interests or *good* rather than public interest, and that this would not cause any problem as long as private actions did not violate the rights of others. Mill's emphasis was on liberty as it provides opportunities for self-development, the freedom to choose how one lives, and to express opinions as long as they do not threaten the freedom or well-being of others.[16] Mill declares, 'No society in which these liberties are not, on the whole, respected, is free, whatever may be its form of government; and none is completely free in which they do not exist absolute and unqualified'.[17] Mill was nonetheless wary of the tyranny of the majority, as it could inhibit people from developing their individuality. Mill also objected to the use of utility as the basis for distinguishing between right and wrong as consequences of an act stretch into the future and could be too distant to the time when individual needs to make his or her decision.

However, in another context, Mill wrote,

Whoever said that it was necessary to foresee all the consequences of an individual action 'As they go down into countless ages of coming time?'—Some consequences of action accelerate others are its natural result according to known laws of the universe. The former for the most part cannot be foreseen; but the whole course of human life is founded upon the fact that the latter can ... The commonest person lives according to maxims of prudence wholly founded on foresight of consequences.[18]

By bringing in subjectivity and individual judgements about one's own actions, Mill enhanced the utilitarian framework within the fold of its own logic. Subsequent extensions to the utilitarian debate were made by Henry Sidgwick and later by G.E. Moore, who challenged hedonism and questioned the *good* as some state of consciousness such as pleasure.

When viewed in its overall logic, utilitarianism continues to be biased towards individuals who overvalue material well-being (for example, commodities, goods, and services). The appeal of the utilitarian school lay in the fact that it was a philosophy that professed core values and a normative system with a strong legal slant. It adopted a uniform method of analysis that could be applied comprehensively in the social sciences. These features contributed to its being established as a fundamental principle of the then-budding discipline of economics.[19] The utilitarians succeeded in transforming ethical debates about happiness by adding numerous economic, legal, and political dimensions to it. At a practical level, they formulated ethical theoretical foundations for an emerging legal system that could test the extant laws using the principle of utility. The extent of its sway on economic analysis is evident to the present day, when utilitarianism is considered to be a mainstream paradigm and any analyst seeking to deviate from it would need to justify the reasons for doing so![20]

Utilitarianism deeply influenced the foundations of thinking about development. Over time, however, the ethical basis and the subjective conceptualization of utility as satisfaction or happiness was forgotten; income and wealth became the metric of measuring utility, and welfare came to be simplistically recognized and judged by the metric of incomes and wealth alone. In large part, Amartya Sen's critique of the utilitarian theory revolves around the loose conceptualization of utility and the problems it poses in building a framework that is adequately sensitive to distributional concerns and interpersonal comparisons.

One major challenge in using the utilitarian logic is that the term *utility* has been used with differing connotations by analysts. Utility can be interpreted in the sense that Mill did in *Utilitarianism*—as 'happiness' or 'fulfilment'—or as Kenneth Arrow[21] interpreted, as 'preferences'. Thus, maximization of utility could, depending on the connotation used, mean maximization of pleasure, happiness, or fulfilment of preferences. Whichever connotation is chosen, it is clear that it deals with a mental attitude, as utilities derived by different people from the same commodity could vary substantially depending on their perceptions of the *good* and its contribution to their utility. Perceptions, in turn, are often shaped by circumstances, with expectations tailored to the situations within which individuals are compelled to live. For example, a poor and undernourished woman may be deprived of material necessities but may have voluntarily restrict her desires to the realm of what is feasible under the circumstances she faces and, thereby, be quite content with life. Judging such a person's situation from the point of view of utility—perceived as desire fulfilment or happiness—would lead us to judge her to be *happy*, though this has been arrived by ignoring her physical conditions, a phenomenon that Sen terms as 'physical condition neglect'.[22]

Further, the utilitarian metric is subject to what Sen calls 'valuation neglect', as it fails to take into account the motivations that underlie the choice of individuals.[23] The choices that people make are influenced by societal norms and other social obligations, and are not always made as per personal choice. A glaring example in this regard is provided by the preference for male child in patriarchal societies where women have fewer rights. In such societies, women often exhibit a preference for male children and may even choose to voluntarily, and often illegally, abort female foetuses to ensure that the child that is born is male. So, while they gain greater utility from choosing to give birth to a male child, their motivations and choices are not really their own, but guided by societal preferences for male children. The failure to pay attention to such factors leads to 'valuation neglect'.

Apart from the operational difficulty in applying the utilitarian principles to real-world situations, there is also an issue of the information base on which the approach bases its judgements. Sen argues that by focusing only on utility, the approach misses out important aspects, such as an individual's rights and freedoms. Sen criticizes the utilitarian paradigm for its preoccupation with consequences, ignoring completely the processes that lead to the consequences.[24]

Both Sen and Rawls also find fault with the neoclassical approach for its use of the principles of 'welfarism' and 'sum-ranking', as both these principles ignore the fundamental fact of diversity of individuals—their preferences and needs. According to Rawls,[25] the main idea of classical utilitarianism is that 'society is rightly ordered, and therefore just, when its major institutions are arranged so as to achieve the greatest net balance of satisfaction summed over all the individuals belonging to it'. This assumption wishes away distributional concerns.

The main drawback of the utilitarian framework is its preoccupation with the maximization of total utility, largely ignoring the distributional aspects of utility among individuals. The simple fact that high aggregate utility may be largely due to the utility of people at the top of the income ladder, while many at the bottom of the social ladder may be doing not so well, or even suffering greatly, does not enter the utility calculus. Extreme inequalities may exist as a result of the maximizing the total utility criterion, which can lead to the argument that a perverse distribution seems to be a natural outcome of the utilitarian approach. Such a distribution may come into existence as those who are better able to convert resources into utility are able to garner a larger share of resources—in turn, an efficient way of ensuring the generation of the highest quantum of utility. However, this approach does not consider those with severe disabilities whose need for resources is much greater, although their efficiency in converting resources to utility may be far less than that of those who are not similarly challenged. To argue for efficiency at the cost of humanitarian considerations seems to vitiate the very spirit of equity and justice in the process of development. The pursuit of such policies may in effect lead to worsening of inequalities in the economy.

THE RAWLSIAN APPROACH

Rawls contested the utilitarian understanding of justice, and presented an alternative conception of justice in the Kantian tradition. His focus was on the principles of justice that govern a well-ordered society where everyone is presumed to act justly. Adopting the notion of justice as fairness, he laid down the basic principles that people in a society would adhere to in their own interest. Situating his theory of justice within the contract theory, wherein the principles of justice are chosen by rational persons, he identified two distinct components involved: (a) understanding the initial situation or what he calls the 'original position'; and (b) problem of choice in choosing a set of principles that are agreed upon.[26]

The original position is a hypothetical situation that is more of an analytical tool that facilitates the understanding of conditions under which moral relationships can be interpreted. A requirement of the original position is that people in a society are unaware of their social position, assets, and abilities, though they have general awareness about the society and its conditions. This *veil of ignorance* is considered necessary so that one's prior attributes with respect to wealth and social standing are unable to influence the design of the principles of justice.

Given these initial conditions, Rawls argues that persons in a society would choose two principles: (a) 'equality in the assignment of basic rights and duties'; and (b) 'social and economic inequalities ... of wealth and authority are just only if they result in compensating benefits for everyone, and in particular for the least advantaged members of society'.[27]

Principle (b) is called the difference principle. Applying the difference principle requires interpersonal comparison of relative advantage, which is defined in terms of social primary goods that include 'rights, liberties and opportunities, income and wealth, and the social bases of social respect'.[28]

Social and economic inequalities are subject to two conditions: (a) they must be attached to offices and positions that are open to all people under equality of opportunity; and (b) they are to provide the greatest benefit to the least advantaged people in society. Justice is ensured through 'equal liberty' and 'equality in distribution' of primary goods. The premise is that people would co-operate with each other as each one's well-being depends on this scheme of co-operation.

Rawls improved upon the neoclassical framework on two issues: (a) he replaced utility as a basis of justice by 'social primary goods'; and (b) he paid attention to the *process* of arriving at the principles of justice.

The social contract has an embedded commitment from the concerned individuals to honour its principles. Thus, the vision of Rawls of a well-ordered society is one wherein individuals agree to and accept the principles of justice. The principles are enforced in basic social institutions and all those involved comply with the chosen principles because of their inherent sense of justice.

In his critique on the Rawlsian approach, Sen points out that the informational base used in terms of primary goods is inadequate for a freedom-oriented assessment of justice. Rawls's focus is on the means to freedom, not the extent of freedom that the person actually enjoys. Given that conversion of primary goods and resource into freedoms differs from person to person, the same or equal holding of primary goods can coexist with serious inequalities in actual freedom enjoyed by different persons.[29] Further, Sen points out that 'by concentrating on the *means* to freedom rather than on the *extent* of freedom, his theory of the just basic structure of the society has stopped short of paying adequate attention to the freedom as such'.[30]

The theory ignores variations in 'health, longevity, climatic conditions, location, work conditions, temperament, and even body size (affecting food and cloth requirements)', and judges advantage purely in terms of primary goods leading to a partially blind morality.[31] Sen forcefully argues that equality of freedom cannot be generated by equality of distribution of primary goods due to interpersonal variations in the way in which primary goods are converted into respective capabilities. Under the Difference Principle, a disadvantaged person is likely to get just as much income as a normal person. However, Sen is of the opinion that to take disabilities or special health needs, or physical or mental defects as morally irrelevant is especially hard and undesirable.

Both primary goods and utilities miss out crucial aspects such as freedoms. Sen's attempt in developing the capability approach was to treat freedoms as being intrinsically valuable in all such assessments.

ON LIBERTARIANISM: THE ROLE OF ENTITLEMENTS

The libertarian approach, as advocated by its prominent exponent Robert Nozick, through the entitlement theory developed in *Anarchy, State and Utopia*,[32] accords priority to liberties that are to be equally guaranteed to each individual. This would imply rejecting equality, or any *patterning* of end states such as the distribution of incomes or happiness.

For Nozick, social justice is an entitlement which forms part of the *basal core* of entitlements.[33] The concept relies on Locke's concept of natural state wherein each individual has a claim to certain natural rights with respect to physical objects as well as to other persons.

A *just* distribution encompasses acquisition, transfer, and rectification, as enunciated below:

1. Justice in acquisition—the appropriation of *unowned* things, as long as enough is left over for others: Individuals have a right to own property and to self-ownership, which gives them the freedom to determine *what to do with what is theirs*. The role of the state is minimal and is confined to protection of individual property rights.
2. Justice in transfer—the acquisition of a holding from someone who is entitled to that holding.
3. Rectification—any unjust transfers are to be rectified by compensation.

Under the libertarian approach, social justice as an entitlement is an essential part of *basal core*. An advantage of Nozick's theory is that if a certain distribution of goods (D1) is just (according to whichever theory) and if people voluntarily move to a different distribution (D2) observing justice in transfer, then D2 will also be just. Whether D2 is patterned according to equality, need or the Difference Principle is irrelevant.

The entitlement theory is historical in approach and is concerned about the process of distribution, though it is not clear as to how long back does one have to go in time so as to ascertain the legitimacy—or otherwise—of the process of acquiring the entitlement. The theory holds that if the processes through which the distribution of assets came about are legitimate, then the current asset holding ought to be considered legitimate. This leads Nozick[34] to make a rather controversial statement that there is 'no presumption in favour of equality, or any other overall end state or patterning. It cannot be merely assumed that equality must be built into any theory of justice'.

Given this belief, any state intervention through (re)distribution of resources—for example, through taxation—is considered *unjust*, as goods and resources are either created by individuals or are pre-owned, and do not constitute manna from heaven, over which the state can exercise control. Nozick sees no role for the state to help individuals who were unluckily born with few resources (that is, those who are poor, weak, sick, and so on), and argues that it is for individuals to decide whether to help such people by giving their resources as a gift. Any redistribution that might occur would, therefore, be only because of voluntary decisions of individuals to transfer some of their assets in pursuit of some moral values.

An illustration may make this principle clear. Suppose Cristiano Ronaldo, a famous footballer whom people love to watch, asks to be paid GBP 25 of each ticket sold for home games. The club agrees, and fans are happy to pay the extra GBP 25. If four million people go to his games in a season, he will be richer by GBP 100,000. According to Nozick, this is not unjust, because everyone gave the extra money voluntarily. Yet the new distribution would be deemed unjust by the other theories of justice. Nozick argued that the crux is about respecting people's (natural) rights—in particular, their rights to property and their rights to self-ownership. He believed that people must have the freedom to decide what they want to do with what they own. Each person is separate, an individual, and their autonomy must be respected. People are 'ends-in-themselves', and they cannot be used in ways they do not agree to, even if that would lead to some supposed greater good (for example, other people getting what they need). This has a radical conclusion: to take property away from people in order to redistribute it according to some pattern violates their rights. But this is exactly what taxation (for the purpose of redistribution) does. To tax Ronaldo's extra earnings and return the money to the poorer fans violates his right to the money. It is interesting to note that the connotation of *ends* in the Nozickian society is about leaving individuals to decide what kind of a just outcome they would like to be part of, rather than seeing the well-being of each individual in society as being equally important. Nozick's concept relies on Locke's notion of natural state, where each individual has a claim to certain natural rights with respect to physical objects and to other persons.

Nozick's ideas have evoked strong reactions, with several scholars such as Buchanan,[35] Drèze and Sen,[36] Sandel,[37] and Schaefer[38] objecting to his views on several grounds. Specifically, Buchanan contests the way in which the libertarian framework, without any reference to considerations of equality, considers as just any entitlement as long as it is obtained through just means. He sees no reason in 'why ... a young Kennedy or Rockefeller "entitled" to an inheritance merely because it was voluntarily bequeathed to him'.[39]

On similar lines, Sandel argues that the libertarians deem any distribution resulting from the play of market forces to be just, and fail to acknowledge the 'arbitrariness of fortune'.[40] Schaefer points out that there is no reason to imagine that any individual's present holdings are the result of a series of 'just' transactions emanating from the origins of human history, and maintain that by adopting an excessively theoretical approach to justice, Nozick ignores the human and political circumstances under which issues of justice arise.

Sen raises a fundamental issue with respect to the discourse of Nozick and his basal space, where there is a combination of rights of the *zero–one* type, such that if there is a violation of any of the rights, it is deemed to be a denial of justice. Equal assignment of libertarian rights for all is at the top of the hierarchy of spaces that are of importance. Sen[41] argues that the assignment of equal rights may not guarantee equality in other spaces that may be important for the lives of the individuals—for example, in avoiding morbidity, being well nourished and healthy, being able to read, and so on. The libertarian approach is based on a narrow informational base. The virtual absence of the state implicitly means weak political presence and lack of accountability with respect to distributional losses.

Reconceptualizing the notion of entitlements, Drèze and Sen[42] argue that entitlements can be ensured through provisions for the right to *use* some commodities without owning them outright. But this would entail a process of justice in the presence of an active state. For example, free distribution of state-owned food for the purpose of public consumption might be construed as falling in the category of *use* without ownership. Deaths due to famine which considered to have been tackled as pre-globalization phenomenon in most countries have resurfaced in their own distinctive forms in several countries. The food crisis in the twenty-first century in East Africa (Ethiopia, Sudan), southern Africa (Malawi), and West Africa (Niger) has been an outcome of catastrophic distributional failures; ineffective response of the market and state action led to rise in malnutrition and under-nutrition levels as well. It has been argued that although often market failures have been considered as a *proximate* cause of disrupted food, the underlying cause of input, output and commodity market failures is to understood as a 'liberalisation failure'; that is, a flawed policy process.[43]

Libertarianism is insensitive to the social consequences of such constraints and requirements. Most disturbingly, the libertarian structure tends to perpetuate inequities in society as there can be severe limitations to basal space, and when this is combined with the absence of trade-off in the social combination, it makes this type of libertarianism inadequate as a theory of justice.

The weak informational base of the neoclassical approach is unsatisfactory in ensuring equity. The Rawlsian framework perceives justice through *equal liberty* and *equality in distribution* of primary goods. These resources need to be free and equal to all in order to enable the individual to pursue his or her various objectives. The entitlement framework measures well-being through entitlements, but not does not ensure equality of other spaces. The basal norms of the capabilities ethic are based on capabilities and functionings that can evolve over a period of time.

Selection of the basal norm influences justice. The array of base information in most frameworks prior to the capabilities approach included physical goods, fundamental rights, income and wealth, and so on, which were arrived at on the premise that equal liberties would help achieve equal outcomes. This assumption also implied that these *resources* are useful for the pursuit of different objectives that the individuals may have, need to be free, and available equally to all. The capabilities approach rejects this postulate. Sen argues that the assignment of equal rights may not guarantee equality in other spaces that may be important for the lives of the individuals, for example in avoiding morbidity, being well-nourished and healthy, being able to read, and so on. The ambivalence to distributional errors on individual losses, too, has its imprints on the evaluative metric. The narrow basal selection of primary goods would provide an evaluative outcome of limited inequalities, whereas the expansion to capabilities and entitlements broadens the metric to encompass rights, liberties, choices, and opportunities that enhance human freedom. The role of affirmative action by the state in ensuring an appropriate socio-legal framework is seen as equally important in achieving distributive justice in the society.

NOTES AND REFERENCES

1. Bentham, J. [1781] 2000. *The Principles of Morals and Legislation*. Kitchener: Batoche Books.

2. Kant, I. 1956. *Critique of Practical Reason*, trans. L.W. Beck. Indianapolis: Bobbs-Merrill.

3. For more discussion on this issue, see Sen, A. 1987. *Commodities and Capabilities*. Oxford: Elsevier Science Publishers.

4. Rawls, J. 1971. *A Theory of Justice*. Cambridge, Mass: Belknap Press of Harvard University Press; Galston, W.A. 1982. 'Moral Personality and Liberal Theory: John Rawls's "Dewey Lectures"'. *Political Theory* 10 (4): 492–519. Accessible at http://www.jstor.org/stable/190960; Sen, A. 1977. 'Social Choice Theory: A Re-examination'. *Econometrica* 45 (1): 53–89.

5. In an unpublished manuscript, Bentham states 'I dreamt t' other night that I was a founder of a sect ... It was called the sect of the utilitarians' (as cited in Burns, J.H. 2005. 'Happiness and Utility: Jeremy Bentham's Equation'. *Utilitas* 17 [1]: 46–61, 49. doi: 10.1017/S0953820804001396). John Stuart Mill, Bentham's student, also makes a claim to have been the first person to use the term utilitarian. Mill states in *What Utilitarianism Is*, 'the author of this essay has reason for believing himself to be the first person who brought the word utilitarian into use. He did not invent it but adopted it from a passing expression in Mr Galt's *Annals of The Parish*' (Mill, J.S. [1863] 2003. 'Utilitarianism', in *Utilitarianism and on Liberty: Including Mill's 'Essay on Bentham' and Selection from the Writings of Jeremy Bentham and John Austin*, ed. M. Warnock, pp. 181–235. Malden: Blackwell Publishing, p. 186). For details, see Burns, 'Happiness and Utility'; Mill, 'Utilitarianism'.

6. As cited in Warnock, M. 2003. *Utilitarianism and On Liberty: Including Mill's 'Essay on Bentham' and Selections from the Writings of Jeremy Bentham and John Austin*. Malden: Blackwell Publishing, p. 6.

7. Bentham, *The Principles of Morals and Legislation*, p. 14.

8. Bentham, *The Principles of Morals and Legislation*, p. 30. Further, Bentham identified pleasures including as those of sense, wealth, skill, amity, a good name, power, piety, benevolence, malevolence, of memory, of imagination, expectation, association, and relief. The pains specified included pains of privation, senses, awkwardness, enmity, an ill name, piety, benevolence, malevolence, memory, imagination, expectation, and pains dependent on association (Bentham, *The Principles of Morals and Legislation*, p. 35).

9. As Schumpeter comments, in this respect, utilitarians were similar to the philosophers and the natural law system whose characteristic feature was to 'derive "laws" about society from a very stable and highly simplified (understanding of) human nature'. See Schumpeter, J. 1954. *History of Economic Analysis*. New York: Oxford University Press, p. 128.

10. Bentham, *The Principles of Morals and Legislation*, p. 15.

11. Burns, 'Happiness and Utility'.

12. Mill, 'Utilitarianism', p. 194.

13. As Guidi states, 'there are reasons to trust John Stuart Mill for attributing to Bentham the "dictum" in its literal phrasing. The only passage in which the rule of impartiality is formulated in similar terms is in *Rationale of Judicial Evidence*, a work edited by young John Stuart under Bentham's guidance. Nonetheless, the rule as such is clearly implied in Bentham's most known formulations of the greatest happiness principle' (Guidi, E.L.M. 2008. '"Everybody to Count for One, Nobody for More Than One"': The Principle of Equal Consideration of Interests from Bentham to Pigou'. *Revue d'études benthamiennes* n°4 (Numéro special): 40–69, p. 41).

14. Rothbard, M.N. 2002. *The Ethics of Liberty*. New York; London: New York University Press, p. 201.

15. Rosen, F. 2003. *Classical Utilitarianism from Hume to Mill*. London: Routledge, p. 6.

16. Liberty, according to Mill, comprises at the first level the 'inward domain of consciousness', and at the second level the 'liberty of tastes and pursuits'. Liberty of consciousness includes liberty of thought and feeling including the freedom to express opinion on all subjects, whereas the liberty of tastes and pursuits includes the freedom to choose a life of one's own liking, as long as such pursuits do not form an impediment to fellow human beings. The liberty of individuals in these two senses logically leads to the liberty enjoyed by a group of individuals and it includes the freedom to unite and act together for common purposes which do not cause harm to others. See Riley, J. 1998. *Routledge Philosophy Guidebook to Mill on Liberty*, as a part of *Routledge Philosophy GuideBooks*. London; New York: Routledge, pp. 48, 49.

17. Mill, J.S. [1859] 2003. 'On Liberty', in *Utilitarianism and on Liberty: Including Mill's 'Essay on Bentham' and Selection from the Writings of Jeremy Bentham and John Austin*, ed. M. Warnock, pp. 88–180. Malden: Blackwell Publishing, p. 97.

18. Mill, 'On Liberty', p. 12.

19. For details on these aspects, see Schumpeter, *History of Economic Analysis*.

20. Indeed, much of Sen's writings have been directed towards showing how and when utilitarian calculus is inappropriate and misleading.

21. Arrow, K. 1959. 'Rational Choice Functions and Orderings'. *Operations Research* 5: 765–74.

22. Sen, A. 1985. *Commodities ad Capabilities*. New Delhi: Oxford India Paperbacks, Oxford University Press, p. 14.

23. Sen, *Commodities ad Capabilities*, p. 14.

24. However, it is necessary to understand that classical utilitarians never confined themselves to considering only consequences, and did take into

account several other aspects of the human condition such as 'motives, intentions, dispositions, virtues, circumstances, the will, passions, feelings and habits'. See Rosen, *Classical Utilitarianism from Hume to Mill*, p. 5.

25. Rawls, *A Theory of Justice*, p. 22.

26. Rawls, *A Theory of Justice*, p. 17.

27. Rawls, *A Theory of Justice*, p. 13.

28. Rawls, *A Theory of Justice*, p. 54.

29. Sen, A. 1992. *Inequality Reexamined*. Oxford: Oxford University Press.

30. Sen, *Inequality Reexamined*, p. 86.

31. Sen, A. 1980. 'Equality of What?', in *Tanner Lectures on Human Values* (Vol. 1), ed. S. McMurrin, pp. 195–220. Cambridge: Cambridge University Press, pp. 215–16.

32. Nozick, R. 1974. *Anarchy, State, and Utopia*. Oxford: Basic Books.

33. We are concerned here only with Nozick's theory of entitlement and will not address his framework for utopia. His arguments for minimal state are also considered only in passing.

34. Nozick, *Anarchy, State, and Utopia*, p. 233.

35. Buchanan, J. 1975. 'Utopia, the Minimal State and Entitlement'. *Public Choice* 23 (1): 121–6.

36. Drèze, J. and Sen, A. 1989. *Hunger and Public Action*. Oxford: Clarendon Press.

37. Sandel, M.J. 1984. 'The Procedural Republic and the Unencumbered Self'. *Political Theory* 12 (1): 81–96.

38. Schaefer, D. 2007. 'Procedural versus Substantive Justice: Rawls and Nozick'. *Social Philosophy and Policy* 24 (1): 164–86.

39. Buchanan, 'Utopia, the Minimal State and Entitlement', p. 124.

40. Sandel, 'The Procedural Republic and the Unencumbered Self', p. 88.

41. Sen, A. 1999. *Development as Freedom*. Oxford: Oxford University Press.

42. Drèze and Sen, *Hunger and Public Action*.

43. Devereux, S. and Tiba, Z. 2007. 'Malawi's First Famine, 2001–2002', in *The New Famine—Why Famines Persist in an Era of Globalisation*, ed. S. Devereux. pp. 143–77. Abington: Routledge.

Annexure B

Discussion on Development Paradigms

The human development concept had several influential front-runners such as the Basic Needs Approach, the Human Resource Development Approach, the Human Rights Approach, and the Human Security Approach. While some of these approaches provided the building blocks for the emergence of the concept of human development, others were an offshoot of it. The concept of human development, while building on earlier approaches, has carved out a distinct place for itself as a wider approach with a broader conceptual sweep and distinct articulation in terms of freedoms and capabilities of people.

However, since often the human development approach is treated either as a substitute or as an extension of the above approaches, it is useful to understand clearly the basic features of these related approaches and understand how similar or distinct they are from the human development approach. The following section does precisely this in an effort to clarify *what the human development approach is and what it is not.*

HUMAN RESOURCE DEVELOPMENT

As mentioned earlier, the human resource development approach is built around the concept of human capital proposed by Theodore Schultz, Gary Becker, and Jacob Mincer during the 1960s. Human capital implies that just as investment in physical capital yields returns over a period of time, individuals also contribute to production through their embodied education, skills, and training. Thus, education, health, and on-the-job training should be considered as investment in the formation of human capital. This is in contrast to the then prevailing practice of considering education and health services as consumption goods. By treating them as investments that individuals make in themselves in anticipation of higher rates of return in future, Schultz, Becker, and Mincer transformed the way in which individuals and their embodied education, health are perceived.

A characteristic feature of the human resource development approach is that people are considered *means* to an end, which is ensuring higher incomes. Human beings are viewed instrumentally as useful for something else. This is in sharp contrast to the human development approach, which recognizes the contributions of individuals to the production process, but goes beyond the instrumental dimension to treat individuals as *ends* in themselves.

Streeten[1] describes the difference between the two approaches as one of focus on 'means' and 'ends'. He highlights seven points of difference between what he terms the 'human resource developers' and the 'humanitarians' who subscribe to the human development viewpoint. The human resource developers are mainly concerned with those who can contribute to the production process, and hence focus primarily on the workforce. The humanitarians, on the other hand, are also concerned with the old, the infirm, the disabled, and the sick. Human resource developers, unlike the humanitarians, overlook the concept of differential needs and abilities of people—that individuals vary in their ability to convert resources (means) to desirable ends. The means approach deduces humans as *passive targets*, whereas the ends approach regards them as active and *participating agents*. The two approaches vary in their outlook towards education and learning, as well as the educational content to be used. The former concentrates on education for skill development, vocational training, and training for flexibility. The latter considers learning as valuable for its own sake and to gain a larger understanding of the world. They also differ in terms of determining gender roles and, thereby, gender equality. The human resource developers confine women them to stereotyped roles of reproduction, nurturing, and care work, whereas the humanitarians strive for equal opportunity in employment. Further, differential weights are assigned to priorities like housing. The human resource developers attribute it as being essential for production purpose, while in the human development approach, it is associated with shelter and as a fundamental need. Finally, they appeal to different categories of people and groups, wherein the former appeals to economists, financial experts, banks, and others, while the latter appeals to moral philosophers, NGOs, and development planners.

BASIC NEEDS APPROACH

The concept of basic needs came into prominence in 1976 at the World Employment Conference of the International Labour Organisation (ILO) and as a reaction to the prevailing development paradigm. Its critical contribution lies in moving beyond the income component as a measure of poverty and to emphasize the importance of physical services and commodities, such as health, sanitation and hygiene, nutrition, education, shelter, and other prerequisites in order to enhance the productivity of the poor.[2] Haq[3] describes the basic needs approach as the 'conceptual forerunner of human development' approach.

The basic needs approach has four different interpretations, each broader than the previous.[4] The narrowest interpretation of the basic needs approach confines it to the minimum required physical quantities of *food, clothing, shelter, and water* in order to protect a person's survival, which could get affected by illness, loss of job, or any such contingencies. The second interpretation is more inclined towards neoclassical school of thought, wherein a subjectivist perception of the basic needs by the consumers themselves is emphasized instead of a list of commodities and services prescribed by experts. Here, the *focus is on the opportunities that people have to earn income that satisfies their basic needs*. The third approach takes a paternalistic view based on the fact that consumers are not rational in taking their decisions. Accordingly, public authorities take the lead in planning and providing basic services and *also guide private consumption in the light of public consideration,* as in the case of food subsidies. In the fourth interpretation, individual and collective participation forms the basis for deviating from the earlier focus on economic and material aspects of human self-sufficiency. It emphasizes that *basic needs are essential human rights and 'freedom from want is like the right not be tortured'*.[5] It focuses on the larger goal of *non-material needs*, such as more fulfilling life, as ends, and *material needs,* such as good health and good education, to achieve the larger goal.

The human development approach is more inclined to the last interpretation of the basic needs approach, though it is the first interpretation that is universally associated with the basic needs approach. Therefore, it is heavily criticized for having a 'commodity fetish'.[6] It must be noted, however, that the basic needs approach refers to the provision of *opportunities of fuller life* to all individuals, but particularly the poor. The human development approach, on the other hand, is applicable to all humans irrespective of their economic status (poor or rich) and geographic location (high-, middle-, or low-income countries).[7] The human development approach emphasizes freedom and choices, whereas the basic needs approach, at least in its implementation, is paternalistic and top-down in nature treating individuals as *recipients* or *beneficiaries.*

HUMAN RIGHTS

The human rights approach, which attained prominence after the Universal Declaration of Human Rights was adopted in 1948, is inextricably linked to the human development approach, as it emphasized economic, social, and political cultural freedoms that all people are entitled to. Although, initially, the human rights approach paid more attention to civil and political freedoms, its scope expanded subsequently to encompass economic social and cultural rights.

The Human Development Report 2000 brings out the commonality between the two approaches by stating that '*[h]uman rights and human development share a common vision and a common purpose—to secure, for every human being, freedom, well-being and dignity*'.[8] The human rights approach, by articulating the fundamental rights of citizens, promotes individual and collective agency, and thus strengthens the principles of equity and empowerment in human development. The human development approach complements the human rights approach by reinforcing people's development and the role of the state in ensuring fundamental freedoms. The human development approach provokes a debate on the priority and goals of development, just as human rights approach underscores specific rights from a moral and ethical viewpoint.

The difference between the two approaches is one of emphasis: the human rights approach focuses on entitlements and articulates the demands of the citizens, whereas the human development approach concentrates more on public provisioning and ensuring adequate supply of social services as an entitlement. Clearly, the success of both approaches depends on the complementarity between them.

Six features of human rights are important from the capability perspective.[9] Human rights are essentially *ethical demands* and not primarily legal commands. While they often trigger legislation, that is not their constitutive characteristic. The approach includes *both opportunity and process aspects of freedom*, though not all freedoms can claim to be human rights. To be classified as such, human rights need to satisfy the threshold conditions of being of special importance and have the ability to influence social arrangements. It *triggers action by agents* who are able to help in promoting or safeguarding underlying freedoms. The obligations induced by the rights may be in the nature of perfect or imperfect obligations.

Implementation of human rights is not confined to those recognized legally, and many imperfect obligations—such as public agitation and recognition—can be part of human rights. While legislation is one means through which human rights are implemented, it is not the only means. Indeed, public discussion and advocacy may be better means of their promotion. In the case of human rights, where there may not be a single identifiable duty holder, their enforcement could be a challenge. Under such circumstances, public action in the form of agitations may be required to assert the rights of the poor and vulnerable people.[10] Very often, economic and social freedoms are not realized because of institutional weaknesses. For example, the right to health is not often realized in many developing countries due to the lacunae in the institutional set-up that is responsible for its implementation. However, this should not prevent its being recognized as a human right. Human rights are universal and, therefore, are not restricted in terms of debate and discussion on them by national boundaries. This feature also entails a free flow of information and ensuring unrestricted opportunity to discuss various points of view that may arise in this process.

The capability approach provides an analytical and practical framework in which tangible human rights can be better explained and evaluated with respect to a group or an individual. The capability approach attempts to analyse the freedoms and opportunities that are available in a person's capability set using variables such as conversion factors, endowments, and entitlements. The mechanisms to safeguard human rights are essentially treated as one such variable that further explains the capability set. In turn, this provides a vast body of empirical evidence (famine prevention, right to avoid premature morbidity, right to education, right to property) ascertaining that human rights play a crucial instrumental role in public policy that expands the individual's capability. Not only do human rights facilitate capability analysis, but capability facilitates human rights analysis as well, through the provision of a framework wherein '*a range of factors that influence the realization of human rights in practice can be more fully investigated and better understood*'.[11]

Another instrumental role of human rights is that it enhances and reinforces public accountability, as it enables people to *voice* their demands because of the *countervailing power* that is provided to them. The capability discourse also strengthens the human rights dialogue. The language of capabilities gives important precision and supplementation to the language of rights. A right to citizens in the areas of, say, political participation, right to free exercise of religion, right to free speech, and so on, is best secured when the relevant capabilities to function are present in people. This is in sharp contrast to the notion of negative freedoms being perceived as rights. The capability approach is also well placed to address inequalities through its focus on *beings and doings* of people. Importantly, it can highlight inequalities that women suffer inside the family, particularly in access to resources and opportunities, educational deprivations, failure of household work to be recognised as 'work', and insults to bodily integrity. Another advantage of the capability approach over the language of rights is that it not linked sharply to any particular cultural or historical tradition—a shortcoming that the language of rights suffers from as it is often associated with the European Enlightenment, though its component ideas have deep roots in many traditions.

A crucial difference between the human rights and capability approaches relates to the role of the state. The traditional language of rights distinguishes between the public sphere, which the state regulates, and a private sphere, which it must leave alone. For the capability approach, non-interference by the state is not always considered a virtue and, indeed, affirmative action by the state to address inequality is not only justified but strongly recommended as part of public action.[12]

HUMAN SECURITY

The concept of human security came into prominence after it was proposed by UNDP in the 1994 Human Development Report, although the concept was already in existence earlier.[13] Following Beveridge, human security was defined as '[f]reedom from want and freedom from fear'.[14] The important contribution of the human security concept was that it shifted the focus from territorial security to people's security.

Four features of the human security concept were highlighted by Amartya Sen. The human security concept focuses on *what happens to human beings* rather than to territories such as nations, *promotes an understanding of the individual person in his or her total context of living, focuses on basic principles* including life-and-death and dignity, and on *stability or instability of fulfilment of basic priorities.*[15]

Human security also serves as a bridge between the human development and peace themes, though the merger has been somewhat awkward and uneasy.[16] What is interesting is that human security broadens the conventional view of security from a military perspective of 'freedom from fear' to include 'freedom from want'. It also enables the human development approach to prioritize better, and thus represents a via media between broad and narrow interpretations of the vital dimensions of human life.

Human security is anchored in freedoms, and connects different types of freedoms—freedom from want, freedom from fear, and freedom to take action on one's own behalf. Human security 'tries to combine human development's broad focus and stress on reasoned freedoms, basic human needs discourse's stress on prioritization, and human rights' discourse's unwillingness to sacrifice anyone'.[17]

Human security was proposed as a companion concept to that of human development. While human development is concerned with functionings, capability, and agency of individuals, the human security concept pays attention to the context in which 'functionings of basic importance are promoted and sustained, or endangered and thwarted'.[18]

Both concepts are concerned with basic capabilities, the difference being that while the former focuses on the changes in levels of human development, the latter is concerned with conditions that influence those levels and the stability of the attainments per se. To illustrate, a human development policy on poverty will attempt to reduce the extent of poverty in a particular region by focusing on people living below the poverty line, and ensuring reduction in multidimensional deprivation and expansion of multidimensional capabilities like health outcomes, educational outcomes, living in safe environment, and social and political liberties. On the other hand, a shock in any of these dimensions can push a person back into poverty. A health shock that requires hospitalization of one of the family members, for example, can push the family back into poverty due to the high costs of seeking health care when public health facilities are inadequate and/or unavailable, as well as due to the opportunity costs incurred in terms of loss of income. Human security in such a case will ensure the stability of basic capabilities required for human development. Human security as a concept deals with the vulnerability of human development outcomes to downside risks of economic growth, climate change, and conflict.

NOTES AND REFERENCES

1. Streeten, P. 1994. Human Development: Means and Ends. *The American Economic Review* 84 (2): 232–7.

2. Streeten, P., Burki, S.J., Haq, U., Hicks, N., and Stewart, F. 1981. *First Things First: Meeting Basic Human Needs in the Developing Countries*. New York: Oxford University Press.

3. Haq, M. ul. 1995. *Reflections on Human Development*. Oxford: Oxford University Press, p. vii.

4. For details, see Streeten et al., *First Things First*.

5. Streeten, P., Shahid, J.B., ul Haq, M., Hicks, N. and Stewart, F. 1981. *First Things First: Meeting Basic Human Needs In the Developing Countries*. Washington, DC: The World Bank, Oxford University Press.

6. Sen's critiques the BNA for being commodity centred as it revolves around the minimum quantities of essential commodities required by people, thereby leading to commodity fetishism. Commodities perspective could be a proxy for certain holdings, but does not capture the conversion of commodities into capabilities. He argues that the approach lacks a conceptual base

for the term 'need'. A person's need for a commodity is taken over by the commodity needed, say food. For details, see Sen, A. 1989. 'Development as Capability Expansion'. *Journal of Development Planning* 19: 41–58.

7.   Haq, *Reflections on Human Development*.

8.   Alkire, S. 2010. 'Human Development: Definitions, Critiques and Related Concepts', Human Development Research Paper 2010/01, UNDP, New York, p. 56.

9.   Sen, A. 2004. 'Elements of a Theory of Human Rights'. *Philosophy and Public Affairs* 32 (4): 315–56.

10.   Drèze, J. 2005. *Tribal Evictions from Forest Land*. Note submitted to the National Advisory Council Government of India, New Delhi.

11.   Vizard, P., Fukuda-Parr, S., and Elson, D. 2011. 'Introduction: The Capability Approach and Human Rights'. *Journal of Human Development and Capabilities* 12 (1): 1–22, p. 5.

12.   Drèze, J. and Sen, A. 2013. *An Uncertain Glory: India and Its Contradictions*. Princeton; Oxford: Princeton University Press; Nussbaum, M. 2000. *Women and Human Development: The Capabilities Approach*. Cambridge: Cambridge University Press.

13.   Rothschild, E. 1995. 'What Is Security?'. *Daedalus* 53–98.

14.   Report by Beveridge, Sir W. 1942. *Social Insurance and Allied Services*. London: HMSO.

15.   Commission on Human Security. 2003. *Human Security Now*. New York.

16.   Gasper, D. 2005. 'Securing Humanity: Situating "Human Security" as Concept and Discourse'. *Journal of Human Development* 6 (2): 221–45.

17.   Gasper, 'Securing Humanity', pp. 233–4.

18.   Gasper, D. and Gómez, O.A. 2014. *Evolution of Thinking and Research on Human and Personal Security 1994–2013*. New York: Human Development Report Office, United Nations Development Programme, p. 12.

Annexure C

Tracing Women-Centric Explanations in Various Development Approaches

The cause of the Women in Development (WID) approach was strengthened by Boserup's[1] historic publication, *Women's Role in Economic Development*. In her exploration of women's contribution to economic development in Africa, she found that differences in women's work participation rates reflected in different stages of development. In the initial stages of development, with the expansion of the industrial sector that predominantly employs men, women's labour force participation in the agricultural sector increases in response to increased demand for food. The WID approach reasons that women's labour force participation continues to be confined to the subsistence economy and productive processes, and away from market-driven processes. Gender relations at the household level control women's participation and mobility within the household (in the case of agricultural households, they remain in the rural areas), while men migrate to the modern sectors in the urban areas. These choices get further strengthened when public policies also keep women *in situ*. Boserup[2] further cautions that when women are kept away from the industrial and developing sectors, it dampens growth rates. Although her work has been critiqued, it still remains a significant contribution that drew attention to the differential gendered impact of development and modernization strategies in an era of androcentric dominance over policy and academic theorization.[3]

Over the years, issues pertaining to women's contribution to the productive labour market gained prominence and shaped the political agenda in the direction of anti-discrimination laws and equal opportunities programmes. High discrimination was attributed to economic factors. Akerlof[4] studied the creation of low-level equilibrium resulting from caste segregation of labour markets, which allocates resources in pre-decided, skewed fashion. Klasen[5] discussed gender-based discrimination in accessing education, with spillovers across health, nutrition, employment opportunities, and most critically, on the outcome of the larger growth process. WID approach limited the discussion largely to the disadvantages that women faced in the productive sphere. There was limited evaluation of the power relations between women and men that affected women in their social and reproductive spheres.[6]

The Women and Development (WAD) discussion came as a critique of the capitalist relations between patriarchy and development. The WAD discourse is rooted in the neo-Marxist feminist approach that emerged in the latter half of the 1970s. Drawing from the explanatory limitations of the modernization theory and its proselytization of the idea that the exclusion of women from earlier development strategies had been an inadvertent oversight, it extends the dependency theory to argue that women have always been a part of the development process, and their inclusion is not a sudden occurrence.[7] WAD scholars highlighted the secondary status of women in society by drawing parallels from the Marxist analysis of subsistence labour of peasantry under capitalism.[8] They pointed out that gender inequalities and the rise in precarious employment results in a disadvantaged position for women, thus pointing to the type of development needed to integrate women into mainstream development.[9] Placing women's agency at the core, the WAD approach sought to underline the structural basis of exploitation based on differences in gender, class, and nations.

Since WID and WAD shared a static conceptualization of women as a homogenous undifferentiated group whose condition was predetermined by their sex,[10] there was a need to reincorporate distinctions by placing a value on gender needs and interests in both strategic and practical terms.[11] The nuanced contextual differences in the gendered structures of constraints and opportunities need to be comprehended for analysing the pathways to women's freedom. These reflect differences in the political, social, and economic conditions that prevail across the world, giving rise to what Benería and others[12] call the 'geography of gender'. This concept deals with the distribution of resources and opportunities in different contexts, including both availability and acceptability of different kinds of work for women and men.

The organization of kinship and family relations is a central aspect of the gendered structures of constraints faced in most societies. Thus, the Gender and Development (GAD) paradigm, which represented the intersectional analysis between gender and other dimensions of identity like social class, race, ethnicity, and sexual identities, emerged as a conceptual framework in the early 1980s. It stressed that policies and initiatives could modify socially constructed gender roles and relations, with a focus on addressing strategic gender needs and interests. Thus, GAD focused not only on examination of gender relations and sexual division of labour, but also sexual division of responsibility.

REFERENCES

1. Boserup, E. 1970. *Woman's Role in Economic Development*. London: Earthscan.
2. Boserup, E. 1975. 'The Changing Role of Women in Developing Countries'. *India International Centre Quarterly* 2 (3): 199–203.
3. Rathgeber, E.M. 1990. 'WID, WAD, GAD: Trends in Research and Practice'. *The Journal of Developing Areas* 24 (4): 489–502.
4. Akerlof, G. 1976. 'The Economics of Caste and of the Rat Race and Other Woeful Tales'. *The Quarterly Journal of Economics* 90 (4): 599–617.
5. Klasen, S. 2002. 'Low Schooling for Girls, Slower Growth for All? Cross-Country Evidence on the Effect of Gender Inequality in Education on Economic Development'. *The World Bank Economic Review* 16 (3): 345–73.
6. Razavi, S. and Miller, C. 1995. *From WID to GAD: Conceptual Shifts in the Women and Development Discourse* (Vol. 1). Geneva: United Nations Research Institute for Social Development.
7. Rathgeber, 'WID, WAD, GAD'.
8. Kabeer, N. 1994. *Reversed Realities: Gender Hierarchies in Development Thought*. London: Verso.
9. Benería, L., Berik, G., and Floro, M. 2015. *Gender, Development and Globalization: Economics as if All People Mattered*. New York: Routledge.

10. McIlwaine, C. and Datta, K. 2003. 'From Feminising to Engendering Development'. *Gender, Place and Culture* 10 (4): 369–82.

11. Molyneux, M. 1985. 'Mobilization without Emancipation? Women's Interests, the State, and Revolution in Nicaragua'. *Feminist Studies* 11 (2): 227–54.

12. Benería, Berik, and Floro, *Gender, Development and Globalization.*

Annexure D

Setting the Global Agenda for an Equitable World: Then and Now

This note discusses the major developments in the global policy architecture and dialogue that have influenced human development attainments.

The formation of the Bretton Woods institutions—the World Bank and the IMF[1]—in the 1940s led nation-states for the first time to pool their resources for global commitments. The idea was to establish a post–World War II economic order based on the notions of consensual decision-making and co-operation in the realm of trade and economic relations. The war-ravaged countries, in their anxiety to improve the living standards of their people, perceived in economic growth a sure way of achieving their aim in the shortest possible period. It was believed that during the initial stages, development should focus on building up capital, productive capacity, and infrastructure of the economy, which may disproportionately benefit the rich. The poor would gain over a period of time from capital investments, savings, and innovations.[2] Sadly, and much to the chagrin of the developing countries, benefits of rapid economic growth did not percolate as expected, and challenges such as poverty, deprivation, and exclusion became persistent.

The Marshall Plan of 1947 was one instance when the reconstruction process of development in the European countries aimed at resurrecting industrial and infrastructural development, and also worked towards addressing issues such as homelessness, unemployment, hunger, and loss of real wages.[3]

The Non-Aligned Movement (NAM) was born in 1961, with most of its members from the developing countries of the Third World. This project was deeply embedded in the values of egalitarianism and sought strength from the charter of the UN. Its aim was to renegotiate the deplorable situation in the developing world.

The oil shock of the early 1970s had far reaching implications for the nascent world economic order. Following the demonstration of the economic power of oil-exporting countries through the formation of cartels and collective bargaining, the NAM called for a special session of UN General Assembly to demand the establishment of the New International Economic Order (NIEO).[4] The NIEO had a significant role in shaping the demand for nations to focus on the human condition rather than per capita GDP. The essence of the NIEO movement was in securing equality of opportunity, including the right to sit as equals around the bargaining tables of the world.[5] It rested on three main planks: finance, technology, and production. Finance encompassed reduction in debt and facilitation of financial trade from developed to developing countries, and differentiated investment for commerce and development. Technology included assistance in technological transfer, research opportunities, and development of educational systems. Production referred to guarding of the prices of raw materials, facilitating the processing of raw materials, creating markets for the products from developing countries, and spreading the commerce from these nations.

Between 1974 and 1990, at least thirty countries in Europe, Asia, and Latin America transited to democracy.[6] This nearly doubled the number of countries that adhered to democratic governance structures globally, even though there were wide differences in the type and extent of democracy actually practised. However, the grand ambition of the developing countries fizzled out due to the counter-initiatives of the developed countries. The prevailing economic paradigm, with its emphasis on free functioning of the markets, proved grossly inappropriate for situations riddled with structural constraints, while technology imported from the developed countries proved to be singularly unsuitable for labour-surplus economies, particularly in South Asia. At such a juncture, the human development approach emerged as an alternative viewpoint that seemed to be closer to the lived reality of the poor and disadvantaged in developing countries.

Haq provided leadership to a series of dialogues between the North and South to facilitate the demand for a just international economic order by the Global South, requiring the Global North to be a party to the change. The series of North–South dialogues, which took place under the aegis of the Society of International Development, initiated by Barbara Ward with Haq as a principal steering force, fostered debate on people-centric development and identified several pathways that could be adopted by national governments.[7] In a bid to maintain its independence, the NSRT raised funds for its activities from national governments, international organizations, and foundations.[8] Membership was by invitation only and influential policymakers and academics were chosen by the governing board. Starting in 1978 with over 100 people drawn equally from developed and developing countries, its membership steadily grew to reach a strength of 200.

These independent global dialogues, conducted over a period of three decades from late 1970s on a variety of issues confronting the world, were hugely influential. The policy papers and publications[9] from the over forty Round Tables crystallized the presented ideas, and lent credence to the idea of a development paradigm that was more humane, equitable, and sustainable. Since this viewpoint arose from a process of dialogue involving thought leaders and politicians from *both* the North and the South, it became more acceptable as a global agenda.

The idea of a human-centred development paradigm found its natural expression in these Round Tables. The NSRT organized three Round Tables specifically on 'Development: The Human Dimension' to spell out the idea in greater detail. The first such Round Table in 1985 in Istanbul, 'The Human Development: The Neglected Dimension', focused specifically on education and training, nutrition and health, role of women, and new technologies. It was at the statement issued at the end of this Round Table that articulated the *importance of human being as both the means and end of development* was articulated in the statement issued. It asserted that people were the objective of development. While the process of development could be measured in economic aggregates or technological and physical achievements, what is intrinsically valuable is the human condition. Further, it was at this NSRT that the recommendation was made that

The organizations of the U.N. system might together collaborate:

a) On research focused on specific aspects of the changing human condition, in the context of both past trends and future prospects and challenges.

b) In the production of a periodic report on 'The State of the Human Condition' covering the changing human situation in all parts of the world.[10]

The second NSRT in 1986 in Salzburg dealt with issues of adjustment policy and explored how human concerns could be made an integral part of objective mechanisms and modalities of structural adjustment packages. The Round Table focused on neglected dimensions and called for a reordering of development priorities by countries towards the human dimension, including the development and use of quality of life indicators alongside economic indicators. The third Round Table (1987) paid attention to the longer-term issues of human development. It stressed the need for assessing the economic policies on human welfare from a long-term perspective. This Round Table also drew particular attention to universal primary education and the subsequent need for a major restructuring of investment to the priority sectors. Subsequently, it also encompassed the urgency for alleviation of poverty and attainment of basic human needs through development policy.

Thus, it is evident that the concept of human development was shaped over a number of years through a process of active deliberation and reflection at the highest levels in global forums. It represented an aspiration for a changed development paradigm that accorded to people their rightful centrality. The process of arriving at the meaning and connotation of the term was equally important as both the Global North and South were partners in the shaping of this idea. As Desai points out, the human development approach emerged from 'the area of economic inequality, social choice and poverty' and '[i]t is from this ... literature on inequality and poverty and especially the notion of capabilities that the concept of human development traces its strongest roots'.[11] The approach was not confined to examining issues of the poor in poor countries, but equally applied to the disadvantaged and excluded in the middle-income and high-income countries.

The broad consensus on the concept of human development that placed *people* at the centre of development and focused on factors that would strengthen human flourishing, enhance freedoms and strengthen well-being led to its emergence as a possible alternative to the mainstream neoclassical paradigm. The intellectual alliance between Haq and Sen, along with the strong support provided by the UNDP, ensured the formal debut of the human development paradigm. The anchoring in UN ensured its bipartisan roots and enabled widespread dissemination through annual HDRs.

HUMAN DEVELOPMENT REPORTS AS AN ADVOCACY TOOL

Since 1990, more than over twenty-five global and over 700 national, sub-national, and regional HDRs have been published. These reports have widened the policy discussions by addressing the neglected dimensions of development. These HDRs have facilitated the government and non-governmental stakeholders, as well as civil society organizations in designing appropriate policy decisions and creating public awareness on pressing issues.[12] These HDRs have gone beyond the conventional HDI in their attempt to measure the broader concept of human development, by addressing the missing dimensions of the global report. In the process, while focusing on regional specificities, the reports have spurred a movement towards devising newer composite indices by introducing newer dimensions and indicators, adopting different methodology and newer data sources. Some have even advocated for a completely different paradigm of assessing human progress.

These HDRs have been instrumental in shaping methodologies that have been used in the capability approach to measure well-being of an individual or a group. For instance, McGregor[13] elaborates on the methodology used by ESRC research group on well-being in developing countries while conducting empirical research concerning social and cultural well-being in Bangladesh, Ethiopia, Peru, and Thailand. The emphasis is on outcomes, structures, and processes to gather data on aspects of well-being. The tools included are community profiling, resources and needs profiling, quality of life, income and expenditure survey and diaries, process research, and structures and regimes.

The HDRs have spurred a plethora of innovations in the measurement arena. In addition to the attempts made by the HDRs,
several academicians and research organizations have also proposed
composite indices measuring a particular aspect of human progress.[14]
The Human Development Atlas in Brazil serves as a guiding tool
in resource allocation irrespective of incumbent government. The
HDI has been utilized in selecting beneficiaries at state, municipality, and household levels for its main federal project, the Alvarado
Project, which was launched in 2000 and aims at improving the living
conditions of the needy within a short term. A further disaggregated
municipal-level HDI has been utilized in targeting social programmes
in Brazil. The Colombia HDR 2002 calculated HDI corrected for
violence, and its recommendations were adopted by local authorities
on prevention of guerrilla recruitment, mine action, and strengthening of local institutions. Numerous such policy initiatives inspired by
the analysis in the HDRs can be cited.

The HDRs have also spurred collection and analysis of data that
were otherwise not available on socio-economic dimensions. For
instance, for Kosovo HDR 2004, a survey covering 6,000 households
across thirty municipalities was conducted, as there was an absence of
census data for more than two decades. The analysis and the data itself
were of particular importance to locate the communities that needed
development support.

Even as some critics argue that the UN has hijacked the human
development agenda, there is certainly a need to give due credit
to the institutional backing of the UNDP, which has anchored the
cause of human development over the years. This support from
the global development institution led to an easy acceptance of the
idea by national governments. It also led many governments to
reorient their agenda towards development recognizing peoples'
choices and well-being.

However, it must be noted that as useful as the HDR exercise has
been, and while the HDRs have over the years been adept at describ-
ing the ground situation in detail, they have not stretched themselves
adequately to provide policy options and engage with policymakers to
explore feasible alternatives. In the absence of systematic follow-up
to the themes presented in the HDRs, and with no institutional mechanism that takes up the issues for action, much of the work of HDRs

has been to advocate for action with no clear roadmap on who is going to take this action and how it is going to take place.

UN CONFERENCES ON SOCIAL SECTORS, GENDER, AND SUSTAINABLE DEVELOPMENT

UN agencies have also been facilitating global agenda-setting dialogues for social sectors, gender, and sustainable development, which need to be dealt with in some detail. As part of the agenda to bring back social sectors into the policy arena, numerous conferences were organized by the UN agencies in the 1980s and early 1990s. The Alma Ata Declaration in 1978, which defined health as not merely absence of disease but as a fundamental human right, was an important landmark that set the tone for several other such conferences. The 134 national health ministries that participated in the conference set the year 2000 as the goal for achieving a level of health that would enable all of the world's people to lead a socially and economically productive life. The focus was on primary health care with emphasis on community participation and tackling underlying causes of disease such as poverty, illiteracy, and poor nutrition. A similar movement was initiated at the World Conference at Jomtien in 1990 on 'Education for All' by UNESCO, UNDP, UNICEF, and the World Bank. The participants endorsed an expanded vision of learning, and committed themselves to universalize primary education and eradicate illiteracy by the end of the decade.

The year 1990 also witnessed the World Summit for Children, which set goals and targets for improving the condition of children globally. In 1992, the Earth Summit at Rio de Janeiro raised awareness on the links between environment and development, whereas the 1993 World Conference on Human Rights advanced the causes of human rights, especially that of women. The 1994 International Conference on Population and Development in Cairo put forth arguments to safeguard reproductive rights and set time-bound targets for reduction in infant, child and maternal mortality. The 1995 UN Summit on Social Development at Copenhagen articulated eradication of poverty as a global priority, and the UN Fourth World Conference on Women, popularly known as the Beijing Conference, led to the formulation of goals towards gender equality and gender empowerment.

These numerous conferences not only succeeded in raising public awareness on important human issues, but also led to the emergence of a consensus that action should be taken towards improving human well-being. The subsequent initiative of the Development Assistance Committee (DAC) of the OECD, which came up with a list of International Development Goals, compelled the global community to think more seriously about specific goals and targets that could be collectively addressed.

A remarkable feature of these developments was the subtle shift in focus from a narrow goal of eradicating poverty defined in monetary terms to the broader goal of reducing multidimensional poverty and deprivation encompassing education, health, food security, and gender inequality. This consistent work by numerous agencies and the prevailing consensus for a global agenda, combined with the UN's ambition to chart out a new vision in the Millennium Summit, culminated in the Millennium Declaration in September 2000, wherein heads of 189 countries reiterated their commitment to the principles of human dignity, equality, and equity at the global level. The values that were emphasized included freedom, equality, solidarity, tolerance, and respect for nature.

One of the foremost platforms that sought to negotiate the position and status of women at the global level was the Commission on the Status of Women (CSW), which was established in 1947 under the UN's Economic and Social Council (ECOSOC). The objective of the Commission was to provide benchmark goals to generate awareness and to eliminate discrimination against women in various national legislations. Some of the initial issues dealt by the Commission included negotiating for political rights of women, old age protection, consent and registration of marriage.[15]

The work of the UN in agenda-setting and bringing sensitive issues to the forefront has been very visible in the area of gender-related policy. Concerns pertaining to discrimination against women came into sharper focus during the 1970–80s with the announcement of the UN Decade of Women. During this period, the Declaration on the Elimination of Discrimination against Women (DEDAW) of 1976 and the Convention on Elimination of All Forms of Discrimination against Women (CEDAW) of 1979 provided a universal template for policy action. Governments that ratified these conventions could choose to measure women's progress, even as women were included within the development discourse. These ideas were further shaped in the *four* UN Conferences that articulated the complex landscape within which women's development was to be established. The UN dealt with issues relating to knowledge base, work, access, and opportunities in development, and led to the emergence of the contemporary understanding of gender-specific location of women in all spheres of development.[16]

While CEDAW and the Beijing Declaration garnered global support and ratification, there were only *soft* legal requirements on the part of the member states to take necessary action that could drive gender mainstreaming. The mixed response that the conventions and the declarations evoked lies in the very nature of the commitments and the lack of legally binding responsibilities on the signatory nation-states. In Southeast Asia, all the governments have ratified and made progress towards their obligations under the CEDAW Convention. Indonesia operationalized the rights of marginalized groups and Thailand shaped the draft Gender Equality Law. After a UN Women-supported training for a network of women living with HIV in the Philippines and Thailand, a UN Women and UNAIDS collaboration on the relevance of CEDAW to the HIV response also enabled women living with HIV across Vietnam to connect with other advocacy networks on women's rights and improve their rights-based advocacy skills. This progress was achieved because of the facilitating role played by UN Women and UNAIDS.

However, such a momentum has not been achieved in other countries. For instance, several Islamic countries have expressed reservations on the acceptance of CEDAW in confirmation to the *Shariah* law, thereby not allowing women equal rights in accessing property, marriage and divorce.[17] Thus, the suggestion that national-level gender policies should interpret and implement gender-based Conventions and Declarations in accordance with their socio-religious cultures is extremely pertinent, and needs further evaluation.

The UN also played a significant role in fostering debate, broadening the definition and helping countries to arrive at a shared understanding on sustainable development. Drawing on this vast literature, Table D.1 highlights some of the landmark conferences organized by UN agencies that shaped the development of the concept of sustainable development.

TABLE D.1 UN Conferences that Shaped the Concept of Sustainable Development

Year	Milestone	Details	Impact on the Evolving Connotations
1972	UN Conference on the Human Environment, in Stockholm (Stockholm Conference)	• Called for common principles and outlook to influence and lead the world for conservation, protection and enhancement of the human environment. • Led to the establishment of UNEP as well as the creation of numerous environmental protection agencies at the national level.	Highlighted environmental concerns on the global agenda and linked it with ongoing political discourse.
1980	World Conservation Strategy: Living Resource Conservation for Sustainable Development	• Prepared by IUCN, emphasized the need to conserve and protect living resources in order to make human life sustainable on the planet.	The term sustainable development was used for the first time.
1987	'Our Common Future': UN World Commission on Environment and Development Report (Brundtland Commission Report)	• Defined sustainable development as 'development that meets the needs of the present without compromising the ability of future generations to meet their own needs'.	Provided the first formal definition for sustainable development.
1992	UN Conference on Environment and Development (UNCED) in Rio de Janerio (Earth Summit)	• More than 178 governments adopted 5 main documents: Rio Declaration; Agenda 21; Convention on Climate Change; Convention on Biodiversity; and Principles for the Sustainable Management of Forests.	Led to the institutionalization of sustainable development at global level and emphasis on intergenerational environmental sustainability.

Year	Event	Details	Significance
2000	UN Summit on the Millennium Development Goals (MDGs)	• Adoption of a global action plan to achieve the eight anti-poverty goals by the target year 2015.	Focused on economic, social, and environmental issues of development, thereby highlighting the pillars of sustainable development.
2002	World Summit on Sustainable Development (WSSD), in Johannesburg (World Summit)	• Adoption of the Johannesburg Declaration and the Johannesburg Plan of Implementation, focusing on poverty reduction as part of sustainable development strategy that reaffirmed the principles of Agenda 21 and the Rio Principles.	Developed a comprehensive approach to sustainable development by including its three pillars and focusing on both inter- and intra-generational sustainability.
2012	Rio+20 Summit	• Essential outcome was the agreement among the member states on the formulation of Sustainable Development Goals (SDGs) by December 2015, based on Agenda 21, drawing upon but going beyond the MDGs.	Reinforced the three pillars of sustainability and formally highlighted the essential elements of the human development approach in its final outcome document, 'The Future We Want'.
2015	UN General Assembly	• Adopted the report of the Open Working Group on SDGs that elaborated an agenda for 2030 constituting seventeen goals and 169 targets.	Multidimensional integrated notion of sustainability, based on the three pillars.

Source: Adapted from Fuentes-Nieva, R. and Pereira, I. 2010. 'The Disconnect between Indicators of Sustainability and Human Development', Human Development Research Paper No. 34, Human Development Report Office, UNDP, New York.

NOTES AND REFERENCES

1.   It is noteworthy here that the original Bretton Woods agreement included plans for an International Trade Organisation (ITO) but they laid dormant until the World Trade Organisation was created in the early 1990s.

2.   Streeten, P., Shahid, J.B., ul Haq, M., Hicks, N., and Stewart, F. 1981. *First Things First: Meeting Basic Human Needs in the Developing Countries.* Washington, DC: The World Bank, Oxford University Press.

3.   For details, see Cini, M. 2001. 'From the Marshall Plan to EEC: Direct and Indirect Influences', in *The Marshall Plan: Fifty Years After*, pp. 13–37. New York: Palgrave; Judt, T. 2001. 'Introduction', in *The Marshall Plan: Fifty Years After*, pp. 1–9. New York: Palgrave.

4.   This demand was accepted in April 1974 in the 6th Special Session of the UN General Assembly.

5.   Haq, K. and Jolly, R. 2008. 'Global Development, Poverty Alleviation and North South Relations', in *Mahbub ul Haq and the Human Development Revolution*, pp. 63–87. New Delhi: Oxford University Press.

6.   Some of these countries were Portugal, Greece, Spain, Ecuador, Peru, Bolivia, Honduras, Argentina, Turkey, El Salvador, Guatemala, Uruguay, Brazil, Philippines, South Korea, Taiwan, Chile, Former Soviet States, South Africa, and Paraguay. For details, Huntington, S.P. 1993. 'The Clash of Civilizations?'. *Foreign Affairs* 71 (3): 22–49.

7.   A few of the eminent scholars who played an active role in NSRTs include the chairmen and vice-chairmen: Mahbub ul Haq, Khadija Haq, Maurice Strong, Saburo Okita, Enrique Iglesias, and Richard Jolly. This group of economists also included Gustav Ranis, Frances Stewart, Paul Streeten, and John Williamson from the North, and Adebayo Adedeji, Nafis Sadik, Lal Jayawardena, and Carlos Massad from the South. For details, see Haq and Jolly, 'Global Development, Poverty Alleviation and North South Relations', p. 73.

8.   Some of the agencies that contributed funds include Canadian International Development Agency, Inter-American Development Bank, Swedish International Development Authority, Governments of Japan, The Netherlands, and Norway. This is also discussed in Chapter 1.

9.   The output was prolific: as many as twelve books were published, more than forty roundtable sessions were held, and eight roundtable papers, and twenty-five roundtable reports were issued.

10.   Haq, K. and Kirdar, U. 1986. *Human Development: The Neglected Dimension.* Islamabad: North South Roundtable. Accessible at https://nsrt.lums.edu.pk/sites/all/themes/nsrt/books/Human_Development.pdf; 4 June 2016.

11.   Desai, M. 1991. 'Human Development: Concepts and Measurement'. *European Economic Review* 35 (2–3): 350–7, p. 352.

12. For a detailed review of impact of HDRs at the national policymaking, refer to Pagliani, P. 2010. 'Influence of Regional, National and Sub-National HDRs', United Nations Development Programme, Human Development Reports, Research Paper 2010/19 July 2010, HDRO, New York.

13. McGregor, J.A. 2007. 'Researching Wellbeing: From Concepts to Methodology', in *Wellbeing in Developing Countries From Theory to Research*, ed. I. Gough and J.A. McGregor. New York: Cambridge University Press.

14. See Yang, L. 2014. 'An Inventory of Composite Measures of Human Progress', Occasional Paper on Methodology, UNDP Human Development Report Office, New York.

15. U.N. Women. n.d. 'Short History of the Commission on the Status of Women', Background paper. Accessible at http://www.un.org/womenwatch/daw/CSW60YRS/CSWbriefhistory.pdf; 25 July 2017.

16. Jain, D. 2005. *Women, Development, and the UN: A Sixty-Year Quest for Equality and Justice*. Bloomington: Indiana University Press.

17. For a detailed list of reservations of member-states to the CEDAW, refer to United Nations. 2009. *Declarations, Reservations, and Objections to CEDAW*. Accessible at http://www.un.org/womenwatch/daw/cedaw/reservations-country.ht; 23 July 2017.

Name Index

Subject Index

About the Authors

K. Seeta Prabhu is a development economist and a leading exponent of the human development approach, and was, until recently, Tata Chair Professor at the Tata Institute of Social Sciences, Mumbai. She has been senior advisor to the Prime Minister's Rural Development Fellows Scheme of the Ministry of Rural Development, Government of India. Prabhu has worked with the India country office of United Nations Development Programme (UNDP) for thirteen years, playing a key role as the head at Human Development Resource Centre and as UNDP senior advisor in the preparation of state- and district-level Human Development Reports and implementation of policy recommendations therein at various levels in government. She was professor of development economics at the Department of Economics, University of Bombay and was engaged in teaching and research on themes ranging from social security, health, gender, poverty, budget analysis, and human development for twenty-two years. She has published numerous books and articles in leading national and international journals on these themes. She has been an advisor to several national and international organizations and a member of governing bodies of Indian Council for Social Science Research (ICSSR), Giri Institute of Development Studies, Lucknow, and Institute of Livelihood Research and Training (ILRT), Basix Group, Hyderabad.

Sandhya S. Iyer is associate professor at and chairperson, Centre for Public Policy, Habitat and Human Development at the School for Development Studies, Tata Institute of Social Sciences, Mumbai. As a development economist, her focus is on poverty, inequality, gender equality, Agenda 2030, and other human development issues. She is involved in the global governance processes at the German Development Institute, and visiting fellow at the Institute for Development Studies, Sussex. She is also a member of the T20 Taskforce of Inequality and Prosperity, German and Argentinian Presidencies. Iyer has led numerous project teams aligned and funded by the Government of India such as Ministry of Panchayati Raj, Ministry of Rural Development, Government of Chhattisgarh, District Collectorate, Ministry of Health and Family Welfare, and national and international agencies such as UNDP, World Bank, Institute for Participatory Practices (PRAXIS), and Confederation of Indian Industry (western region). She has several publications to her credit in the areas of human development estimation, modelling on multidimensional poverty, institutional analysis and decentralization, social security, and social protection policies.